WOMEN AND THE CANADIAN WELFARE STATE
CHALLENGES AND CHANGE

Canadians can no longer expect as much from their governments. Rights formerly guaranteed by our 'welfare state' are disappearing. Social spending has been cut drastically in an attempt to combat recession, globalization and restructuring, and the deficit.

The decline of the welfare state poses special risks for women. The policies, benefits, and services of the welfare state are directly linked to women's basic freedoms. The welfare state employs women to deliver services such as child care, home-help, nursing, and social work. In turn, these services have meant that women can enter the paid labour force, provide for dependants, and leave abusive relationships. Access to political resources has helped women to form solidarities, alliances, and organizations. In *Women and the Canadian Welfare State*, scholars from environmental studies, law, social work, sociology, and economics explore the changing relationship between women and the welfare state. They examine the transformation of the welfare state and its implications for women; key issues in the welfare state debates such as social rights, family and dependency, and gender-neutral programs and inequality; women's work and the state; and the role of women as agents of change.

Women and the Canadian Welfare State explains not only how women are affected by changes in policy and programming, but how they can take an active role in shaping these changes. It bridges an important gap for scholars and students who are interested in gender, public policy, and the welfare state.

PATRICIA M. EVANS is a professor of social work and Associate Dean of Graduate Studies at York University.
GERDA R. WEKERLE is a professor of environmental studies at York University.

EDITED BY
PATRICIA M. EVANS AND GERDA R. WEKERLE

Women and the Canadian Welfare State: Challenges and Change

UNIVERSITY OF TORONTO PRESS
Toronto Buffalo London

© University of Toronto Press Incorporated 1997
Toronto Buffalo London
Printed in Canada

ISBN 0-8020-0663-9 (cloth)
ISBN 0-8020-7618-1 (paper)

Printed on acid-free paper

Canadian Cataloguing in Publication Data

Main entry under title:

Women and the Canadian welfare state : challenges and change

ISBN 0-8020-0663-9 (bound)   ISBN 0-8020-7618-1 (pbk.)

1. Welfare state.   2. Women – Government policy – Canada.
3. Women – Canada – Social conditions.   4. Canada – Social
policy.   I. Evans, Patricia M. (Patricia Marie), 1944–   .
II. Wekerle, Gerda R.

HQ1236.5.C2W628 1997   361.6'5'0820971   C97-931401-1

University of Toronto Press acknowledges the financial assistance to its
publishing program of the Canada Council for the Arts and the Ontario
Arts Council.

Contents

Acknowledgments

This book has had a long gestation, and we owe debts of gratitude to a number of people who have helped us along the way. First, to Thelma McCormack for her valuable contributions at the early stages of this project. Second, to the contributing authors for their good humour and tolerance of deadlines and editorial suggestions. We are also grateful to Virgil Duff at the University of Toronto Press for his help from the initial submission of the manuscript through to its publication. Special thanks to Carina Hernandez for her care and attention in the last stages of manuscript preparation, and the Faculty of Environmental Studies at York for supporting this work. Finally, to our families, Slade and Bryn Lander, and John, Katharine, and Caroline Evans, for their encouragement all along the way.

Tables

Contributors

Pat Armstrong Professor and Director, School of Canadian Studies, Carleton University

Monica Boyd The Mildred and Claude Pepper Distinguished Professor of Sociology and Research Associate, Center for the Study of Population, Florida State University

Marjorie Griffin Cohen Economist, Professor of Political Science and Chair of Women's Studies, Simon Fraser University

Patricia M. Daenzer Associate Professor, School of Social Work, and Director of Women's Studies, McMaster University

Patricia M. Evans Associate Professor, School of Social Work, and Associate Dean, Faculty of Graduate Studies, York University

Sue Findlay Private scholar, Toronto

Hester Lessard Associate Professor, Faculty of Law, University of Victoria

Meg Luxton Professor of Social Science and Women's Studies, York University

Morag MacLean Legal Editor, Professional Legal Training Course, Continuing Legal Education Society of British Columbia

Mary Jane Mossman   Professor of Law, Osgoode Hall Law School of York University

Sheila Neysmith   Professor, Faculty of Social Work, University of Toronto

Norene Pupo   Associate Professor, Department of Sociology, York University

Ester Reiter   Associate Professor of Social Science and Women's Studies, York University

Gerda R. Wekerle   Professor, Faculty of Environmental Studies, York University

PART I

Welfare State in Transition

1

The Shifting Terrain of Women's Welfare: Theory, Discourse, and Activism

PATRICIA M. EVANS AND GERDA R. WEKERLE

The idea for this book began several years ago at a time when the steadily consistent, but relatively quiet erosion of the Canadian welfare state during the Mulroney government, was well advanced. By the time this book is in the hands of readers, this 'social policy by stealth' (Gray, 1990) approach has been replaced by explicitly articulated, rapidly paced, and radical changes. Against a background of economic restructuring, globalization, and the overriding imperative of deficit reduction, the Canadian 'welfare state' is in retreat. This retreat continues a direction that has been apparent since the mid-1970s and one that advanced significantly in the 1980s. However, the 1990s are characterized by a more fundamental challenge to the welfare state that has been fuelled by recent recessions, growing concerns about trade globalization, the restructuring of the labour market, and a focus on cuts to social spending as the dominant solution to the problem of the deficit. The challenge to the welfare state, however, is not simply a reduction in costs. Canadians are being told that they must scale down the expectations they hold of their governments and accept a significant curtailment in the scope and comprehensiveness of state-provided services.

This book explores, from the perspective of women, some important changes, tensions, and issues that characterize women's experience with the contemporary welfare state. Following other feminist literature (see, for example, Gordon, 1990), we use the term 'welfare state' to encompass much more than social services and income support programs designed for those 'in need.' We use the term also to include those policies, programs, and legislation that redistribute status, rights, and life opportunities. As Orloff (1993) points out, the ease or difficulty with which women can enter paid work, the way in which the unpaid work of caring for others is treated, and the regulation of marital and family relationships are all central arenas where gender relations are constituted, and these are all influenced in significant ways by the nature and extent of state intervention.

There are at least five reasons why there needs to be a special focus on women's experience with the welfare state. First, policies, services, and the benefits of the welfare state frequently incorporate significant, though implicit, assumptions about gender roles. The type and amount of home care services allocated to the frail elderly, for example, often depend upon assumptions about women's availability, and obligation, to care. Similarly, whether single mothers are viewed primarily as 'workers' or 'mothers' has an important influence on the terms and conditions of their social assistance benefits. Second, the welfare state provides an important, though declining, source of employment for women, some of whom work as child care workers, home-helps, and nursing assistants as well as the better paid nurses and social workers. Third, women are not only at the front lines of delivering welfare services, they also are their chief consumers, although the services they seek and receive are often on behalf of others, such as their children or their aging parents. Fourth, the services and policies of the welfare state do not simply reproduce the problematic assumptions about gender that are held in the broader society, they also actively shape gender relations as they help or hinder women to enter the paid labour market, to exit from abusive relationships, and to provide care to dependent family members. Finally, the welfare state has the potential to generate political resources for women by creating new solidarities, alliances, and organizations (Fox Piven, 1990).

The transformation of the welfare state that is occurring is moulded by ideological challenges and shaped in response to economic, political, and demographic pressures. And this transformation has profound implications for women's lives. This book explores some of these important changes, drawing upon a variety of disciplinary traditions and perspectives. The authors, whose backgrounds include environmental studies, law, social work, sociology, and economics, bring their specific expertise, and some common concerns, to an exploration of the changing relationship between women and the welfare state. Some of the common themes that resonate through the chapters include:

1 Restructuring is simultaneously occurring in the state, labour markets, and families. These changes have interacting effects and women frequently bear a disproportionate share of their costs.

2 Gender is not the only, or necessarily the most important dimension of inequality – class and race interrelate with gender to further disadvantage women.

3 Women's relationship to the welfare state is imbued with important tensions and contradictions. These can operate in favour of, as well as in opposition to, women's interests.

4 Women have acted, and continue to act, across diverse arenas to articulate their claims to gender equality and social benefits.

In this Introduction, we do not explore the meaning and impact of the specific changes and shifts – this has been the challenge that each author takes up in her chapter. Rather, the task that we attempt here is to address the recurring themes and tensions that underpin this transformation and to examine the feminist understandings of the challenges this poses for women in the 1990s. The first section highlights the essential components of the transformation in the Canadian state. Second, the major themes in the feminist critique of the welfare state are examined. Next, we explore the struggle over language and meaning in the discourse and debate which accompany the restructuring of welfare. In the fourth section, the challenges for women's activism are considered. The concluding section previews the individual chapters that follow, by introducing the central issues that the authors explore in their different arenas as they consider the challenge of increasing gender sensitivity in policies and the implications for feminists organizing for change.

The Hollowing Out of the Welfare State

The Canadian version of the welfare state, until recently, appeared to rest – if not firmly, at least with a measure of stability – on the assumption that governments in Canada had a positive role to play in alleviating some of the worst effects of the inequities of the free market and operating as a buffer for some of its most vulnerable citizens. From the mid-1960s to the early 1970s, a number of important programs were introduced that provided services and income benefits to many more people than ever before. This was the period when a much more comprehensive unemployment insurance scheme was introduced, post-secondary education expanded, medicare was established, and benefits for seniors were made universal. Under the aegis of the 1966 Canada Assistance Plan, social services were extended and federal guidelines for welfare benefits were put in place. Women and children were particular beneficiaries of this expanded safety net. At the same time, it is important not to overstate the degree of consensus about this expansion, or the progress that an expanded social safety net made in alleviating the class, race, and gender inequities that persisted during this period. Programs and policies that comprised the 'welfare state' have always been contentious, and, with the exception of the elderly, poverty rates among other Canadians have not diminished. Nonetheless, it is also important to recognize the radical nature of the changes that are currently taking place and the fundamental challenges they pose.

Globalization, restructuring, and downsizing are redefining the relationship between Canadians and their governments, and these have particular impacts on women. The mounting influence of international regulatory bodies, the increased concern of government and the private sector about the 'flight' of capital, and the primacy placed on the need to be more competitive, lead to an identification of social spending as the problem, rather than part of the solution to the inequities of unregulated markets. Gone is the belief in the corrective potential of government intervention that characterized the postwar period. Governments have embarked on several related solutions to the problems of globalization and competitiveness, and these include downsizing and deregulation. Jessop (1993) has identified the impact of these trends as the 'hollowing out' of the state, a phrase which suggests that although the exterior shell appears relatively unchanged, the core functions of the state are disappearing.

The hollowing out of the central functions of the state have important and particular implications for women. As in other industrialized countries, Canada's public sector has provided full-time, relatively well-paid, and often unionized jobs; women have also benefited from the pay equity programs that are more likely to apply to public than private employment. The downsizing of the public sector has a clear and direct impact on jobs that comprise a significant source of women's employment (see Luxton and Reiter, this volume). Some jobs simply disappear while others are replaced by lower paid and less secure employment. But downsizing is about much more than a loss of jobs. It is also closely linked to a disappearing federal presence that is exemplified by the passage of the 1996 Canada Health and Social Transfer (CHST). The CHST combines all federal spending on health, education, welfare benefits, and social services into a single, and reduced, transfer. This 'megablock' transfer to the provinces virtually eliminates all cost-sharing conditions and, along with them, any significant leverage that might be used to promote national standards. Those programs and services that enjoy the least support are the most vulnerable as provinces attempt to cushion themselves from the growing demands on their purse, unfettered by federal regulations or cost-sharing mechanisms. In this environment of deregulation, shelters and other services for women fleeing domestic violence, child care subsidies, and homemaker services for the elderly and those with disabilities are made even more vulnerable (Torjman and Battle, 1995).

In addition to reductions in public services, and a devolution of powers to the provinces, a third aspect of downsizing involves reprivatization. These are the initiatives that transform programs and services, formerly provided in the public sector, and make them available through the private sector, or embed them anew as the private responsibility of the family or the voluntary sector (Rekart, 1993). Reprivatizing takes these programs and services out of the realm of mandated, collectively provided services and makes their provision a matter of individual choice and ability to pay, or personal or community responsibility. Perhaps the most dramatic example of this trend is the abolition of publicly provided kindergarten in Alberta, but the shifts in health care provision that are increasingly requiring families to provide treatment that was formerly confined to hospitals (intravenous feeding, for example) also come sharply to mind (Armstrong, 1995). This same retreat from the public sector to a renewed emphasis on market and the family is also apparent in the provision of income benefits, as unemployment insurance is curtailed, social assistance benefits are reduced, and income-testing of Old Age Security is introduced.

The Canadian welfare state is in the process of dramatic structural transformation. It is important, however, not to leave the reader with the impression that the *only* change occurring is in the welfare state. The changes that are described here – the decentralizing, deregulating, and privatizing in the welfare state, do not occur in a vacuum. Nor is Canada's welfare state alone in undergoing fundamental change. The internationalization of markets, deregulation, and privatization, and the erosion of social benefits, are trends that are evident, in varying degree, across the 'developed' countries. And, as Patricia Connelly and Martha MacDonald (1996) suggest, the pursuit of international competitiveness and deficit reduction has had profound implications for the quality of jobs and the process of collective bargaining, and these also have particular impacts for women.

Economic restructuring takes its toll on individuals and families as the good jobs that disappear are increasingly replaced by non-standard employment. The erosion of the minimum wage and the increasing tax burden on low-income families also helps to make welfare rates more competitive with market wages, despite the fact that these rates fall well below the levels of Canada's unofficial poverty line (National Council of Welfare, 1993; Battle, 1990). Robert Mullaly (1994) suggests that the current welfare wars are constructing a new dual social order, with a labour market divided between full-time, well-paying jobs with related benefits and a secondary sector of part-time, low-wage jobs and a flexible labour pool formed by volunteer and unpaid workers. By tying social programs into the labour market and decreasing benefits in the general welfare system for those who cannot compete in the market, workers become even more reliant on a marketplace which can offer low wages.

Although the so-called postindustrial strategies that can include cooperatives and community enterprises have an appeal, Jocelyn Pixley (1993) argues convincingly for the necessity of full employment policies as the key component of political and social citizenship. This does not mean 'more of the same,' but instead suggests the importance of a 'right to a job' approach that maintains and restructures paid work, rather than reduces, or seeks alternatives to it. The changes, so briefly highlighted in this section, are wide-ranging, but the way ahead is not to be found in what has been referred to as 'nostalgic welfarism' (Brodie, 1995a). This was, after all, a state of affairs that feminists have long critiqued, as we discuss in the following section.

Feminist Understandings of the Welfare State

Welfare State Perspectives

A substantial feminist literature has developed over the past twenty years that stands as an important challenge to mainstream scholarship on the welfare state. This traditional scholarship has focused on state–market relations, but paid little attention to the family, stressing the significance of class, but neglecting gender. It emphasizes the role of the state in regulating market work through levels of welfare and unemployment benefits, but ignores the regulation of women's paid work through, for example, child care policy. An emphasis on class, and class with a male cast, also pays particular attention to the important role played by political parties and the labour union movement in social change, but ignores the activity of women in the early reform movements who generated and shaped policies through their own organizations (Kealey, 1979; Mitchinson, 1987; Prentice, 1988; Skocpol, 1992; Koven and Michel, 1993). Class is of enormous significance in welfare state analysis, but to marginalize gender and to neglect the sexual division of labour cannot provide an adequate framework for understanding the welfare state. A parallel concern is, of course, the general absence of race in welfare state analyses, and the significant challenge that exists in attempting to integrate race, class, and gender into a welfare state framework (see Williams, 1989, for example). We recognize the importance of this theoretical challenge, but our contribution is more modest in scope. We highlight the significance of gender, while recognizing the critical ways that class and race intersect. Although we do not resolve the tensions, we reject a position that places gender in contestation to, or ranked in a hierarchy with class and race.

Several important and interrelated themes characterize the development of efforts to situate gender as a significant component in welfare state analysis. Part of this literature, the early work in particular, has been rooted in the important task of revealing and documenting the ways in which the welfare state discriminated against women in its support of capitalism and patriarchy through the reinforcement of the sexual division of labour. Elizabeth Wilson (1977) writing in England, Mimi Abramowitz (1988) presenting a U.S. perspective, and Jane Ursel (1986, 1992) in her discussion of the Canadian state are examples of this approach. An identification of the welfare state as 'public patriarchy' provides fruitful insights into the regulatory and monitoring aspects of state intervention in production and reproduction, but it may tend to suggest a monolithic and reductionist view of the complex entities that comprise 'the state,' to neglect the way in which state provisions might vary in their impacts on women, and may also operate to their benefit. More apparent in the recent literature are views that accommodate, with greater readiness, the tension between the positive and negative aspects of the state's involvement in the lives of women, and a growing (but still underdeveloped) attention to its differential impacts by class and race (see Quadagno, 1994; Daenzer, 1993, and this volume).

An important counterweight to the literature which suggests a functional, somewhat invariant, and generally pessimistic approach to the welfare state are studies that examine its variability over time and place. A rapidly expanding body of comparative work is revealing the great diversity, as well as some stubborn commonalities, in the way welfare states respond to women (see, for example, Sainsbury, 1994, 1996; Lewis,

1993). Much recent comparative work stems from the 'politics matters' or 'power resources' school, that emphasizes the political nature of the struggles to secure social provision and argues that welfare states, in addition to their regulatory aspects, also include emancipatory elements with potential to alter power relations. Gösta Esping-Andersen's (1990) framework has received considerable attention, both in the mainstream literature and in the feminist efforts to integrate gender into it (O'Connor, 1993; Orloff, 1993). Central to his framework is the concept of social citizenship, originally developed by T.H. Marshall, a British political economist. According to Marshall (1964), citizenship rights include not only civil and political rights, but also social and economic rights. Social citizenship entails the right to a prevailing standard of living and a reduction in the inequalities associated with the market through state provision of some economic goods and services, including education and social services (Barbalet, 1988: 6). Marshall identified the struggle for the recognition of social rights as a characteristic of the twentieth century, in contrast to earlier periods when civil and political rights gained ground. Jane Jenson (1993: 127) concludes that 'definitions of citizenship establish the boundaries of inclusion and exclusion, thereby providing access to full membership in a nation state and the grounds for making claims to that state for rights and welfare.'

Building on Marshall's work, Esping-Andersen (1990) identifies the 'de-commodification' of labour as an important function of the welfare state and a central component of social rights. Welfare states de-commodify labour as they enact provisions, such as unemployment insurance, which allow workers some protection against the necessity of selling their labour at any price. In addition to de-commodification, Esping-Andersen also compares welfare states on the range and nature of state activity directed towards meeting needs, as well as their stratifying effects. Based on these dimensions, he identifies 'three worlds of welfare capitalism' including the social democratic Scandinavian countries that represent the most de-commodified, comprehensive, and least stratified of welfare states. Conservative–corporatist countries (France, Germany, and Italy, for example) also embrace the idea of social rights but structure their welfare provisions in ways that maintain, rather than diminish, class differences. In contrast, the 'liberal' regimes (the United Kingdom, Canada, and the United States, for example), with their emphasis on the market, offer an extremely circumscribed range of social rights and make much greater use of welfare provisions that are minimal and stigmatizing.

As feminist critiques point out, Esping-Andersen's framework breaks down when women are taken into account, and integrating gender into it requires considerable analytic reworking. For a woman, it may be at least as important that the state helps to 'commodify' her labour by promoting her access to paid work and enhancing her personal autonomy. To consider primarily the state–market dimension in meeting needs and to subsume women in the unit of 'family' ignores the distribution of labour within the household and between the family and the state. To reflect adequately the position of women, an understanding of stratification must move from an almost exclusive emphasis on class relations to incorporate attention to the way that the state may privilege the male 'worker–citizen' status (for further discussion, see Orloff, 1993; O'Connor, 1993; Daly, 1994; Evans, this volume).

It comes as no surprise, as Julia O'Connor (1993) notes, that feminist literature from the English-speaking countries has paid more attention to the state's oppressive aspects, while Scandinavian writers, though far from unanimous, have been more optimistic about the welfare state as a site of women's empowerment. Sweden is widely regarded as a 'woman-friendly' state, and indeed its rate of women's labour force participation, and infrastructure of child care, parental leave, and comparatively generous income support programs have all served to improve significantly the position of women and children in comparison with Canada and other countries (Hauser and Fischer, 1990; Hobson, 1990). Nonetheless, the persistence of inequality is underlined by the comparatively high levels of occupational segregation that Swedish women experience, women who continue to carry primary responsibility for children (OECD, 1988). This leads Scandinavian writers such as Birte Siim (1994; see also Hernes, 1987) to conclude that although a social democratic approach has helped women's welfare, it has done significantly less to alter the distribution of power.

The Struggle over Language and Meaning

The control over language and the naming of issues and solutions, while often neglected, are key elements in welfare debates and becoming increasingly important as the welfare state retreats. These 'discursive struggles' are over much more than language, but language plays an important role in the creation of new discourses and new claims, and it is often used to reinterpret long-standing problems. As Taylor and Whittier (1995: 183) explain, 'The public discourse about an issue can be thought of as a set of interpretive packages that frame or give meaning to an issue.'

According to Nancy Fraser and Linda Gordon (1994a, 1994b), 'keywords,' those words which become increasingly focal and critical in defining social reality, permeate and influence discourses in powerful ways. These authors trace the shifts in the meaning of 'dependency' from historical periods when it was not inflected with notions of deviance, to the present, when 'welfare dependency' is a stigmatized and pathologized status that is conferred on all, including single mothers, who were once regarded as the 'deserving' in the hierarchy of the poor. Picking up on the critique of dependency on the welfare state initially articulated by the left, the new right emphasizes the desirability of independence offered by wage work in the market economy, even if this entails mandatory workfare that subsidizes private industry. Participation in the labour force, and the associated reliance on entitlements based on worker contributions rather than general welfare, are glorified and characterized as contributing to the wider society, while the work of caring for young children is equated with privatized, individual choice.

A second example of the way in which a feminist discourse on gender equality and rights has been appropriated and stood on its head by the new right relates to employment equity legislation and programs. In the province of Ontario, where the most advanced employment equity law in Canada was passed in 1994, the newly elected Conservative government promptly eliminated the legislation when it came to office in 1995. Ironically, the discourse of equality and rights that supported the claims of the women's movement and other groups for employment equity legislation is now used by the new right to argue, instead, that employment equity is, itself, a creator of new inequalities. In a perversion of equality discourse, the new right labels its own proposals to eliminate employment equity as 'equality policies,' arguing that equal treatment of individuals should take precedence over equality of treatment for disadvantaged groups.[1]

Governments are both the targets of these struggles over meaning and the key actors in the ongoing articulation, interpretation, and implementation of claims. Through legislation, regulation, rules, and access to media, governments attempt to gain acceptance for their framing of problems and solutions. Writers on the Canadian welfare state, including Lightman and Irving (1991), Evans (1994), and Mullaly (1994) have pointed out that the vehement and vitriolic rhetoric of the new right in the United States and the United Kingdom has not been evident in

Canadian government discourse. The relative civility of the language of the welfare state debates has been abandoned in the mid-1990s, and the restructuring discourse has been taken up with aggressive energy by the federal Liberals. This energy is no doubt exacerbated by the emergence of the Reform party in federal politics and the ascendance of Conservative provincial governments in Manitoba, Alberta, and Ontario.

The welfare state is also challenged by oppositional groups from both the left and the right. The state was often seen as providing a 'free space' for feminist interventions, particularly through policies such as equal opportunity legislation (Pringle and Watson, 1992: 58). To the new right, on the other hand, the state is viewed as interfering in market forces and creating new inequalities. While the left seeks to include previously excluded interpretations of needs, the right aims to redefine what constitutes legitimate needs, who has the authority to define them, and how they are to be satisfied in ways that challenge social rights and the state's obligation to meet them. The anti-government and anti-public sector focus of the neo-conservative agenda shares some common ground with critiques from the left which point to the regulatory and social control nature of the welfare state. However, instead of empowering clients and changing the workplace, the proposed solution is privatization and new profits for the private sector. These 'reprivatization discourses' (Fraser, 1989: 170) seek to enclave issues in the market, the family, or the voluntary sector, thereby declaring them politically off-limits and depoliticizing the welfare state. The discourse on rights and citizenship which has been front and centre in feminist theories of the welfare state has been pre-empted to focus on the individual's rights to freedom from government regulation and property rights. As Resnick (1994: 27) points out, the neo-conservative view of liberty is one of a minimalist state freeing market actors.

The dominant discourse in Canada in the 1990s reframes societal problems in terms of market forces, global competitiveness, and individualism. Brodie (1995b: 27) urges us to evaluate dominant discourses as the biased and historically specific assertions of political agents, rather than accepting them as the natural order of things that is not contestable. Current discursive struggles over keywords and concepts in the welfare state are indicators of changing cultural assumptions and a shifting terrain of political struggles.

The struggle centres around which paradigms are to emerge as authoritative and the accepted conventions that shape the narrative debate. Some discourses may be 'hegemonic, authorized, and officially

sanctioned on the one hand,' while others are 'nonhegemonic, disqualified and discounted' (Fraser, 1989: 165). The spectre of the deficit, the
powerlessness of nation states to counter the forces of the global economy, and the need to alter fundamentally the expectations that Canadians have of their governments comprise the current foundations of the
dominant discourse that must be challenged if the welfare state in Canada is not to be dismantled (examples of such challenges include,
Cohen, this volume; McQuaig, 1995; Canadian Centre for Policy Alternatives, 1995). The challenge for feminists is not to lose sight of the
socialist–feminist perspective on the state that links race, class, and
patriarchy as mutually reinforcing systems of domination in the current
welfare wars.

Women's Activism

A significant theme in feminist work on the welfare state is the inter-
meshing of political and social rights, of empowerment and material
well-being. One of the most problematic impacts of the prevailing discourse of economic restructuring is the implication that these global economic forces are inevitable, unable to be influenced or controlled by
citizens. In contrast, we find that women globally, and in Canada, are
actively engaged in developing sites of resistance, both to the dominant
restructuring discourse and to the impacts of restructuring on women's
day-to-day lives.

Engaging with Governments: Institutional Feminism

In Canada, women's political activism has had a major impact on the
shape and direction of the welfare state. Across Canada, at both the federal and provincial levels, women's movement organizations have been
actively engaged in 'political conflicts over the interpretation of
women's needs' (Fraser, 1989: 146). Engaging directly with the state,
institutional feminism, represented by national organizations such as
the National Action Committee on the Status of Women (NAC), has
been instrumental in shaping government policies such as pay equity
and employment equity. This has been reinforced by women working in
the public sector who have actively pressed their claims for equality.
Outside the formal state welfare system, women's movement organizations have developed a parallel structure of services to meet women's
unmet needs, including battered women's shelters, rape crisis services,

and women's centres. And finally, the political activism of Aboriginal and racial or ethnic minority women has shifted the focus of women's movement organizations to issues such as immigration and refugee policies, women's health, and job retraining.

In pressing their claims, women are not simply attempting to improve the position of women, critical though this objective may be, but they are also attempting to 'expand the spaces of politics and generate more democratic politics' (Jenson, 1993: 138). Feminist visions of the welfare state go beyond responses to 'traditional' women's concerns (child care and employment equity, for example). As the NAC campaigns of the 1980s against Free Trade and the Meech Lake and Charlottetown accords have demonstrated, women in Canada have engaged in a struggle to develop the political resources to press their position and the language to express it (Jenson, 1992: 26).

As they work together to develop the political resources to combat the erosion of the welfare state in Canada, women face several important challenges. The devolution of control over social programs from the federal to the provincial governments, discussed earlier in this chapter, is one such challenge.[2] There have been important differences, however, in the orientation of women's movements to the devolution in English Canada and in Quebec. Sylvia Bashevkin (1994: 145) points out that women's organizations in English Canada have long argued that the federal government should protect national standards and uniform social programs across the country. Relinquishing federal leadership and widening provincial jurisdiction over social programs, would, they feared, water down the progress that women have made over the past decades. In contrast, during the constitutional debates of 1981–2, Quebec women's organizations supported proposals to grant provinces jurisdiction over family law, arguing that Quebec's family law was more favourable to women than was federal legislation. This pattern repeated itself during the debates over the Meech Lake Accord, when English Canadian women's groups again opposed devolution of power to the provincial governments, a proposal supported by the Fédération des Femmes du Québec.

The disappearing presence of the federal government in social programs presents new challenges to national women's organizations. For example, NAC has opposed the implementation of the CHST, which replaced the federal Canada Assistance Plan with block grants to the provinces to fund social programs, and other federal proposals to allow provinces more autonomy in setting standards for social programs.

With the exception of Quebec, women's movement organizations are not as well organized to fight cutbacks to social programs in the provinces and territories as they have been at the federal level. Instead of a single focus for organizing and lobbying – the federal government – the political arena has shifted to twelve jurisdictions. To have an impact, women's organizations will need to organize and coordinate resistance strategies both at the provincial and territorial levels and across the country.

In response to cutbacks in social programs, women's organizing has started to focus more directly on women's material conditions. In the summer of 1995, women's movement organizations in Quebec organized a ten-day Bread and Roses March Against Poverty from Montreal to Quebec City. Almost 1,000 women marched, and they were joined by another 10,000 when they arrived at the Quebec legislature. The march drew attention to women's issues and elicited promises from the Parti Québecois government that included an increase in the minimum wage, the creation of a special job creation program for women, and the tabling of provincial pay equity legislation (Canadian Press, 1995; Picard, 1995).

Between 14 May and 15 June 1996, NAC and the Canadian Labour Congress (CLC) jointly organized a cross-country caravan, called the Women's March Against Poverty: For Jobs and Justice! For Bread and Roses. An estimated 100,000 women were involved in educational events, public protests, and marches in communities along the route, making this one of the largest public events sponsored by the Canadian women's movement. The caravan culminated in Ottawa with a march of 10,000 people on Parliament Hill. Linking the March to the International Year for the Eradication of Poverty, NAC articulated its aims in terms of social welfare: 'We are marching to show governments we oppose their policies which create unemployment, poverty and the destruction of our social programs' (CLC and NAC, 1996). Confronting head on the perceived contradiction between women who support devolution of federal jurisdiction to the provinces and those who support standardized national programs, NAC's call to action states: 'We recognize that aboriginal peoples and the people of Quebec have distinct needs which must be respected in all programs brought in by the federal government. We reject the suggestion that respecting the unique needs of these communities requires off-loading federal responsibility for social programs in the rest of Canada onto provincial and municipal governments and onto individual families' (CLC and NAC, 1996).

Over the past two decades the Canadian women's movement has

developed a range of self-help, advocacy, and social services. Now women find that even these minimally funded and precarious services are at risk: non-profit day care centres have closed down (in Ontario); some battered women's shelters have had to close or to revert to volunteer staffing (in British Columbia). In Ontario, funding for women's job training programs (and associated funding for child care) was eliminated in 1995. Those agencies that both serve women and employ women are at risk as funding is cut back, and programs are rationalized or services are contracted out to the private sector.

Coalition Strategies

Although relatively insignificant in the amounts saved to provincial treasuries, these funding cuts have managed to seriously undermine and destabilize a system of feminist services that women had painstakingly developed over decades. Canadian women's movement organizations have provided an independent voice in evaluating seemingly gender-neutral changes to the Canadian social welfare system and in highlighting the dissimilar policy outcomes for women and for men. Increasingly, NAC and other women's organizations have engaged in alliance strategies with other social movements, including anti-poverty groups, unions, and anti-racist movements to challenge national policies that will reshape Canadian society and women's lives. At a time when an increasingly influential neo-conservative stance makes 'government' suspect and argues for decentralizing decisions to the community, it is important to remember that civil society is expressed in social movement and voluntary sector organizations. Within the Canadian women's movement these include not only the large nationally visible organizations like NAC, but also the women's caucuses in trade unions, the services such as women's shelters, women's housing projects, and Aboriginal and ethno-racial minority women's organizations.

The reassertion of the significance of class, and of class-based alliances, also becomes of mounting importance. Increasingly, feminist movements are engaged in coalition politics, finding common ground with labour movements, social justice groups, and people of colour in mobilizing against the cutbacks to the welfare state. Involvement in such coalitions has been a survival strategy for feminist agencies that fear reprisal from government for taking a stand against government policies. Participating in coalitions gives feminist service providers both protection and a collective voice. But reliance on coalition politics as a major strategy of feminist resistance also has drawbacks. Feminist goals may be watered down in order to find common ground with other movements and gender inequalities may be de-emphasized within a broader social justice agenda (Briskin, 1992). Within coalition politics, feminist politics may make an indirect, and less visible, contribution, giving the impression that feminist movements are less active than in the past, as Verta Taylor and Leila Rupp (1993) have suggested.

In Canada, progressive movements have had a history of forming broad-based coalitions on such issues as opposition to free trade or to implement pay equity. Coalitions have often been viewed as defensive, oppositional strategies in response to perceived threats rather than being constituted as a transformative revolutionary politics (Bleyer, 1992: 108). In response to the demands of global capital for massive economic and social restructuring within nation states, Canadian social movements are attempting to band together to create a counter-hegemonic bloc of alliances functioning at the level of civil society and directed at generating alternatives to restructuring by the state (Bleyer, 1992: 103). Grounded in the workplace, the community, and within the politics of race and class, women's activism in relation to the state in the mid-1990s responds more contextually and strategically to shifting frameworks of power and resistance. As Pringle and Watson (1992: 67) have noted, women's activism has taken a poststructuralist turn. It is characterized by a 'multiplicity of forms of resistance' which goes far beyond the human rights tradition associated with liberal feminism.

Prelude to the Chapters

This book was born out of the frustration we encountered in finding an adequate range of Canadian materials when we taught, in different years, a course on 'Women and Public Policy.' This volume is intended to help to bridge this gap for others particularly interested in gender issues and policy as it relates to the 'welfare state.' As our introductory chapter suggests, the transformation of the Canadian welfare state is occurring at a very rapid rate, with important consequences for women, who are, at the same time, also altering the welfare state. In an effort to develop the themes of change and activism, we have organized this volume around three major sections.

Part I, entitled 'Welfare State in Transition,' addresses the current transformation of the Canadian welfare state and its implications for women. In addition to our introductory chapter, Marjorie Cohen in

'From the Welfare State to Vampire Capitalism' (chapter 2) explores the roots of the deficit crisis and the shift in power to the corporate sector. She critiques the perceived inevitability and apolitical nature of the processes of globalization and economic restructuring and its supporting pillars, such as NAFTA. Arguing that the deficit is a problem, but more of a political problem than an economic one, Cohen makes the point that feminists must more effectively tie their analytic understanding of the importance of economic policy in the modern capitalist state to the politics of their activism.

In Part II, 'Challenging the Bases of Claims,' the authors focus on the key issues in current welfare state debates: social rights and changing conceptions of citizenship; redefining family and dependency; how gender-neutral programs can perpetuate gender inequality. Hester Lessard's chapter 3, 'Creation Stories: Social Rights and Canada's Constitution,' outlines the contradictions for women of pursuing the rights-based strategy of entrenching social rights through constitutional changes which leave intact existing relations of subordination. Drawing upon the example of the Charlottetown proposals, social charters are critiqued for their problematic imagery of 'contract,' the assumption of a split between public responsibility and private economic interactions, and the myth of state neutrality. Lessard concludes that proposals for the constitutional entrenchment of social rights may perpetuate existing inequalities unless they are linked to issues of political participation and empowerment.

Patricia M. Evans's chapter 4, 'Divided Citizenship? Gender, Income Security, and the Welfare State,' focuses on the changes to the 'dual' welfare state in which women have tended to rely more heavily on a social assistance system which recognizes them as 'mothers' and 'wives,' while men have drawn upon the employment-related social insurance benefits. However, the bases of claims are changing. In social assistance, 'gender-specific' policies are giving way to 'gender-blind' policies as mothers are redefined as 'workers.' Meanwhile, the gender-blind policies based on a 'citizen–worker' model continue to disadvantage women by failing to address their caring responsibilities within the household or the gender-segregated labour market. The formulation of gender-sensitive policies, Evans argues, requires moving beyond the dichotomy of either 'sameness' or 'difference.'

Mary Jane Mossman and Morag MacLean, in 'Family Law and Social Assistance Programs: Rethinking Equality' (chapter 5), contrast the principles that define the 'private' financial responsibilities in divorce with those that underpin the 'public' provision of income assistance to 'needy' mothers. Exploring the commonalities and differences between these two policy arenas, usually not juxtaposed but treated separately, the authors reveal the differing assumptions regarding women who are entitled to 'private' support and those who receive welfare. Their examination suggests that the definition of 'the family' in both cases is very problematic. While recognizing that shifting to an individual basis of entitlement is not a panacea, they suggest that it does offer a greater potential to achieving equality goals, particularly in relation to single mothers on social assistance.

Monica Boyd addresses the contested concept of 'female dependency' in chapter 6, 'Migration Policy, Female Dependency, and Family Membership: Canada and Germany.' She focuses on an arena not generally discussed as part of the welfare state – migrant and immigration policies – and argues that immigration policies are part of the larger domain of state policies which assume and sustain female dependency and grant differential access to social rights for men and women. The meaning of citizenship is called into question when immigration policies systemically hamper immigrant women's access to both political citizenship rights and social citizenship by linking rights and entitlements to family relations. A comparison of Canadian and German immigration and migrant policies, two countries representing different welfare state regimes and immigration histories, shows how immigration and/or migrant policies in both countries perpetuate gender stratification through linking family and entitlements and create conditions of economic marginality for immigrant women.

In chapter 7, 'The Shift to the Market: Gender and Housing Disadvantage,' Gerda R. Wekerle argues that housing represents a relatively unexamined aspect of welfare state restructuring that reflects the wider trend of privatization. Just as women are concentrated on the social assistance side of social welfare, their lower incomes also make them disproportionately reliant on publicly funded social housing. However, as federal and provincial governments withdraw from supplying and subsidizing housing, more women are forced to compete for housing in the private market, and their housing security is further undermined. Women are systemically disadvantaged within a housing regime that is organized around property ownership and ability to pay. Within the overall restructuring of the welfare state, a discourse on the 'right to housing' has been replaced by notions of individual choice and efficiency. Although housing has been a focus for women's activism in the past decade, Wekerle argues that the gains made by women's organizations in developing and managing non-profit housing for women are seriously threatened by the withdrawal of government support for these programs.

Part III addresses the relationship between women's work and the state. In their chapter, 'Double, Double, Toil and Trouble ... Women's Experience of Work and Family in Canada 1980–1995,' Meg Luxton and Ester Reiter provide a careful exploration of the restructuring that is taking place of women's work in the home and the workplace. They argue that the political and economic changes are 'putting women in double jeopardy by intensifying their toil in both spheres.' Their discussion focuses particularly on the downsizing of the public sector and its consequences for women. Not only has the expanded public sector provided women with an important source of employment, but through the union movement, it has also been an important location of concrete achievements in wages and conditions of employment. In addition, public sector service provision has helped to lay the groundwork for alternatives to home-based care for looking after people who need care, and is helping to alleviate the many and contradictory demands on women. The erosion of the public sector in the name of welfare state restructuring raises important questions for feminists, questions that are not easily resolved, but that must continue to be addressed.

In chapter 9, 'Towards a Woman-Friendly Long-Term Care Policy,' Sheila Neysmith explores the changing terrain of policy with respect to the frail elderly. The transformation of the institutionally based care model to the home care model in the 1990s is assessed, along with the gender-neutral language that accompanied this shift. Neysmith's analysis includes attention to the women at home whose caregiving will increase, those who are receiving care, and the women who confront deteriorating conditions in their employment as home- and institutionally based care workers. In order for policies to be 'woman-friendly,' Neysmith argues, the debate must be reconstructed to place women at the centre. This means that for the women who so often provide the care, the issue must extend well beyond the parameters of both health policy and employment policies. Practices need to be responsive, and the option of non-family care must be available. This will require not the formal and perfunctory participation often incorporated into policy 'reform,' but concerted and determined activism by organizations focused on the interests of their members that would include unionized workers in home care agencies as well as organizations of kin carers.

Pat Armstrong's discussion in chapter 10, 'The State and Pay Equity: Juggling Similarity and Difference, Meaning, and Structures,' questions whether Ontario's legislation, viewed as path breaking when implemented, serves women's interests. This legislation encourages local determination of pay equity plans, and Armstrong suggests that the emphasis on locality and difference is in keeping with a postmodernist aversion to 'universalizing' and attention to struggles over meaning. Yet, as she points out, it is important for strategies to also attend to what women share. A failure to do this may exacerbate some of the very aspects the legislation set out to alleviate, and her examination reveals many of its uneven and contradictory impacts.

The welfare state has always been a site of struggle and contestation for Canadian women. Today it frequently appears that women are fighting a rearguard action as hard-won gains are dismantled by economic restructuring and public sector cutbacks. In this climate, in which women often seem to bear a disproportionate share of the costs, it is easy to lose sight of how women have been and continue to be active agents in constituting and redefining the welfare state. The chapters that comprise Part IV, 'Women Challenging the Welfare State,' focus on women's agency in working for change in the Canadian welfare state as clients, workers, and activists. A theme that is raised throughout this book is the unresponsiveness of the social welfare system to adapt to meet the needs of a diversity of women. Patricia Daenzer in chapter 11, 'Challenging Diversity: Black Women and Social Welfare,' addresses Black women's challenge to the mainstream social welfare system. Daenzer traces the historical roots of Black women's activism in Ontario, an activism that emphasizes access to education and the improvement of economic conditions. Through a case study of a participatory action research project involving Black women in one community, Daenzer shows how the group became a site for community identity and resistance. Her discussion of Black women's activism provides a very important contribution to the debates on the integration versus separation of minority services from the mainstream services of the welfare state.

Women's mobilization and activism has been most apparent in the public sector, a sector in which women have made inroads both as workers and in obtaining programs and legislation directed at promoting greater gender equality. Norene Pupo, in 'Women, Unions, and the State: Challenges Ahead' (chapter 12), shows that women workers are increasingly militant, challenging both the state and the unions. As members of public sector unions, they are engaged in fights to maintain job security, and within their own unions they are attempting to broaden the scope of unionism to incorporate social welfare issues.

In chapter 13, 'Institutionalizing Feminist Politics: Learning from the Struggles for Equal Pay in Ontario,' Sue Findlay focuses on women's sites of resistance within the state, specifically the agencies created to implement Ontario's Pay Equity Act. Findlay's chapter examines the question of what happens when feminist policies are institutionalized within the state and what the role of feminist organizations is in mediating women's interests. The chapter raises questions about the marginality of women's offices within the bureaucratic structure of government and the limitations of coalition politics in representing the diversity of women's experience. The lessons to be learned from the experience of implementing equal pay legislation in Ontario are particularly pertinent today when pay equity and employment equity programs are under attack and in the process of being dismantled by neo-conservative governments.

The themes addressed by the authors of this book go beyond the traditional social welfare debates. Restructuring at the global and local levels is connected to the reframing of discourses and concepts of citizenship. The fluidity of boundaries between the public and private is revealed in changes in such arenas as family law and long-term care policies. The ongoing shifts from gender-specific social policies to gender-blind policies that further disadvantage women is another theme. The contributors to this volume portray women engaged in a continual struggle to claim and reclaim the welfare state within the workforce and in the community, through legislation or from political spaces established within the state itself, or through separatist and alternative organizations outside the state. During this period of rapid change and shifting social and political agendas, close attention to the policies of the welfare state and their impacts on all women is imperative.

Notes

1 In the summer of 1995, the Republican Governor of California repealed his state's affirmative action legislation and substituted for it 'equal rights legislation,' which progressive social movements and women's movement organizations have organized statewide to have repealed.
2 When the federal government anounced a Social Policy Review, NAC sponsored a conference to highlight the impact on women and the Canadian

Advisory Council on the Status of Women released eight research papers showing how women would be disproportionately and adversely affected by proposed changes to unemployment insurance, welfare, the child tax benefit, and post-secondary education funding. The shift to block funding of social programs through the Canada Health and Social Transfer (Bill C-76) effectively undercut this opposition by women's organization and anti-poverty groups at the national level.

References

Ambramowitz, M. 1988. *Regulating the Lives of Women*. Boston: South End Press.

Armstrong, P. 1995. 'Unravelling the Safety Net: Transformations in Health Care and Their Impact on Women.' In Janine Brodie, ed., *Women and Public Policy*. Toronto: Harcourt Brace, 129–49.

Barbalet, J.M. 1988. *Citizenship Rights, Struggle and Class Inequality*. Minneapolis: University of Minnesota Press.

Bashevkin, S. 1994. 'Building a Political Voice: Women's Participation and Policy Influence in Canada.' In Barbara Nelson and Najma Chowdhury, eds., *Women and Politics Worldwide*. New Haven: Yale University Press, 142–60.

Battle, K. 1990. 'Clawback: The Demise of Universality in the Canadian Welfare State.' In I. Taylor, ed., *Social Effects of Free Market Policies*. New York: St Martin's Press, 269–96.

Bleyer, P. 1992. 'Coalitions of Social Movements as Agencies for Social Change: The Action Canada Network.' In W.K. Carroll, ed., *Organizing Dissent: Contemporary Social Movements in Theory and Practice*. Toronto: Garamond Press, 102–17.

Briskin, L. 1992. 'Socialist Feminism from the Standpoint of Practice.' In Pat Connolly and Pat Armstrong, eds., *Feminism in Action: Studies in Political Economy*. Toronto: Canadian Scholars Press, 267–94.

Brodie, J. 1995a. 'Canadian Women, Changing State Forms, and Public Policy.' In J. Brodie, ed., *Women and Public Policy*. Toronto: Harcourt Brace, 1–28.

Brodie, J. 1995b. *Politics on the Margin: Restructuring and the Women's Movement*. Halifax: Fernwood Publishing.

Canadian Centre for Policy Alternatives. 1995. *The Alternative Federal Budget*. Ottawa: CCPA.

Canadian Labour Congress and the National Action Committee on the Status of Women. 1996. 'Women's March Against Poverty: For Jobs and Justice! For Bread and Roses!' Press release.

Canadian Press. 1995. 'Women Boo PQ Ministers.' *Toronto Star*, June 5.

Connelly, M.P., and M. MacDonald. 1996. 'The Labour Market, the State, and the Reorganizing of Work: Policy Impacts.' In I. Bakker, ed., *Rethinking Restructuring: Gender and Change in Canada*. Toronto: University of Toronto Press, 82–91.

Daenzer, P. 1993. *Regulating Class Privilege: Immigrant Servants in Canada, 1940s–1990s.* Toronto: Canadian Scholars' Press.

Daly, M. 1994. 'Comparing Welfare States: A Gender Friendly Appproach.' In D. Sainsbury, ed., *Gendering Welfare States.* London: Sage.

Esping-Andersen, G. 1990. *Three Worlds of Welfare Capitalism.* Princeton, NJ: Princeton University Press.

Evans, P. 1994. 'Eroding Canadian Social Welfare: The Mulroney Legacy, 1984–1993.' *Social Policy and Administration* 28, 2: 107–19.

Fox Piven, F. 1990. 'Ideology and the State: Women, Power and the Welfare State.' In L. Gordon, ed., *Women, the State, and Welfare.* Madison: University of Wisconsin Press, 250–64.

Fraser, N. 1989. *Unruly Practices.* Minneapolis: University of Minnesota Press.

– and L. Gordon. 1994a. '"Dependency" Demystified: Inscriptions of Power in a Keyword of the Welfare State.' *Social Politics* 1, 1: 4–31.

– 1994b. 'A Geneaology of Dependency: Tracing a Keyword of the U.S. Welfare State.' *Signs* 19, 2: 309–36.

Gordon, L. 1990. 'The New Feminist Scholarship on the Welfare State.' In L. Gordon, ed., *Women, the State and Welfare.* Madison: University of Wisconsin Press, 9–35.

Gray, G. 1990. 'Social Policy by Stealth.' *Policy Options* 11, 2: 17–29.

Hauser, R., and I. Fischer 1990. 'Economic Well-Being among One-Parent Families.' In T. Smeeding, M. O'Higgins, and L. Rainwater, eds., *Poverty, Inequality and Income Distribution in Comparative Perspective.* Washington, DC: Urban Institute, 126–57.

Hernes, H. 1987. 'Women and the Welfare State: The Transition from Private to Public Dependence.' In A. Showstack Sassoon, ed., *Women and the State.* London: Unwin Hyman, 72–92.

Hobson, B. 1990. 'No Exit, No Voice: Women's Economic Dependency and the Welfare State.' *Acta Sociologica* 33, 3: 235–50.

Jenson, J. 1992. 'Getting to Morgenthaler: From One Representation to Another.' In J. Brodie, S.A.M. Gavigan, and J. Jenson, eds, *Politics of Abortion.* Toronto: Oxford University Press, 15–55.

– 1993. 'De-Constructing Dualities: Making Rights Claims in Political Institutions.' In G. Drover and P. Kerans, eds., *New Approaches to Welfare Theory.* Aldershot, Hants: Edward Elgar, 127–42.

Jessop, B. 1993. 'Towards a Schumpeterian Workfare State? Preliminary Remarks on Post-Fordist Political Economy.' *Studies in Political Economy* 40: 7–39.

Kealey, L., ed. 1979. *A Not Unreasonable Claim: Women and Reform in Canada, 1880s–1920s.* Toronto: Women's Press.

Koven, S., and S. Michel, eds. 1993. *Mothers of a New World: Maternalist Politics and the Origins of Welfare States.* New York: Routledge.

Lewis, J. 1993. 'Introduction.' In J. Lewis, ed., *Women and Social Policies in Europe: Work, Family and the State*. Aldershot, Hants.: Edward Elgar, 1–24.

Lightman, E., and A. Irving 1991. 'Restructuring Canada's Welfare State.' *Journal of Social Policy* 20, 1: 65–86.

Marshall, T.H. 1964. *Class, Citizenship and Social Development*. Chicago: University of Chicago Press, 71–134.

McQuaig, L. 1995. *Don't Shoot the Hippo: Death by Deficit and Other Canadian Myths*. Toronto: Viking.

Mitchinson, W. 1987. 'Early Women's Organizations and Social Reform: Prelude to the Welfare State.' In A. Moscovitch and J. Albert, eds., *'Benevolent' State: The Growth of Welfare in Canada*. Toronto: Garamond Press.

Mullally, R. 1994. 'Social Welfare and the New Right: A Class Mobilization Perspective.' In A. Johnson, S. McBride, and P.J. Smith, eds., *Continuities and Discontinuities: The Political Economy of Social Welfare and Labour Market Policy in Canada*. Toronto: University of Toronto Press, 76–96.

National Council of Welfare. 1993. *Incentives and Disincentives to Work*. Ottawa: NCW, Autumn.

O'Connor, J. 1993. 'Gender, Class and Citizenship in the Comparative Analysis of Welfare State Regimes: Theoretical and Methodological Issues.' *British Journal of Sociology* 44, 3: 501–18.

Organization for Economic Cooperation and Development (OECD). 1988. 'Women's Activity, Employment and Earnings: A Review of Recent Developments.' *Employment Outlook*. Paris: OECD, September, 129–72.

Orloff, A. 1993. 'Gender and the Social Rights of Citizenship: The Comparative Analysis of Gender Relations and Welfare States.' *American Sociological Review* 58: 303–28.

Phillips, A. 1992. 'Feminism, Equality and Difference.' In L. McDowell and R. Pringle, eds., *Defining Women: Social Institutions and Gender Divsions*. Cambridge: Polity Press, 205–22.

Picard, A. 1995. 'How Politicians Greeted the Marchers against Poverty.' *Toronto Star*, 8 June 1995.

Pixley, J. 1993. *Citizenship and Employment: Investigating Post-Industrial Options*. Cambridge: Cambridge University Press.

Prentice, A. 1988. *Canadian Women: A History*. Toronto: Harcourt, Brace, Jovanovich.

Pringle, R., and S. Watson 1992. 'Women's Interests and the Post-Structuralist State.' In M. Barrett and A. Phillips, eds., *Destabilizing Theory: Contemporary Feminist Debates*. Stanford: Stanford University Press, 53–73.

Quadagno, J. 1994. *The Color of Welfare. How Racism Undermined the War on Poverty*. New York: Oxford University Press.

Rekart, J. 1993. *Public Funds, Private Provision*. Vancouver: University of British Columbia Press.

Resnick, P. 1994. 'Neo-conservatism and Beyond.' In A. Johnson, S. McBride, and P. Smith, eds., *Continuities and Discontinuities: The Political Economy of Social Welfare and Labour Market Policy in Canada*. Toronto: University of Toronto Press, 25–35.

Sainsbury, D. 1996. *Gender, Equality and Welfare States*. Cambridge: Cambridge University Press.

– ed. 1994. *Gendering Welfare States*. London: Sage.

Siim, B. 1994. 'Engendering Democracy: Social Citizenship and Political Participation for Women in Scandinavia.' *Social Politics* 1, 3: 287–305.

Skocpol, T. 1992. *Protecting Soldiers and Mothers: The Political Origins of Social Policy in the United States*. Cambridge: Harvard University Press.

Taylor, V., and S. Rupp. 1993. 'Women's Culture and Lesbian Feminist Activism: A Reconsideration of Cultural Feminism.' *Signs* 19, 1: 32–61.

Taylor , V., and N. Whittier. 1995. 'Analytic Approaches to Social Movement Culture: The Culture of the Women's Movement.' In H. Johnston and B. Klandermans, eds., *Social Movements and Culture*. Minneapolis: University of Minnesota Press, 163–87.

Torjman, S., and K. Battle. 1995. *Dangers of Block Funding*. A Caledon Commentary. Ottawa: Caledon Institute of Social Policy.

Ursel, J. 1986. 'The State and the Maintenance of Patriarchy.' In J. Dickinson and B. Russell, eds., *Family, Economy, and State*. London: Croom, 150–91.

– 1992. *Private Lives, Public Policy*. Toronto: Women's Press.

Williams, F. 1989. *Social Policy: A Critical Introduction*. Cambridge: Polity Press.

Wilson, E. 1977. *Women and the Welfare State*. London: Tavistock.

2

From the Welfare State to Vampire Capitalism

MARJORIE GRIFFIN COHEN

Social policy as a progressive force has been more or less dead in Canada for the past ten years.[1] The optimism of feminists in the 1970s – that government policy could be changed to reflect women's needs – has been replaced by the desperate realization that even the few redistributive gains women worked so hard to achieve are being reversed.[2] Women's political activism focused on the state continues, but it is activism to hold on to what remains of the welfare state.[3]

The relationship between women and the welfare state has been an ambiguous one, and feminists are now in the unenviable position of defending programs and whole systems we have criticized in the past. This criticism focused mainly on the ways in which the institutions of the welfare state have been shaped by ideologies and practices which perpetuate inequalities. Too frequently, the state's responses to feminists' demands, when actually realized, turned out to be frustratingly crude imitations of what women truly wanted. In some bizarre way, the program women struggled for would be twisted so that it truly did seem as though women had replaced private patriarchy with state patriarchy.[4] This does not mean that the welfare state was unimportant to women, but rather, that the specific demands of women were probably less significant in bringing about redistributive policies in women's favour than were the general programs which shaped the economic climate which, in turn, made redistributive policies possible.

Much of the feminist critique of the relationship between women and the welfare state deals with the ways in which state programs have reinforced women's dependence and subordination (Kealey, 1979; Wilson, 1977; Hartmann, 1981). These have been important critiques for understanding how social policy might be more inclusive and also for bringing about changes in the ways in which society, in general, thinks about women's rights. In demanding that state policy be more responsive to women's needs, feminist activism has been successful, occasionally, in bringing about more women-centred programs. The problem is that these types of programs often do conflict with what is perceived as rational within the system itself. As a result, when economic circumstances change, the indulgence of the state in meeting the needs of 'special interest groups' is more easily challenged. The kinds of arguments feminists successfully had used to bring about expanded programs became less effective as the ideological logic of the market as the best regulator of all needs, including social ones, has come to dominate social discourse.

The dramatic changes associated with economic restructuring and the consequent attacks on the welfare state have necessitated reactive political mobilization.[5] Generally this reaction among feminist groups has focused on understanding the impacts of the policy changes on women and how change will affect either the way women relate to the state as providers or recipients of social welfare or how well the state protects individual group rights.[6]

In this chapter, I argue that social welfare relies as significantly on economic policy which affects the way the market works, including government monetary and fiscal policy, budgets, taxation, trading relationships, and development policy, as it does on those state programs more normally associated with feminist actions directed towards redistributive policies. This does not mean that the struggle over women's rights and specific programs has been irrelevant or misguided or even that the effort to preserve what exists should be abandoned.[7] But it does mean that the public policy affecting all disadvantaged groups goes far beyond the implications of specific social programs, labour market policies, and the legal status of these groups. Feminists certainly have recognized this, but there is a distinction to be made here between a feminist *analysis* of the constraints of modern society which have been constructed by capitalist economics, and feminist action which has tended to pursue changes in social, rather than economic institutions. Feminist literature abounds with the knowledge of the structural nature of inequality, but the day-to-day feminist activity and confrontation with the state has tended to focus pragmatically on remedying specific injustices.[8] Less clear is how to develop a strategy for dealing with the interrelatedness of social programs and regressive economic policies and to more specifically focus action on the institutions and ideologies which are shaping the ways the welfare state operates.

My discussion will focus on the ways in which social changes are being shaped by the expansion of international capital through 'globalization.' These economic changes are perceived by those advancing the dismantling of the welfare state as both inevitable and desirable and are related to their notion of what is an appropriate role for the state. The term 'vampire capitalism' fits this activity because all the arguments used to describe the 'inevitability' of the market as the main regulator of social life focuses on the necessity, in order to maintain corporate health, to perpetuate activities which are life-draining activities for the welfare state. The intention here is to not only discuss the logic of 'vampire capitalism,' but also to show the fallacies in the financial arguments which maintain that social welfare can no longer be sustained. This chapter will end with a discussion of the ways feminists might proceed to change what is often presented as inevitable.

The Terms: Globalization and Restructuring

The idea that the globe is a small place where people are increasingly interdependent first captured the public imagination with Marshall McLuhan's concept of the 'global village.' The village metaphor no longer fits, particularly because the driving force behind the space contraction is the antithesis of the village dynamic, but the implications of a compression of both space and economic interests has become central to public policy decisions: 'globalization' is the justification for a revolution in the economic and social policies of the welfare state. It refers to the dramatic increase both in the mobility of capital and in the international organization of production and distribution. Related to economic 'globalization' are cultural and ideological changes which support the spread of global economic systems. The values entrenched by globalization and their conflict with those values feminists have identified as essential for a just society are what is at stake in the defence of the welfare state.

'Restructuring' is the act of implementing the values of globalization within a nation's economic, social, and political systems.[9] Both globalization and restructuring are terms which imply a kind of inevitability to the policy changes which are occurring, changes beyond the control of people. In this sense restructuring appears apolitical and outside the purview of social analyses dealing with gender, class, and racial issues. While economic change has been a consistent feature of all modern industrial societies, normally, in the past, the conditions ushered in by economic depressions or recessions have been criticized and seen as temporary, at best. But with restructuring, the implications are distinct: unemployment, greater inequalities, and the contraction of social programs are not part of a temporary phase which will disappear with the end of a specific economic crisis. Rather, the changes which are being made to economic, social, and political systems are more fundamental and are considered and stated by the political and economic elites to be normal features of globalization. This is the critical difference between economic change now and economic change in other eras. However disruptive and unhappy the consequences of economic restructuring in the past, the elites always held forth the promise of a better life for the masses, in the long run. This progressive idea of economic change is no longer the justification for restructuring. The promise, rather, is a harmonization of social and economic life so that no nation will be disadvantaged because its corporate sector cannot compete internationally. A consistent theme of the corporate sector, that the economy can no longer support expensive social programs, is directly linked to the downward spiralling of social welfare through the harmonization process.

Free trade is the central supporting apparatus of globalization. In order to achieve the objective of creating a single market worldwide, international corporations consider essential the need to establish conditions so that they are free to produce and distribute goods and services without interference from governments throughout the world.[10] This ultimate objective is a long way from being fully realized, but the recent free trade agreements such as the Canada–U.S. Free Trade Agreement (FTA), the North American Free Trade Agreement (NAFTA), and the General Agreement on Tariffs and Trade (GATT) have made major advances towards this end.[11] Their main stated purpose is to eliminate practices within countries that constitute barriers to trade. Some people may be inclined to feel that this is reasonable and sensible because their notion of what constitutes barriers to trade are outright prohibitions against imports or exports or high tariffs designed to keep trade from occurring. But these trade agreements are much more than simply agreements about tariffs and import quotas because they involve the regulation of economic and social behaviour which goes far beyond trading relationships.[12]

Within these trading agreements, the concept of trade has been expanded beyond the notion of production of a good or service in one country for sale in another. Rather, the concept of free trade now involves institutions and rules which are designed to facilitate capital mobility as well. A distinction between the two types of international economic integration is sometimes made, with the spread of market linkages through greater trade flows referred to as *shallow integration*, and the type of integration associated with foreign direct investment and the internationalization of production referred to as *deep integration* (United Nations, 1994). The deep integration which is fostered through the liberalization of investment is accomplished through a conditioning framework which has been set up to harmonize the economic and social structures of countries.[13] This homogenization is accomplished partly through the direct dictates of the trade agreements themselves which very specifically restrict the ways in which the state can construct its economic and social policies.[14] Related to these requirements are the new competitive pressures which are created by the deep integration of economies on a global scale, and it is these pressures, coupled with ideological force, which are the most effective in reducing the scope of the welfare state.

The Justification for Government Retreat

During the initial years of welfare state constriction in the mid-1980s, Canada appeared to be approaching this process of change in a markedly different way from that which was done in England and the United States. To many analysts this difference was characterized by the absence of the anti-welfare state rhetoric so characteristic of the Reagan and Thatcher era (Lightman and Irving, 1991; Evans, 1994). In some sense the conservative forces in Canada seemed not to be so brutal as elsewhere, but were merely responding to the international pressures in such a way that the welfare state appeared to be 'restructuring,' rather than dismantling. To some commentators this indicated that there was a resilience in the welfare state which created a certain imperviousness to attempts by various governments to dismantle its main features (Mishra, 1990; Myles, 1988). In particular, the business elites, at least for a time, did not rail against the largess of the state, preferring, instead, to indicate their support for social programs and generally arguing not for their elimination, but for economic policies which would strengthen the capitalist class so that the programs could be assured funding in the future.[15]

This qualified support for the welfare state by the corporate sector was politically pragmatic and in hindsight can be understood not to have been rooted in a social welfare ideology. It appears the Canadian corporate sector understood that careful planning over a period of time was necessary in order to shape the political climate to tolerate the dismantling of the welfare state.[16] People in Canada have been strongly supportive of the country's social programs and governments were particularly attuned to the political danger which could result from changes to these programs.[17] To overcome this obstacle, a conditioning framework needed to be established so that the withdrawal of the state from performing functions people had come to expect could be seen as logical and inevitable. The economic logic for deconstructing the welfare state had to become part of the subconscious way people understood the working of the economic system in order to be able to erase the public's attachment to 'expensive' social programs. Ultimately, the argument that 'we can't afford' these programs had to become part of the culture of the nation.

Two main approaches were used to saturate the public with the notion that the welfare state could not continue to exist in the form people liked. One line of argument related to the logic of international trade as a result of the increased competitiveness associated with the free trade agreements. The other was to whip up concern about public finances by focusing on the 'tax wall,' the threat of inflation, the problems of maintaining a deficit, and the huge size of the public debt.

Competition

If Canadian businesses were to continue to compete in international arenas, it was argued that they could not be disadvantaged because they paid more taxes or were forced to abide by stricter equity, labour, and environmental laws than their rivals in poorer countries. While this was not a new argument from the corporate sector, the increased mobility afforded to these corporations with the trade agreements lent more weight to their complaints. They simply threatened to leave Canada to locate in countries which had more attractive business climates if their demands for changes were not met. A more attractive business climate would be one with low taxes and few restrictions on a firm's activities which affected labour and the environment.

The development of the social welfare state, particularly in the shape it took after the Second World War, required the cooperation of the corporate sector. But with trade liberalization the logic through which the state extracted corporate cooperation was loosened. For a while economic policies which focused on full employment, high wages, and social support systems made sense to the corporate community as a group.[18] Individually, each business knew that it could make higher profits than its competitors if it could reduce costs by paying low wages to its workers and avoiding taxes. But, collectively, the corporate world understood that if selling products or services meant a reliance on people within the nation to buy them, it would be important that these people had the money to do so. The welfare of the people within a nation was intrinsically linked to the ability of mass production to find a mass of customers to purchase the things produced. Individually, corporations could do well by high rates of unemployment because then workers would be competing for jobs, and wages would fall, but this low-wage strategy could not work for all producers simultaneously if they wanted to sell all they produced. Individually, firms would have higher profits if they did not pay taxes, but collectively they would suffer if the state could not afford an infrastructure to support business activities.

With the uncoupling of the production of a nation from its markets, as is the intention with trade liberalization, the logic of maintaining a high standard of living within a nation begins to lose its saliency with the corporate sector. The growth in the significance of export markets means that higher rates of unemployment and lower wages can be tolerated, since the people within the country will not be required to buy all that is produced within the country in order for the corporate sector to maintain itself. Unemployment and low wages can become a permanent feature of an export-led economy.[19] From the perspective of corporations, not having to rely on selling what they produced within the nation is ideal because costs can be lowered sigificantly without danger of creating economic conditions which would negatively affect their ability to sell, as would be the case in a more closed economic system. Internationally the corporations can become 'more competitive.'[20]

Public Finances[21]

The desire of the corporate sector to pay little, or no, taxes comes into direct conflict with the problem of how to provide for social welfare. The corporate sector's solution to this problem is to reduce the size of government and to shift as much as possible of the services government provides to the private sector. As noted above, people's attraction to government services made this politically difficult, particularly when the elimination of some service or part of a service became part of public discussion. The easier way to accomplish the dismantling of the welfare state would be by creating a perception among the public that the kinds of government Canadians liked was no longer affordable and to shift the debate onto budgetary issues, while at the same time maintaining that services were being protected.

The campaign to convince Canadians that the government was hopelessly in debt because of overspending on social programs began soon after the Mulroney government's re-election in 1988, partly as a deflection of public attention from the obvious economic downturn which was occurring as a result of free trade. Public advertising on television showed the Loonie divided up to indicate how government spent money, with the intention of riveting the public's attention on the fact that spending on social programs was a huge portion of total government expenditure. This is true, but then this is precisely what government is supposed to do, and even if government shrinks the proportion spent on social programs would still be large.

The intention over the next few years was to establish the idea firmly that government deficits were out of control and that the debt was escalating to such dangerous heights that Canada was in danger of bankruptcy. This was skilfully managed by the government with the help from the corporate sector and the corporate-controlled media. A debt certainly existed, but the impression created that excessive spending on redistributive programs was its cause was clearly false. Also false is the conviction that the country is in a desperate state because of the debt crisis. But those supporting conservative economic policies in successive governments have been successful in convincing almost *everyone* that the debt crisis requires that Canadians begin to live within our means, a requirement that would mean either higher taxes or cutting government programs.

The problem now is that virtually every political party and government throughout the country seems to agree that the debt and the deficit issues are the main parameters which should shape all government policy. As one critic of this deficit hysteria notes, while *everyone* agrees that Canada has a debt crisis, it is possible that *everyone* can be mistaken. This critic then reminds us that there was a time when *everyone* knew the earth was flat, when *everyone* thought witches should be burned, and when *everyone* knew sunbathing was healthy (Rosenbluth, 1995).

For a while those on the progressive side of the political spectrum were united in recognizing that the size of the debt and the deficit had become a handy justification, by right-wing governments, for cutting spending on socially useful programs. As long as this type of action was confined to conservative political governments, the left was fairly uniform in its criticism of program-slashing behaviour. Since the election of several NDP provincial governments in Canada, this left(ish) unity on economic policy has dissipated – particularly as these governments have tended, almost uniformly, to adopt the same language and surprisingly similar policies as their politically conservative rivals. As a result, there appears to be an inevitability to the economic arguments of the right, producing consensus on the need to eliminate government deficits and to reduce all governments' debt as the first and most important economic problems to be addressed.[22]

Because of the capitulation of the left to the economic arguments of the right, the deficit is now the problem – the political problem, that is. It is not the major economic problem facing this country, and the policies which have been followed to eliminate the deficit and reduce the debt are precisely the ones which helped to create the problem in the first place and will compound it in the future.

The identification of the debt as more of a political problem than an economic one is not to dismiss its significance. The political nature of highlighting the deficit and the debt as key economic issues is tied up with the entire perspective of conservative economic thinking: it reinforces the notion that the disappointing performance of the Canadian economy is not a result of the failure of conservative economic policies, which have been guiding this country for over a decade now, but rather arises because these policies were not stringent enough. Despite their overt political demise, in the political battle to win the minds and souls of the Canadian electorate the Conservatives appear to have won. People, in general, do seem to believe that taxes are bad (because presumably individuals receive less from government than they pay to it), that any activity undertaken by government will be inefficient, that the market is the best and most efficient guide of economic activity, that government spending is out of control and therefore evil, and that government deficits cause economic problems.

An understanding of the cause of the 'debt crisis' is critical for women's ability to refute the arguments used to reduce spending on those areas which are crucial for women and to refuse to increase taxes on the wealthy.[23] As long as social spending is targetted as the problem, and *everyone* believes taxes cannot be raised, the arguments of neo-conservative economics will appear to make sense.

The Deficit and the Debt

The federal government has a large deficit and spends about a third of its revenues, amounting to over $48 billion in 1995–96, just to pay interest payments on the money it owes for past borrowings. The deficit (the excess of expenditures over revenues each year) exists primarily because of the need to pay interest payments on the debt. Without interest payments on the debt (the sum of past deficits) there would be a substantial surplus in government accounts. This is because in all but two years since 1988 the government has taken in more money in taxes and other revenues than it has spent on all government programs and administration. In some years the operating surplus has been over $10 billion, but over the period between 1988 and 1995 the government has received a total of $31.1 billion in revenues above what was necessary for expenses on social programs, other programs (like defence), and government administration (Bank of Canada, 1995–6).

Obviously, at some point, the government spent more on programs and administration than it received, otherwise a deficit would not have arisen. This it did in the early 1980s, but it was neither irresponsible action nor evidence of spending beyond the country's means, as is often the criticism leveled when governments generate a deficit. The rise in government deficits in the 1980s was a response to a severe recession, one which affected Canada more than any other developed country.[24] During this period real output declined and unemployment rates soared to 12 per cent and remained high, averaging over 10 per cent for most of the time since then. The decline in output and employment was the result of dramatic decreases in capital spending which then resulted in large increases in private savings.[25] The cyclically sensitive components of program spending (unemployment insurance and social assistance payments) increased government expenditures more dramatically than revenues during this period. The critics of government spending would maintain that the problem with the debt arose because the government did not cut back spending enough during this period of high unemployment. But excess government spending then was not really the problem, and without it things would have been worse. The low capital spending during this period and excessive savings were mainly responsible for the decline in employment and production levels. Under these circumstances, government counter-cyclical measures in the form of unemployment benefits and welfare payments prevented the economy from experiencing an even more severe recession.

Certainly a debt was being created, but it would not have escalated and become the problem it has become were it not for the excessively tight monetary policy pursued at this time. The government's obsession with fighting inflation through high interest rates meant that each year the government paid more in interest payments for the money it had borrowed in the past. In addition to initiating chronic deficits, the high interest rates damaged economic performance: the recession of the early 1980s was a result of this problem. By 1981 treasury bill rates were almost 18 per cent and long-term government bonds yielded 15 per cent, making Canada's interest rates among the highest among all developed countries, a distinction which has been retained since then.

This high interest rate policy had long-term economic consequences. It depressed the recovery in private capital spending, since borrowing was much more costly. This meant that unemployment levels remained high, and since income levels were depressed so were government revenues. In addition to affecting government revenues, the amounts paid in interest on the debt increased yearly deficits.

Another consequence which has had long-term political implications was the increased attractiveness of Canadian bonds to foreign investors because of their extraordinarily high yield. Less than 3 per cent of Canada's government debt was foreign held in 1970. And although this had increased to about 10 per cent by 1980 as a result of the inflation-fighting policies of the late 1970s, this was still moderate compared with the proportion of the debt held outside the country now, which stands at about 25 per cent (Bank of Canada, 1995). The increased foreign debt holdings further accentuates the need to keep interest rates high as foreign bondholders' opinions of appropriate Canadian economic policy have increasing significance with policy makers.

Other problems affecting government revenues and therefore compounding the debt problem were generated by additional misguided policies towards the end of the 1980s. Three of these were most significant. First, reduced taxes on the corporate sector directly affected government revenues. Second, the large rise in the value of the Canadian dollar in the late 1980s made Canadian items too costly on foreign markets and thereby considerably reduced economic activity in those industries which rely on the export market. Third, the introduction of the Free Trade Agreement with the United States brought about the beginnings of large capital drains from Canada. The increase in the value of the dollar and the results of free trade negatively affected both government revenues from corporate and individual taxes as well as the level of employment.

Throughout all of this Canada has persisted with a restrictive monetary policy. Even though the rate of inflation fell from over 11 per cent in the early 1980s to about 4.5 per cent when the Conservative government took power in 1984, inflation fighting through high interest rates remained a crucial part of economic policy. Even today, during a deflationary period, the threat of inflation guides the Bank of Canada's interest rate policy. Real inflation does not exist. Still, the present governor of the Bank of Canada, Gordon G. Thiessen, has explained that the bank could not hold interest rates down because this would shake confidence in the belief that 'we will keep inflation low into the future. We cannot offset the risk premiums demanded by savers and investors because of their concerns about future fiscal and political developments.' Thiessen's strategy (remarkably similar to that of his predecessor) is that 'over time, by maintaining confidence in monetary policy, we seek to provide a stable environment in which financial markets can operate,' (Thiessen, 1994: 11). Under John Crow the Bank of Canada's goal was zero inflation. Now that this has been achieved even zero inflation appears to be too high.

Canada has now had ten years of remarkably stable price levels. The strategy so ardently followed by the Bank of Canada and successive governments, despite party changes, simply has not worked.[26] Monetary policy designed solely around price stability does not automatically bring about confidence in economic performance. If anything, the results have been the opposite of those promised by the zero inflation strategy and some markets, most notably the labour and housing markets, are in a chronic state of instability.[27] In the name of stability, the Bank of Canada has created a very volatile economy: any increase in economic activity (particularly decreases in unemployment rates) brings quick reaction from the central bank to trigger the mechanisms (higher interest rates) which generate further instability.

The politics of solving a non-existent problem (inflation) may seem smart, but the economic price is a high one. The pain caused by the persistently high interest rate policy, in the form of high rates of unemployment, lower government revenues, income inequality, and real human misery, has not generated the stable state so long touted as the necessary route to inspire business confidence. Any politically convenient scapegoat, such as uncertainty about Quebec or even the threat that programs like medicare may be maintained, can be found at any particular moment to explain lack of confidence in the Canadian economy and to justify still further restrictive economic policy.[28] But whatever is said about economic confidence and various routes towards inspiration, the most consistent way to generate a stable economy is through both creating among the population the expectation that their incomes will be maintained in the future and creating among producers the expectation that they will be able to sell what they have produced and that expanding production will result in even higher sales in the future. These two expectations are related, and the disassociation of one from the other inevitably creates lower expectations for both. If we want a stable economy, we must have stable institutional structures, particularly with regard to employment and income security. In the past, the stability sought through monetary policy was really generated by the institutions which have been swept away in the marketization process. Restrictive monetary policy is not creating stability, but it does have a function, and that function is to reduce the scope of the welfare state by challenging income security. Reducing income security is, in the words of one critic, the 'epicentre of the marketisation process' (Hutton, 1994: 21).

The main point to be made about the deficit is that it has not arisen from reckless government spending. The deficit exists because of an ideologically driven, recklessly restrictive monetary policy which has created conditions resulting in both higher costs for government and reduced revenues. The cure, of reducing spending on counter-cyclical programs and maintaining high interest rates, which the present government seems to want to pursue and which does not differ from that of the policies of the previous ten years, cannot solve either the deficit problem or the economic morass experienced by most of the country. Attempts to control the federal deficit have failed because the very tools used to control it have a perverse effect on the economy. It undermines the revenues the government receives, and the result is greater deficits and a growth in the debt.[29] Any cut in spending means someone's income is reduced or eliminated altogether. When that person is forced to spend less, someone else's income falls. Ultimately, everyone affected has less income and, as a consequence, pays less tax. The deficit problem cannot be solved unless the underlying economic weaknesses are eliminated. This is where the policy procedures bog down. Economic orthodoxy suggests that just letting the market take its course will ultimately right a dismal situation. Perhaps some external event could occur to stimulate economic activity, but waiting for this to happen is not a wise strategy. An active economic strategy to ensure full employment and to meet other social and economic goals, as so often has been said, is needed.

The distinction now, between this and any other time in Canadian history, is that the ability for a government to act takes a great deal more political courage than it ever did. This is because the economic tools to discipline the market are not as readily available as they were in the past, and the decision to reassert the right to use these tools requires a bold political step.

The most serious economic problem facing Canada is the inability to design policy necessary to foster an economic system which accommodates the specific conditions here. The results of two different, although related, international trends have restricted whatever economic autonomy Canadian governments could use to this end. One is the extraordinarily artificial economic results which occur from the wildly speculative nature of international finance. The other is the artificial economic conditions imposed by international free trade agreements. Pressure from both have generated government policy and institutional responses which have little relationship to those which are needed to meet Canadian conditions.

The Pressure of Finance Speculation

The speculative nature of international financial markets has uncoupled the relationship between a nation's economic viability and its attractiveness as an international investment risk. International financial markets are not about investment: only a small proportion of international currency exchanges actually pays for real goods or services. Most of the currency trading is betting.[30] Anything (rumour, greed, sentiment, prejudice, manipulation) can be the driving force determining whether a country is in favour or not, but these speculative currents have little to do with how healthy an economy is. The speculation is about the future, and if some government does not behave according to the way international traders want it to behave, it will have no future. Governments are increasingly guided by the actions of offshore actors who have little, or no, knowledge of the actual circumstances of the countries they bet on: economic and political (at best) orthodoxy will guide their actions.[31] The new technologies which allow instantaneous responses to decisions about Canada taken in the United States, Europe, or Asia means greater and greater volumes of money can be brought to bear on a government to behave the way that international finance wants it to. The sheer volume of the money traded daily gives these speculators political clout: an estimated $1 trillion was traded daily on international exchange markets in the early 1990s, or almost forty times the amount of money which arises daily from international trade (Helleiner, 1996). The governor of the Bank of Canada maintains that 'the basic monetary and economic foundations for a solid and sustained growth in the economy are in place,' (Thiessen, 1994: 11), but this does not seem to matter much to international financial markets which demand very specific kinds of economic behaviour from this country.

Recognizing the need to regulate international finance is not confined to the mumbling fringe of a dissatisfied left. Even the International Monetary Fund (IMF), not widely known for its hostility to international finance, cautiously counsels a reassessment of the uncontrolled actions of the speculators: 'The increasing complexity and volume of contemporary financial intermediation, its international scope, the speed with which disturbances spread, and the breakdown of geographic and functional barriers that potentially insulate markets, are now leading supervisory authorities ... to reassess the adequacy of prudential arrangements both nationally and internationally' (IMF, 1989: 12). The voices for an independent financial system are certainly subdued in Canada, and while a few recognize the necessity for action to bring this about this has yet to become a political issue.

Our system is more vulnerable to manipulation than that of any other industrialized country, and this should be public knowledge. Even a figure as unsympathetic to financial regulation as Gordon G. Thiessen recognizes that Canada is peculiarly placed when he observes that 'when international markets take on a negative tone, there is a much more critical assessment of Canadian events' (Thiessen, 1994: 11). Other commentators would go much farther and target international financial pressure as the main economic problem Canada faces.[32] As long as it is believed that the increased power of financial speculation is mainly a result of technological changes which permit rapid transfers of massive amounts of money, it would appear that the anarchy in this highly volatile sector will continue. But countries like Canada have made conscious political decisions, as a result of lobbying from the corporate sector, which have supported and encouraged international financial speculation. Technological change has facilitated the cross-border exchange of financial assets, but without state actions such as the withdrawal of currency controls and the deregulation of banking and other financial institutions the technological changes alone could not have produced these changes in financial power over governments.

Why It Matters for Women

The new power given to the corporate sector – through trade agreements and unregulated financial speculation – places nations in about the same stage of control over capital as they were at the dawn of the industrial revolution. Then the power of capital grew faster than the power of nation states. Yet, over time, institutions were developed, as a result of pressure from people, to humanize the most brutal aspects of this phase of economic 'restructuring.'

There was a long period between the establishment of forces to attempt to control the worst aspects of the power of the market and the establishment of institutions which we have come to label as the welfare state. And, however critical feminists have been of the welfare state, it has been the one instrument through which women have been able to exercise their equality rights as citizens. It is through the redistributive aspects of the welfare state that women have been able to achieve the policies necessary so that their needs can be met and so that conditions could be created for women's equal participation in public life.

However, this piecemeal approach, which attempts to control the worst aspects of the power of the market, took centuries. It is a much too long-term approach in the face of international finance, WTO, the FTA, and NAFTA. People can fatalistically accept the framework which says that nothing can be done and that we must accept the fact that economic policy will be removed from the democratic process. If we do, the best to be hoped for is a policy approach which simply organizes all institutions to service the corporate sector so that they themselves can be more aggressive internationally: and then hope it works. What is more likely to occur under these circumstances is the full playing out of the logic of vampire capital. If we submit to international capital, our natural and human resources will be mercilessly exploited, eventually depleted, and then capital will simply move on. In this process, all that women have worked for to establish the recognition that other values, other than those of the market mechanism are critical ones for social life, will become simply utopian notions of the past – much in the way we view the attempts at establishing egalitarian communes in the nineteenth century. These efforts will be a colourful part of our feminist history.

There are alternatives to submission and the reduction of state functions to minimalist activities. Nations and people are not paralyzed from acting in response to the increased strength of the power of the corporate private sector. But it is important that this action occur soon, before all the institutions have changed to accommodate the new international order. In what follows I will discuss some ways in which the activism of feminism can proceed in the face of what appears to be an inevitable dismantling of the welfare state. This discussion of alternatives is meant not to be definitive, but to raise, in the context of the march towards 'vampire capitalism,' the approaches which will be necessary to reinstate feminist values in political debates about economic and social structures.[33]

Alternatives

In showing how the ideology of the right has reshaped international and domestic institutions in ways which condition our behaviour, we run the risk of contributing to its assertion that the changes which are occurring are inevitable and that 'there is no alternative.' The notion that the globalization process is incompatible with strong systems of social welfare, group rights, and states' sovereignty is one issue on which there often is not much disagreement between the left and the right.[34] In the case of the right, the argument about the obsolescence of the welfare state serves its purpose of ensuring that the obligations and constraints demanded by national governments are replaced by international economic rights.[35] The analysis of the left, on the other hand, has focused on the incompatibility between social welfare and democracy and trade liberalization in order to gain political support for public opposition to the globalization process. As usual, for the political groups in the weaker position, there is a fine balance between messages of despair and those which inspire action. An analysis which shows the dangers in the new conditions will lead to despair if the alternatives to it are not sufficiently compelling and if there is nothing concrete which can be suggested for action in the normal course of daily lives. Changing the world, or at least the trajectory which is now apparent, is an important goal, but most people will be unable to respond to this long-term initiative if there is not some relationship between it and their immediate political concerns. I see feminists well positioned to provide leadership on both the perspective for change at the international level and for political action in concrete immediate terms.

At the National Level

It is critical that feminists maintain their actions which focus on supporting social welfare, equitable distribution systems, and making the state more democratic. The overwhelming nature of the internationalization process has made this a reactive, rather than a proactive, position and as such it is often the target of criticism of the feminist movement by both its supporters and detractors.[36] But, as is frequently noted, there is no consensus in Canada about the vision of the future, and public support for some of the central institutions of the social system continues to be strong; so although resisting the dismantling of social programs is 'reactive,' it nonetheless can be successful. While the new international structures supporting trade liberalization give the corporate sector a great deal of leverage over public policy within nations, there are sufficiently different possible courses of action that the uniform race to the bottom can be resisted with credibility. As Ramesh Mishra (1990) points out, the substantial national differences in social policies in countries within the European Community, despite free trade and the free movement of capital, indicate that the convergence of social welfare policy is not inevitable. The decisions taken in Canada, for example, to reduce the number of women receiving Unemployment Insurance benefits, to reduce drastically federal funding for health and education, and to ignore promises to provide a national child care scheme are political decisions based on ideological and cultural values which can be contested on moral and democratic bases.

The power of nation states, although constrained, is still strong, and the government is the primary avenue people within a nation have for addressing their interests at the international level. For this reason it is important that feminists work to resist the political fragmentation which is occurring in Canada as each region demands more and more autonomy over social and economic programs. While the Canadian government continues to be a champion of trade liberalization and, in some circumstances, is far more ardent than even the United States in pursuing new free trade deals, this does not mean that sometime in the future Canada could not take a different lead in shaping international institutions. For this we will need not only a strong federal government, but also one which is truly democratic and represents, at the international level, the will of the nation. This representation has not occurred with trade liberalization issues: people within Canada repeatedly have voiced their opposition to free trade, yet the government continues to support the interests of the corporate sector. The response of government certainly raises the contradiction of calling for national sovereignty when the national government does not respond to popular sovereignty.

At the International Level

At the international level three main interrelated initiatives should be the focus for action of progressive groups.

First, there is an urgent need to begin what will be a long-term project

to counter the ideological hegemony of the right with regard to the efficiency of the self-regulating market. This could begin with analysis
which shows the economic inefficiencies and real human misery which
follows from imposing a uniform economic system around the world.
The call would be for an ability to recognize economic pluralism in
international trade agreements. What this means is allowing for a differentiation in economic systems in order to respond to distinct problems
faced by countries. The need for a differentiation in economic and social
institutions can result from a variety of factors, related to, for example,
the ways the country developed historically, its cultural objectives, and
its geographic constraints. The attempt of international trade agreements to impose uniform economic and social policy worldwide creates
impossible positions for people in countries which have vastly different
problems and resources, in addition to different values and goals. We in
Canada have devised an economic and social system which is different
from the United States because, in part, we have needed to accommodate the needs of few people living in a huge and often hostile geographic area. We are being forced to change many of these systems as a
result of trade liberalization, and, however difficult it will be for many
groups in this country, the problems arising from conformity are infi-
nitely more serious for poor countries with very different types of social
and economic organizations.

Without economic pluralism, any attempts to enforce labour and
environmental standards internationally will either fail, or if truly
enforced, will unduly punish some of the poorest places on earth. In the
process of demanding economic uniformity, the corporate community
has taken away from poor countries any innovative ways in which they
might be able to find unique solutions to their problems. If poor countries must both abide by the employment and environmental standards
of wealthy countries and maintain the same economic system without
any ways of circumventing the impossible through collective, public
policies, they most certainly will be made even poorer.

Feminists' recognition of difference among women and the concomitant need for social policy to recognize the different needs for different
circumstances is an important starting point for an analysis which recognizes the need for pluralism in social and economic systems. Any
attempt to change the international rules seems an Amazonian task, particularly because the power of the corporate sector has been so
enhanced by the changes in the trading rules so far. However, the very
real likelihood of failure of these policies to meet the needs of most of

the people in the world is going to give new approaches a chance to flourish. A project which begins to analyse the ways in which international institutions could be organized to allow for economic and social welfare pluralism would be well positioned to be accepted when the promises of the existing trade regimes are not fulfilled.

Second, it is important to initiate action to demand the creation of international institutions to control capital. The current unwillingness or inability of nation states to assert the kind of control over capital which is necessary to protect employment levels, the environment, and conditions of life reflects the power which corporations have to intimidate or otherwise gain the cooperation of national governments. With the new trading arrangements, new international institutions of governance are being created, but these are market-creating institutions, rather than a replication of market-controlling institutions of the nation state. The current attempt to initiate standards, such as the labour and environmental side agreements in NAFTA or the social charters such as exist in Europe, tend to operate by focusing on each nation's responsibility.[37] As I noted above, this disadvantages the poorest nations in the international economy who have little real power to bring about progressive changes under the free-market system. Rather, the focus for discipline must be the international corporation. Their very rationale for capital mobility is to take advantage of the economic climate in countries which are either politically corrupt or too weak to protect their people or their environments. International institutions which disciplined corporations, rather than countries, would begin to replicate some of the work of national institutions which was effective when nations had more power over corporate behaviour.

In addition to designing international institutions to control capital, there is also a need to imitate the redistributive functions of the nation state at the international level. As long as the enormous disparities which exist worldwide continue, the corporate sector will be able to blackmail nations into submitting to their demands for a 'favourable' climate for business. This redistributive function requires an ability for an international governing institution to raise money and to decide where money should go. The recent interest in developing a tax on international financial speculation (the Tobin tax) in order to both discourage excessive speculation and to raise money could be the starting point for new international institutions to control and redistribute capital.

Finally, it is essential for women in Canada to work with other people in nations which also are negatively affected by the rule of international corporations. In this, feminists throughout the world are well positioned to lead discussions for a future which would make a global economy viable socially as well as economically: few popular sector groups have the kinds of international connections which have been made by feminists through huge international conferences like those in Nairobi and Beijing. Women have begun to make important innovative use of U.N. conventions to pressure nations on economic and social reform. For example, women have pursued poverty issues as human rights violations. This is an approach which, if developed further, squarely confronts the economic demands of capital mobility.

While the opposition of women in Canada to the initial Free Trade Agreement was not successful in getting the support of women in the United States, the links did begin to develop between the women there and in Mexico during the political debates associated with NAFTA.[38] As the trajectory of trade liberalization continues to unfold, the experiences of women in different parts of the world will be distinct, but the ability to learn from each other and to explore ideas for collective action could lead to significant political initiatives for change.

Appendix

Deconstructing Social Welfare:
The Federal Government Chronology, 1985–1995[*]

The idea of a 'welfare state' went through a metamorphosis during the bleak years of the Mulroney government. The progressive notion that the state should be responsible for how well its citizens fare has degenerated to a sense that 'welfare' means government handouts to the unfortunate or the lazy. With depressing uniformity governments in Canada have rejected a sense that collectively providing services is good for everybody and that social institutions are necessary so that people are in a position to care for themselves. Providing universal medical care, education, pensions, inexpensive transportation and communication systems, affordable housing, work at reasonable wages, and adequate child care are the things that make a decent life possible and keep a large proportion of people out of poverty. While none of these programs occurred in a way and to the extent that fully recognized either the contribution or

[*]This chronology was constructed with the help of Judy Morrison and Darcian Smith.

the needs of women or disadvantaged minorities, the idea that they should exist, at least, was the notion of the welfare state.

During the past ten years even the programs which seemed secure because of their popularity have been either eliminated or eroded so badly that they are in danger of withering away. In some cases some debate has taken place before the government initiated a change. This was most notable on issues leading to free trade and changes in the patent monopolies for drug companies. More common was a steady erosion of programs and institutions which was achieved by introducing a thousand little budget cuts, tax changes, and hard-to-explain technical manipulations to existing legislation. These small changes were not ignored by popular sector groups, but each change in itself was not significant enough to generate either media interest or heated public debate. Altogether the changes have been significant and are related to an ideological shift to the right which has swept the entire continent.

The following is a list of the changes the federal government has made which has made the tax system more favourable to the wealthy, cut government programs and employment, and increased the power of the private sector by privatizing social and economic activities. The first term of the Mulroney government began the process of deconstructing Canada's social welfare systems, a process which was accelerated dramatically after their 1988 re-election. The election of a Liberal government in 1993, despite its election promises, did not change the downward trajectory. The 1995 budget indicated the determination of the federal government to accelerate the move towards minimalist government. The 1996 budget is not included because there were no new cuts to programs, since the ones which were to occur during the year had been announced in the 1995 budget.

1985

Budget Cuts

- Canada Mortgage and Housing Corporation (CMHC) budget reduced by $26 million
- Steady cut of funding for affordable housing (1980–1984 government spent 1.7 per cent of the budget on housing; after 1984, 1.4 per cent on average)
- 15,000 civil service jobs to be cut by 1990
- Initiatives to limit public sector pensions to those comparable to the private sector announced

- Official Development Assistance reduced by $50 million
- Glace Bay and Port Hawkesbury heavy water plants closed

Tax Changes

- Partial deindexing of family allowance (indexing for inflation established by the average rate of inflation minus 3 per cent)
- Partial deindexing of Old Age Security announced (resisted by seniors and not accomplished until 1989)
- Capital gains exemption of $500,000 to be phased in over 6 years with $20,000 exemption in 1985, $50,000 in 1986, and $100,000 additional each subsequent year until 1990 (amended in 1988 to limit the exemption levels to $100,000)
- Federal sales tax general increase of 1 per cent effective 1 January 1986, plus expanded list of taxable items to include candy and confectionery, soft drinks, pet foods, certain goods related to energy efficiency, beauty, and health goods
- RRSP contribution limits to be increased each year from 1986 to 1990

Privatization

Nanisivik Mines
Northern Transportation Company
- Privatization plans announced for the Canadian Development Corporation (CDC) plus thirteen other entities

1986

Budget Cuts

- Established Programs Financing limited to GNP minus 2 per cent (2 per cent cut)
- $500 million reduction in non-statutory spending
- First 5,000 civil service jobs eliminated (of 15,000 announced in 1985 budget)
- Canada's aid program reduced by $1.6 billion over next 5 years

Reduced funding to:
Canada Mortgage and Housing Corporation
Canadian Broadcasting Corporation

CN Marine
Via Rail

Tax Changes

- Corporate tax rate reduction from 36 per cent to 33 per cent of taxable income by 1989 announced
- Increase in sales tax of 1 per cent for 1 April 1986
- Manufacturing companies' taxes to be reduced from 30 per cent to 26 per cent by 1989
- Tax rate for small business to fall from 15 per cent to 13 per cent
- Surtax of 3 per cent on all personal incomes and corporations
- Partial deindexation of personal tax exemptions, including child benefits (exemptions would be indexed only for the rate of inflation minus 3 per cent)

Privatization

Canada Development Corporation
Canadair
Canadian Arsenals
CN Route
de Havilland
Eldorado Nuclear
Northern Transportation Company
Pecheries Canada Incorporated

1987

- Changes to Drug Patent Act (Bill C-22) to increase monopoly power of drug companies and limit availability of generic drugs

Privatization

Fishery Products International
Northern Canada Power Commission (Yukon)
Post Office privatization:
- Parcels and registered mail pick-up moved to privately operated sub-post offices
- Cleaning and trucking contracted out

- Announced plans to close all 734 city and town post offices and stations

Teleglobe Canada
Varsity Corporation

1988

Budget Cuts

- 300 rural post offices closed
- Federal cap on contribution to federal-provincial cost-sharing for programs under the Young Offenders Act
- $300 million decrease in federal budget for 'non-statutory' items announced

Tax Changes

- Massive change in personal income tax structure by reducing ten tax brackets to three and substantially lowering tax rate for top brackets (the ten tax brackets had ranged from 6 per cent to 34 per cent; rates changed to 17 per cent, 27 per cent, and 29 per cent)
- Child care income tax expense deduction increased (from $2,000 to $4,000) and child care tax credit increased (to replace promised national child care program)

Privatization

Air Canada
CN Hotels
Northern Canada Power Commission (Northwest Territories)
Northwestel Incorporated
Terra Nova Telecommunications

1989

- Canada–U.S. Free Trade Agreement

Budget Cuts

- Rental rehabilitation assistance program (used by many municipal

non-profit housing groups to maintain low-cost rental housing and rooming houses) eliminated; funding for cooperative housing cut
- $4 billion promised to provinces for child care to be dropped (would have provided 200,000 new child care spaces over 7 years)
- Regional development programs cut by $400 million per year for 4 years
- Foreign aid cut by $400 million per year for 4 years
- Established Programs Financing cuts of 1 per cent; additional $2 billion to be cut during following 3 years
- Grants to advocacy groups cut by $10 million, including:
  $2 million cut from women's groups
  $3 million cut from Native groups
  $2 million cut from visible minority groups
- Cuts in environmental programs, including:
  National Conservation and Alternative Energy Initiative phased out in 1990–91
  12 regional conservation and renewable energy offices closed (saving $10 million in 1989–90)
- Cuts to health and safety training: $10 million cut annually from the Canadian Centre for Occupational Health and Safety (in an attempt to end all public funding to this body by 1992)
- Cuts in agriculture support, including:
  Crop insurance system cut by $90 million in 1989–90, then $110 million in 1990–91
  Railway branchline rehabilitation program to be cut by $48 million and ended 1 year early
  Interest subsidy on grain payments cut by $27 million
  Dairy special export program cut by $7 million annually
  End to subsidized farm loans
  Skim milk powder programs cut by $7 million
- Postal subsidy to Canadian publishers cut by $10 million in 1989–90 and $45 million in each subsequent year until it is eliminated
- Cuts to Via Rail of $100 million each year for 5 years
- Cuts to CBC of $20 million in first year and $10 million in next 3 years, totaling $50 million

Tax Changes

- Claw-back of family allowance and Old Age Security for recipients with annual incomes of more than $50,000

- Goods and Services Tax of 7 per cent announced (to be effective 1991)
- Personal income tax surtax increase from 3 per cent to 5 per cent
- Increased sales taxes on gas, alcohol, tobacco, communications, and construction materials
- Large Corporation Tax of 0.175 per cent in corporate capital in excess of $10 million (affected only 4 per cent of corporations)

Privatization

- Airports in Vancouver, Calgary, Edmonton, and Montreal to be privatized

Unemployment Insurance Changes

- Complete federal government withdrawal from funding arrangements (amounting to $2.9 billion annually); future funding by employers and employees only
- $800 million diverted from UI fund for retraining programs
- Changes to qualifying periods of work (from 10 to 14 weeks minimum work – depending on regional unemployment rates to 14 to 20 weeks in most cases)
- Minimum duration of benefits reduced to 17 weeks from 20 weeks, with a decrease in benefits (from 46–50 weeks to 35–50 weeks)
- Disqualifying period for 'voluntary job-leavers' extended and benefits reduced

1990

Budget Cuts

- Cuts in grants to advocacy groups of $16 million, including a cut of $1.6 million to Secretary of State Women's Programs
- Some 80 women's centres in Newfoundland, Nova Scotia, the Yukon, and British Columbia lost all operation funding
- 39 women's centres in Quebec lost federal core grants
- Four national women's organizations lost 100 per cent of their funding (including funding for three feminist periodicals)
- Funding to Native groups' programs cut, including:
Secretary of State removal of core funding for all twelve First Nations newspapers; budgets of native radio and TV outlets severely reduced;

Native communications programs cut by $9.8 million

Aboriginal languages funding in the northern territories cut by $800,000

Funds to 28 Native organizations cut, including core funds for Native friendship centres, women's groups, and other Native associations (totaling $8 million)

Social housing capped at $90 million in 1990–91 and $86 million in 1991–92, representing a 15 per cent decrease in spending

- Cap on Canada Assistance Plan (increases in funding to wealthiest provinces, that is, Ontario, Alberta, and British Columbia, limited to 5 per cent regardless of size in growth of population and numbers needing social assistance)
- Established Program Financing to be frozen between 1990 and 1995 (per capita amount thus reduced to smallest since EPF was first established in 1977)
- Open House Canada, a youth exchange program, funding reduced from $9.8 million to $3.3 million
- $12.2 million cut from Health and Welfare grants and contribution program to citizens' groups
- Seniors Initiatives Program reduced by $3.5 million
- Child Care Initiatives Program reduced by $1.75 million

1991

Budget Cuts

- Court Challenges Program eliminated
- Canada Assistance Plan 5 per cent cap for Alberta, Ontario, and British Columbia, due to expire in 1991, extended 3 years
- Established Program Funding freeze, due to expire in 1991, extended another 3 years
- Canada Jobs Strategy cut by $100 million
- Grants to popular sector groups cut by $75 million in 1991 and $125 million in 1992 (Native and Inuit programs exempted)
- Green Plan cut by 20 per cent
- Operating and salary budgets for all government departments frozen for 1991–92:
  Any wage increases to be offset by lay-offs
  In following 2 years, wages to be constrained by a 3 per cent cap
  Government plans to contract out more work

- Social housing cut from already announced levels by 15 per cent, for a total of $411 million cut over 5 years
- Science and Technology and Official Development Assistance (ODA) spending reduced to 3 per cent growth
- Canada Film Development Corporation and Export Development Corporation funds frozen

Taxes

- Implementation of Goods and Services Tax of 7 per cent on all purchases except groceries, drugs, and some medical devices
- UI premiums increased by 24 per cent with worker contribution rising $.55 per $100 of earnings

Privatization

Cameco
Canada Oil and Gas Lands Administration
CN Exploration
Nordian International
Petro-Canada (42 million shares)
Petro-Canada International Assistance
Telesat Canada

1992

Budget Cuts

Government organizations eliminated:
Advisory Committee for le Musée des arts et du spectacle vivant
Advisory Committee on La francophonie
Advisory Committee on le Musée de la Nouvelle France
Advisory Council on Lay Members of the Competition Tribunal
Agricultural Products Board
Canada Employment and Immigration Advisory Council
Canadian Environmental Advisory Council
Canadian Institute for International Peace and Security
CN Steamships Limited
Demographic Review Secretariat
Economic Council of Canada

International Aviation Advisory Task Force and Committee
International Centre for Ocean Development
Law Reform Commission
Marine Advisory Board on Research and Development
Montreal Science and Technology Museum Advisory Committee
National Advisory Committee on Development Education
Pay Research Bureau
Petroleum Monitoring Agency
Science Council of Canada
Veterans Land Administration

Taxes

- UI premiums raised by 7 per cent
- RRSP withdrawal of up to $20,000 tax free for house purchase
- Capital cost allowance for manufacturing and processing machinery increased to 30 per cent from 25 per cent
- $230 million tax incentives to encourage research and development
- Small business financing program to provide loans at a lower interest rate and the ceiling on loans doubles to $200,000
- Manufacturing and processing tax rate drops to 22 per cent from 23 per cent in 1993 and to 21 per cent in 1994

Privatization

- Co-operative Energy Corporation (held the federal government's 32.5 per cent share in Co-Enerco, a publicly traded energy company)
- Dosimetry Services United (part of the Health Department that provided radiation monitoring services to workers across the country)

1993

- Drug Patent Legislation (C-91) changed to extend the monopoly patent period for brand-name drugs

Budget Cuts

- Social housing funding cut by $660 million from 1993 through to 1997–8

- 6-month postgraduate interest subsidy on student loans to be eliminated
- Student Employment Program funding cut by $61.3 million (funding cut five times between 1985 and 1993)
- Established Program Financing cash portion to be phased out

Taxation

- Family allowance to be replaced with Child Tax Benefit, based on income

Unemployment Insurance Changes

- 'Voluntary' job-leavers and those fired for misconduct cut off from UI benefits
- Benefits reduced from 60 per cent to 57 per cent of insurable earnings

1994

- North American Free Trade Agreement

Budget Cuts

- Federal government employees' salary freezes extended to the end of 1997:
  Freeze extended to all Crown corporations
  No increments based on progression through a pay range
- Funding to women's groups and all non-government organizations cut by 5 per cent
- Overseas development assistance cut by 2 per cent
- Transfers to provinces cut by $1.5 billion each year

Taxes

- $100,000 lifetime capital gains exemption to be eliminated (for gains after 1994):
  25 per cent of capital gains still exempt from taxes, as well as $500,000 for small business and farm capital gains
- First $25,000 of employers' contribution to life insurance included in the taxable income of the worker

- Age credit eliminated for people with incomes over $49,100

Unemployment Insurance Changes

- $725 million cut in first year and budget reduced by $2.4 billion for the following years
- Minimum qualifying period raised from 10 to 12 weeks
- Regional benefits cut from 32 to 26 weeks:
  Move to two-tiered benefits – benefits drop from 57 per cent to 55 per cent of insurable earnings, except for low-income claimants whose benefits will be 60 per cent of insurable earnings
- UI premiums cut from $3.07 to $3.00

1995

Budget Cuts

Unprecedented cuts of $29 billion to occur over three years including the following:
- $2.5 billion in 1996–7 and a further $4.5 billion in 1997–8 cut from transfer payments to provinces (now called the Canada Social Transfer)
- 45,000 jobs cut in the public sector (14 per cent)
- 19 per cent funding cut from government departments, including
  $550 million for international assistance
  $600 million at Natural Resources
  $900 million at Human Resources Development
  $200 million at Fisheries
  $900 million at Industry
  $550 million at Regional Agencies
  $450 million at Agriculture
  $1.6 billion at Defence
  $1.4 billion at Transport
- Western Grain Transportation Act, an act to assist grain handling and transportation in effect since 1897, rescinded
- Atlantic freight subsidies eliminated

Taxation

- $950 fee instituted for immigration applications (refugees will be offered repayable loans)

- Minor increase in corporate taxes to raise $300 million
- Interest on taxes owed to be increased by 2 per cent
- Temporary tax (until October 1996) on banks to raise $100 million
- Gasoline tax increased 1.5 cents per litre
- RRSP allowable contributions reduced for 1 year, then increased so that the maximum contribution will be increased by $1,000 in 1998

Unemployment Insurance Changes

- 10 per cent minimum cut in size of program announced
- Legislation to reform program to occur later in year

Privatization

Air Navigation System (ANS) to be commercialized
All airports to be commercialized
Canada Communication Group (formerly the Queen's Printer)
Canadian National Railways to be sold
Petro-Canada share (70 per cent) owned by the government to be sold

Other opportunities for privatization to be pursued include part or all of the following government services:

Canada Space Agency
Canadian food inspection systems of the Department of Health, Agriculture, Fisheries, and Oceans and Industry[*]
Department of National Defence
Environment Canada's weather services
Inspection and regulation activities of the Department of Agriculture
Management of capacity, licensing and compliance activities of the Department of Fisheries and Oceans
National Capital Commission
Natural Resources Canada

[*]*Sources*: Federal Budgets 1985–1995; Canadian Council on Social Development, *Canada's Social Programs Are in Trouble* (Ottawa, 1989); Stephen McBride and John Shields, *Dismantling a Nation: Canada and the New World Order* (Halifax: Fernwood Publishing, 1993), Table 2.4, p. 59.

Notes

1 I recognize that there have been some important improvements to social security programs, such as the introduction of parental leave to Unemployment Insurance leave provisions, improvements in labour legislation in British Columbia, and some changes to provincial pay equity schemes. My point, however, is that the overall direction of social policy has been to support market activities, rather than social welfare. For an inventory of recent program changes, see Katherine Scott, *Women and Welfare State Restructuring: Inventory of Canadian Income Security and Employment Related Initiatives* (North York: Centre for Research on Work and Society, May 1995).

2 I use the term 'redistribution' to include more than the redistribution of income, but also the redistribution of power and resources.

3 In other cases this activism ignores the state altogether and focuses only on the relationship between men and women in the private sphere. As will become clear as this essay continues, ignoring the power of the state is a dangerous route for feminism to follow.

4 This is the approach some feminists take to explaining the relationship between women and the modern state. For a discussion of this approach see Linda Gordon, 'The New Feminist Scholarship on the Welfare State,' in Linda Gordon, ed., *Women, the State, and Welfare* (Madison: University of Wisconsin Press, 1990), 9–35.

5 Janine Brodie's discussion of restructuring and the women's movement notes that at the same time that feminists are defending the welfare state they had criticized it for being 'inadequate, patriarchal, classist and racist.' In contrast, the neo-liberals are blaming this very state for being responsible for the economic crisis. Janine Brodie, *Politics on the Boundaries: Restructuring and the Canadian Women's Movement* (Toronto: Robarts Centre for Canadian Studies, 1994), 31–2.

6 These kinds of analyses of the implications of policy changes are very important for women's activism. For an analysis of the absence of a consideration of gender issues in social security reform, see Therese Jennissen, 'The Federal Social Security Review: A Gender-Sensitive Critique,' in Jane Pulkingham and Gordon Ternowetsky, eds., *Remaking Canadian Social Policy: Social Security in the Late 1990s* (Halifax: Fernwood Publishing, 1996), 238–55.

7 For a discussion of the trajectory this focus on redistributive programs has taken in Canada, see Marjorie Griffin Cohen, 'Social Policy and Social Issues,' in Ruth Roach Pierson, Marjorie Griffin Cohen, Paula Bourne, and Philinda Masters, eds., *Canadian Women's Issues*, vol. I, *Strong Voices* (Toronto: Lorimer, 1993), chapter 4, 264–320.

8 There have been some important exceptions, however, such as the activism of women in Canada against free trade. See Sylvia Bashevkin, 'Free Trade and Canadian Feminism: The Case of the National Action Committee on the Status of Women,' *Canadian Public Policy* 15, 4 (1989): 363–75; Matthew Sparke, 'Negotiating National Action: Free Trade, Constitutional Debate and the Gendered Geopolitics of Canada,' *Political Geography* (1996): 615–39.

9 'Restructuring' is a term which has been used in a variety of ways and is, therefore, problematic. For an interesting discussion of the ways in which the word 'restructuring' itself has facilitated the shift in the political atmosphere to the right, see Ray Broomhill and Rhonda Sharp, 'Gender Economic Restructuring Discourse in Australia,' unpublished paper presented to the Women and Restructuring Network's Roundtable on Regulating Restructuring in Canada and Australia, Toronto, 27 June 1996.

10 For a discussion of why the strategy of a single market has been pursued by the corporate world, see my article, 'New International Trade Agreements: Their Reactionary Role in Creating Markets and Retarding Social Welfare,' in Isa Bakker, ed., *Rethinking Restructuring: Gender and Change in Canada* (Toronto: University of Toronto Press, 1996), 187–202.

11 The FTA went into effect 1 January 1989, and NAFTA went into effect 1 January 1994. The last GATT agreement instituted a new international organization to facilitate trade. This organization, the World Trade Organization (WTO), was instituted in 1 January 1995.

12 I have attempted in other places to analyse the implications of free trade for people and have specifically focused on women. Some of these are as follows: 'Democracy and the Future of Nations: Challenges for Disadvantaged Women and Minorities,' in Robert Boyer and Daniel Drache, eds., *States against Markets: The Limits of Globalization* (London and New York: Routledge, 1996), 319–414; *Free Trade and the Future of Women's Work: Manufacturing and Service Industries* (Toronto: Garamond, 1987); 'Americanizing Services,' in Ed Finn, ed., *The Facts on Free Trade* (Toronto: Lorimer, 1988), 63–7; 'Services: The Vanishing Opportunity,' in Duncan Cameron, ed., *The Free Trade Deal* (Toronto: Lorimer, 1988), 140–55; 'Women and Free Trade,' in Duncan Cameron, ed., *The Free Trade Papers* (Toronto: Lorimer, 1986), 143–8; 'The Lunacy of Free Trade,' in Jim Sinclair, ed., *Crossing the Line: Canada and Free Trade with Mexico* (Vancouver: New Star, 1992), 14–25; 'Exports, Unemployment and Regional Inequality: Economic Policy and Trade Theory,' in D. Drache and M. Gertler, eds., *The New Era of Global Competition: State Policy and Market Power* (Montreal: McGill-Queen's, 1991), 83–102.

13 The way in which the trade deals work as a conditioning framework to constrain social and economic policy was the core of the political activism

against free trade in Canada. For an excellent analysis of the comprehensive nature of the international trade agreements as conditioning agents, see Ricardo Grinspun and Robert Kreklewich, 'Consolidating Neoliberal Reforms: "Free Trade" as a Conditioning Framework,' *Studies in Political Economy* 43 (Spring 1994), 33–62.

14 There are now a considerable number of studies which have explained the various ways in which state actions are inhibited by trade agreements. See, for example, various articles in the following collections: Ricardo Grinspun and Maxwell Cameron, eds., *The Political Economy of North American Free Trade* (Montreal and Kingston: McGill-Queen's University Press, 1993); Duncan Cameron and Melville Watkins, eds., *Canada Under Free Trade* (Toronto: Lorimer, 1993); Daniel Drache and Meric Gertler, *The New Era of Global Competition: State Policy and Market Power* (Montreal and Kingston: McGill-Queen's Press, 1991); John Calvert with Larry Kuehn, *Pandora's Box: Corporate Power, Free Trade and Canadian Education* (Toronto: Our Schools/Our Selves, 1993); Isabella Bakker, ed., *The Strategic Silence: Gender and Economic Policy* (London: Zed Books, 1994); Robert Boyer and Daniel Drache, eds., *States against Markets: The Limits of Globalization* (London and New York: Routledge, 1996).

15 For a discussion of the political tactics of the business elites up to and including free trade, see David Langille, 'The BCNI and the Canadian State,' *Studies in Political Economy* (Autumn 1987), 4–86.

16 The strategy of the Fraser Institute is an example of the understanding that long-term planning is necessary to change the intellectual consensus of the nation. See Marjorie Griffin Cohen, 'Neo-cons on Campus,' *This Magazine* (July 1995), 30–2.

17 This is a support which continues, according to a survey conducted on behalf of fourteen public and private sector clients by Ekos Research Associates Inc. 'Maintain Services, Canadians Tell Survey,' *Globe and Mail*, 25 February 1995.

18 The devotion to full employment tended to be more rhetorical than practical in Canada, in contrast to Western European governments in the postwar period. Ramesh Mishra (1990: 17) points out that no government in Canada has been fully committed to full employment as a policy objective. Nevertheless, the rhetoric about full employment meant that governments in the past felt compelled to shape public policy in this direction. Today not even the rhetoric of full employment exists in policy statements.

19 In Canada there is convincing evidence that unemployment associated with recession has become a permanent feature of the economy. The average rate of unemployment from 1950 to 1980 was 5.3 per cent. This average increased to 9.8 per cent in the 1981–94 period. For a discussion of the 'permanent

recession,' see Jim Stanford, 'The Economics of Debt and the Remaking of Canada,' *Studies in Political Economy* 48 (Autumn 1995), 113–36.

20 Canada's economy has been more export-oriented than that of most wealthy, industrialized countries, with generally between one-quarter and one-third of its national income coming from export sales. Since NAFTA, the significance of trade has increased subtantially so that in 1995 38 per cent of the national income came from trade. This is in comparison with other wealthy industrialized countries like the United States, which receives only about 10 per cent to 12 per cent of its income from exports and Japan, which receives less than 15 per cent of its income from exports. In some sectors, particularly the resource-extracting sectors, Canada has been highly competitive.

21 The material in this section on Public Finances was adapted from my paper prepared for the NDP Renewal Conferences in 1994–5, entitled 'Debt and Deficit: A Problem or The Problem.'

22 The concurrence of socialist governments to the economic policies of the political right is a phenomenon not confined to Canada. For a particularly interesting discussion of the effect of the Hawke Labour government in Australia on women's relationship to the welfare state, see Rhonda Sharp and Ray Broomhill, *Short Changed: Women and Economic Policies* (Boston: Allen and Unwin, 1988).

23 For an excellent and readable account of how the right has manipulated the debt debate, see Linda McQuaig, *Shooting the Hippo: Death by Deficit and Other Canadian Myths* (Toronto: Viking Penguin Books, 1995).

24 For a discussion of why Canada is more severely affected by economic crises than other industrialized countries, see my article entitled 'Exports, Unemployment and Regional Inequality: Economic Policy and Trade Theory,' in D. Drache and M. Gertler, eds., *The New Era of Global Competition: State Policy and Market Power* (Montreal: McGill-Queen's, 1991), 83–102.

25 Much of the data for this section comes from Clarence L. Barber, 'Monetary and Fiscal Policy in the 1980s,' in Robert C. Allen and Gideon Rosenbluth, eds., *False Promises: The Failure of Conservative Economics* (Vancouver: New Star Books, 1992), 101–20.

26 This strategy was so crucial to the Conservative government that it attempted to incorporate a constitutional requirement in the Charlottetown Accord to make inflation control the sole focus of the Bank of Canada.

27 For a discussion of changes to labour markets, see Leah Vosko, 'Irregular Workers, New Involuntary Social Exiles: Women and UI Reform,' in Jane Pulkingham and Gordon Ternowetsky, *Remaking Canadian Social Policy*; Gordon Betcherman, 'Globalization, Labour Markets and Public Policy,' in Robert Boyer and Daniel Drache, *States Against Markets*, 250–69.

28 I am writing this as the future of medicare in Canada is being debated. As the country's health ministers meet, the major bond rating services have downgraded Canada's credit rating (making borrowing more expensive), explaining that social spending is still too high, despite the federal budget which generally received their approval. The speculation that these agencies were attempting to influence the future direction of this social program in Canada is not unwarranted.

29 A progressive way of dealing with the debt has been offered by popular sector groups. Canadian Centre for Policy Alternatives and CHO!CES: A Coalition for Social Justice, *Alternative Federal Budget 1995* (Ottawa: CCAP, 1995).

30 For a discussion of the power of international financial markets see John Dillon, 'Monopolizing Money,' *Canadian Forum* (June 1994), 8–12.

31 Even the Economic Council of Canada, which favours deregulation of financial markets, recognizes this problem. In a report entitled *A New Frontier: Globalization and Canada's Financial Markets* (Ottawa: 1989), it said: 'Because the quality of information on which all financial decisions must rely tends to deteriorate with distance, institutions headquartered in Europe, Asia, or the United States are often less familiar with the needs of Canadians than are domestic institutions.' Cited in Manfred Bienefeld, 'Financial Deregulation: Disarming the Nation State,' *Studies in Political Economy* 37 (Spring 1992), 31–58.

32 Manfred Bienefeld is one of these. He maintains that 'the speculative excess of interlocking, deregulated financial systems are at the heart of the current economic crisis in which debt, asset price inflation and high interest rates are combining to destroy governments, businesses, jobs and farms.' Manfred Bienfeld, 'Financial Deregulation: Disarming the Nation State,' *Studies in Political Economy* (Spring 1992): 31–58.

33 I have discussed alternatives to the marketization process in 'Feminism's Effect on Economic Policy,' in Ruth Roach Pierson and Marjorie Griffin Cohen, *Canadian Women's Issues*, Vol. 2, *Bold Visions* (Toronto: Lorimer, 1995), chapter 4, 263–359; 'Democracy and the Future of Nations: Challenges for Disadvantaged Women and Minorities,' in Robert Boyer and Daniel Drache, eds., *States against Markets*, 319–414; 'New International Trade Agreements: Their Reactionary Role in Creating Markets and Retarding Social Welfare,' in Isabella Bakker, ed., *Rethinking Restructuring*, 187–202.

34 For a discussion of this 'new functionalism,' see Ramesh Mishra, 'The Welfare of Nations,' in Robert Boyer and Daniel Drache, eds., *States against Markets*, 316–33. Janine Brodie also raises this issue and makes the important point that 'we perhaps have been too quick to accept the determinism and unrestrained economism of the restructuring discourse. We have not suffi-

ciently challenged its impositional claims as "impositional" – that is, as vested interpretations of reality which are open to political contestation and moral evaluation.' Janine Brodie, 'New State Forms, New Political Spaces,' in Boyer and Drache, *States against Markets*, 383–98.

35 For an analysis of the methods through which the ideology of the right has gained legitimacy, see Seth Klein, *Good Sense Versus Common Sense: Canada's Debt Debate and Competing Hegemonic Projects*, MA Thesis, Simon Fraser University, 1996.

36 See, for example, Diana Ralph, 'How to Beat the Corporate Agenda: Strategies for Social Justice,' in Pulkingham and Ternowetsky, eds., *Remaking Canadian Social Policy*, 288–302; Jill Vickers, 'The Intellectual Origin of the Women's Movement,' in Constance Backhouse and David H. Flaherty, eds., *Challenging Times: The Women's Movement in Canada and the United States* (Montreal and Kingston: McGill-Queen's Press, 1992), 39–60.

37 For a discussion of why social charters cannot replicate the disciplinary function of nation states, see Wolfgang Streck 'Public Power beyond the Nation-State: The Case of the European Community,' in Boyer and Drache, eds., States against Markets, 219–315; Tony Clarke, 'Free Trade and Social Charters Don't Mix,' *CCPA Monitor* 3, 2 (1996), 15.

38 For a discussion of this, see Christina Gabriel and Laura Macdonald, 'NAFTA, Women and Organizing in Canada and Mexico: Forging a Feminist Internationality,' *Millennium* 23, 3 (1994), 535–62.

References

Bank of Canada. 1995. *Bank of Canada Review*, Autumn.
– 1995–6. *Bank of Canada Review*, Winter.
Evans, Patricia. 1994. 'Eroding Canada in Social Welfare: The Mulroney Legacy, 1984–1993.' *Social Policy and Administration* 28, 2: 107–19.
Hartmann, Heidi. 1981. 'The Unhappy Marriage of Marxism and Feminism.' In Lydia Sargent, ed., *Women and Revolution*. London: South End Press, 1–41.
Helleiner, Eric. 1996. 'Post-Globalization: Is the Financial Liberalization Trend Likely to Be Reversed?' In Robert Boyer and Daniel Drache, eds., *States against Markets: The Limits of Globalization*. London: Routledge, 193–210.
Hutton, Will. 1994. 'Stability Remains a Tory Pipedream.' *Manchester Guardian Weekly*, 10 July, p. 21.
International Monetary Fund (IMF). 1989. *International Capital Markets: Developments and Prospects*. April, p. 50.
Kealey, Linda, ed. 1979. *A Not Unreasonable Claim: Women and Reform in Canada 1880–1920s*. Toronto: Women's Press.

Lightman, Ernie, and Allan Irving. 1991. 'Restructuring Canada's Welfare State.' *Journal of Social Policy* 21, 1: 65–86.

Mishra, Ramesh. 1990. *The Welfare State in Capitalist Society.* Toronto: University of Toronto Press, 73–99.

Myles, John. 1988. 'Decline or Impasse? The Current State of the Welfare State.' *Studies in Political Economy* 26 (Summer).

Rosenbluth, Gideon. 1995. *The Debt/Deficit Crisis.* Pamphlet. Vancouver: B.C. Teachers' Federation.

Thiessen, Gordon G. 1994. 'Steering Canada through Unsettled Financial Waters.' *Globe and Mail*, 4 July p. A 11.

United Nations. 1994. *World Investment Report: Transnational Corporations, Employment and the Workplace.* New York and Geneva: United Nations, 118.

Wilson, Elizabeth. 1977. *Women and the Welfare State.* London: Tavistock.

PART II

Challenging the Bases of Claims

3

Creation Stories: Social Rights and Canada's Constitution[1]

HESTER LESSARD

In this essay, I set out to examine the constitutional entrenchment of social rights as a strategy to advance social justice and, in particular, to redress the material and social inequalities which characterize women's lives in Canada. The issue of entrenched social rights came to the forefront of public debate in Canada during the negotiation in 1992 of the Charlottetown Accord proposals to amend the Constitution. Part III.1 of the Accord contained recognition of a number of governmental commitments to social policy objectives. The Accord proposals fell far short of the inclusion of a charter of social rights called for by anti-poverty activists (Nedelsky and Scott, 1992). However, it provided the occasion for a public discussion of such an initiative. The Accord was ultimately rejected in a public referendum in October 1992. Nevertheless, it remains important for groups committed to social justice to reflect upon and consider the underlying strategic issue of whether entrenchment of a governmental obligation to fulfil basic social needs addresses social inequalities effectively, and, if so, on what terms should such a commitment take place.

This essay analyses constitutional strategies in light of the lessons of the Charlottetown Accord. However, before doing so, it is important to briefly clarify what is meant by social rights and by the related concepts of entrenchment and justiciability. Patrick Macklem and Craig Scott provide the following definition of social rights:

[Social rights are] those rights that protect the necessities of life or that provide for the foundations of an adequate quality of life. The necessities of life encompass at a minimum rights to adequate nutrition, housing, health, and education. All of these rights provide foundations upon which human development can occur and human freedom can flourish. In addition, such basic social rights should be conceptualized in terms of an entitlement both to be equal as humans and to be equal as members of society. (Macklem and Scott, 1992: 9–10)

Entrenchment of such rights means that they cannot be altered or repealed by ordinary legislative activity. Once they find their place in the Canadian constitution, they can only be altered by means of the constitutional amending process. Thus entrenched social rights represent a firmer commitment to the provision of benefits than that contained in a statutory regime such as Canada's current health care program or the provincial regimes which provide income assistance. The question of whether social rights, in addition to being entrenched, should be justiciable raises questions about the institutional and ideological character of courts and the judiciary. Justiciable rights refer to rights which can be interpreted and enforced by courts. Justiciability became a key issue among the groups supporting entrenchment of social rights in the discussions leading up to the Charlottetown Accord. Some proponents argued that social rights should not be treated differently than political rights and should be enforceable through litigation before the courts (Lamarche, 1992; Jackman, 1992). Others took the position that a monitoring agency with authority to review government compliance as well as hear individual complaints would provide a better forum for upholding a social charter of rights (Brodsky, 1992; Nedelsky and Scott, 1992). I shall not enter into the justiciability debate in this essay. Rather my focus will be on the more fundamental question of how social rights fit into the map of political relationships and aspirations contained in the Canadian constitution.

My overall thesis is that the social rights strategy must be carefully examined in light of the contradictory experiences of women and subordinated groups with respect to rights based strategies. In particular, I would argue that social rights, as they were finally articulated in the Charlottetown Accord, would have reinforced rather than transformed the structural and institutional oppression of women and other subordinated groups. This claim is in tension with the positive aspects of constitutionalizing the social welfare state which at first glance seem obvious and irrefutable. For example, the prospect of entrenched social rights seems to offer an immediate and urgently needed basis on which to challenge the steady erosion of social welfare regimes which has characterized the past fifteen years in Canada (Bakan and Schneiderman, 1992: 5). The inclusion of social rights in a constitution gives public visibility and moral and political authority to the claims of the most dispossessed within Canadian society. Even without any mechanisms for enforcement, such provisions, at the very least, change the terms of public debate with respect to the dismantling of social supports. A set of social rights which is fully enforceable, either through the courts or a monitoring agency with the power to bind governments, would seem to contemplate the possibility of a significant redistribution of resources and to give some concrete content to the comparatively abstract and empty guarantees of civil and political rights. Indeed, only the economically secure can afford to turn away from a constitutional entitlement to food, shelter, health care, collective bargaining, education, and environmental protection.

The account of social rights sketched above, however, can also be viewed as simply adjusting our existing constitutional structures to take account of the latest casualties of macro-economic shifts without rethinking the assumptions on which those structures are founded. From this latter perspective, entrenched social rights leave intact the liberal vision of a social contract between state and citizen, a contract which preserves a natural, and apparently necessary, division between public and private and which presupposes the neutrality of the state. Meanwhile, what Carole Pateman calls the sexual contract remains invisible and submerged, and its terms remain essentially the same (Pateman, 1988). It is as if the liberal creation story is being re-enacted by the same actors with just a slightly different script.

In this essay, I argue that the social rights strategy needs to be reconsidered and, at the very least, placed alongside other constitutional strategies for addressing the political disempowerment of socially marginalized groups. In the first section I will draw on the work of Pateman to examine the imagery of contract which, in general, pervades discussions of constitution making and which has been particularly prominent in recent considerations of entrenched social rights. In the second section, as a way of further exploring and elaborating on Pateman's insights, I will examine the extent to which the conception of social rights which emerged from the Charlottetown Accord proposals leaves intact the relations of subordination. I will argue that the Accord proposals are best understood in terms of the relocation of the ideological split between public and private at the split between the social and economic spheres. In the third section I will examine the assumption that the state remains neutral in its performance of the expanded responsibilities of the social welfare state. In this latter section, I will illustrate my point by examining the contradiction between the formal commitment in Canada to publicly funded health care and the denial of reproductive health services to women seeking to control their fertility. In my view, to constitutionalize the present structure of social welfare benefit provision, at least in the area of health care, will simply entrench the bureaucratic form of public responsibility without the substance of material support and political empowerment. This is not to reject the general strategy of obtaining a constitutional commitment to universal health care and other social entitlements, but simply to stress the importance of linking such commitments to issues of political participation and empowerment. I explore this final point in the conclusion.

The Language of Contract and Constitution Making: The Example of the 1992 Social Charter Debate

As in most Western democracies, women in Canada have engaged in long and difficult struggles to attain the status of legal persons with the formal rights of citizens. In many respects, these struggles, which we usually associate with nineteenth-century Western feminism, are not over. However, if we move beyond the realm of the formal and inquire into the ways in which the law effectively and indirectly maintains sexual subordination – in domestic relations, employment relations, and political participation – the story becomes depressingly repetitive. Carole Pateman explains the contradiction between the social reality of subordination and the official story of equality and full citizenship in terms of the sexual contract. In Pateman's view, the classical accounts of the origins of the state in a social contract between naturally free individuals presumes that the basis of political right was originally in the relationship of father to son. However, Pateman argues that the paradigm of political right is not paternal power but the conjugal power of husbands over wives which preceded the power of fathers over sons. Thus the liberal creation story of classical theory must be retold. It is a story about naturally free male individuals overthrowing the structures of paternal patriarchy and replacing them with the structures of fraternal patriarchy in which the male sex right is extended equally to all men. This is the sexual contract. Its terms are reflected in the experiences of women within relationships set in place by marriage, employment, prostitution, and surrogacy contracts.

Pateman's retelling of the familiar parable about the foundations of modern civil society can be faulted for ultimately speaking in images that oversimplify, and portray as universal, experiences which are complex, multilayered, and socially differentiated. In effect, she replaces contract, as the archetype of freedom, with male/female relations, as the archetype of subordination.

Nevertheless, her unpacking of the myth of contract as the emblem of freedom remains a powerful critique of political authority and of the use of consent to legitimate the exercise of both private and public power. It is particularly useful for Canadians at a time when the imagery of constitutions as social contracts seems to have captured our political imaginations. Quebec and First Nations have argued that they were left out of, or they never consented to the constitutional arrangements of 1982 and the terms of the 1990 Meech Lake discussions (Milne, 1991: 186–317). Similarly, the proposed entrenchment of social rights in 1992 was described as a way of bringing economically marginalized groups within the terms of the renegotiated Canadian social contract (Schneiderman, 1992: 126). This language is powerful. When deployed by those who experience Canadian political and social life as outsiders, it lends authority to claims of belonging and to challenges to the legitimacy of the Canadian state as it is currently constituted. However, there has been very little reflection on the underlying assumption that consent, the central idea of contract, will transform social and political domination into social and political equality.

Pateman's central thesis is that contract is a device whereby freedom is transformed into subjection, civil subjection in the social contract, civil slavery in the employment contract, and sexual subordination in the marriage contract. She faults feminists and socialists alike for implicitly accepting the political meaning of contract as the paradigm of freedom and equality in their critiques of exploitive and unconscionable contracts. She observes: 'Contract theory is primarily about a way of creating social relationships constituted by subordination, not about exchange ... The new relationship is structured through time by a permanent exchange of obedience for protection ... The peculiarity of this exchange is that one party to the contract, who provides protection, has the right to determine how the other party will act to fulfill their side of the exchange' (Pateman, 1988: 58–9).

Pateman develops her thesis in the context of certain civil contracts in which an individual's property in the person – her mobility, her sexual integrity, her time and physical labour, comes under another party's control. This transformation into legitimate, because consented to, subordination is worth exploring further in the context of constitutions, which we still persist in thinking and talking about in contractual terms.

Pateman's work provides a basis on which to question the extent to which the recent proposals in Canada rely on a notion of constitutional bargaining and consent to ratify and legitimate a social system of subordination. In particular, the story about consent and contract typically submerges the background conditions of the contract. They become invisible, simply part of 'the natural,' in the sense of non-negotiable, backdrop against which the political actors formulate their bargain.

For example, much of the literature urging adoption of a social charter during the Charlottetown negotiations used the language of social contract while appearing to accept that subjection in the private sphere of a globalized market is the 'state of nature' from within which we must try to get the best contract or deal possible in terms of imposing public responsibility for social and economic protection. The Ontario government's discussion paper, which in many respects launched the notion of social rights as a viable and necessary feature of a new constitution, described such rights as 'a strategy for ensuring that growing interprovincial and international economic competitive pressures do not become an excuse for weakening or abandoning our social contract' (Ontario Ministry of Intergovernmental Affairs, 1991: 3). Indeed, social rights are sometimes viewed as facilitative of economic integration and efficiency. The Ontario paper goes on to observe: 'National standards are very important in the promotion of the Canadian economic union. The efficiency of the Canadian economy is improved by the free movement of people, trade and investment across the country. Differing standards for health care or social assistance can act as a barrier to interprovincial labour mobility. By increasing labour mobility and strengthening the economic union, productivity growth and international competitiveness are also strengthened' (Ontario Ministry of Intergovernmental Affairs, 1991: 7–8).

A number of academic commentators also urged support for a social charter on the basis that recent economic changes require a social buffer to protect against the inevitable deepening of the divide between social groups, a divide that is neither race neutral nor sex neutral. In this regard, Lars Osberg and Shelley Phipps, economists who write from a perspective that is sensitive to issues of equity and economic equality, stress the fact that recent social and demographic changes in the labour market, household composition, poverty, and inequality have rendered many features of the Canadian welfare state inadequate or obsolete. In particular, they argue that the growth of the low-paying, part-time, temporary, and self-employed sector of the Canadian labour market in the past decade has meant that many of Canada's social insurance programs are ineffective, especially for women who 'constitute a large fraction of non-standard employment' (Osberg and Phipps, 1992: 12). In their view, a constitutional reform that prohibits government interference in market transactions would only strengthen this trend, and thus social rights should be viewed as the necessary *quid pro quo* for giving up the democratic accountability of private power. Thus they link a social charter not only to larger, freer, more globalized markets, but also to 'a decreased role for the democratic process in restraining the impact of market forces' (Osberg and Phipps, 1992: 2). The following passage starkly illustrates the assumption that the Constitution should be understood as a trade-off of political power for security: 'A social charter is also required because private market transactions are increasingly unable to meet the economic needs of many Canadians ... Thus we argue very strongly that the Constitution should provide protection of the free market only on condition that effective guarantees for social and economic rights are received in return' (Osberg and Phipps, 1992: 19).

Osberg and Phipps usefully bring concerns about historical and demographic change and about issues of poverty, racism, and sexism into the constitutional discussion. However, what is disturbing about the shape of these arguments is the acceptance, first of all, that the market is a force, much like a force of nature, rather than an institution or a form of social ordering in itself which is subject to a multitude of variations and qualifications; second, that this force is inevitably beyond the realm of democratic control and regulation; and, third, that it is appropriate to treat fundamental entitlements to social well-being as simply another set of interests to be traded off against economic interests.

The bargain implied by these discussion papers, namely, a social charter in exchange for an unregulated market, is mapped out in the formal language of the constitutional proposals which were placed before Canadians in 1992. However, in order to obtain the full picture of the bargain, one must pull together, not only different parts of the Accord, but two different accords. The fragmented presentation of the key terms of the constitutional proposal obfuscated, to some extent, the terms of the offer which Canadians were being asked to accept. In the next section, I describe the basic components of the proposed social contract contained in the 1992 proposals in order to illustrate the way in which such proposals often simply renegotiate rather than reject the boundary between private oppression and public responsibility.

Relocating the Public/Private Split at the Economic/Social Split: The Example of the Charlottetown Accord

The articulation of a set of commitments to the social and material well-being of Canadians in the final version of the 1992 proposals combined an extremely qualified endorsement of the importance of social and material supports for full membership in a political community with comparatively firm protections for the negative liberty of economic actors. It is useful to explore this reconfiguration of the Canadian political community in terms of a relocation of the ideological split between public and private at the divide between the social and economic spheres of life. In other words, the proposals gave more recognition than the existing Constitution to the principle that social needs should be acknowledged as community or 'public' responsibilities, rather than constructed as 'private' individual burdens. However, this was accompanied by a much clearer commitment to a 'private' sphere of freedom for economic actors.

The starting point is the Beaudoin-Dobbie Report which was issued in February 1992 (Canada, House of Commons and Senate, 1992). The report was the product of a special joint committee of the Senate and the House which was formed to 'inquire into and make recommendations' regarding federal proposals to amend the Constitution (ibid.: vii). The committee held hearings across Canada. Its report not only identified and discussed the issues and themes that, in its view, emerged from the hearings but also submitted a draft set of amendments to the Constitution. The Beaudoin-Dobbie draft amendments, for the most part, provided the starting point for the Charlottetown negotiations.

The Beaudoin-Dobbie Report proposed to formally recognize constraints on the reach of democratic politics by entrenching the principle of free movement of 'persons, goods, services, and capital' in a revised section 121 of the Constitution Act 1867. The revised section 121 was presented in its own section called 'The Common Market' which immediately preceded the section called 'The Social Covenant and the Economic Union' (ibid.: 121–4). The free market principle set out in the revised section 121 specifically prohibited governments from actions in relation to provincial and territorial boundaries which 'impede the efficient functioning of the Canadian economic union.' The provision also had a number of exceptions, including one for laws relating to public protection, safety and health. Finally, the introduction to the section stated that a dispute resolution mechanism for the section was required but not yet drafted.

The Charlottetown Accord appeared to drop the 'common market' provisions. However, the proposal to entrench a free market principle was simply buried in a less publicly visible document, the Political Accord, and consideration of the details postponed to a less politically volatile time. The Political Accord was issued as a companion document to the Charlottetown Accord, but it received very little public attention. It committed First Ministers to reviewing and implementing a set of economic proposals which almost exactly mirrored those which appeared in the Common Market section of the Beaudoin-Dobbie Report. To enforce the economic provisions, the Political Accord also gave First Ministers the authority to create a dispute resolution agency with the power to bind governments. The agency was described in the text as independent and as having an obligation to report to the First Ministers (Consensus Report, 1992: 31–2).

Meanwhile, the proposed social charter found its place in the much publicized Charlottetown Accord under the title, 'The Social and Economic Union.' The protections were presented as policy objectives rather than rights. The social policy objectives, which again closely resembled provisions in the Beaudoin-Dobbie Report, announced five governmental commitments: provision of health care that is 'comprehensive, universal, portable, publicly administered and accessible,' 'reasonable access to housing, food and other basic necessities,' provision of high quality public education at the primary and secondary levels and reasonable access at post-secondary levels, protection of collective bargaining for workers, and 'protecting, preserving and sustaining the integrity of the environment' (Consensus Report, 1992: 5; Draft Legal Text, 1992: 44–6).

These provisions were presented together with the Economic Union provisions which committed governments to five economic objectives: strengthening the economic union, 'free movement of persons, goods, services and capital,' full employment, ensuring 'a reasonable standard of living' for all Canadians, and 'ensuring sustainable and equitable development.'

Unlike the common market provisions contemplated in the Political Accord, both the social and economic provisions in this section, were clearly non-enforceable. Instead, the establishment of an agency was contemplated which would 'monitor the progress' made in relation to the social and economic objectives. This obscured the fact that the Political Accord contemplated a body with the power to enforce the economic objectives under another part of the Constitution. Although enforceability would have by no means cured the defects in the Charlottetown proposal, the difference in treatment revealed a difference in how seriously the two types of commitments were being taken.

In addition, the effect of combining the social objectives in the same provision as the economic objectives was that each modified the other on an equal basis. This supposedly integrated approach was again misleading because of the much more forceful commitment to non-interference in markets in the Political Accord's common market proposal. Furthermore, the social objectives presented in the Charlottetown Accord were, for the most part, rooted in an equal opportunity or proceduralist understanding of equality rather than a substantive or redistributive notion of equality. The goals were reasonable accessibility, universality, and portability rather than the health and well-being of all persons. To the extent that substantive goals were articulated, they consisted of benefits that are already provided under existing regimes such as primary and secondary education and a comprehensive public health care system. No doubt a constitutionalized exhortation to respect the importance of these benefits as an aspect of membership in the Canadian community would assist in the struggle to keep them in place in the face of the trend towards budgetary restraint, fiscal conservatism, and individualism (Bakan and Schneiderman, 1992: 5). However, Canada's existing benefit regimes were much more clearly and forcefully protected by another provision in the Charlottetown proposals which would have made intergovernmental agreements regarding, among other things, cost-sharing arrangements for government programs, binding for a five-year term (Consensus Report, 1992: 14–15; Draft Legal Text, 1992: 27–8).

What can we learn from this complicated set of declarations, commitments, and objectives? Viewed in the setting of all the relevant texts, the Social Covenant which was placed before the Canadian public in 1992 arguably had more to do with the consolidation rather than the democratization of social and economic privilege. One way of understanding the rewriting of the constitutional map in the 1992 accords is in terms of a reconfigured public/private split. In this respect, the accords reflect the notion, which pervades the literature discussed in the preceding part of this essay, of constitutions as bargains. Any gains in the proposals in terms of democracy and social justice are effectively undermined by the acceptance of a larger, stronger, less democratically accountable, and, therefore, more 'private,' market. In other words, the constitutional blueprint for the arena of public responsibility has been ostensibly expanded by the commitment to a set of social 'policy objectives.' However, these are not only qualified in some yet-to-be-determined way by the economic 'policy objectives,' but, in fact, are secondary to a much more clearly delineated and firmly entrenched sphere of negative economic liberty contemplated by the Political Accord. As Osberg and Phipps (1992) point out, within this enlarged and constitutionally enshrined private sphere of freedom, a purportedly natural relegation of female, youth, immigrant, and First Nations workers to the non-standard employment sector will occur. Within this sector, workers receive wages that are well below the poverty level, are structurally precluded from collective action such as collective bargaining, and are often explicitly excluded from minimum benefits conferred by statute (Fudge, 1991: 73–89). As Judy Fudge has observed: 'Women and young workers presently comprise the majority of those employed in what are euphemistically called "non-standard" work forms: part-time employment, short-term work, own-account self-employment and temporary-help agency work, more accurately known as "bad jobs."' Fudge links the trend towards increased polarization of the workforce to the restructuring of the economy in the wake of the mid-1970s recession. However, she argues that a number of factors including the commitments to deregulation, privatization, and free trade 'suggest that the current process of economic restructuring is ongoing.' The arrangements in the 1992 accords appear designed to formally recognize and enshrine that process. Furthermore, the *quid pro quo* for the renegotiation of the social contract presented in the accords is a set of social and economic objectives which reflect the past accomplishments of the now eroding Canadian welfare state. However, even more important than the question of whether this was a bad bargain is the question of whether constitutions should be understood as bargains at all, especially as bargains in which political power is given up in return for extremely meagre promises of security, or as Pateman (1988: 58) puts it, as 'a permanent exchange ... of obedience for protection.'

In sum, although the Social and Economic Union proposal contained in the Charlottetown Accord may very well become a minor footnote in the history of constitutional change in Canada, it is an example that provides strong lessons and a starting point from which to critically examine and assess future discussions of Canada's constitutional framework.

The Myth of State Neutrality: The Example of Abortion Access

In the foregoing sections, I attempted to sketch out the connection between the contractual language of bargaining and exchange and the assumption of a split between public and private which underlies the classical liberal vision of social and political prosperity. In this section, I wish to examine a further way in which the ideology of public and private re-emerges in the social rights debate, namely, with respect to what I have called 'the myth of state neutrality.'

The promise of a set of social rights appears, at first glance, to challenge radically the principle that the liberal state should remain neutral in relation to the articulation of social goods. As Alison Jaggar has written, 'Liberalism views the state as a politically neutral instrument whose function is to guarantee to all individuals an equal opportunity for moral development and self-fulfilment' (1983: 33–5). Neutrality is thus determined by reference to the notion of what is properly the realm of private individual choice and initiative and what is properly the realm of public responsibility. Within classical liberalism, neutrality is compromised where, for reasons other than external defence or internal peace, the state interferes in individual pursuits and preferences. However, liberal democracies have for many years accepted the role of the state as the provider of social welfare and the concomitant notion of an enlarged public realm. Thus, positive state action to provide material supports for the meaningful pursuit of autonomy and self-fulfilment is widely viewed as consistent with liberal principles rather than as a compromise of state neutrality. It is appropriate but certainly not radical for liberal democratic constitutions to reflect finally that reality. This is what the entrenchment of social rights purports to do.

However, notwithstanding the express recognition of the material needs of the citizen, the neutrality of the welfare state is still understood in terms of deference to the private pursuits and preferences of individuals. Within the classical framework, this notion of neutrality is mythic in the sense that what is often deferred to are the pursuits and preferences of the most powerful and privileged interests within society (Hutchinson and Petter, 1988; Lessard, 1986). Thus, at the level of design, the relationship between state and society inevitably removes from public visibility any consideration of the inequalities that structure private relations. My argument is that by constitutionally enshrining the welfare state, the myth of state neutrality is at least partially dispelled at the level of constitutional design, but, at the same time, becomes more likely to be invoked to legitimate patterns of oppression at the level of administration and particular social interactions with the state. In this manner, statutory commitments to welfare provision, while satisfying immediate and urgent needs, have, at the same time, often provided a more extensive arena for the management and control of social groups under the guise of neutrality in the provision of social services and benefits (Ursel, 1992). Thus, although state benefit schemes are clearly better than the Elizabethan Poor Law regimes and reliance on private charity that they replaced, the experiences of the beneficiary groups have been, in many ways, contradictory (Gordon, 1990). It is important to bring these historical lessons to bear on any proposal to constitutionalize the welfare state. In this regard, the experience of women in Canada with the provision of state-administered reproductive health services, in particular abortion services, provides an example of what I would describe as the contradiction between the official story of benevolent neutrality and the unofficial and multiple stories of subordination.

During the years when access to abortion in Canada took the form of a therapeutic exception to otherwise criminal behaviour, women were required by section 251 of the Criminal Code[2] to obtain permission for the procedure before a committee of doctors at an approved or accredited hospital. The committee was required to certify that the continuation of the pregnancy would endanger the life or health of the applicant. By constructing the abortion decision as a health exception to a crime and, therefore, as a decision involving proper hospital facilities and medical diagnosis rather than moral or political concerns, Parliament was able to take the anti-choice stance required by conservative morality while at the same time maintaining neutrality towards the pro-choice exception. However, state neutrality was belied by the actual operation of section 251. Women had extremely limited and difficult access to abortion services because of the decisions by hospitals not to set up committees, varying interpretations of the criterion of danger to life or health, and the limited number of hospitals that qualified as approved or accredited. In addition, many of the health decisions by the committees were founded on a familial ideology which presumes that women are untrustworthy, especially with regard to their reproductive lives, and that the state through the delegated authority of doctors should maintain the natural hierarchy of sex-differentiated roles within the family. A survey of committee practices found: 'More than two thirds (68%) of the hospitals surveyed by the Committee required the consent of the husband. A few hospitals required the consent of a husband from whom the woman was separated or divorced and the consent of the father where the women had never been married' (Gavigan, 1992: 134).

The Criminal Code regime was struck down in R v Morgentaler[3] as a violation of section 7 of the Charter of Rights and Freedoms. This was perceived as a victory for those who had argued for an understanding of abortion access in terms of women's social equality. For the purposes of my essay, it is useful to understand the *R v Morgentaler* case in its broadest terms, namely, as a recognition that state neutrality towards the individual choices of women with respect to their reproductive lives was compromised by the direct action of the state in the form of the Criminal Code provisions. Thus, the action of the Court in striking down the Criminal Code in the name of constitutional rights ostensibly restored state neutrality, at least, to use my earlier terminology, at the level of constitutional design.

However, it soon emerged that what had been so dramatically swept away was only the most visible aspect of the complex arrangement of private and public interests that control reproductive decision making. Hospitals and doctors, both considered 'private' actors with many of the same claims under the Charter to individual autonomy as their patients, remained firmly in control of the delivery of abortion services under Canada's 'public' health care program. Entitlements under that program are statutory rather than constitutional in nature. However, the comprehensiveness of the regime as well as its commitment to universal access renders it not only a key feature of the Canadian welfare state, but also very similar in nature to a constitutional entitlement or right to health care. Thus, the shift in the arena of struggle over abortion access from that of the Criminal Code to that of the administration of the health care program provides a glimpse into the manner in which a constitutionally entrenched social right to health care might be understood and applied.

In the aftermath of *R v Morgentaler* some professional medical associations asserted control of the issue by formulating guidelines which significantly restricted access to abortion for patients. Provincial governments also moved to limit access by imposing extra fees, requiring approval from anywhere from two to five doctors, de-insuring abortion services obtained within the province, de-insuring abortion services outside the province, and requiring abortions to be performed only in approved hospitals (Gavigan, 1992: 140–5).

The actions of hospital boards were particularly interesting because of the way in which notions of community autonomy and local management of institutions eclipsed the issue of the structure of power within communities and institutions. Some boards filled the vacuum left by *R v Morgentaler* by putting in place requirements which were more burdensome than those contained in section 251 of the Criminal Code or by refusing to provide abortion services at all. The example of Dauphin

General Hospital is especially instructive. On 27 February 1991 the board of directors of Dauphin General Hospital in Manitoba voted to ban all abortions except those where the patient was obviously threatened by death because of the pregnancy. The policy was subsequently endorsed at a shareholders meeting attended by more than one thousand people who had acquired voting rights by paying a $3.00 fee. Although there were complaints that the vote had been stacked by anti-choice activists brought in from outside the community, the hospital by-laws contained no residency requirements for voting shareholders (Lessard, 1993: 141–4). Legal doctrine developed under the Charter prevented any recourse to the principle underlying the R v Morgentaler case to challenge the hospital board's decision. Under the Charter, hospitals are considered 'private' actors and therefore potential rights holders rather than potential rights violators. In addition, events like that at Dauphin General frequently become cast as stories about self-regulation by local communities rather than about the gendered nature of power within communities.

The key question raised by the story of Dauphin General Hospital is whether an entrenched social right would provide the legal basis for a rights challenge where the Charter has failed to do so. The answer can only be guessed at. However, the delineation under the Charter of a sphere of private autonomy for the day-to-day management decisions of otherwise public institutions such as hospitals suggests that there would be similarly powerful arguments for community and local institutional control under a social charter of rights.

In addition, the doctor–patient relationship provides an even more traditionally private location for the denial of abortion access than the notion of community autonomy. Indeed, without the superstructure of administrative decision making imposed by the Criminal Code, individual medical decisions with respect to abortion become very difficult to scrutinize, even when the pattern of denial of services raises issues of systemic oppression. In this context, state neutrality takes the form of deference to the claims of professional autonomy and of technical expertise.

This final point is illustrated by the following account of the provision of abortion services at Stanton Hospital in the Northwest Territories. Stanton Hospital is located in Yellowknife, the capital of the Northwest Territories. The Territories cover roughly one-third the land mass of Canada and have a majority Aboriginal population (Coates and Powell, 1989: 2–3). Stanton Hospital, at the time in question, was the only facility in the Northwest Territories providing abortion services on a regular basis. During the period which stretched from 1985, before the decision in *R v Morgentaler*, until 1992, several years after the decision, women patients were routinely provided abortions with little or no accompanying pain control. Thus, the vindication of women's rights represented by *R v Morgentaler* had no effect on the practice which, in addition to being cruel, was presented and explained in racist and misogynist terms. For example, one explanation proffered to a complaining patient was that 'the man in charge of [the hospital] doesn't approve of abortion' (Certenig, 1992). Other women were subjected to remarks that implied they were being punished for their promiscuity, that they were not in control of their fertility, or that they needed lessons in hygiene (Lessard, 1993: 156–9). The practices were eventually investigated and discontinued. However, the report of the body set up to inquire into the situation portrayed it as one involving faulty medical procedures and gaps in bureaucratic processes (Northwest Territories Ministry of Health, 1992). Although the recommendations for new procedures and practices remedied the immediate need for a more humane and acceptable approach, ultimately the articulation of the problem as a technical and managerial one obscured the fundamental political issues of racism, sexism, and colonialism (Lessard, 1993).

In sum, the removal of the obviously coercive presence of the state in the form of the criminal law in *R v Morgentaler* in some ways has merely shifted the terms on which women are denied meaningful control over their reproductive lives. Since *R v Morgentaler*, the complicity of the state in the continued disempowerment of women in the area of reproduction has become increasingly submerged in the fragmentation of decision making among individual and institutional actors, many of whom are considered 'public' actors for one or several purposes, but 'private' actors for constitutional purposes. The complex intertwining of private and public power combined with the resort to the technical discourses of medical science or bureaucratic efficiency and propriety to justify denial of services, renders the experience of systemic oppression invisible or seemingly irrelevant to public debate and action. The official face of state involvement either takes the indirect forms of inaction and indifference, deference to the expertise of medical and health professionals, and deference to local autonomy, or the more direct form of the imposition of onerous but ostensibly neutral health criteria for the delivery of abortion services.

In this situation legal challenges to the apparently benevolent neutrality of the state must meet the narrow doctrinal tests of a charge of colourability or of some other form of jurisdictional excess. Shelley Gavigan describes this as jumping from 'the "criminal frying pan" only to be burned by the "health care fire"' (1992: 145). For women seeking control over their reproductive lives, this has meant that the goal of establishing a network of abortion clinics continues to face deeply entrenched resistance. In some provinces, women still have to travel thousands of miles, often at their own expense, in order to obtain safe abortions; in others, clinics face harassment and violent confrontations in order to keep their doors open (*Pro-Choice News*, 1992: 5; 1993: 4–5; 1994: 1, 7; 1995: 1, 8; 1996: 4, 8). In sum, women's experience of a statutory entitlement to publicly funded health services demonstrates the limits of a concept of social rights which presumes state neutrality and which operates within a contractarian vision of political legitimacy. The proposed constitutionalization in the Charlottetown Accord of the main features of the existing scheme did not purport to address those limits, but rather to sanctify them as constitutionally permissible.

Conclusion: Changing Our Constitutional Visions

As Shelley Gavigan has written, 'It will continue to be critical for feminists, activists and academics together, to explore and expand the social right to health care envisioned by the early advocates of comprehensive health care' (1992: 145). To do that we need, first of all, to examine the 1992 Social Charter debates and the Charlottetown proposals in light of what they assume about the background conditions of a renegotiated social contract. In particular, the assumption that globalized markets are a 'natural' force in the sense that they can no longer be made accountable to political communities needs to be questioned and challenged. Thus, to the extent that extra-constitutional instruments such as free trade agreements fundamentally reconfigure democratic politics, those instruments should be included in the constitutional debate and ratification process (Bakker, 1988). In addition, the assumption that constitutional change is simply about a trading off of interests obscures the relative power of those interests and deflects discussion away from the substance of constitutional agreement onto the goal of simply reaching agreement. At the very least, the conditions of consent must inform notions of political legitimacy rather than simply the fact that consent has occurred through the amending process. In strategic terms this means that not only should material support be provided to a wide range of groups for meaningful participation in constitutional discussions, but that the various histories of oppression and deprivation that groups have experienced must be accounted for in the design of constitutional entitlements. For example, in the area of abortion services, discussed earlier in this essay, the strategy of entrenching a social right to health care must account for the way in which differently positioned women currently experience significantly divergent levels of self-determination as political actors within the Canadian community.

Second, the categorical separation between the economic and the social spheres as well as the primacy accorded the economic sphere in the Charlottetown and Political accords must be critically examined in light of the larger ideology of public and private which informs and gives it coherence. In terms of strategic implications, this means that the social rights strategy should challenge rather than reinforce the separation between the social and the economic spheres and develop an analysis that is rooted in the concerns of social equity.

Finally, the political lessons of women's experiences in the various arenas of social benefit provision should inform and shape a feminist constitutional strategy. Thus, for example, in the area of reproductive health care, the experiences of women seeking abortion services should provide the material on which to base a social right to health that is designed to support women as health care decision makers as well as ensure their access to a service. While this may entail different institutional structures for differently situated women, the fundamental linkage between material support and political self-determination must be maintained rather than severed. Only then will the political ideal of good health come to signify empowerment rather than an inducement to accept a 'natural' state of chronic disempowerment.

Notes

1 An earlier version of this chapter appeared in *Social Justice and the Constitution*, edited by J. Bakan and D. Schneiderman (Ottawa: Carleton University Press, 1992), 101–14.
2 RSC 1970, c. C-34
3 [1988] 1 SCR 30.

References

Bakan, J., and D. Schneiderman. 1992. 'Introduction.' In J. Bakan and D. Schneiderman, eds., *Social Justice and the Constitution*. Ottawa: Carleton University Press, 1–16.

Bakker, I. 1988. 'The Social Wage and the Canada–U.S. Free Trade Agreement.' In M. Gold and D. Leyton-Brown, eds., *Trade-Offs on Free Trade*. Toronto: Carswell, 407–14.

Brodsky, G. 1992. 'Social Charter Issues.' In J. Bakan and D. Schneiderman, eds., *Social Justice and the Constitution*. Ottawa: Carleton University Press, 43–58.

Canada, House of Commons and Senate. 1992. *A Renewed Canada. Report of the Special Joint Committee of the Senate and House of Commons*. G. Beaudoin and D. Dobbie, joint chairpersons, 28 February.

– Consensus Report on the Constitution. 1992. Charlottetown. Final Text, 28 August.

– Draft Legal Text. 1992. Charlottetown Accord, 9 October.

Certenig, M. 1992. 'NWT Orders Abortion Inquiry.' *Globe and Mail*, A1.

Coates, K., and J. Powell. 1989. *The Modern North: People, Politics and the Reflection of Colonialism*. Toronto: Lorimer.

Fudge, J. 1991 'Reconceiving Employment Standards Legislation: Labour Law's Little Sister and the Feminization of Labour.' *Journal of Law and Social Policy* 7: 73–89.

Gavigan, S. 1992. 'Beyond Morgentaler: The Legal Regulation of Reproduction.' In J. Brodie, S. Gavigan, and J. Jenson eds., *The Politics of Abortion*. Toronto: Oxford University Press, 117–46.

Gordon, L. 1990. 'The New Feminist Scholarship on the Welfare State.' In L. Gordon, ed., *Women, the State, and Welfare*. Madison: University of Wisconsin Press, 9–35.

Hutchinson, A., and A. Petter. 1988. 'Private Rights / Public Wrongs: The Liberal Lie of the Charter.' *University of Toronto Law Journal* 38: 278–xx.

Jackman, M. 1992. 'Constitutional Rhetoric and Social Justice: Reflections on the Justiciability Debate.' In J. Bakan and D. Schneiderman, eds., *Social Justice and the Constitution*. Ottawa: Carleton University Press, 17–28.

Jaggar, A. 1983. *Feminist Politics and Human Nature*. New Jersey: Rowman and Allanheld.

Lamarche, L. 1992. 'Le debat sur les droits sociaux au Canada: respecte-t-il la juridicité de ces droits?' In J. Bakan and D. Schneiderman, eds., *Social Justice and the Constitution*. Ottawa: Carleton University Press, 29–42.

Lessard, H. 1986. 'The Idea of the Private: A Discussion of State Action Doctrine and Separate Sphere Ideology.' *Dalhousie Law Journal* 28: 107–37.

– 1993. 'The Construction of Health Care and the Ideology of the Private in Canadian Constitutional Law.' *Annals of Health Law* 2: 121–59.

Macklem, P., and C. Scott. 1992. 'Constitutional Ropes of Sand or Justiciable

Guarantees?' *Social Rights in a New South African Constitution. University of Pennsylvania Law Review* 141: 1–148.

Milne, D. 1991. *The Canadian Constitution.* Toronto: Lorimer.

Morris, C. 1994. 'Abortion.' *National General News* (CP), 28 June.

Nedelsky, J., and C. Scott. 1992. 'Constitutional Dialogue.' In J. Bakan and D. Schneiderman, eds., *Social Justice and the Constitution.* Ottawa: Carleton University Press, 59–83.

Northwest Territories, Ministry of Health. 1992. *Report of the Abortion Services Review Committee.* Yellowknife, June.

Ontario, Ministry of Intergovernmental Affairs. 1991. *A Canadian Social Charter: Making Our Shared Values Stronger.* Toronto.

Osberg, L., and S. Phipps. 1992. 'A Social Charter for Canada.' In H. Echenberg A. Milner, J. Myles, L. Osberg, S. Phipps, J. Richards, and W.B.P. Robson, eds., *A Social Charter for Canada?.* Ottawa: C.D. Howe Institute.

Pateman, C. 1988. *The Sexual Contract.* Stanford: Stanford University Press.

Pro-Choice News. 1992. 'Across Canada.' Summer: 4–5.

– 1993. 'Across Canada.' Spring: 4–6.

– 1994. 'Clinics Fight for Access.' Winter: 1, 7.

– 1995. 'Stiffer Measures Needed After Romalis Shooting.' Winter: 1, 8.

– 1996. 'Justice Denied: B.C. "Bubble Zone" struck down.' Spring: 4, 8.

Schneiderman, D. 1992. 'The Constitutional Politics of Poverty.' In J. Bakan and D. Schneiderman, eds., *Social Justice and the Constitution.* Ottawa: Carleton University Press, 135–8.

Ursel, J. 1992. *Private Lives, Public Policy.* Toronto: Women's Press.

4

Divided Citizenship? Gender, Income Security, and the Welfare State[1]

PATRICIA M. EVANS

Social assistance and unemployment insurance are among the most prominent and visible income support programs of the modern Canadian welfare state. Income security has been termed a 'paradigmatic social right' (Shaver, 1993: 103), although, with the exception of a few universal benefits, the right to income benefits has never been unconditional. Welfare states define the particular needs and circumstances that create legitimate claims on the state for income support, and, in this process, the terms and conditions that govern their citizens' access to benefits are articulated, and different distributive principles in the claiming process are invoked (Peattie and Rein, 1983). The claims that are recognized as legitimate and the principles that are used as a basis for these claims change over time, both reflecting, as well as shaping, the shifting terrain of social, political, and economic values and priorities. Income security represents, then, an ideological marker that constructs entitlements to benefits and confers different categories of statuses that are embodied in the language of claimant, beneficiary, and recipient. The nature of the benefit, then, can constitute 'either a badge of poverty or a badge of citizenship' (Lister, 1990: 453).

For more than twenty years, feminist scholarship has been uncovering the extent to which income claims on the state are problematically gendered for women. In particular, priority is given to paid work over unpaid work, while the work of caring for others, overwhelmingly the work of women, is typically regarded as a private responsibility. When played out in the arena of income security, these ideological assumptions and material realities produce a differential construction of claims and claiming processes for men and women in which women traditionally have been more likely to claim on the gender-specific basis of their family status as mothers or wives, and less likely than men to claim directly as 'workers.' At the same time, it is clear that the policy principles that govern women's claims are changing. Writing in the Australian context, Sheila Shaver (1993: 3) suggests that this trend 'is redefining the underlying basis of social security from a logic of gender difference to one of gender neutrality in rules and conditions of entitlement to benefits.'

The contours of income security are being reshaped as Canada, along with other nations, positions itself to respond to a transformed political and economic landscape increasingly sculpted by the pressures of deficits, unemployment, and the globalizing and restructuring of economies. Once regarded as a response to the inequities and 'diswelfares' of a capitalist economy, the welfare state is now depicted as the problem, not the solution. In what has been described as a shift from the 'welfare' to 'workfare' state, the promotion of full employment in a relatively closed economy gives way to increasing the competitiveness of open economies. The emphasis changes from demand- to supply-side measures, and wages are viewed, not as a source of demand, but as a production cost (Jessop, 1993). In this environment, the claims to social citizenship are particularly fragile.[2]

The terms and conditions that govern a woman's rights and claims to income from the state constitute, then, an important arena for exploring the changing relationship of women to the welfare state. It provides a critical nexus where her identities as citizen, mother, and worker converge, often in confusing and contradictory ways. Women, of course, do not hold common identities, and important factors such as class and race influence the stakes women hold and the claims they make to income support; see Quadagno (1994) and Amott (1990) for the influence of race in U.S. programs. Within this diversity, however, the changing images of women as 'mothers' and women as 'workers' that underpin income security play a defining role in relations between women and the welfare state and help to construct the contemporary reality of women's social citizenship.

In this essay, I pose and attempt to respond to several broad questions. How have women been incorporated as 'social citizens' into the Canadian welfare state? Is the basis of their social citizenship changing? What are the particular challenges for women as social policy is reconfigured to meet what are regarded as the imperatives of globalization, economic restructuring, and fiscal restraint? To address these questions, the first section begins with a brief exploration of the literature on women's social citizenship. This sets the stage for examining the changing basis of women's claims to income security from gender specificity to a formal gender neutrality. The third section assesses the implications for women of recent changes to income security. The final section considers how gender might be sensitively incorporated into income security without either disadvantaging women or reinforcing inequalities. While the primary focus is on Canada, some attention is also given to other countries which illustrate both commonality and difference.

Gender Claims and Social Citizenship

The idea of social citizenship is most closely associated with T.H. Marshall, whose now classic formulation suggested that the development of social rights in the twentieth century, exemplified by the postwar welfare state, constituted a third 'layer' of citizenship that, for men at least, rested upon the establishment of civil rights (property, personal liberty, and due process) in the eighteenth century, and the extension of political rights (voting, right to hold elective office) in the nineteenth century. Social rights, Marshall suggests, range from the right to 'economic welfare and security to the right to share to the full in the social heritage and to live the life of a civilized being according to the standards prevailing in society' (1964: 78). There has been a resurgence of interest in this pioneering work, spurred in part by the current tenuousness of the social rights component of citizenship.

Gøsta Esping-Andersen's (1990: 21) typology of welfare state regimes represents the most ambitious of the recent attempts to examine empirically the notion of social citizenship, which he calls the 'core idea of the welfare state.' Welfare states, he proposes, cluster into broad groupings, partially distinguished by the extent to which benefits are 'decommodified' – that is, the degree to which an individual can maintain a livelihood, as a matter of right, outside of any attachment to the labour market. Esping-Andersen classifies Canada, and the other English-speaking countries, as 'liberal welfare regimes,' in which social rights are significantly circumscribed by a market ethos, resulting in an income security system that emphasizes means-tested benefits, delivers low levels of benefit, embodies stringent eligibility conditions, and involves considerable individual scrutiny and stigma.

As feminist scholars have suggested, the archetypal model of the 'citizen' in income security policy is neither free of gender bias, nor is it gender sensitive. As expressed by Marshall and typologized by Esping-

Andersen, social citizenship has a distinctly male cast. The relationships between class, the welfare state, and capitalism are prominent, while the other important domain of inequality, the family, is largely ignored. The link between paid work and welfare is emphasized, but the welfare regime classification begins to break down when unpaid work is taken into account (Lewis, 1992; Fraser and Gordon, 1992). As Orloff (1993) points out, the idea of the welfare state implies a loosening of the ties to the marketplace, but this is not sufficient to ensure the social citizenship of women, whose position may well require access to paid work (or the right to be 'commodified') as well as the right to form autonomous households (see also O'Connor, 1993). Social citizenship, then, 'is shaped by women's roles as mothers, carers and paid workers and is constricted by the ideology and reality of women's economic dependency' (Lister, 1990: 446).

The language of social citizenship has undergone a sea change since Marshall introduced this phrase in 1949, ten years after the term 'welfare state' was first used in opposition to the 'warfare' state, and at a time of great optimism about the postwar state as a vehicle for positive social change (Pateman, 1992). In the general discourse of today, social citizenship may resonate as distinctly unfashionable. In the same way that 'welfare' has been translated over time to equate with ill-being instead of well-being (Gordon, 1994), and 'dependency' has come to refer to a highly pejorative, and distinctly constricted range of relationships, so social citizenship has come to be inflected with notions of obligation, rather than entitlement (Fraser and Gordon, 1994). The view that social citizenship is not to be achieved through state provision or intervention, but through 'exhorting the citizenry to assume a greater responsibility for taking care of themselves and others' (Marston and Staeheli, 1994: 843), has gained great momentum since the 1980s. This is particularly evident in the increasing emphasis on work obligations in Canadian income security (Evans, 1995a) and the calls for 'community' care for the elderly (Neysmith, 1991). This type of discourse, with its particular implications for women to pick up the slack, has been viewed as 'an attempt to apply a thin varnish of community to essentially an atomistic view of society' (Lister, 1990: 454).

Despite the efforts to reconstitute and restrict the meaning of social citizenship, it is important not simply to abandon this contested terrain of language. As Fraser and Gordon (1992: 46) suggest, social citizenship is a powerful and evocative phrase that resonates with three major political traditions: 'liberal themes of rights and respect; communitarian norms of solidarity and shared responsibility; and republican ideals of participation in public life.' The remainder of the essay assesses the Canadian context of women's social citizenship, attending to the 'practices' of citizenship, not simply those that are embodied in a formal articulation of rights and obligations (Turner, 1993).

'Two-Track' Income Security?

Elizabeth Wilson (1977) is usually given credit for turning the attention of critical feminist scholarship to gender relations and the welfare state. The burgeoning work that followed her initial lead all lends support to the gendered nature of the welfare state, although interpretations about its particular construction, and its causes, vary considerably. In general, the early work emphasized the 'patriarchal' aspects of the welfare state and the ways in which it reinforced women's disadvantage. The assumption of dependency, for example, has been critical to women's incorporation into the welfare state. The notion of the 'family wage,' which assumed that male wages should be sufficient to support several dependents, has a long history as a justification for the exclusion of women from paid industrialized work. Similarly, assumptions of dependency are built into a social insurance system in which women traditionally have been more likely to benefit indirectly, as wives of unemployed or retired men, rather than as direct claimants on the basis of their own work record.

Recently, feminist literature has shifted from an emphasis on the negative effects of the welfare state on women to a greater attention to its ambiguous and contradictory aspects. Income benefits, for example, do structure women as men's dependents. Social assistance is typically claimed by the male 'head' in a married-couple household. At the same time, however, social assistance provides an escape route, albeit a minimal and stigmatizing one, from the necessity to remain tied, economically and in other ways, to individual men. While some argue that this replaces 'private' patriarchy with 'public' patriarchy (Hernes, 1987), others point out that women do not have to 'live with the state' as they do with men (Gordon, 1990: 23). Other writers also emphasize the potential of the welfare state to provide women with a political resource and a focus of collective action (Fox Piven, 1990).

While there are differences in interpretation, there is general agreement that the incorporation of women into income security programs has been different from men. Carole Pateman (1992: 229) describes what is often referred to as the two-track income support system: 'First, there are the benefits available to individuals as "public" persons by virtue of their participation, and accidents of fortune, in the capitalist market ... Second, benefits are available to the "dependants" of individuals in the first category, or to "private" persons, usually women.' Ann Shola Orloff (1993) argues that the analytical distinction in social security is not primarily between men and women, but different types of households: the household headed by a male breadwinner and an economically dependent wife, and households maintained by women who cannot participate in the labour market, and so make their claims based on their family status. Whichever distinction is preferred, the anticipated outcome remains the same: women are more likely to benefit from the inferior tier of income security – social assistance, where claims are made on the basis of 'need,' benefits are low, stigma is considerable, and scrutiny is intense. In contrast, men are more likely to claim benefits based on their participation in the labour market, and these benefits are typically more generous, less stigmatized, and the process of claiming is less onerous (UI, Workers' Compensation, and public and private retirement benefits). Evidence of a 'two-track' system has come largely from the United States (see, for example, Pearce, 1985; Fraser, 1989; Nelson, 1990), where social assistance is particularly limited in coverage and meagre in benefits. Diane Sainsbury (1993: 89) suggests that the extent of women's dependence on means-tested benefits should be regarded as a dimension of welfare state variation rather than an inherent feature of it.

To what extent are the current claims of Canadian women to income support structured along the lines of gender? Limited data make it difficult to explore the gendering of the Canadian welfare state, and it is especially problematic in the arena of social assistance, where data are regularly reported by age, but not by sex. However, it is possible to make some estimates of the proportion of men and women who are receiving social assistance, either in their own right or as a 'dependant.' Caseload data from British Columbia for March 1993, excluding individuals over 60 and those with disabilities, indicate that women are somewhat more likely than men to depend upon income from social assistance – 52 per cent versus 48 per cent (National Council of Welfare, 1994, calculated from Table 2). These figures probably underestimate women's profile in social assistance in non-recessionary times, and, indeed, in 1988 and 1989, 54 per cent of the province's caseload comprised adult women, and 55 per cent in 1990 (Canada, Health and Welfare, 1991: 130–1, Tables 4.23a, b, and c).[3] Quebec data also reveal that women are considerably overrepresented on the welfare rolls: they constituted fully 57 per cent of the caseload in 1988 and 1989, and 56 per cent in 1990 (Canada, Health and Welfare, 1991: 84–5, Tables 4.9a, b, and c). Unfortunately, it is not possible to update the Quebec data because the province no longer organizes their publicly available statistical data by sex. The only other province that does report social assistance data by sex is Saskatchewan, and the most recent data available show that women comprised 55 per cent of the 1992 caseload (Canada, 1994, Tables 4.16, 4.17a, b).

Poverty appears to be even more sharply gendered than the 'welfare track': in 1994 women comprised 62 per cent of the adult, non-elderly and non-disabled poor in Canada (National Council of Welfare, 1996: 71, calculated from Table 15).[4] These differences are even more pronounced among the elderly. Four out of ten (44 per cent) women living on their own are poor, compared with one in four (25 per cent) of single, elderly men (National Council of Welfare, 1996: Graph D).

As the two-track model suggests, women tend to be both overrepresented in the social assistance system and underrepresented in social insurance. In December 1995 40 per cent of all regular Unemployment Insurance claimants were women, whereas, as noted earlier, they constitute over half of the social assistance caseload. While their 40 per cent share of UI beneficiaries is nearly the equivalent of their 41 per cent representation among the unemployed (Statistics Canada, 1996a, 1996b), it does appear that Canadian men and women are 'tracked' differently in the income support system. Women are more likely than men to be recipients of social assistance, and they are considerably less likely to benefit from unemployment insurance. However, the Canadian welfare state may be somewhat less gendered than its counterparts in other liberal welfare states. In Britain, for example, women comprise about two-thirds of the adults who are on social assistance, in part because the low incomes of many elderly persons make them eligible for social assistance, and many of these individuals are women. In the United States, nearly eight in ten of the adult recipients of the U.S. federal means-tested program are women because many men are systematically excluded (for estimates, see Sainsbury, 1993: 85, Table 4).[5] Canadian social assistance has also become less gendered over time. The cost-sharing provisions of the Canada Assistance Plan (CAP), instituted in 1966, encouraged provinces to adopt more comprehensive schemes and thus improved men's access to social assistance. At the same time, women's expanded labour market activities have also increased their use of unemployment insurance. Nonetheless, gender remains an important dimension of income security.

The 'citizen–worker' model of social insurance provides a formally equivalent entitlement to men and women, but benefits are cast with a male worker in mind. A woman's entitlement *may* equal a man's, but only if her behaviour with respect to paid work and family is like a man's, and if she is also able to escape the general effects of wage discrimination and occupational segregation. In contrast to social insurance which emphasizes the role of paid work, social assistance incorporates many women according to claims based either directly on their status as mothers without husbands, or indirectly, as wives of male recipients. Claims made through social assistance on the basis of 'citizen–mother' are accorded neither the degree of legitimacy nor the level of benefits that accompanies 'worker' claims through social insurance. The claims to income security, therefore, can be gender-specific and explicitly treat men and women differently. They can also be gender-neutral and provide benefits to men and women on formally equal terms and conditions. Gender-neutral benefits may be gender-blind and embody gendered impacts, typically to women's disadvantage. Gender-neutral benefits may also be gender-sensitive, and while not explicitly incorporating gender have differential but positive impacts for women. The following sections explore the implications of the increasing trend to gender neutrality in social assistance and its long history in social insurance.

Gender Specificity to Gender Neutrality: Social Assistance

In the early days of Canadian social provisions, attention to gender was typically explicit and direct. The first modern social assistance programs in Canada were the provincial 'mothers' allowances' or 'mothers' pensions' that began in Manitoba in 1916. These programs marked a slight shift from charity to entitlement by providing a small but regular source of income to poor mothers (but not fathers) who were rearing children on their own and were deemed to be 'worthy' (Strong-Boag, 1979). The names of these programs have long since been divested of their gendered titles, but explicitly gendered practices take longer to disappear, and the changes that have occurred are not necessarily to women's advantage.

Social assistance programs continue to reflect the assumptions of the 'breadwinner/dependent' model of the family that views men as the primary economic providers and women as the central caregivers. When present in a household, men traditionally have been considered its 'head' for purposes of social assistance. This practice is changing, and in some provinces couples can elect which individual, or whether both, will be considered as the applicants. The traditional assumptions held about the gendered division of labour are also aptly illustrated by the situation of single custodial fathers in Ontario, who, until a 1984 change in legislation, were not eligible to receive long-term social assistance on the same terms and conditions as single mothers (Little, forthcoming).

The strength of the breadwinner/dependent model of the family is particularly apparent in the 'man in the house' rule, a regulation which automatically deems a woman ineligible for social assistance in her own right if she is living with a man, even if the man has no obligation for her financial support. The assumption that any woman who lives with a man ought to be supported by him forms the basis for highly intrusive investigations into the personal circumstances of single mother applicants and recipients of social assistance (Little, forthcoming).

Practice regarding 'man in the house' is also changing, but not necessarily in a linearly progressive manner. In 1987 Ontario adopted the same definition of 'spouse' for social assistance that is found in family law. As a result, men and women who were living together, but not married, were not assumed to owe a financial obligation to each other's support until they had borne a child or lived together for a period of three years (the length of time required to establish legal relationship of cohabitation). However, under the welfare cutbacks that have accompanied the arrival of a Conservative government in Ontario in 1995, the province has now reverted to its former practice which excludes cohabiting women from claiming social assistance as single mothers. Quebec uses a similar principle to the one used in Ontario between 1987 and 1995, although in Quebec the support obligation begins when a man and woman have lived together for one year. A case decided in Nova Scotia, where the 'man in the house' rule was still in force, involved a single mother who was charged with fraud for failing to reveal that she was cohabiting with a man, who neither contributed in fact to her support, nor owed any support obligation. The Nova Scotia Supreme Court held that the man-in-the-house rule violated the equality clause of the Canadian Charter of Rights and Freedoms. A Charter challenge to Ontario's 'man-in-the-house' regulation was recently dismissed, but on procedural rather than substantive grounds.[6]

An area that is more consistently moving from gender specificity to gender neutrality is the expectation of employment that may accompany a single mother's entitlement to social assistance. This is an obvious arena in which the shift to gender neutrality, through ignoring women's child care responsibilities, actually represents a deterioration of the gender-based claims that have been made as mothers. In the current climate, single mothers on social assistance are increasingly subjected to the same work requirements that pertain to married men and single women. Alberta, for example, now defines a single mother as employable once the youngest child is six months old, and Quebec reduces the benefit level for single mothers when their youngest child enters school, unless they are participating in employment-related activities. Ontario's recently announced mandatory workfare program does not incorporate single mothers in its first phase of operation, but it does plan to include them as the program expands, and at that time only single mothers with very young children (i.e., under the age of three) will be exempt. Social assistance, then, has become increasingly gender-neutral and single mothers, a large and expanding group of recipients, are increasingly viewed as 'workers' rather than 'mothers' (Evans, 1995b). This shift in definition from 'mothers' to 'workers' is occurring at the same time that child care provision is deteriorating across most provinces, when training dollars for women are in decline, and job opportunities are increasingly limited to those that offer non-standard employment (Friendly and Oloman, 1996; Cameron, 1996).

It is not only compulsory work requirements or workfare programs that raise concerns for single mothers. Even programs that are 'voluntary' are problematic when they are not grounded in the realities of women's paid and unpaid work. Programs that encourage single mothers on social assistance to volunteer for community service jobs help to institutionalize women's unpaid work and may contribute to the erosion of women's paid employment. The recent Metro Toronto Job Incentive Program, for example, was designed to extend help to non-profit organizations which were struggling with budget cutbacks that reduced the number of their staff (Evans, 1995a).

Further examples of the problems of voluntary participation are found in the British Columbia and New Brunswick wage supplement programs designed for single mothers who leave social assistance to take up paid work. In these pilot projects, women who volunteer and are selected for participation have one year to find a job (or jobs) that offers at least 30 hours of paid work a week. If they are successful in gaining employment, their wages are supplemented by an amount that is half of the difference between their annual earnings and a benchmark figure, set in 1994 at $37,500 in British Columbia and $30,600 in New Brunswick. They may continue to receive the supplement for a maximum of three years, by which time it is assumed that their wages will have increased to offset the supplement. However, the size of the supplement, in relation to average earnings, suggests that this assumption is highly unrealistic. In February 1994 the average supplement paid was $794, amounting to 71 per cent of participants' average earnings (Social Research and Demonstration Corporation, 1994: Table 4). It is unlikely that many women will be able to increase their earnings by the magnitude required to make up for their lost supplement at the end of the three-year period. Given the realities of women's low-wage employment, this program of temporary assistance seems destined to leave many women in the lurch.

Although the English-speaking countries are grouped into 'liberal welfare state regimes' (Esping-Andersen, 1990), there are also important differences among them. As indicated earlier, social assistance in the United States is even more sharply gendered than in Canada. The recently abolished federal social assistance program, Aid to Families with Dependent Children (AFDC), only became available to two-parent families in 1962, and only in 1988 were states required to provide this aid. Aid to single-father families was not generally available through AFDC, and the 'man in the house' provision remained in force. In contrast to the United States and Canada, Britain never developed the 'mother allowance' model, and social assistance has never identified poor sole-support mothers as a separate category of recipients. Nonetheless, women comprise about two-thirds of the adults on social assistance. This different pattern of development has led Theda Skocpol (1992) to distinguish the 'paternalist' British welfare state, which recognized much earlier those dependencies created by unemployment, from the 'maternalist' welfare system in the United States (and Canada), where needs related to family structure were acknowledged long before those arising from unemployment. Ironically, the 'maternalist' emphasis in the United States and Canada appears to provide the single mother with less protection from the 'stick' of work requirements in social assistance than has been the case in Britain (Evans, 1992).

Gender Neutrality? Unemployment Insurance and the 'Worker–Citizen'

In contrast to the household 'needs test' which determines claims to social assistance, eligibility for UI is based on an individual record of employment, and historically it has embraced a greater degree of formal gender equality than has social assistance. UI was established in Canada in 1940 following a constitutional amendment that resolved a jurisdictional wrangle which had doomed an earlier proposal. The 1940 act, a 'cautious piece of legislation' (Struthers, 1994: 166), covered approximately 40 per cent of the labour force. Unlike an earlier proposal, or the British program, benefits were 'classed' and geared to earnings, rather than set at a single flat rate; it also included a married worker supplement which was later revoked. UI became explicitly gendered in 1950 when more stringent eligibility conditions were imposed on newly married women to prevent them from claiming benefits too easily when, it was thought, they were really withdrawing from the labour force. An estimated 12,000 to 14,000 women each year were excluded from receiving benefits until the provision was abolished in 1957, amid concerns about its discriminatory nature (Dingledine, 1981).

In 1971 major changes were made to UI that increased its coverage from approximately 80 per cent to 96 per cent of the employed population (Dingeldine, 1981) and introduced 15 weeks of maternity leave. In 1990 parental leave was instituted, providing an additional 10 weeks of leave to care for infant children. This gender-neutral title, however, is spectacularly at odds with its take-up: since its introduction, not more than 3 in every 100 of its monthly claimants has been male (Statistics Canada, various years). While the take-up of parental leave may be the most obvious instance of the gendered implications of policies that are formally gender-neutral, there are other, less visible consequences that result from the triage of women's position in the labour market, the inequitable division of domestic responsibilities, and the lack of attention in our social policies to countering these disadvantages. Policies constructed with the 'regular' worker in mind do not serve women well (Vosko, 1996).

As a result of gendered disadvantage in the home and in the labour market, women are less likely than men to claim non-maternity-based UI benefits. The majority of women (59 per cent) become unemployed for the same reasons men do: they lose their jobs (Statistics Canada, 1995). But unemployment also has a gendered dimension, and women's traditional responsibilities help to exclude them from UI benefits. Unemployed women, for example, are much more likely than men (10 per cent versus 6 per cent) to be either new entrants or re-entrants to the labour market. They also lose more time on the job because of personal and family responsibilities than men do: in 1993 women lost, on average, almost seven days a year in comparison with men who lost just under one day (Akyeampong, 1995). They are also six times more likely than men (6 per cent versus 1 per cent) to leave their jobs because of personal or family responsibilities (Statistics Canada, 1995: 68), contingencies typically covered by UI include only the birth or adoption of a child and the care of an infant.

To the extent that women are overrepresented in 'non-standard' employment, they are also less likely to be covered by UI. Women are certainly disproportionately represented in part-time employment and multiple job-holding (Krahn, 1991: 37, calculated from Table 1). In 1990, for example, they constituted 64 per cent of the part-time workers excluded from UI eligibility (Canada, 1994b: 74). And when women are eligible for UI, the earnings-related basis of benefits ensures that their disadvantaged position in the labour market is replicated in their UI benefits. In December 1995 the insurable earnings of 57 per cent of the women who received UI benefits amounted to less than $400 per week, while this was true of only 25 per cent of men. Conversely, 13 per cent of women had insurable earnings in excess of $600 a week, in comparison with 43 per cent of men (Statistics Canada, 1996b).

The capacity of gender-neutral social insurance provisions to operate without gendered disadvantage depends, of course, upon the degree of substantive equality in the labour market. Over time, women have certainly increased their representation in the labour force and their presence in higher education, and they have seen a diminution in the wage gap. However, the percentage of women employed part-time has increased, and fully one-third of them work part-time because they cannot find full-time work (Statistics Canada, 1994). In addition, women's labour force participation, which had been steadily increasing, has now begun to decline with the recession, although it has fallen less than men's. As Pat Armstrong (1996) notes, some of the recent gains attributed to women are illusory and are partly accounted for by the fact that men's work is deteriorating. Economic restructuring makes men's paid work look more like women's as the global economy 'harmonizes down.'

Recent Directions

The revamping of social security was the most important plank in the federal Liberal party election platform, and it has been a primary focus of domestic policy since the Chrétien government came to power in 1993. The Social Security Review was officially launched in January 1994 and was buttressed by a ministerial task force to develop proposals and a standing committee to receive briefs and review options for reform. The February 1995 budget provided further specifics of the government's plans for changes to Canadian income security, and it demonstrated to anyone who might have been in doubt that the goal of deficit reduction was its major driving force.

The reform process has been marked by language that has increasingly provided Canadians with individualized definitions of, and solutions to, structural problems. Thus, social programs needed to be made 'active' rather than 'passive,' which has translated into a greater emphasis on work and training requirements as conditions to income benefits; it did not mean more attention to ensuring the availability of jobs. The federal approach takes as a given that the fiscal deficit is *the* problem, while neglecting to attend to the accumulating social deficit apparent in the rising rates of child poverty.[7] In this respect, most provincial governments have followed the federal lead.

At a time when gender consciousness is supposedly on the rise, it has been remarkably absent in the review of social security. Neither the ministerial task force nor the standing committee included a member who was primarily accountable to women. In addition, women were not targeted for particular attention, as were the categories of employable adults, families with children, those with disabilities, and youth (Nemiroff, 1994). The standing committee's report (House of Commons, 1995: 100), however, did recommend that proposals for social security reform should be subject to a gender analysis. Given the very high poverty rates of adult women, especially single mothers (57 per cent) and elderly women on their own (44 per cent) (National Council of Welfare, 1996: 17, 19), no genuine or meaningful reform can occur without concerted efforts to improve the situation of women.

The major targets for reforming income security that are especially relevant to this chapter include UI and the arrangements for financing social assistance through the Canada Assistance Plan (CAP). In May 1996, in keeping with an emphasis in language on 'active' rather than 'passive,' Unemployment Insurance was renamed Employment Insurance, in the largest single overhaul of UI in twenty-five years. Although the new legislation emerged from the political process with the rejection of some of the more retrogressive proposals, the changes, nonetheless, continue a general direction of retrenchment in UI policy that has been pursued with particular vigour over the past five years. The changes to UI between 1990 and 1995 lengthened qualifying periods and reduced the duration and the level of benefits. In addition, 'voluntary' leavers were completely disqualified from benefits, and these are often women who leave jobs because of difficulties with child care and sexual harassment (National Association of Women and the Law, 1993). Data from the Canadian Labour Congress indicate that the effect of these changes has been dramatic: prior to the 1990 changes, 87 per cent of the unemployed claimed benefit, in contrast to 58 per cent by the end of 1994 (cited in Vosko, 1996). Despite predictions that the UI account will be in surplus, the 1996 legislation will reduce the size of the UI program by a *minimum* of 10 per cent (emphasis in original, Canada, 1995: 16).

The 1996 changes continue the erosion of benefits by shortening their duration and reducing benefits for 'frequent' users. Short-term workers also find their benefits reduced because the earnings calculations now include weeks with zero earnings for workers in areas where the unemployment rate is less than 9 per cent. The most radical change, however, is that eligibility is based on a calculation of the number of hours rather than the number of weeks worked. This has the positive value of including some part-time workers who were formerly excluded from coverage because they worked in their jobs for less than 15 hours a week. However, the number of hours now required for eligibility has more than doubled, and it has tripled for those who have recently entered the labour market.[8] These changes will particularly affect women, who are disproportionately represented in part-time and insecure work.

The continuing contraction of the ability of workers to claim benefits when unemployed increases reliance on social assistance, the 'safety net' of last resort. This shift is completely consistent with a trend to 'target' benefits to those 'in need,' a trend that has been particularly apparent in Canadian social policy since the Mulroney government came to power in 1980 and is exemplified by the abolition of the Family Allowance and the erosion of universality in Old Age Security (Evans, 1994; Lightman and Irving, 1991).

The second important area of change in federal social security policy, relevant to this chapter, is the elimination of the Canada Assistance Plan (CAP), the federal transfer program to the provinces which funded social assistance and social services to those 'in need' (day care subsidies, for example). In April 1996 CAP was replaced by the Canada Health and Social Transfer (CHST). The CHST creates a 'mega' transfer by folding into one envelope the funding for welfare and social services and the block funding that was already in place for health care and post-secondary education. The shift from a cost-shared to a block-funding approach has potentially very serious consequences for income-tested social programs. It decreases the visibility of the federal government in social assistance spending, and it increases provincial flexibility in spending because the provinces are no longer required to spend on social assistance in order to receive matching federal funds. The CHST also eliminates the specific conditions that were attached to CAP cost sharing. These included the requirement to base eligibility on a determination of 'needs,' which has had a 'powerful impact in ensuring the presence of an income safety net' (Torjman and Battle, 1995: 2). In addition, provinces are no longer required to provide access to an appeals system, and they are no longer prohibited from requiring social assistance recipients to work in exchange for benefits. Although the CHST embodies the CAP ban which prohibits provinces from imposing residence requirements as a condition of social assistance, it is not at all obvious how easily or effectively a financial penalty can be imposed.

The abolition of CAP removes the federal presence from social assistance, and it can only widen the holes in an already tattered social safety net. The reduction in federal transfers, and the removal of all but one of the existing cost-sharing conditions related to social assistance, means that women and men on welfare are considerably more dependent on the goodwill of the individual provinces not to 'beggar' their social assistance systems to generally reduce costs or to divert funds to health and education (National Council of Welfare, 1995). The prospects do not look good in a climate that is characterized by increasing calls for work-for-welfare, concerns about welfare fraud, and a belief that welfare benefits are too high. Alberta's social assistance cutbacks have already removed large numbers of recipients from the caseload (Feschuk, 1994) and the Conservative premier of Ontario, elected in 1995, has introduced mandatory workfare and implemented a 22 per cent across-the-board cut in welfare benefits. As we have seen, women make up the majority of adults who benefit from social assistance. They are particularly affected when benefits are decreased and, at the same time, increased efforts are made to move single mothers into the paid workforce without a commitment to provide the necessary resources for additional child care and training and to ensure the availability of jobs.

Towards Gender-Sensitive Social Citizenship

A major response to globalization, economic restructuring, and the deficit has been to reduce spending on social programs, programs that are viewed as too expensive, too 'passive,' and too 'unresponsive' to the pace of change. Paid work, the critical nexus for the modern construction of social citizenship, is becoming more difficult to obtain in the global economy, while at the same time it is increasingly viewed as a 'badge' of citizenship. As Ostner (1994: 129) notes, 'Those who care for dependents during their life course or who are among those groups ascribed such roles can easily become "laggards" in a competitive market economy.'

The analysis I present in this chapter suggests that a shift is occurring in income security policy that, with few exceptions, increasingly emphasizes the formal notion of gender equality. At the same time, the gendered disadvantages that accompany the actual operation of income security are exacerbated by the budget cuts, the abolition of CAP, and the restructuring of UI. The notion of social rights is eroding in both layers of the income security system, including the traditionally more privileged contributory social insurance. In social assistance, the direction of policy is to 'degender' the employment expectations of single mothers with an emphasis on an equality that redefines them as 'workers' rather than 'mothers.' Unemployment Insurance, or its more recent title, Employment Insurance, continues to reflect the formal notion of gender equality with which it began. However, it becomes increasingly insensitive to both gender and class as it contracts and reshapes conditions of entitlement in ways that are even less responsive to the growing numbers of marginalized workers. Intertwined in these trends is a discourse of dependency that builds on the opposition between two types of exchanges: a contractual exchange among equivalents ('independence') versus the unreciprocal and unilateral charitable relationship ('dependence'). Thus, an ever-tightening boundary is drawn around 'the deserving,' the notion of interdependence fades, and the possibility of an 'honorable' entitlement disappears (Fraser and Gordon, 1992). For women, this opposition of independence and dependence is particularly problematic and paradoxical. Women's 'dependence' is often the outcome of efforts to support the 'independence' of others, including children and the frail elderly as well as able-bodied men. The downsizing of public services under the rubric of encouraging self-reliance and deficit reduction increases the 'dependence' of others upon women and decreases their own opportunities for 'independence.'

Women's claims to social citizenship are not served well by either the maternalist gender-specific provisions of the past, which tended to enshrine women's domestic obligations, or the current emphasis on formal gender neutrality, which ignores the very different material conditions that shape the lives of men and women. Neither past maternalism nor the present gender-neutral emphasis addresses the gendered division of labour which forms the core of women's economic disadvantage; both approaches offer to women a social citizenship that is inflected with patriarchy. And yet the tradition in income security has been to treat women as either 'mothers' or 'workers.' As Pateman (1992: 236) points out, in these dichotomous alternatives 'either women become (like) men, and so full citizens; or they continue women's work, which is of no value for citizenship.'

Feminists debate the nature of the appropriate welfare state strategy to recognize women's unpaid labour in looking after family members. The terminology used reflects their different approaches. Writers working from a marxist tradition tend to refer to women's unpaid work as 'reproductive' labour, stressing the functions it serves for capitalism, in an emphasis that has been called 'economistic' (Pascall, 1986: 21). Others from the social democratic and liberal perspectives have typically been more disposed to recognize the affective, as well as instrumental, dimensions of this work and refer to it as 'care work' or 'caring labour' (Baines, Evans, and Neysmith, 1991; Ungerson, 1990; Dalley, 1988). This perspective has been criticized for a tendency to celebrate the aspects of women's lives that form the base of their disadvantage. Perhaps 'compulsory altruism' is the phrase that most accurately captures the nature of this hidden work and the constraints on women's freedom to refuse to undertake it (Land and Rose, 1985). But language is important, and lurking underneath these different uses of terminology lie much larger contested issues that include the primary cause of women's subordination and the way it may best be redressed. While feminists agree on the significance of unpaid labour to women's oppression generally, and to the gendered impacts of the welfare state more specifically, there is considerable debate regarding what to do about it. At the core of this controversy is whether sameness or difference provides the best foundation for constructing the road to gender equality.

Anne Phillips (1992) identifies the views that represent the polarities of the sameness–difference continuum. At one end are those who argue that to acknowledge any difference is to exacerbate the separation of private and public spheres that has been so damaging to women's interests. At the other end are those who challenge a pursuit of gender equality that simply means that women must construct their experience to fit the lives of men. Noting that many feminists remain 'agnostic' about whether, and to what extent, there are essential and irradicable differences between women and men, Phillips suggests that 'feminists will continue to debate and disagree over how far the inequality stems from the difference and how far the difference can or should be eliminated' (1992: 222). A shift in focus to the meaning of language suggests that the oppositional use of equality and difference is itself part of the problem, and it is their interdependence that must be recognized. Arguing that we cannot give up either difference or equality, Joan Scott (1992: 261) suggests that 'it makes no sense for the feminist movement to let its arguments be forced into pre-existing categories and its political disputes to be characterised by a dichotomy we did not invent.'

Whether women's interests are better served through an emphasis on sameness or difference has posed an important dilemma for feminists, but comparative experiences in different types of welfare states help to make this debate less abstract by examining the different approaches that have been used to address women's inequalities. As Jane Lewis (1993) points out, most countries have tried to counter inequalities in employment, and some countries have attempted to address the problem of attaching value to unpaid labour, but no country has done anything significant in terms of sharing unpaid labour. In a similar vein, Bettina Cass (1994) suggests that it is not women's dependence that constitutes the problem for public policy, but rather men's independence.

The gendered division of caregiving and market work, then, cuts across welfare state classifications and extends well beyond the traditional 'laggards' in welfare state development, a designation that includes Canada, along with other English-speaking countries. Jane Lewis and Gertrude Åström (1992) suggest that, while Swedish policy may not transcend the equality–difference dichotomy that Scott suggests is necessary, 'It has constructed a distinctive equal opportunity strategy by grafting the right to make a claim on the basis of difference onto a policy based on equal treatment.'

The Swedish social democratic tradition, Lewis and Åström argue, has paid more attention to 'difference' than the equal opportunity formulation. characteristic of liberal welfare state regimes that attends almost exclusively to the public world of employment, neglecting the private world of domestic labour. Recognition of difference was built into the strategies of the 1960s and 1970s when Swedish policy, partly in response to labour shortages, was altered to increase the incentives to attract women into the labour force and change the basis of their entitlements from mothers to workers. A generous parental leave was introduced, tied to a history of labour force participation, and public child care provisions were expanded. Because of this, it is argued, the benefits paid are 'first class' rather than the meagre benefits that traditionally have been paid to women as 'carers.' The 'Swedish model' has created significant gains for women, but it also represents a 'cautionary tale' (Lewis and Åström, 1992: 61). Although Swedish policy has been very important in helping women to better accommodate paid and unpaid work, the sharing of 'caring' work remains largely untouched, and women still remain primarily responsible for the care of children. As a result, while the wage gap in Sweden is relatively small, the labour market remains highly segregated, and the policies may serve to accentuate these divisions. Nonetheless, as Lewis and Åström (1992) suggest, Sweden offers the most attractive example of the existing models.

National policies are rarely 'exportable,' and Sweden and Canada are sharply distinguished on a range of dimensions, including their commitment to full employment. Given this, what, if any, are the lessons to be learned from the Swedish example? I suggest there are several, and the lessons grow in importance as the claims to social citizenship erode, along with public services and income support, while the pace of globalization and deficit-cutting mount. First, it is essential to reassert the claims of women to paid employment and to recognize that women's responsibilities for caring for others will not be adequately compensated in the absence of labour force attachment. Second, it is important to recognize that the claims to paid employment that do not acknowledge women's caring responsibilities are claims that only the most affluent of working women can benefit from, and these same claims are likely to entrap many single mothers and others who are most vulnerable. Third, the full exercise of women's citizenship requires an equitable division of unpaid labour, and this goal may be the most difficult to achieve through public policy initiatives.

These lessons suggest, in turn, that a primary objective of a feminist agenda, as NAC has long held, must be to vigorously oppose the erosion of public services that curtail an important source of women's employment while also constricting the services, such as child and elder care, that make paid work possible. Child care demands can no longer be made as simple appeals to equity, but must be situated in a critical analysis of the broader political and economic issues which so tightly constrain its development. 'Women's' issues are not only gender-specific; strategies for full employment, unfashionable as they may seem in the current climate, are critical to men's and women's citizenship (for discussion, see Pixley, 1993).

Welfare states, whether highly gendered or not, whether liberal or social democratic, are all experiencing varying degrees of erosion. Canadian women are now having to defend with renewed vigour those policies, such as social assistance, that have been long-standing targets of criticism. It is a particularly difficult time to press women's social citizenship claims, but at a time when these claims appear so fragile and contingent, they have never been more important.

Notes

1 The research for this chapter was supported by the Social Sciences and Humanities Research Council, network grant 816-94-003.
2 The claims of social citizenship extend beyond a minimum level of economic security to include participation in the full life of a society. It is a concept that is rooted in issues of social inequality, social class, and power (Turner, 1993: 3).
3 These calculations include an assumption that 95 per cent of the single parents on social assistance are women, as indicated by the Quebec data (Canada, Health and Welfare, 1991).
4 The table includes 'single mothers' but not single fathers. As a result, female poverty rates are *slightly* overestimated (see note 2).
5 In August 1996 the United States ended its commitment to aid families with children when it abolished Aid to Families with Dependent Children (AFDC) and replaced it with a block grant that, among other things, imposes a general five-year lifetime limit on welfare receipt.
6 *R* v *Rehberg* (1994) 111 DLR (4th), 336; *Falkiner v Ontario Ministry of Community and Social Services* (1996) 140 DLR (4th), 115
7 In February 1997 the Ministry of Finance announced the new Canada Child Tax Benefit, which will improve child-related benefits for some families. It is criticized, however, for its failure to address the situation of Canada's poorest children – those whose families depend on social assistance (Pulkingham and Ternowetsky, 1997).
8 Previously, individuals needed to work between 180 and 300 hours to qualify for benefits, depending upon the regional unemployment rate. This is now increased to between 420 and 700 hours. New entrants and re-entrants must now have 910 hours of work to establish eligibility rather than the previous minimum of 300 hours.

References

Akyeampong, E. 1995. 'Missing Work.' *Perspectives on Labour and Income* 7, 1: 12–16.

Amott, T. 1990. 'Black Women and AFDC: Making Entitlement Out of Necessity.'
In L. Gordon, ed., *Women, the State, and Welfare*, Madison: University of Wisconsin Press, 280–98.

Armstrong, P. 1996. 'The Feminization of the Labour Force: Harmonizing Down
in a Global Economy.' In I. Bakker, ed., *Rethinking Restructuring: Gender and
Change in Canada*. Toronto: University of Toronto Press, 29–54.

Baines, C., P. Evans, and S. Neysmith. 1991. 'Caring: Its Impact on the Lives of
Women.' In C. Baines, P. Evans, and S. Neysmith, eds., *Women's Caring: Feminist Perspectives on Social Welfare*. Toronto: McClelland and Stewart, 11–35.

Cameron, B. 1996 'From Equal Opportunity to Symbolic Equity: Three Decades
of Federal Training Policy for Women.' In I. Bakker, ed., *Rethinking Restructuring: Gender and Change in Canada*. Toronto: University of Toronto Press, 55–91.

Canada, Department of Finance. 1995. *Budget Speech*. Ottawa: Finance Canada
Distribution Centre, 27 February.

Canada, Health and Welfare. 1991. *Inventory of Income Security Programs in Canada, July 1990*. Ottawa: Minister of Supply and Services.

Canada, Human Resources Development. 1994a. *From Unemployment Insurance
to Employment Insurance: A Supplementary Paper*. Ottawa: Minister of Supply
and Services Canada.

– 1994b. *Improving Social Security*. Ottawa: Minister of Supply and Services,
October.

– 1994c. *Inventory of Income Security Programs in Canada January 1993*. Ottawa:
Minister of Supply and Services.

Cass, B. 1994. 'Citizenship, Work, and Welfare: The Dilemma for Australian
Women.' *Social Politics* 1, 1: 106–24.

Dalley, G. 1988. *Ideologies of Caring*. Basingstoke, Hampshire: Macmillan Education.

Dingeldine, G. 1981. *A Chronology of Response: The Evolution of Unemployment
Insurance from 1940 to 1980*. Ottawa: Employment and Immigration Canada.

Esping-Andersen, G. 1990. *Three Worlds of Welfare Capitalism*. Princeton, NJ: Princeton University Press.

Evans, P. 1992. 'Targeting Single Mothers for Employment: Comparisons from
the United States, Britain, and Canada.' *Social Service Review* 66, 3: 54–67.

– 1994. 'Eroding Canadian Social Welfare: The Mulroney Legacy, 1984–1993.'
Social Policy and Administration 28, 2: 107–19.

– 1995a. 'Linking Jobs to Welfare: Workfare, Canadian Style.' In P. Evans, L.
Jacobs, A. Noël, and E. Reynolds, eds., *Workfare: Does It Work? Is It Fair?* Montreal: Institute for Research on Public Policy, 75–104.

– 1995b. 'Single Mothers and Ontario's Welfare Policy: Restructuring the
Debate.' In J. Brodie, ed., *Women and Public Policy*. Toronto: Harcourt Brace,
151–71.

Feschuk, S. 1994. 'Klein's Policies Go Beyond Bottom Line.' *Globe and Mail* (3 October): A4.

Fox Piven, F. 1990. 'Ideology and the State: Women, Power and the Welfare State.' In L. Gordon, ed., *Women, the State, and Welfare*. Madison: University of Wisconsin Press, 250–64.

Fraser, N. 1989. *Unruly Practices: Power, Discourse, and Gender in Contemporary Social Theory.* Minneapolis: University of Minnesota Press.

– and L. Gordon. 1992. 'Contract Versus Charity: Why Is There No Social Citizenship in the United States?' *Socialist Review* 22: 45–67.

– 1994. '"Dependency" Demystified: Inscriptions of Power in a Keyword of the Welfare State.' *Social Politics* 1, 1: 4–31.

Friendly, M., and M. Oloman. 1996. 'Child Care at the Centre: Child Care on the Social, Economic and Political Agenda in the 1990s.' In J. Pulkingham and G. Ternowetsky, eds., *Remaking Canadian Social Policy: Social Security in the Late 1990s*. Halifax: Fernwood, 273–85.

Gordon, L. 1990. 'The New Feminist Scholarship on the Welfare State.' In L. Gordon, ed., *Women, the State, and Welfare*. Madison: University of Wisconsin Press, 9–35.

– 1994. *Pitied but Not Entitled: Single Mothers and the History of Welfare*. New York: Free Press.

Hernes, H. 1987. 'Women and the Welfare State: The Transition from Private to Public Dependence.' In A. Showstack Sassoon, ed., *Women and the State*. London: Unwin Hyman, 72–92.

House of Commons. 1995. *Security, Opportunities and Fairness: Canadians Renewing Their Social Programs*. Report of the Standing Committee on Human Resources Development.

Jessop, B. 1993. 'Towards a Schumpeterian Workfare State? Preliminary Remarks on Post-Fordist Political Economy.' *Studies in Political Economy* 40: 7–39.

Krahn, H. 1991. 'Non-standard Work Arrangements.' *Perspectives on Labour and Income*. Ottawa: Statistics Canada, Cat. 75-001E, Winter: 35–45.

Land, H., and H. Rose. 1985. 'Compulsory Altruism for Some or an Altruistic Society for All?' In P. Bean, J. Ferris, and D. Whynes, eds., *In Defence of Welfare*. London: Tavistock.

Lewis, J. 1992. 'Gender and the Development of Welfare Regimes.' *Journal of European Social Policy* 2, 3: 159–73.

– 'Introduction.' In J. Lewis, ed., *Women and Social Policies in Europe: Work, Family and the State*. Aldershot: Edward Elgar, 1–24.

– and G. Åström. 1992. 'Equality, Difference, and State Welfare: Labor Market and Family Policies in Sweden.' *Feminist Studies* 18, 1: 59–87.

Lightman, E., and A. Irving. 1991. 'Restructuring Canada's Welfare State.' *Journal of Social Policy* 20, 1: 65–86.

Lister, R. 1990. 'Women, Economic Dependency and Citizenship.' *Journal of Social Policy* 17, 2: 445–67.

Little, M. Forthcoming. *No Car, No Radio, No Liquor Permit: The Moral Regulation of Single Mothers in Ontario, 1920–1997.* Toronto: Oxford University Press.

Marshall, T.H. 1964. *Class, Citizenship and Social Development.* Chicago: University of Chicago Press.

Marston, S., and L. Staeheli. 1994. 'Citizenship, Struggle and Political and Economic Restructuring.' Guest Editorial in *Environment and Planning* 26: 840–8.

National Association of Women and the Law. 1993. NAWL Submission to the Legislative Committee on Bill C-113, An Act to Provide for Government Expenditure Restraint. Ottawa: NAWL, 15 March.

National Council of Welfare. 1994. *Who Are the People on Welfare?* Backgrounder No. 2.

– 1995. *The 1995 Budget and Block Funding.* Ottawa: NCW.

– 1996. *Poverty Profile 1994.* Ottawa: NCW.

Nelson, B. 1990. 'The Origins of the Two-Channel Welfare State: Workmen's Compensation and Mothers' Aid.' In L. Gordon, ed., *Women, the State, and Welfare.* Madison: University of Wisconsin Press, 123–51.

Nemiroff, G. 1994. *Women and Social Security Review: General Principles for Social Policy.* A Report by the Expert Task Force on Women and Social Security Review, chaired by the Joint Chair of Women's Studies, Carleton University and the University of Ottawa (July).

Neysmith, S. 1991. 'From Community Care to a Social Model of Care.' In C. Baines, P. Evans, and S. Neysmith, eds., *Women's Caring: Feminist Perspectives on Social Welfare.* Toronto: McClelland and Stewart, 272–99.

O'Connor, J. 1993. 'Gender, Class and Citizenship in the Comparative Analysis of Welfare State Regimes: Theoretical and Methodological Issues.' *British Journal of Sociology* 44, 3: 501–18.

Orloff, A. 1993. 'Gender and the Social Rights of Citizenship: The Comparative Analysis of Gender Relations and Welfare States.' *American Sociological Review* 58: 303–28.

Ostner, I. 1994. 'Independence and Dependency: Options and Constraints for Women Over the Life Course.' *Women's Studies International Forum* 17: 129–39.

Pascall, G. 1986. *Social Policy: A Feminist Analysis.* London: Tavistock.

Pateman, C. 1992. 'The Patriarchal Welfare State.' In L. McDowell and R. Pringle, eds., *Defining Women: Social Institutions and Gender Divisions.* Cambridge: Polity Press, 223–45.

Pearce, D. 1985. 'Toil and Trouble: Women Workers and Unemployment Compensation.' In B. Gelpi, N. Hartsock, C. Novak, and M. Strober, eds., *Women and Poverty.* Chicago: University of Chicago Press, 141–61.

Peattie, L., and M. Rein. 1983. *Women's Claims: A Study in Political Economy.* Oxford: Oxford University Press.

Phillips, A. 1992. 'Feminism, Equality and Difference.' In L. McDowell and R. Pringle, eds., *Defining Women: Social Institutions and Gender Divsions.* Cambridge: Polity Press, 205–22.

Pixley, J. 1993. *Citizenship and Employment: Investigating Post-Industrial Options.* Cambridge: Cambridge University Press, 1993.

Pulkingham, J., and G. Ternowetsky. 1997. 'The New Canada Child Tax Benefit: Discriminating between the "Deserving" and "Undeserving" among Poor Families with Children.' In J. Pulkingham and G. Ternowetsky, eds., *Child and Family Policies: Struggles, Strategies and Options.* Halifax: Fernwood, 204–8.

Quadagno, J. 1994. *The Color of Welfare: How Racism Undermined the War on Poverty.* New York: Oxford University Press.

Sainsbury, D. 1993. 'Dual Welfare and Sex Segregation of Access to Social Benefits: Income Maintenance Policies in the U.S., the Netherlands, and Sweden.' *Journal of Social Policy* 22, 1: 69–98.

Scott, J. 1992. 'Deconstructing Equality-Versus-Difference: Or, The Uses of Post-Structural Theory or Feminism.' In L. McDowell and R. Pringle, eds., *Defining Women: Social Institutions and Gender Divsions.* Cambridge: Polity Press, 253–64.

Shaver, S. 1993. *Women and the Australian Social Security System: From Difference Toward Equality.* Discussion Paper No. 44, Social Policy Research Centre. Sydney: University of New South Wales.

Skocpol, T. 1992. *Protecting Soldiers and Mothers: The Political Origins of Social Policy in the United States.* Cambridge: Harvard University Press.

Social Research and Demonstration Corporation. 1994. *Making Work Pay Better Than Welfare: An Early Look at the Self-Sufficiency Project.* Vancouver, BC: SRDC, October.

Statistics Canada. 1994. *Women in the Labour Force.* Ottawa: Minister of Industry, Science and Technology, Cat. 75-507E.

– 1995. *Women in Canada.* Ottawa: Minister of Industry. Cat. 89-503E.

– 1996a. *The Labour Force, December.* Ottawa: Minister of Industry, Cat 71-001.

– 1996b. *Unemployment Insurance Statistics, December 1995.* Ottawa: Minister of Industry, Cat. 73-001.

Strong-Boag, V. 1979. '"Wages for Housework": The Beginnings of Social Security in Canada.' *Journal of Canadian Studies* 14, 1: 24–34.

Struthers, J. 1994. *Limits of Affluence: Welfare in Ontario, 1920–1970.* Toronto: University of Toronto Press.

Torjman, S., and K. Battle. 1995. *Dangers of Block Funding, A Caledon Commentary.* Ottawa: Caledon Institute of Social Policy, February.

Turner, B. 1993. 'Contemporary Problems in the Theory of Citizenship.' In B. Turner, ed., *Citizenship and Social Theory.* London: Sage, 1–18.

Ungerson, C., ed. 1990. *Gender and Caring: Work and Welfare in Britain and Scandinavia.* New York: Harvester Wheatsheaf.

Vosko, L. 1996. 'Irregular Workers, New Involuntary Social Exiles: Women Non-Standard Workers and UI Reform.' In J. Pulkingham and G. Ternowetsky, eds., *Remaking Canadian Social Policy: Social Security in the Late 1990s.* Halifax: Fernwood Publishing, 256–72.

Wilson, E. 1977. *Women and the Welfare State.* London: Tavistock.

5

Family Law and Social Assistance Programs: Rethinking Equality[1]

MARY JANE MOSSMAN AND MORAG MACLEAN

With increasing numbers of sequential marriages, solutions to the financial crisis of marriage breakdown must be sought not only within the parameters of family law but also in social and economic policies that promote the financial viability of all persons in need, including the economic victims of marriage breakdown. The war on the feminization of poverty must be won by innovative and coherent socioeconomic policies.
Payne, 1994: 27.

Payne's comment usefully highlights increasing recognition in Canada that marriage breakdown is no longer simply a 'private' dispute. Instead, the end of a marriage shatters the economic interdependence of family members in an ongoing family unit, leaving some of them less able to assume economic independence post-divorce than others. In general, women and children experience economic disadvantage disproportionately to men at marriage breakdown, thereby contributing to the feminization of poverty. In this way, most of the 'costs' of Canada's policy of accessible divorce are unfairly borne by individual women and children in post-divorce families and relatively less by their husbands and fathers – or by society as a whole.

A decade ago we explored this phenomenon (Mossman and MacLean, 1986) by examining the first decade of statistics on divorce following the enactment of federal divorce reform legislation in 1968: the Divorce Act. We concluded that there was an emerging pattern of gender difference in post-divorce economic circumstances in Canada and that family law principles (that emphasized the formal equality of the spouses at marriage breakdown) did not adequately address the differing economic realities experienced by men and women, either in relation to their work-force opportunities or to the burdens more often assumed by mothers for primary care of children after divorce. We also tried to show how social assistance (welfare) programs had adopted principles of entitlement based on familial relationships, principles that were frequently not at all congruent with those emerging in family law based on the formal equal-ity of spouses. Thus, women were frequently assumed to be equal (and economically independent) by family law principles applicable at divorce and thus were not always entitled to spousal support. At the same time, however, they were often viewed by social assistance pro-grams as having a continuing entitlement to familial support and were thus considered ineligible for welfare. In this way, their disentitlement to either familial support or welfare assistance contributed to economic insecurity, and often poverty, for many women and children after divorce. Moreover, even those women who received spousal support or welfare assistance after marriage breakdown often lived in poverty because their post-divorce resources were diminished, especially by con-trast with the resources of their former husbands.

Our assessment led us to rethink ideas about dependency and inde-pendence in the family law context and to assess the consequences of using 'the individual' or 'the family' as the basis of entitlement to income security programs in the context of marriage breakdown. We concluded that accessible divorce policies should be augmented by fam-ily law and social assistance principles which can ensure fairer distribu-tions of economic burdens and advantages for individual family members at divorce. We made tentative recommendations for reform in light of the data from this first decade after divorce reform.

In the intervening decade there have been numerous legislative changes in family law and some interesting court decisions, with some confirming and others challenging, at least to some extent, our earlier analysis. There have also been some changes in policies in federal and provincial income security programs and significant court challenges by same-sex families claiming entitlement to employment and governmen-tal benefits on the basis of 'family status.' Yet, most of the changes have not altered legal principles in fundamental ways. And, most impor-tantly, women and children remain significantly disadvantaged, in contrast to men, in terms of their relative post-divorce economic circum-stances (Lemprière, 1992; Dooley, 1993). Thus, the work of rethinking policies about family law and social assistance to promote goals of sub-stantive gender equality in Canada remains an important task. This reassessment focuses on the issues identified in our work a decade ago and the extent to which more recent changes in common law provinces in Canada (all provinces except Quebec) have contributed to greater gender equality for post-divorce family members.

The Feminization of Poverty: Marriage and Marriage Breakdown

The Second Decade of Post-Divorce Act Statistics

As is now well-known, the rate of divorce rose sharply after the enactment of comprehensive federal divorce legislation in 1968. Indeed, 'between 1965 and 1988, Canada moved from having one of the lowest divorce rates to having one of the highest among industrialized nations' (Vanier Institute, 1994: 48). The sharpest increases occurred just after 1968 and again after 1986 when the current divorce legislation (the Divorce Act, 1985) took effect. Although the rate of divorce decreased somewhat in the late 1980s, it is still significantly higher than prior to 1968. To illustrate, in 1951 one couple divorced for every twenty-four couples that married, but in 1987, when the rate of marriage dipped and the rate of divorce peaked, one couple divorced for every two who married. In 1990 one couple divorced for every 2.4 who married (Vanier Institute, 1994: 47). According to Statistics Canada (1993: 17), there were 78,152 divorces in Canada in 1990, a rate of 294 per 100,000 population. Thus, the possibility of divorce continues to be a real fact of family life in Canada in the 1990s.

The increased rate of divorce does not itself confirm the differential impact of divorce on husbands and wives. However, other data suggest that the experience of divorce continues to occur at a time when women and men may be at relatively different points in their lives in terms of their ability to become economically independent. According to Payne (1994: 14), for example, the average duration for marriages ending in divorce is 12.5 years, and Statistics Canada (1990: 2) figures for 1985 to 1988 indicate that the mean age at divorce for those years was about 38 for men and 36 for women. In 1991 the largest number of divorced persons in Canada were between ages 35 and 49 (Statistics Canada, 1993: 44). Overall, therefore, the statistics confirm that large numbers of spouses divorce in their mid- to late 30s or 40s, after about twelve years of marriage.

The significance of the data for assessing the potential differential impact on former husbands and wives is related to a number of other factors. One of the most important is that in marriages with children the data suggest that there will be many situations where there will be dependent children who require ongoing care. As was the case a decade ago, 'mothers have been, and continue to be, more likely than fathers to receive custody of the children. For instance, mothers were given custody of 73% of children [affected by court orders] in 1990, while 14% of cases involved joint awards to both parents. In only 12% of cases did the father receive custody' (Statistics Canada, 1993:11). The absence of accessible and affordable child care in Canada (Duxbury and Higgins, 1994: 31) thus has a direct impact on the ability of mothers to enter or remain in the full-time paid workforce after divorce.

In addition, the provincial schemes for dividing property, or the value of assets, between spouses at divorce may not contribute to the economic well-being of men and (especially) women after divorce. Except where the spouses have already accumulated significant amounts of debt-free assets, a situation which is not very likely for the average couple divorcing after about twelve years of marriage, a division of assets will not be sufficient to provide substantial financial security for either spouse. Thus, continuing access to full-time, well-paid work with employment benefits, a situation which is more often available to men than to women (Statistics Canada, 1993: 22), is critical to economic well-being even after a division of assets between divorcing spouses. In 1990, however, divorced women working full-year, full-time earned an average of about $29,000, while men in the same category earned about $38,000; the divorced women thus earned 76 per cent of divorced men's earnings (Vanier Institute, 1994: 82). Since these figures refer only to 'divorced' rather than 'divorced or separated' spouses, they may not fully reflect the levels of poverty for women who separate without having been in a legal marriage.

In some families, moreover, there will be no assets at all for division between the spouses, making income-earning potential even more critical. Yet, for those women who have been out of the paid workforce to care for infants and young children, a reasonable decision for many families in light of the lack of affordable and available child care (Knetsch, 1984; Lero and Brockman, 1993), there may be career 'costs' at divorce which are either not recognized by family law principles of formal equality, or compensated only partially, if at all, by orders for spousal support.

All of these factors contribute to the greater risk of poverty for mothers post-divorce and post-separation. They are part of the increasing numbers of female lone parents in Canada; indeed, of almost one million lone parents in Canada in 1990, 83 per cent were female. The average family income of families headed by female lone parents in 1990 was $26,550, an amount which was 65 per cent of the average income of $40,792 for families headed by male lone parents (Vanier Institute, 1994: 83). As the Vanier Institute noted: 'There are many reasons for the economic differences between male and female lone parents. On average, women earn less than men. In addition, lone fathers tend to be older and better-educated, have more labour force experience, and have older children. Their careers are often established before they become lone parents and their children are often already school-aged' (1994: 83).

The same report also noted that tax data for 1990 showed that, on average, divorced women received $4900 in alimony payments (spousal and child support payments combined), representing 14 per cent of their average total family income of $33,500, while the amount of these payments represented, on average, only 9 per cent of men's total incomes of $55,400 (Vanier Institute, 1994: 84; Zweibel, 1993).

Lone parents' incomes generally lag behind the family incomes of two-parent families. The proportion of lone parents who are 'divorced' or 'never married' has greatly increased in recent decades, while 'widowhood' as a cause for lone parenthood has declined; the proportion of lone parents who are 'separated' has remained constant (Vanier Institute, 1994: 50–1). In 1991 the average income for female lone-parent families was 38 per cent of the average income of two-parent families (under age 65) with children under age 18. Compared with elderly families, historically among the poorest in Canada, the position of families headed by lone parents worsened in the 1980s (Statistics Canada, 1993: 35), while the position of elderly families improved. Thus, although families with female lone parents represented only 6 per cent of all family units in Canada, they constituted 29 per cent of 'low-income families' as defined by Statistics Canada (1993: 35). And while 33 per cent of all poor children in 1980 lived in families headed by single-parent mothers, the percentage of poor children with single-parent mothers increased to 40 per cent by 1994 (National Council of Welfare, 1996: 74).

Overall, these statistics generally confirm that Canada's increased rate of divorce since 1968 has contributed to the creation of a substantial number of families headed by female lone parents with dependent children. Since the data also suggest that lone parents' families are generally less well-off than two-parent families, and that those headed by female lone parents are especially vulnerable, there is evidence that women are more likely than men to be economically disadvantaged as a result of divorce or marriage breakdown. This conclusion has also been supported by statistics about welfare recipients, at least in Ontario, where our earlier data indicated substantial increases in the numbers of families headed by female lone parents receiving welfare after 1968 (Mossman and MacLean, 1986: 88). More recently, the provincial government's study of social assistance in Ontario explained that 'single-parent families ... have grown faster than any other part of the ["family benefits"] caseload, increasing from 33% to 41% of cases from 1969 to 1987' (Ontario Ministry of Community and Social Services, 1988: 37).

All of these data suggest that divorce is one of the important causes of poverty for mothers and their children: the 'feminization of poverty.' And, although female lone parenthood may also occur because of widowhood or the birth of a child 'out of wedlock' (Eichler, 1993), the poverty of women and children post-divorce remains an important phenomenon:

For most women, separation or divorce results in drastic reductions in income and a decline in living standards. They feel the financial effects of divorce much more harshly than men do. But divorced women, of course, are not alone in their discomfort. Their children usually accompany them on their slide into poverty. So while the children of these families represent just 3 per cent of all Canadians, they constitute more than one quarter of all persons in low-income families. [Moreover,] despite legislative attempts to improve the disadvantaged position of divorced women and their children, things have not gotten much better for them ... Even without counting the many who do not receive court-ordered support payments, our high rates of separation and divorce and the paltry nature of most support payments consign many Canadian women and children to poverty. (Vanier Institute, 1994: 85)

Thus, the context of post-divorce poverty for women and children which we described a decade ago has not measurably changed for the better. In this context, we turn again to an examination of the principles of family law and social assistance and a reassessment of their congruence (or not).

The Evolution of Basic Principles: Family Law and Social Assistance

The principles of family law which currently define spousal rights and responsibilities at divorce in Canada have evolved over several centuries, responding to both changing social patterns of family relationships and differing legal approaches to intervention in 'private' family life. By contrast, current arrangements for providing income assistance to indigent Canadians developed primarily in the twentieth century and especially after the Second World War. In our assessment a decade ago, we identified the separate evolution of these two sets of principles, based on differing policy objectives and without substantial coordination, as a partial explanation for the lack of congruence between family law principles of formal equality and independence, on the one hand, and social assistance principles based on familial entitlement, on the other. At the same time, we suggested that changes in family life in Canada since 1968, evidenced by both the increased frequency of divorce and the severe economic consequences for dependent family members post-divorce, signalled a need to re-examine fundamental principles and to rethink ideas about dependency and independence in the post-divorce context. In the 1990s such rethinking of fundamental principles remains an essential task in the search for solutions to the feminization of poverty at marriage breakdown.

The Family Law Context

In the context of early English common law, the family was part of the social structure of feudalism, a system of land ownership which ensured that wealth and status derived from land would remain intact within the family (Spring, 1993; Erickson, 1993), usually passing from one generation to the next by way of the eldest son (Hamilton, 1988). Since land was the basis of wealth, the social position of individuals was dependent on their positions in the family feudal structure. According to Frances Olsen, this arrangement meant that 'the feudal family was not perceived to be separate from the rest of economic life' (Olsen, 1983: 1516).

Mary Ann Glendon has asserted, however, that this early pattern of the family changed as the feudal system of societal organization was replaced by capitalism. As capital increased in importance and displaced land as the major form of wealth, the family became increasingly defined as a husband–wife marriage bond with dependent children: the modern nuclear family (Glendon, 1981: 138). In the twentieth century, moreover, the emphasis on income and employment in the modern welfare state (sometimes referred to as 'new property') has become a more important defining characteristic of status for individuals, with a corresponding diminution in the family's role. According to Glendon, the transformation of wealth from land (in feudal society) to capital (in the eighteenth and nineteenth centuries) to income and employment (in the modern welfare state) has contributed to increasing independence among members of the modern nuclear family.

These changes in family structure and forms of wealth were reflected in changing legal principles concerning spousal rights and responsibilities. According to common law principles in the feudal period, the husband and wife became one, and the one was the husband. This principle meant that on marriage, the husband acquired the right to manage and control all land owned by his wife, to collect all rents and profits from such land, and to grant or withhold his consent to its sale or other disposition (McCaughan, 1977; Holcombe, 1983).

In the eighteenth and nineteenth centuries, trust settlements were sometimes adopted by fathers in order to avoid property passing to their sons-in-law at marriage, but full reform of these principles occurred only in the late nineteenth century with the enactment of Married Women's Property acts in most common law jurisdictions, including Canada (McCaughan, 1977: 17; Holcombe, 1983: 37; Backhouse, 1988). Even then, however, while women had the right to hold property, only a minority had the means by which to acquire it, thus confirming their continuing dependency in the marriage relationship. At the same time, a husband generally had an obligation to support his wife and dependent children during marriage and to ensure continued support for an innocent wife (that is, one not guilty of a matrimonial offence) after divorce (Hovius, 1982: 379). In this way, women's lack of property in marriage was compensated by a right to financial support during and often after the marriage.

Since the Second World War, women's roles have undergone profound changes in terms of workforce participation and fertility, as well as in relation to marriage and divorce (Ursel, 1992). The Divorce Act of 1968 introduced the concept of 'no-fault' divorce, a concept which was fully embraced in the new divorce legislation in 1986 when 'marriage breakdown' became the only ground for divorce in Canada. According to the new divorce legislation, however, since 'marriage breakdown' must be established either by the separation of the parties or by the commission of adultery or physical or mental cruelty, hidden vestiges of 'fault' remain. The accelerating rate of divorce pursuant to the new legislation, coupled with more acceptance of the impermanency of marriage and new roles for men and women, also led to major reforms in provincial schemes for property and support.

Since 1978 all of the common law provinces in Canada have enacted reform legislation altering the traditional rules of spousal entitlement to property and support. Under most of these statutes, marriage breakdown permits the equal division of property (or its value) between the spouses regardless of which spouse holds legal title and subject to overriding discretionary principles on the part of a presiding judge. However, the concept of marriage as creating a lifelong entitlement to support has declined in importance, and sometimes it has disappeared. In its place, the new statutes frequently provide that each spouse has primary responsibility for his or her own financial support, although each spouse may claim support where there is proof of individual need and available resources on the part of the other spouse. It is need, however, rather than status as a spouse in the family, which determines entitlement under this provincial legislation. Thus, these new principles 'deem' equality and independence for married spouses on divorce, divide their property, and then assume that each of them can become an autonomous individual responsible for financial self-support.

These principles illustrate a classic liberal approach to legal problem solving: legal intervention is restricted to removing legal barriers to full participation, but economic and other barriers are generally ignored. Such an approach fails to achieve substantive equality for women because male and female spouses are not similarly situated at marriage breakdown, particularly in relation to access to financial security (Fineman, 1991).

The explanations for this 'gender gap' are now obvious. First, if there are few or no assets from the marriage, a division of family property may produce equality, but it will result in very little financial security for either spouse. Second, the wife's access to a financially rewarding job may be less than her husband's, either because she has worked less than full-time while shouldering the primary responsibilities for child care or because she agreed to postpone her own training opportunities in order to support her husband's acquisition of further education. Third, even if she is able to obtain 'rehabilitative' support while undergoing further training for employment, there may still be limits imposed on the length of time for such support. Fourth, if she is employed, and whether or not she has experienced job interruption, a woman is statistically likely to earn a salary which is only about two-thirds of that earned by men. Finally, if following marriage breakdown she is unable to work in the paid labour force while caring for children, she is likely to experience immediate impoverished circumstances as a female lone parent, and, in addition, she will not be able to accumulate a pension for retirement, and thereby some financial security in old age (Eichler, 1993).

Thus, the principles of equality and independence reflected in the divorce legislation and the provincial schemes for distributing property and defining support at marriage breakdown do not match the reality of women's unequal and dependent circumstances at divorce. From another perspective, the goals of 'equality and independence' are essentially formal rather than substantive: a declaration of what is legally possible without regard to what is economically feasible. While Madam Justice L'Heureux-Dubé, in a 1992 decision of the Supreme Court of Canada (*Moge*), reinterpreted the divorce legislation so as to take account of the feminization of poverty, the application of these principles in cases where different facts exist remains somewhat unclear. Consequently, our earlier conclusion remains unchanged: the principles of property division and support in Canadian family law have continued to espouse ideas about equality and independence for husbands and wives at marriage breakdown, but they have generally not achieved these goals, especially for women.

The Social Assistance Context

Social assistance programs in Canada are quite recent in origin. Numerous governmental initiatives providing financial and other assistance have been developed within the last century: workers' compensation as early as the 1880s, unemployment insurance in 1940, universal hospital insurance in the provinces between 1947 and 1961, and universal medical care insurance between 1962 and 1971. In addition, the federal Canada Assistance Plan (CAP) of 1966 was designed to permit the federal government to fund 50 per cent of the costs of provincial social welfare schemes (although levels of funding for British Columbia, Alberta, and Ontario were 'capped' unilaterally by the federal government in 1990, and the CAP itself was substantially repealed in 1996). There are also federal old age pensions and numerous income tax deductions, credits, and subsidies. In 1993 the federal government announced its intention to reform social security in Canada, including arrangements for federal funding of social assistance, plans which are likely to affect levels of funding for welfare recipients.

The federal government's report, *Working Paper on Social Security* in Canada, published in 1973, explained the existence of social security programs as a reflection of shared community support for the values of independence, interdependence, and fairness in the distribution of resources. According to the *Working Paper*, Canadians accept the value of independence and expect to 'meet their own needs through their own efforts, and they expect others to do their best to do the same. This sturdiness of outlook is not a matter, it should be said, of sheer selfishness: rather it is a matter of believing that each should contribute, to the extent *he* is able to *his* own and *his* family's well-being' (Canada, 1973: 4–5, emphasis added).

Similarly, the same document stated that the value of interdependence means that '*man* has a responsibility to his fellow *men*' (emphasis added). Moreover, it argued that there was no contradiction between the values of independence and interdependence: 'It is simply a matter of working, if you are able, to meet your family's daily needs, and of saving, to the extent you are able, to meet the contingencies of life.'

As is evident, the *Working Paper*'s explanation of the values of independence and interdependence obscures the role of the family and the obligations of individual family members in relation to these values. The statement concerning independence also clearly assumes a male breadwinner working to support family dependents, including a spouse. It does not assume 'equality' and 'independence' during the marriage. The second quotation similarly assumes that support for family dependents should be provided by accumulated savings in times of contingencies. Although social assistance in the twentieth century has also offered economic security to persons in financial need, the exact relationship between family and social obligations to meet such needs remains unclear in the *Working Paper*.

This confusion represents a historical ambivalence about the provision of income security in the welfare state, an ambivalence which has been compounded by the changing roles of women in Canada since the Second World War (Ursel, 1992; Gavigan, 1993). Historically, there has always been an effort to respond to financial needs on the part of the 'deserving' poor, but this group has been carefully distinguished from the 'undeserving' poor (Pearce, 1984). In simplest terms, there was a perceived need to distinguish those who could not work (deserving) from those who would not work (undeserving) and to ensure that the former were cared for effectively, while the latter were maintained at only a basic subsistence level. However, as the *Working Paper* illustrates, the categories of deserving and undeserving poor (at least for two-parent families) were essentially conceptualized in terms of the 'male head of a household.' Thus, according to Pearce, the deserving poor were those in a family unit with a 'male breadwinner' head, while the undeserving poor were those in a family unit with a 'male pauper' head. Pearce has also suggested that these categories were used to create two different types of welfare benefits, one which was more of a 'right,' usually not means tested and quite often work related, while the other, a 'charitable' payment, was usually means tested and available to those unable to work (Pearce, 1984; Wilson, 1977; Land, 1984).[2]

Applying these categories to the Canadian context, unemployment insurance or workers' compensation would be classified as 'male breadwinner' benefits, while welfare to the unemployable would be assistance in the 'male pauper' category. Since both categories are really directed to male heads of households, moreover, the position of a female lone parent with dependent children seems anomalous at best. Because such a female parent may have no significant workforce experience, she will usually fall into the 'male pauper' category: social assistance which is charitable and means tested and which will not be available to *her* at all if there is a male head of the household (the 'spouse in the house' rule). Significantly, while the definition of 'spouse' in social assistance policy was altered in Ontario in the 1980s to accord with the definition of 'spouse' in the provincial family law statute, the underlying principle that a female lone parent with a 'spouse' (according to the family law definition) was ineligible for social assistance was never changed. Thus, after three years of cohabitation, a cohabitee in Ontario who would have been liable to pay spousal support if the couple separated would also have disentitled a woman to social assistance in the form of welfare if they remained together. Recent reform measures in 1995 have recreated a gap between the family law definition and that in the social assistance context. As of 1995, a woman receiving social assistance becomes immediately ineligible if she cohabits with a man, even though family law principles create no obligation for him to provide financial support to her until they have cohabited for three years.

What is significant here is that the introduction of income security in Canada has created two categories of assistance: the deserving poor who receive work-related benefits and the undeserving poor who receive welfare because they do not 'work.' Moreover, it has also become increasingly clear that current governmental policies in Canada are eroding support for women as workers and in their family roles (Armstrong, 1997). Thus, the dramatic changes in patterns of marriage and divorce over the past two decades show that female lone parents and their children must now become a major focus of reforms, including social security reforms.

In rethinking the conceptual basis for social assistance programs, the relationship between obligations of familial and societal support for dependent individuals is critical. In the context of 'male breadwinner' programs, for example, entitlement is usually defined for individuals without regard to the availability of family support obligations. By contrast, those of the 'male pauper' category tend to define eligibility for individuals *only* after all possible family support obligations have been exhausted. The result is that individuals who qualify for 'male breadwinner' benefits (traditionally male persons) do so without regard to the 'family' income available, while those eligible for 'male pauper' benefits (including many women) will qualify only *after* they have demonstrated the absence of other familial support. In this way, the programs tend to treat males more often as individuals for determining entitlement, while women are more often regarded as members of family units, not as individuals. Margrit Eichler has explained this dichotomy as the 'familialism-individualism flip-flop':

[To] the degree that we make social security programmes available to individuals, we guarantee as a society some income security to individuals. Conversely, to the degree that we let eligibility for the social security programmes be determined by family status, we disentitle individuals from access to social support on the basis of their family status. This disentitlement is usually justified by reference to the support function of 'the family' ... As far as the support function of families is concerned, there is widespread consensus that families not only do support their own, but *should* do so. What is often overlooked is that there tends to be a direct opposition between the notion of the family as a support system and social security programmes: to the degree that the proper locus of support for an individual is seen to lie within that individual's family, the individual becomes *disentitled* from public support.' (Eichler, 1983: 110)

The review of social assistance in Ontario in the *Transitions* report of 1988 focused expressly on the relationship between 'private' support systems in family law and the 'public' support system of social assistance for women and children after marriage breakdown: 'The different policy frameworks underlying the two systems, and the failure of each to recognize the concrete problems facing those who are expected to find relief in the other system, have often resulted in confusion and serious financial hardship (Ontario Ministry of Community and Social Services, 1988: 487).

The report recommended adoption of the same definition of 'spouse' for purposes of family law and for entitlement to welfare, as a means of overcoming some of the problems of the 'spouse in the house rule,' a reform which was in place until the changes adopted in 1995 reopened a gap between legal obligations created in family law and in social assistance principles.

However, the Report also recommended retention of the 'family unit' as the basis of entitlement, concluding that an 'individual-based' system 'would largely ignore the fundamental principle of need' and in addition 'would be prohibitively expensive' (ibid.: 161). The *Report* stressed the need for further research about the financial impact of family law principles about property and support, emphasizing that 'there must be a better understanding of the real problems facing those who are expected to look to the state for relief when support from family members is denied' (ibid.: 491).

These recommendations demonstrate a better understanding of the need for congruence between principles of family law and those of social assistance in relation to the plight of former wives and their children after marriage breakdown. However, they also identify the central problem in the reform of income security programs: the need to define the role of the family in relation to economic dependency. And while social policy must resolve this issue in relation to programs whose benefits are available to individuals in an existing family unit, there is a special urgency to address these questions from the perspective of post-divorce wives and children, dependents whose family unit is no longer intact. In this context, moreover, it is important to confront the fact that many women and children at marriage breakdown are not economically independent, whether their dependency is to be alleviated by former husbands (according to 'private' family law principles) or by social assistance programs ('public' support). In this way, the interdependence of family members in an intact family unit results in 'unmasked' dependency and economic vulnerability at marriage breakdown (Fineman, 1991).

Yet, in practice, the need for congruence in family law and social assistance principles may be more difficult to achieve. Because family law principles have been designed for the division of property and support at marriage breakdown, and at least some spouses will have substantial assets for distribution at divorce, family law principles of equality and independence which limit spousal support may be valid in some cases. By contrast, social assistance principles have been designed for a number of different circumstances in which individuals may experience financial need, and former wives and their children form only one such category. In spite of the separate historical development of these two sets of principles, however, we argue that the dramatic changes in Canadian family life occasioned by the rise in the rates of marriage breakdown and divorce in the past two decades, and the consequential financial insecurity for dependent family members created by this new phenomenon, demand a clear focus on these dependent family members post-divorce. Coordinated policy directions are needed to define principles which accommodate the objectives of both family law and social assistance to meet this challenge.

Merging Principles

In our earlier analysis we identified the point at which the incongruent policies of 'public' support and 'private' family law merged: where the dependent spouse came close to economic dependence on the state. Where such a danger existed, private family law policies began to shift away from goals of equality and independence, reverting to notions of continuing familial obligation. As Smart and Brophy (1985: 13) explained in relation to similar trends in the United Kingdom:

Family law no longer argues, as it once did, that it is against 'public policy' to award maintenance to a guilty wife. On the contrary it now argues that it is in the interests of preserving 'public funds' that all husbands should support their dependents ... But a wife's economic position is not necessarily improved ... because the policy of the courts is not to benefit wives but to protect the 'public purse' and to deflect the economic costs of the disintegration of the family away from the welfare state and onto individuals. [In this way,] family legislation is now moving closer to welfare legislation and is also adopting interventionist strategies that have been more common to the latter.

Since 1986 the Supreme Court of Canada has been involved in a continuing debate over the role of spousal support and, therefore, the appropriateness and feasibility of the goals of equality and independence as they relate to spousal support. The cases seem to fall into two separate groups. In one group are cases where the payor spouse has requested an order to terminate or substantially reduce the amount of support being paid to a dependent spouse pursuant to an earlier court order. In the other group, the recipient spouse has asked the court to assist in revising an agreement previously entered into by the spouses, where the agreement has provided for the termination of support at a predetermined point in time. In these latter cases, the dependent spouse ñas generally argued that assumptions about the spouse's ability to become financially self-sufficient have proved inaccurate because of illness, levels of unemployment, or lack of necessary work skills.

The Supreme Court of Canada has distinguished between two groups in its decisions in the past decade (Bailey, 1989–90; Cossman, 1990; Rogerson, 1989). In general, the court has refused to intervene in settled arrangements where the parties have themselves previously agreed that support payments should cease at a predetermined time. The court has reasoned that, barring a radical, unforeseen change that was somehow connected to the marriage, 'a deal is a deal' (Bala, 1988; *Pelech*; *Richardson*; *Caron*). In these circumstances, the court has attempted to reinforce the principle of independence consistent with classic liberalism (the individual's right to contract).

By contrast, in cases where court orders for spousal support have existed, the Supreme Court has not restricted itself to this policy of nonintervention, at least where the dependent spouse would otherwise become dependent upon the state. In particular, these decisions demonstrate a reluctance to set time limits on a dependent spouse's support where a judge cannot reasonably anticipate a date by which the spouse could be expected to gain self-sufficiency (*Messier* v *Delage*). Furthermore, these decisions have generally rejected the idea that entitlement to support, as well as any subsequent change in the amount payable, is predicated upon some causal connection being established between the economic need of the dependent spouse and the roles assumed during the marriage (*Moge*).

Yet, in cases where the parties have not entered into a separation agreement, and where a dependent spouse is not in danger of becoming a public charge, equality is seen to be achieved simply by dividing marital property, and independence is secured by assessing a quantum and duration of support payments necessary to make the spouse self-sufficient within a reasonable time. Therefore, despite statements that self-sufficiency or a 'clean break' is not the paramount factor to be considered, it seems that self-sufficiency is the preferred goal when reliance upon the state is not at issue.

The obvious conclusion to draw from the past decade is that the principles to be applied depend upon who bears the cost, and not on the ideology. 'Public policy' would seem to require that independence and equality principles apply where a former dependent spouse's income is anywhere above the subsistence level. By contrast, where the state might be called upon to provide income, familial relations and obligations frequently assume primary importance. This conclusion is applied rigorously by the social assistance bureaucracy, and it seems to have been accepted by the judiciary in family law cases. In this way, the family law principles and the social assistance principles merge and gain consistency. However, the consistency is based on societal convenience: so long as women (and children) bear the cost of marriage breakdown, the principles of equality and independence have at least a formal credibility, but once the burden may be shifted to the public purse, the cost of sustaining these principles becomes too demanding. In other words, the cost of public policies assuring spousal equality and accessible divorce is too expensive to be borne by society at large (Mossman, 1994).

Towards Substantive Equality: (Re)defining the Legal Unit

Our analysis of the legal principles concerning marriage breakdown suggests that the economic costs of increased rates of divorce in Canada have been borne, and continue to be borne, disproportionately by women and children, and not by men or by society as a whole. Reform of social policies must therefore start by understanding the economic interdependence of members of intact families and the ways that families provide economic support for their dependent members: children, the elderly, those who are ill, and those whose family responsibilities discourage career aspirations or full-time workforce participation – many of whom are wives (Symes, 1987). In such a context of economic dependency within family units, marriage breakdown may inevitably result in economic crisis. Our analysis has also demonstrated that there continues to be some inconsistency between the principles of equality and independence generally espoused by family law and those of ongoing familial dependence even after marriage breakdown as espoused by social assistance programs.

As is clearly evident, dependent family members do not cease to be dependent at divorce, whether or not their economic hardship is alleviated to some extent by spousal support payments in the family law system or by social assistance. On the assumption that high rates of divorce and marriage breakdown will continue to be the norm for family life in Canada, we argue that the economic costs should be met otherwise than by women and children, that is, 'the feminization of poverty.' In addressing this problem, one of the key issues is what unit of legal entitlement will best achieve this goal: 'the family' unit or 'the individual' unit? Assuming as a starting point that we want to improve economic security, equality, and consistency, what are the implications of adopting each of these options?

'The Family' as a Legal Unit

The lack of congruence between principles of family law and social assistance would be overcome by the consistent use of either 'the family' or 'the individual' as the basic legal unit. In choosing one of them, however, an initial problem of using 'the family' in the context of marriage breakdown is the absence of an intact family unit. Thus, assessing needs of 'the family' in such a context seems practically unworkable.

Yet, there are more fundamental problems with the use of 'the family' as a basic legal unit. The social science literature suggests that there are many different family forms and that the definition of 'the family' depends on both context and purpose (Eichler, 1983). As has been demonstrated, the increased rate of divorce in Canada has contributed to an increasing number of lone-parent families. It has also created large numbers of 'blended' or 'reconstituted' families, those in which a parent and child from a former marriage relationship enter a new family unit with another adult, or with another adult and children from a previous unit. Families may also be recognized increasingly in legislation where there are two adults of opposite sexes with or without children, even though the adults have not married. Further, a recent legislative proposal in Ontario recognizing that same-sex relationships create familial relationships for some purposes (Bill 167) was defeated at second reading in 1994, but entitlement to employment and governmental benefits on the basis of comparable 'family status' for such families has been accepted in a number of cases in recent years (*Leshner*; *Knodel*; *M v H*), although not in all of them (*Egan*). It may also be necessary to take account of 'family' units where one or more family members has a separate household as, for example, where one family member lives and works in another city. Eichler has proposed a useful set of categories for differing sets of familial and household relationships of parents and children in the context of marriage breakdown, emphasizing that all these variations must be taken into account in social policy administration (Eichler, 1993: 143). Such a task is a challenging one indeed.

Anthropological literature which has identified the functional basis for family life has suggested that modern families have emerged in the context of modern states (Collier, Rosaldo, and Yanagisako, 1982). Yet, such an assertion means that a functional approach to defining 'the family' leads to a definition which includes only those family forms which have already been recognized and shaped by state policies. For this reason, others have suggested a need to analyse 'the family' as an ideological unit (Glendon, 1981; Gavigan, 1993). Moreover, in the context of legislation and governmental policy making, it is clear that any definition of family is purposive, not value-free. Any such policies 'implicitly or explicitly ... [discourage] some reactions among citizens and [encourage] others' (Blehar, 1983: 604). In this way, an open-ended definition of 'families' rather than of 'the family' may be more accurate in reflecting the diversity of family forms.

Current family law statutes, while focusing on individual rights and responsibilities of spouses, seem to assume the existence of 'the family' as well. Divorce legislation, for example, applies only to those spouses who are legally married, and most of the provincial statutes concerning property rights at marriage breakdown also apply only to spouses who are legally married. These provincial statutes tend to extend rights to spousal support to cohabiting heterosexual spouses, but not to same-sex spouses (although the Ontario Law Reform Commission (1996) has recommended the extension of these rights to same-sex couples who are Registered Domestic Partners, and a recent case in Ontario has recognized same-sex partners for purposes of spousal support), while child support obligations may be shared among biological and 'social' parents. As is evident, moreover, the rights to spousal and child support mean that 'the family' continues to exist even where a divorce has been granted and although former family members are living in separate households and perhaps even in new 'family' relationships.

Such a legal approach means that some families are recognized while others are not, so that definitions of 'family' are neither neutral nor inconsequential. Moreover, the principles seem designed for a traditional family relationship with a male breadwinner and female housewife, with prescribed roles and economic responsibilities which flow out of this arrangement. The recent recommendations of the Ontario Law Reform Commission for the extension of property entitlement and spousal support obligations to both common law and same-sex couples demonstrate how awkward it may be to apply principles from traditional marriage relationships to those which may involve more elements of choice relating to both roles and economic responsibilities. Moreover, by contrast with these unarticulated assumptions in the family law context, differentiated male and female roles and responsibilities are very clearly delineated in traditional social assistance legislation (Land, 1986).

Overall, therefore, the underlying ideal family form in both family law and social assistance legislation is not neutral, and in the context of diverse family forms, it may be prejudicial. In particular, the use of 'the family' as a basic legal unit undermines the goal of equality by selecting which family forms are to be recognized from among a diversity of choices and by reinforcing gendered social roles and responsibilities within this ideal family form. This latter problem also contributes to a lack of economic security for women at divorce, particularly when they live in lone-parent families. Perhaps most importantly, the use of 'the family' as a basic legal unit assumes beneficial distribution of economic resources within a family unit. Instead, power imbalances within families may severely undermine this assumption (Pahl, 1984). As Olsen has stated: '[Family] law both reflects and helps create an ideology of the family – a structure of images and understandings of family life. This ideology serves to deny and disguise the ways that families illegitimately dominate people and fail to serve human wants' (1984: 3).

An Alternative: 'The Individual' as a Legal Unit

The use of 'the individual' as the basic legal unit overcomes many of the disadvantages which accompany the use of 'the family.' By adopting 'the individual,' there is no need to categorize a diversity of family forms or to distinguish between them. Moreover, since all families are composed of individuals, use of 'the individual' as the basic legal unit simply underlines the component parts of a family unit. By using 'the individual' as the unit for policy administration, interactions between people and family forms could be approached more as processes than as static entities, and it would be easier to overcome prescribed gender roles so that economic responsibilities could be distributed according to needs and abilities rather than sex roles.

It is necessary, however, to be wary of the use of 'the individual' as the basic legal unit, having regard to our recent experiences with this approach in the family law context. In the context of divorce reforms based on no-fault and equality between the spouses, statutory assertions of equality have taken the place of actual achievement of substantive equality goals. In other words, there has been some serious confusion about what equality means in such a context (Westerberg Prager, 1982: 111). More forcefully, Olsen has explained the problem of assuming equality between the spouses on the basis that 'this view treats women's subordination as though it occurred by chance. That men happen to earn almost twice as much as women, and that this affects the social relations between the sexes is, according to this view, not the state's concern. Similarly, that children are economically dependent upon their parents, and that parents sometimes use this dependence to dominate or exploit their children, is likewise not the state's concern. Rather, the mistreatment of wives and children is simply a series of unfortunate individual occurrences' (1984: 10–11).

In addition, using 'the individual' as the basic legal unit may also prevent recognition of the fundamental economic interdependence within families. If such interdependence is not recognized, the value of home labour may be ignored, a factor which may also undermine the goal of equality between spouses, especially in relation to issues about property at marriage breakdown. The individual approach also fails to take account of the ways that people often make certain kinds of choices, especially career choices, because of spousal and family considerations, choices which they might not make at all if they were not members of a family unit (Knetsch, 1984). For example, more often than not, it makes 'economic sense' during an ongoing family relationship for women to engage in limited workforce activity, a 'choice' which permits them to take primary child care and household responsibilities while their husbands pursue career goals and higher family incomes. Yet, these same 'choices' disadvantage women seriously at marriage breakdown if they are then regarded as equal within the relationship. Thus, using 'the individual' as the basic legal unit is not problem-free.

Directions for Further Questing

The goal of equality is not necessarily better served by using 'the individual' as opposed to 'the family,' although the *potential* for accomplishing equality may be greater. It is clear, however, that using 'the individual' would enhance the position of female lone parents in the social assistance context since their entitlement to assistance could be assessed without regard to the resources of other 'family' members such as a cohabiting partner. Even so, however, numerous other reforms would also be needed to improve the position of such women significantly. Recent experience with ideas about equality and independence for individual spouses in the family law context underlines the law's limited conceptual approach to equality ideas and the extent to which it may focus on formal rather than substantive ideas about equality.

The essential point here is that a major societal phenomenon has changed our understanding of the nature of family life in the past two decades, and these changes now appear somewhat permanent. In this context, legal and social policy making must begin to address the problem of the 'feminization of poverty' to which these reforms have contributed, not simply by tinkering with current arrangements, but rather by recognizing the need for fundamental rethinking about them.

Fundamental rethinking in this context requires us to examine more carefully the processes of family law reform which all too often have exacerbated economic inequities among family members rather than assisting them to find solutions; to recognize the limits of formal rather than substantive ideas about equality for individual members of family units; and to confront the law's traditional dichotomy between private family life and public family policies so as to better integrate the purposes of family law and social assistance programs (Mossman, 1994). While Susan Moller Okin has suggested that 'the family ... must be just if we are to have a just society' (1989: 14), we are suggesting that where familial relationships are economically unjust, the state has an obligation to redress the economic inequities through appropriate social welfare and family law policies.

Notes

1 This essay is a revised and updated version of 'Family Law and Social Welfare: Toward a New Equality' by the same authors, published in vol. 5, no. 1 of the *Canadian Journal of Family Law* (1986), 79–110.
2 These concepts of 'deserving' and 'undeserving' recipients of social assistance focus on male recipients for whom the distinction is one of being unable to work or, on the other hand, being unwilling to work – a distinction reflected in recent governmental initiatives to establish 'workfare' programs. By contrast, sole-support mothers were characterized in the early development of mothers' allowance schemes as 'deserving' if they were morally blameless for their circumstances of poverty, but 'undeserving' if they were blameworthy (Chunn, 1994; Abner, 1989). Significantly, women's relationships with men were also important in this context in determining whether they were 'deserving' or 'undeserving.' However, the level of benefits for sole-support mothers, even those who are 'deserving,' has not usually been as high as benefits payable to males in the category of 'deserving' recipients.

References

Abner, E. 1989. 'The Merits of the Use of Constitutional Litigation to Unravel the Fabric of the Feminization of Poverty in Canada. Toronto. LM Thesis, York University.

Armstrong, P. 1997. 'Restructuring the Public and Private: Women's Paid and Unpaid Work.' In S. Boyd, ed., *Challenging the Public/Private Divide: Feminism, Law and Public Policy.* Toronto: University of Toronto Press.

Backhouse, C. 1988. 'Married Women's Property Law in Nineteenth Century Canada.' *Law and History Review* 6: 211–57.

Bailey, M. 1989-90. 'Pelech, Caron, Richardson.' *Canadian Journal of Women and the Law* 3: 615–33.

Bala, N. 1988. 'Domestic Contracts in Ontario and the Supreme Court Trilogy: A Deal Is a Deal.' *Queen's Law Journal* 13: 1–61.

Blehar, M. 1983. 'Families and Public Policy.' In A. Skolnick and J. Skolnick, eds., *Family in Transition*. Boston: Little, Brown, 601–5.

Canada. 1973. *Working Paper on Social Security in Canada*. Ottawa: Queen's Printer.

Chunn, D. 1992. *From Punishment to Doing Good: Family Courts and Socialized Justice in Ontario 1990–1940.* Toronto: University of Toronto Press.

Collier, J., M. Rosaldo, and S. Yanagisako. 1982. 'Is There a Family?: New Anthropological Views.' In B. Thorne with M. Yalom, eds., *Rethinking the Family: Some Feminist Questions.* New York and London: Longman, 25–39.

Cossman, B. 1990. 'A Matter of Difference: Domestic Contracts and Gender Equality.' *Osgoode Hall Law Journal* 28: 303–80.

Dooley, M. 1993. 'Recent Changes in the Economic Welfare of Lone Mother Families in Canada: The Role of Market Work, Earnings and Transfers.' In J. Hudson and B. Galaway, eds., *Single Parent Families*. Toronto: Thompson Educational, 115–36.

Duxbury, L., and C. Higgins. 1994. 'Families in the Economy.' In M. Baker, ed., *Canada's Changing Families: Challenges to Public Policy.* Ottawa: Vanier Institute of the Family, 29–40.

Eichler, M. 1983. *Families in Canada Today.* Toronto: Gage.

– 1993. 'Lone Parent Families: An Instable Category in Search of Stable Policies.' In J. Hudson and B. Galaway, eds., *Single Parent Families*. Toronto: Thompson Educational, 139–55.

Erickson, A.L. 1993. *Women and Property in Early Modern England.* London, New York: Routledge.

Fineman, M. 1991. *The Illusion of Equality.* Chicago: University of Chicago Press.

Gavigan, S. 1993. 'Paradise Lost, Paradox Revisited: The Implications of Familial Ideology for Feminist, Lesbian and Gay Engagement with Law.' *Osgoode Hall Law Journal* 31: 589–624.

Glendon, M.A. 1981. *The New Family and the New Property.* Toronto: Butterworths.

Hamilton, R. 1988. 'Women, Wives and Mothers.' In N. Mandell and A. Duffy, eds., *Reconstructing the Canadian Family: Feminist Perspectives.* Toronto: Butterworths, 3–26.

Holcombe, L. 1983. *Wives and Property.* Toronto: University of Toronto Press.

Hovius, B. 1982. *Family Law.* Toronto: Butterworths.

Knetsch, J. 1984. 'Some Economic Implications of Matrimonial Property Rules.' *University of Toronto Law Journal* 34: 263–82.

Land, H. 1984. 'Changing Women's Claims to Maintenance.' In M.D.A. Freeman, ed., *The State, the Law, and the Family: Critical Perspectives.* London: Tavistock, 25–35.

– 1986. 'Women: Supporters or Supported?' In D. Baker and S. Allen, eds., *Sexual Divisions and Society: Process and Change.* London: Tavistock, 108–32.

Lemprière, T. 1992. 'A New Look at Poverty.' *Perception* 16, 2 & 3: 18–21.

Lero, D., and Brockman, L. 1993. 'Single Parent Families in Canada: A Closer Look.' In J. Hudson and B. Galaway, eds., *Single Parent Families.* Toronto: Thompson Educational, 91–114.

McCaughan, M. 1977. *The Legal Status of Married Women in Canada.* Toronto: Carswell.

Moller Okin, S. 1989. *Justice, Gender and the Family.* New York: Basic Books.

Mossman, M.J. 1994. '"Running Hard to Stand Still": The Paradox of Family Law Reform.' *Dalhousie Law Journal* 17: 5–34.

– and M. MacLean. 1986. 'Family Law and Social Welfare: Toward a New Equality.' *Canadian Journal of Family Law* 5: 79–110.

National Council of Welfare. 1996. *Poverty Profile 1994.* Ottawa: National Council of Welfare.

Olsen, F. 1983. 'The Family and the Market: A Study of Ideology and Legal Reform.' *Harvard Law Review* 96: 1497–1578.

– 1984. 'The Politics of Family Law.' *Law and Inequality* 2: 1–19.

Ontario Law Reform Commission. 1996. *Report on the Rights and Responsibilities of Cohabitants Under the Family Law Act 1993.* MvH, 17 RFL (4th) 365.

Ontario Ministry of Community and Social Services. 1988. *Transitions: Report of the Social Assistance Review Committee.* Toronto: Queen's Printer for Ontario.

Pahl, J. 1984. 'The Allocation of Money Within the Household.' In M.D.A. Freeman, ed., *The State, the Law, and the Family: Critical Perspectives.* London: Tavistock, 36–50.

Payne, J. 1994. 'Family Law in Canada.' In M. Baker, ed., *Canada's Changing Families: Challenges to Public Policy.* Ottawa: Vanier Institute of the Family, 13–28.

Pearce, D. 1984. 'New Knots or New Nets: Toward a Model of Advocacy to Meet the Needs of Single Parent Heads of Household.' Presented to Conference on

Poor Clients Without Lawyers: What Can Be Done?, University of Wisconsin Law School, October.

Rogerson, C. 1989. 'The Causal Connection Test in Spousal Support Law.' *Canadian Journal of Family Law* 8: 95–132.

Smart, C., and J. Brophy. 1985. 'Locating Law: A Discussion of the Place of Law in Feminist Politics.' In J. Brophy and C. Smart, eds., *Women-in-Law: Explorations in Law, Family and Sexuality.* London: Routledge and Kegan Paul, 1–20.

Spring, E. 1993. *Law, Land and Family: Aristocratic Inheritance in England, 1300 to 1800.* Chapel Hill: University of North Carolina Press.

Statistics Canada. 1990. *Health Report*, Supplement 17, vol. 2.

– 1993. *The Nation*, Cat. No. 93-310. Ottawa: Minister of Supply and Services.

Symes, P. 1987. 'Property, Power and Dependence.' *Journal of Law and Society* 14: 199–216.

Ursel, J. 1992. *Private Lives, Public Policy.* Toronto: Women's Press.

Vanier Institute of the Family. 1994. *Profiling Canada's Families.* Ottawa: Vanier Institute of the Family.

Westerberg Prager, S. 1982. 'Shifting Perspectives on Marital Property Law.' In B. Thorne with M. Yalom, eds., *Rethinking the Family: Some Feminist Questions.* New York and London: Longman, 111–30.

Wilson, E. 1977. *Women and the Welfare State.* London: Tavistock.

Zweibel, E. 1993. 'Canadian Income Tax Policy on Child Support Payments: Old Rationales Applied to New Realities.' In J. Hudson and B. Galaway, eds., *Single Parent Families.* Toronto: Thompson Educational, 157–84.

List of Cases

Caron v *Caron* (1987), 7 RFL (3d) 274.
Egan v *Canada* (1995), 12 RFL (4th) 201.
Knodel v *B.C. (Medical Services Commission)* (1991), 58 BCLR (2d) 356.
Leshner v *Min. of A.G.* (1992), 16 CHRR D/184.
M v *H* (1996), 31 OR (3d) 417.
Messier v *Delage* (1983), 35 RFL (2d) 337.
Moge v *Moge* (1992), 145 NR 1.
Pelech v *Pelech* (1987), 7 RFL (3d) 225.
Richardson v *Richardson* (1987), 7 RFL (3d) 304.

6

Migration Policy, Female Dependency, and Family Membership: Canada and Germany

MONICA BOYD

In their examination of female dependency and the patrilocal family as the source of female subordination, contemporary feminists see state policies as perpetuating the dependency of women on men. Considerable attention is paid to welfare programs which determine eligibility to benefits on the basis of family structure and which assume that women and children have access to male wages. However, *immigration policies also are part of the larger domain of state policies which assume and sustain female dependency*. Immigration and migrant policies affect women through dependency relations and family relations, which are administratively embedded in immigration policies governing entry and in migrant policies of integration.

Such policies may be overtly discriminatory. However, as is true of other social policies, discriminatory outcomes can be indirectly generated by sex-specific ideologies and entrenched systems of sex stratification. This essay selects examples of each from postwar immigration and migrant policies in Canada and Germany. Differing histories create differences in the way in which migrant/immigration policy presumes and enhances female dependency. But both countries share a general commonality in the emphasis placed on family and dependency relations by state policies regarding immigration and migrants and in the resulting marginalization of specific groups of migrant women.

Feminist critiques of the welfare state point to assumed or actual dependency relations as an integral part of many social policies and as a source of gender inequality. In this chapter, I argue that immigration and migrant policies[1] place women more than men in positions of dependency. As a result, foreign-born women may face postponed access to legal citizenship-status and are hampered with respect to full participation in the public sphere,[2] which is essential to receiving citizenship based entitlements in most welfare states (see Orloff, 1993; Pateman, 1988). This argument is based on a review of immigration admission categories and in the use of the family unit in migration in two countries: Canada and Germany.[3] Although both countries differ in immigration approaches and in welfare state regimes, both have practices that administratively create dependencies, prorate access to legal citizenship, and connect entitlements to family relations.

Gendering the Welfare State

A welfare state exists when a state takes on the responsibility for promoting and ensuring, either through legislation, budgets, or other state action, the basic well-being of its members (Kuhnle, 1991). Citizenship, broadly defined, is a key concept in discussions of the welfare state, for it both defines who shall receive rights and entitlements and what the content of these rights and entitlements shall be. As developed by T.H. Marshall, citizenship is both a status which indicates equality as a member of a community and a set of civil, political, and social rights (Barbalet, 1988: 17; Marshall, 1981: 92; Mishra, 1981: 28). However, neither citizenship nor the welfare state is gender-neutral. Feminist activists and scholars observe that theories of the welfare state often fail to acknowledge the sexually divided way in which the welfare state is constructed.

The gendering of welfare states is evident in three ways. First, as Pateman (1988) observes, paid employment has become the key to the recognition of an individual as a citizen of equal worth to other citizens and to the social entitlements of citizenship. However, the model of paid employment is constructed largely from the experiences of men, with the result that the male worker is the prototype for much of the conceptualization of citizenship status and of social rights. In liberal welfare states, such as Canada, individual benefits, such as unemployment insurance or the Canada or Quebec pension plan, frequently are premised on labour force participation. However, this conceptualization of citizenship entitlements may have limited application to women, particularly when their labour force experiences differ substantially from those of men with respect to labour force participation, jobs, and wages. A gender perspective on the welfare state thus reveals that a group to whom citizenship is formally extended may be denied access or only partially benefit from the full range of citizenship rights and entitlements. Such denial need not be overt. Instead, denial often is indirectly achieved as a result of prevailing gender ideologies, gender roles (including gender-specific responsibilities for child care and family), and gender-specific labour demands.

Second, although most rights in industrial democracies are individually based, some derive from membership in a larger collective, such as the family (Daly, 1994). Programs and policies governing eligibility for welfare benefits frequently assume a breadwinner-husband and dependant-wife family form and require recipients to demonstrate the presence or absence of family relations (Barrett, 1980; Quadagno, 1990). Social assistance and income security programs also may assume female dependency on husbands or male partners and thus prohibit women's eligibility to benefits as individuals. Many programs are designed with the assumption that women are primarily in the private sphere and as dependants (and thus indirect beneficiaries) of men (Daly, 1994; Orloff, 1993; O'Connor, 1993). Informed by these departures from individually based rights, feminist scholars stress that family, as well as the state and market, have been central organizing principles in the development of welfare states (Daly, 1994; Orloff, 1993; Williams, 1989: xiii).

These two insights into the assumptions and operations of the welfare state reveal gender inequality, to the detriment of women, in the bestowing of membership in a community and in accessing entitlements. For feminist scholars of the welfare state, a third crucial dimension is the impact of such inequalities in reinforcing women's secondary status and dependence on men (Daly, 1994: 104). It is not just that the welfare state has programs that are disproportionately accessed by men (for example, unemployment and work-related pensions) or by women primarily (social assistance such as aid to dependant mothers, public housing supports, or day care benefits). Rather a central concern is that by constructing the amount and type of resources available, state action can sustain women's reliance on male incomes (Bussemaker and van Kersbergen, 1994; Daly, 1994).

Recent critiques of the welfare state literature have exposed the implicit separation of the public and private spheres and the assumption of female dependency. Feminist critics argue that current orthodox thinking on the welfare state contains the following androcentric stances (O'Connor, 1993; Orloff, 1993; Pateman 1988; Gordon, 1990): (1) the separation of the public and private sphere with an emphasis on the former; (2) a focus on the role of the state and the market rather than on state–market and family relations; (3) the treatment of women as dependent on men and frequently thus as outside, and extraneous to, state- and market distribution-based claims; (4) and, as a result of dependency images, the conceptualization of women as second-class workers.

Diversifying the Focus

Two additional inputs extend these revisionary critiques of orthodox approaches to social policies and the welfare state. One criticism is that feminist approaches neglect the role played by the welfare state in creating and/or perpetuating institutionalized racism (Shaver, 1989; Williams, 1989). Not only can policies have gender-specific impacts, but also they can be reconstituted in either different or more intense ways for racially defined groups. In particular, women of colour challenge feminist approaches to the welfare state by noting: (1) the existence of racially based power relations in which white women are simultaneously oppressed compared with men yet privileged compared with women of colour, and (2) the failure of the 'family' underpinning of the welfare state to fully apply to black women (Brand, 1984; Carby, 1982; Collins, 1989; Dill, 1979; King, 1989; Kline, 1989; Shaver, 1989, 1990; Stasiulis, 1990; Thornhill, 1989).

A second modification to recent feminist discussion on social policy and the welfare state is represented by efforts to go beyond the primary focus on gender and welfare programs. The focus on welfare programs is understandable given the attention paid by governments and analysts to social policy developments and their gender implications. However, immigration policies also are part of the larger domain of state policies which assume and sustain female dependency and which differentiate men and women with respect to the types and accessibility of social rights.

Simply put, migration policies stipulate the conditions under which people may legally enter and remain in a country, acquire citizenship status, including legal citizenship, and access the rights and entitlements associated with membership in a community. Type of movement (permanent or temporary) underlies the acquisition (or non-acquisition) of legal citizenship status. Use of family ties in entry can suppress or deny individually based rights and entitlements.

Categories of Migrants

Countries typically distinguish two main types of migrants when classifying legal border-crossers: (1) those who are considered temporary residents and (2) those who have, or eventually will be granted permanent residence, and who thus may acquire legal citizenship and/or rights and entitlements. These two distinctions create many different administratively defined categories of admission. However, three main groupings usually exist, each characterized by different citizenship status and by different access to social entitlements. Visitors are by their very definition limited in the length of their stay, are not considered eligible for citizenship status, and almost never benefit from the social rights and entitlements of a host country. Temporary workers have limited length of residence, although the period of stay may be longer than that of visitors. Their 'right to remain' in a country generally is dependent on a specific job and/or with a specific employer and/or on converting rights of temporary residence into those of permanent residence. Both temporary labour migrants and refugee claimants constitute the majority of temporary migrants in most countries. Access to government-funded health care may be permitted (if for no other reason than illness threatens the health of citizens), but eligibility for unemployment insurance or pensions may not exist or may be provided only under long periods of 'temporary' residence (see Boyd, 1995). Permanent residents are more likely to have citizenship status, broadly defined as civil, legal, and social rights and entitlements, conferred on them, although considerable variation between countries exists in the length of time required and in the prorating of rights and entitlements.

Family Relationships
Family ties also can affect the conferring of citizenship status and the access to rights and entitlements. Migration policies set the terms under which family members may enter or be reunited with a migrant. Family migration often is permitted by industrial democracies under the assumption or legal requirement that families act as safety nets. Access to social entitlements, including those crucial to migrant adaptation and to the enjoyment of social citizenship (for example, labour market access) may then be based on family membership, rather than on individual needs or rights.

While not overtly gender-specific in their wording, such assumptions and entry criteria are more likely to impact upon women than men for two interrelated reasons. First, enactment of the safety net concept requires designating some individuals as 'dependants' within the family unit. This is accomplished by linking 'dependency' to designated administrative categories of admission, often spouses and children of principal migrants or of current citizens and residents. Second, women are less likely to enter as autonomous migrants and more likely to enter on the basis of marital ties. Thus, women, not men, are more likely to be assigned this 'dependency' status. The impact goes beyond the administrative procedure. The congruency between the population in these categories (wives and children) and sex-specific stereotypes of dependency and subordinate status (women = dependants, subordinates) minimizes reactions to any subsequent differentials in entitlements. As a result, the incorporation of family relations in migrant policy can reinforce and perpetuate gender and gender–race disadvantages rather than reducing these disparities. Theoretically, the issue is that of migrant entitlements and the way in which they become 'gendered' in two related ways: through prevailing conceptualizations of the family as the safety net and through the concept of dependency embedded in family relationships.

Immigration and Welfare State Regimes
My analysis of the migration policy–family–female dependency nexus rests on the review of postwar immigration and migrant policies in two countries: Canada and Germany. From the perspective of the welfare state literature, the two countries represent different welfare state regimes. Esping-Andersen's (1990) increasingly cited work distinguishes between three different kinds of welfare states: social democratic (for example, Scandinavian countries); corporatist (Austria, France, Germany, and Italy); and liberal, market-oriented (Anglo-American democracies, including Canada).

While an important summary of major differences in welfare state regimes, Esping–Anderson's typology, however, is less relevant for a discussion of state policies governing migrant entitlements. On the one hand, it is true that the distinction between social democratic welfare regimes and other types appears to capture country distinctions in approaches to migrant adaption. In Sweden, for example, the state plays a more positive role in organizing and funding migrant adaptation services than is the case in many European countries or in Canada and the United States, where market principles prevail.

On the other hand, when the social rights of migrants, and migrant women in particular, are considered for other countries, the fit between the typology and policies governing migrant entitlements is far from perfect. Two examples suggest caution in expecting the liberal–corporatist–social democratic typology of welfare state regimes to accurately compare how governments extend citizenship-based entitlements to new members. First, as Brubaker (1992) shows in his comparison of

France and the Federal Republic of Germany, countries grouped as similar welfare state types can vary in their usage of territory and social community as a basis of nationhood and legal citizenship. These variations in turn are consistent with differences between France and Germany regarding the extension of social entitlements to migrants, despite common categorizations as corporatist welfare regimes.

Second, countries such as Canada and Germany with different welfare regimes and immigration histories, nonetheless perpetuate gender stratification and accentuate gender–race–birthplace interrelationships through administratively defined admission classes and through linking family and entitlements. Note that Canada is considered a settlement country, whereas Germany is a prototype of the non-settlement approach adopted by many European countries. Their different histories do create country-specific manifestations of the way in which entry and migrant policies presume and enhance female dependency. However, as discussed in the remainder of the chapter, both countries also admit workers on a temporary basis. As well, both emphasize family and dependency relations in state policies regarding immigration and migrants. In both countries, these practices of admitting temporary migrants and emphasizing family relations can marginalize specific groups of migrant women.

Modes of Entry: Structuring Dependency

Concepts of nationhood and sovereignty assure that all nations seek to determine who may be allowed to cross borders for permanent or semi-permanent residence. Although a growing convergence exists between settlement and labour-recruitment countries regarding border control, reducing the size of flows, developing strategies to deal with refugee claimants and illegal migrants (de Wenden, 1987), it still is common to distinguish between the regulations and practices of 'settlement' countries (Canada, Australia, New Zealand, and the United States) and countries in Western Europe. This distinction is illustrated by comparing both Canada and Germany, using the past and recently revised regulations.

Canada

Admission to Canada is governed by the universal application of the 1976 Immigration Act and associated regulations, subsequently updated in 1992 (Bill C-86) with new regulations becoming effective during 1993. The Act and regulations stipulate the conditions under which people may enter and reside in Canada on a temporary basis and as permanent residents.

Temporary Admission and Domestic Workers

With the exception of persons from select countries where visitor status is viewed by the Canadian government as a prelude to illegal residence, visitors to Canada are not required to have visas. Temporary visas are issued mainly to two groups: refugee claimants and persons who are employed for periods of short duration in jobs that cannot be filled by resident Canadians. Increasingly most of these temporary visas are granted to refugee claimants as a way of legalizing their stay in Canada until their claims of U.N. Convention refugee status can be heard. Visas issued to non-refugee claimants for employment purposes cover a diverse set of jobs, including rock band performers, football teams, agricultural workers, and domestic servants. A pronounced gender segregation of occupations exists for these temporary workers (Boyd and Taylor, 1986).

Refugee claimants and workers admitted on temporary visas are not granted citizenship status, defined by Marshall (1981) as membership in the (Canadian) community that is equal to the status enjoyed by permanent residents. Refugee claimants eventually may attain this status, if the adjudication of their claims grants them the right to apply for permanent residence. Most workers who are granted visas for the express purpose of working in Canada are expected to leave when the jobs end. Despite popular claims to the contrary, there is no clear evidence that Canada is rapidly adopting the guest worker, short-term labour focus of its European counterparts in the 1970s.[4]

However, there is one program that is both highly gendered and is organized on the principle of postponed acquisition of membership in Canadian society, thus creating conditions of personal dependency. This is the program in which workers are recruited as live-in domestics in a Canadian resident's home. Over 95 per cent of these workers are female, and they are not eligible to apply as permanent residents until they have had at least two years of employment as live-in domestics in Canada.

The migration of domestics is not unique to Canada in the 1990s. Other countries recruit women as caregivers and housekeepers. And from the settlement of New France to the present, the demand for domestic workers has brought young women to Canada (Barber, 1991).

However, from a feminist perspective, the migration of domestics contains at least two troublesome aspects. First, as Bakan and Stasiulis (1994: 16) note, recent programs since 1973 have reversed the right enjoyed historically by domestic workers, namely, the equating of entry to Canada with the right to remain as permanent residents. This represents a movement away from the earlier position of conferring the right to eventually claim legal citizenship simultaneously with initial residence in Canada (applications for legal Canadian citizenship may be made after three years of residence). Second, increasingly this initial exclusion from the right to citizenship has become racially specific.

Prior to 1973 many of the domestic workers in Canada were readily given permanent resident status. Starting in 1973, with the introduction of the Temporary Employment Authorization Program, workers who were recruited as domestics were issued temporary visas. In 1981 this program was replaced by the Foreign Domestic Movement (FDM) program, partly in response to cases in which women had their permits renewed numbers of times but still were subject to non-renewal and thus subject to removal. Under the FDM program, domestics could be admitted if they served as live-in workers. For many women, the attractiveness of the program lay in the fact that they could apply to have their status changed to that of a permanent resident after two years of employment. The success of the application depended on the ability to demonstrate to the immigration authorities that the domestic worker could successfully adjust to Canada. Three important criteria were applied to domestics to demonstrate the likelihood of successful adjustment: (1) successful domestic employment history, usually relying on favourable reports from employers; (2) demonstrated capacity to support themselves economically; and (3) evidence of social adaptation. Indicators of social adaptation included attaining new job skills and/or becoming involved with local communities (Arat-Koc, 1992; Boyd, 1989; 1991; Macklin, 1994). In her review of the program, Macklin (1994) emphasizes that upgrading job skills was essential, partly because domestic wages were so low that continuation in domestic employment would necessitate state income assistance to attain an adequate living standard.

In 1992 a new program was implemented, following a court ruling which prevented the Canadian government from demanding additional criteria for permanent resident status after the issuing of the Foreign Domestic Worker visa. The procedure under the FDM program had been to admit domestics on temporary work permits and later to require meeting of additional criteria in order to qualify for permanent residency after the initial two-year period of employment. The new Live-in Care-giver Program (LCP) went beyond the generally stated FDM program requirements, but applied them at the point of entry and upon the issu-ing of a temporary work permit. These criteria specified in detail the lan-guage, education, and job-related skills that would-be domestic workers must have for admission to Canada (Canada, Employment and Immi-gration Canada, 1992). Initially the program demanded the equivalent of a grade 12 education and at least six months of formal training in a care-giving occupation. In 1994 this latter requirement was dropped from the immigration regulations to make a one-year experience in caregiving as an alternative (Macklin, 1994: 29). Despite the changes in criteria and in the timing of their application, the LCP retained the requirements found in the FDM program that domestics live in and that applicants for per-manent resident status must have two years of employment as a care-giver (this does not include any time away from Canada).

While not insisting that the same employer exist throughout the two-year probationary period, the Foreign Domestic Movement and the Live-in Caregiver programs administratively created a dependency rela-tion between the domestics and employers. Employment authorizations are granted only for a specific job with a specific employer. Changing employers requires that the previous employer provide to the domestic a record of employment under the LCP and a release letter under the FDM. As well, a new employment authorization must be obtained in order to begin work with a new employer.

These bureaucratic rules and regulations lend themselves to bloodless description, and it is all too easy in such recounting to overlook difficul-ties in implementation. Domestics must negotiate with past or still cur-rent employers in order to obtain required documents. They must also have the confidence to terminate employment, in the face of a program that emphasizes the importance of having a job as a domestic worker for two years in order to apply for permanent resident status. Domestics can easily perceive their status and stay in Canada as highly governed by their employers. Interviews by Silvera (1983) and others allude fre-quently to the control exerted by employers through threats that they will refuse to write letters of recommendation for job changes or that they (the employers) will accuse the domestic of contract violation before an officer at a Canada Immigration Centre.

Domestic Workers, Dependency, and Citizenship
To summarize, women who enter Canada under recent domestic worker programs may apply for permanent resident status only at the end of a

two-year work period. During this time, these women are highly dependent on their employers, for it is only through two years of domestic employment that they can acquire the eligibility to apply for permanent resident status. Within the feminist discourse on the welfare state, this situation has two implications: First, there is postponed eligibility for acquiring legal citizenship, with a probationary period necessary before permanent residence status is granted. As Arat-Koc notes (1992: 236), while in domestic employment, these women are members of the economy, but not of the nation. Second, a dependency relationship exists throughout this probationary period that is not only asymmetrical in terms of power (see Boyd, 1991), but also in terms of citizenship rights and race. Migrant domestic workers lack citizenship rights held by permanent residents of choosing the employer and choosing domicile. In contrast, their employers usually have full citizenship rights regarding employment and residence (Bakan and Stasiulis, 1994: 304).

The employer-employee–citizen-non-citizen nexus also includes race, ethnicity and class dimensions. Throughout the history of Canada, the immigration of women as domestics has always had two facets. First, there is the selling of labour by women to other women of the middle and upper classes. Second, these domestics are racially categorized. During the early part of the twentieth century, British domestics were preferred over the Irish, a group frequently viewed as a 'race' and as less desirable. There was also recruitment of approximately 100 women from Guadeloupe in 1910–11, an endeavour that had racist overtones (Calliste, 1989; MacKenzie, 1988). During the 1950s and 1960s, the Caribbean Domestic Scheme was responsible for the migration of between 500 and 1,000 women, primarily Black. The metaphors of the dominant Anglo-French culture which describe these movements are mixed. But it is clear that mistress–servant relationships rested on racial imagery of nurturing Aunt Jemima, and backward colonies (Calliste, 1989).

With the implementation of the Foreign Domestic Worker program in the 1980s, workers from the Caribbean area have been replaced by domestics from the Philippines. Unpublished data from immigration statistics collected by the government show the following:

• In 1982, before the current Foreign Domestic Worker program was fully implemented, women from the United Kingdom or European countries represented about 45 per cent of all foreign domestics in Canada. Another 18 per cent were from Caribbean countries, and approximately 25 per cent were from the Philippines.

• By 1989 domestics from the Philippines had increased to nearly 50 per cent of all new entrants, workers from the Caribbean represented only 6 per cent of all new entrants, and domestics from the United Kingdom or Europe declined to 27 per cent of the new entrants.

These data indicate one important feature of the past ten years of domestic worker migration to Canada – it consists primarily of women of colour. Macklin (1994: 21–2) describes the recasting of earlier racialized stereotypes. Domestics from Britain and Europe are seen as professionals at child care, whereas women from less developed countries are described as having natural affinities for housekeeping tasks and longer hours of work. One implication is that class, race, and colour are intermingled with the asymmetry of citizenship status associated with entering Canada as a domestic.

Permanent Resident Status and Family Dependency
In addition to guidelines for admitting migrants on a temporary basis, Canadian immigration law and regulations also define the classes under which permanent residents may enter and the criteria that must be met for admission in each entry class for entering in each class. In seeking to enter Canada as permanent residents, both females and males must satisfy the criteria of admissibility associated with three major categories: the family class, the refugee class, and the independent class, consisting of assisted (more distant) relatives and others entering on the basis of a point system. Meeting these criteria can be accomplished in two ways: either directly or as an accompanying family member. A male or female seeking permanent resident status may meet all of the criteria associated with admissibility under one of the three major immigrant classes. Alternatively, a male or female may be given permanent resident status as an accompanying family member of another individual who satisfies the criteria of admissibility.

In principle, these rules and regulations are not sex-specific. Males are not required to enter in one class and females in another. However, women often enter Canada to rejoin their families, and when they enter Canada with their spouses they are less likely to be the principal applicant. Between 1981 and 1991 women age 15 and older were more likely than male adult immigrants to enter in the family class and less likely to enter in the refugee class (table 6.1, lines 1–4; also see Boyd, 1989: table 22; Boyd, 1992: table 3; Boyd 1994). Further, excluding the family class where women often are spouses rejoining men already in Canada,[5]

TABLE 6.1

Sex ratios for permanent residents, age 15 and older, by class of admission and family status, Canada, 1981–1991

	Total (1)	Family class (2)	Refugees and designated classes (3)	Assisted relatives (4)	Other class (5)
Age					
>15 (*n*)					
Female	641,046	304,282	80,738	53,874	202,152
Males	612,092	219,418	131,059	56,307	205,308
Distribution (%)					
Females	100	47	13	8	32
Males	100	36	21	9	34
Sex Ratio					
Females per 100 Males	105	139	62	96	98
Sex Ratio					
by Family Status					
Principal					
Applicant	69	124	28	50	49
Spouse	962	2,045	1,766	532	760
Dependant	87	88	80	87	88

Source: Data supplied by Employment and Immigration Canada, Immigration Statistics, 21 January 1993.

women are less likely to enter as principal applicants and far more likely to enter as spouses. This can be seen in table 6.1, which provides sex ratios, defined as the number of women admitted for every 100 men. Overall, among those admitted as principal applicants between 1981 and 1991, 69 women were admitted for every 100 men. Conversely, among immigrants admitted as spouses of principal applicants, 962 women were admitted for every 100 men.

Family-based entry in Canada (and in settlement countries such as the United States and Australia) requires that persons admitted in the family and assisted relatives categories be sponsored. The use of sponsorship in these two classes reflects the view that while family reunification is desirable on social grounds, integration-related matters are the responsibility of the family, and costs are not to be borne by the state. Sponsors agree to provide or assist with lodgings and to provide food, clothing, incidental living needs, and counselling to the sponsored immigrant(s) during the specified period of settlement. They also agree to provide financial assistance so that the sponsored immigrant(s) shall not require financial maintenance support from federal or provincial assistance programs described in the regulations pertaining to the 1976 Immigration Act (Schedule VI of the current regulations). Thus, sponsorship is viewed by the federal and provincial governments as a commitment that the designated immigrants will not require economic assistance. A sponsorship relation may be designated for up to ten years in the family class and for five years in the assisted relative category. Sponsorship relations also may exist in the refugee class where private citizen groups (individuals or institutions such as churches) and the federal government act as sponsors.

The dependency relations associated with the categories of admission are not mandated to be sex-specific. But two interrelated factors make it so. First, gender stratification in countries of origin often privilege men with respect to entry criteria. Women are less likely to have the same education, paid work experience, occupationally related skills, and investment-related income as their male counterparts.[6] Second, partly because of better chances at meeting admission criteria based on education and economic characteristics, and partly because of gender roles, men are more likely to follow a 'scout' model in which they will migrate first and then seek reunification with their families. As a result, women are more likely than men to enter under sponsorship arrangements, such as those inherent in the family class (table 6.1).

Family Ties, Language, and Paid Work
Immigrants to Canada who are issued visas for purposes of permanent settlement are free to enter, or not enter, the labour force. However, this 'freedom' overlooks possible constraining factors that migrants face in finding employment and receiving wages. Knowing the language of the host country is an important criterion of labour market entry and an important factor in earnings. In Canada, for example, not knowing English or French limits the degree to which individuals can utilize their education and previous work experience in a broad array of jobs. Studies find that average annual earnings of immigrants who do not know one or both of the two official languages are below those of immigrants who can converse in English and/or French (Boyd, 1992).

The response of countries to training migrants in the host country's language(s) is varied. In countries such as the United States and Canada, dominant market principles go hand in hand with *laissez-faire* assumptions. Together they generate the expectations that individuals are responsible for obtaining needed 'skills' and that immigrants will learn the language when it pays to do so in terms of getting a job or in obtaining higher earnings. Canada, however, is slightly more proactive than the United States in funding some language training courses. One major program initiative was the language training program which was a part of the Job Entry Component of the Canadian Job Strategy Programme, and which existed between 1986 and 1991. A more recent initiative is the Immigrant Language Training Policy, which was designed to replace the earlier programs beginning in June 1991.

Participation in both of these federally funded language training courses is governed by funding limitations and by rules of eligibility. Neither program explicitly limits participation on the basis of gender. However, during the period the first program was in effect (1986–1992), statistics confirm that foreign-born women who would benefit from language training were not as likely to be enrolled in the programs as men (Canada Employment and Immigration Advisory Council, 1991).

Numerous studies have discussed this program and the reasons for the reduced participation of women (see Boyd, 1989, 1990, 1992; Boyd, deVries, and Simkin, 1994). One important reason arose from linking eligibility for training allowances to the entry status of immigrants. Participants in the program were eligible for five types of income support, including a living allowance called a basic training allowance. However, the basic training allowance was not provided to immigrants who entered Canada in the family class and assisted relative class, the argument being that sponsors agreed to be financially responsible for these immigrant classes. Although gender-neutral in wording, the impact of this stipulation was gender-specific since women more than men were sponsored immigrants (see table 6.1). Ineligibility for the basic training allowance meant that immigrant women who were sponsored would not generate income during the training period. Many Canadian families, including immigrant families, rely on two paycheques, and the absence of training allowances was undoubtedly a deterrent on the participation of immigrant women in the federally funded language training programs of the 1980s.[7]

On 1 June 1992 a new language training initiative by the federal government came into effect. Whereas the previous program had emphasized the delivery of language training programs to persons destined to the labour force, the new program reversed the focus and directed approximately 80 per cent of its budget to language skills for adult newcomers (persons older than the legal school age) under a program called Language Instruction for Newcomers to Canada (LINC). Language training of immigrants destined to the labour force is now handled through a program called Labour Market Language Training (LMLT), accounting for 20 per cent of the language training funds from the Department of Citizenship and Immigration.

Under the new program, the pre-existing guidelines which restrict the provision of training allowances by immigrant entry class are removed, thus severing the link between category of admission and the receipt (or non-receipt) of basic training allowance benefits. Furthermore, the redirection of the program towards teaching basic language skills to newcomers could be viewed as increasing the entitlements of women who might not be intending to enter the labour market immediately and who thus would have been ineligible to participate in Canadian Jobs Strategies language training programs.

However, while the program removes training allowance barriers originating from the family–class of entry nexus and extends language training to the unpaid as well as the paid foreign born population, it actually reshapes old barriers[8] and imposes a new one. Under the new program, the old barrier of having to forego earnings during training is merely recast. Training allowances are no longer part of the program, and they are not available to anyone, thereby making men and women equal in not having access to training allowances. One possibility, as yet undetermined, is that the neutrality of no training allowances will not correct the underrepresentation of women in language training programs simply because higher wages normally paid to men in Canada mean that men still economically benefit more in the long run from participating in such programs than do women.

Consistent with its focus on newcomers, the new program also explicitly excludes immigrants who have received legal Canadian citizenship (obtainable after three years of permanent residency). Entitlement to federally funded language training programs thus is distinct from, and indeed negated by, the acquisition of legal citizenship rights. The rationale for this provision is that successful applicants for Canadian citizenship have to demonstrate enough English or French language knowledge to properly understand their new society and participate in it. Presumably, then, persons who have obtained legal citizenship have already demonstrated levels of language knowledge that would make participation in the program redundant. In fact, of the foreign-born women and men who are between age 15 and 55 and who speak neither English nor French, 60 and 53 per cent, respectively, are Canadian citizens (unpublished tabulations from the 1991 census).[9] These figures reflect the discretion that judges have to award legal citizenship to persons on 'humanitarian' grounds. Such awards are most likely when the entire family is obtaining citizenship, but where English or French may be unevenly known by family members. Under the LINC program, such gestures have disenfranchised individuals with respect to accessing federally funded language training programs. Women are at greater risk for this disenfranchisement since they are less likely than men to know one of Canada's two official languages but they are more likely than men to be Canadian citizens. As a result, the impact, in fact, is gender-skewed, affecting immigrant women more than men.

The difficulties which immigrant women may experience in obtaining language training become all the more consequential when juxtaposed with the changing composition of immigration flows to Canada. Increasingly, immigrant women are coming from regions other than the United States and Northern Europe. Their knowledge of French or English cannot be assumed. Yet, these women frequently are in the labour force where their lack of English or French language knowledge reinforces their location in the lower rungs of the occupational structure (Boyd, 1992; Boyd, deVries, and Simkin, 1994) and segments them from the Canadian-born and from women born in Europe or the United States. As was true for domestic workers, such segmentation of immigrant women by language and origins contains racial and class overtones. Most women from regions other than Europe and the United States are women of colour. A multivariate statistical analysis shows that these visible minority women who are in the labour force and who have poor or non-existent language skills have the lowest earnings of all groups in the 1991 Canadian labour force (groups are defined by gender, language skills, and visible minority status; Boyd, 1996).

Germany[10]

Designating Canada as one of the 'settlement' countries captures the fact that residency rights are synonymous with being granted entry as a permanent resident. However, this orientation and related immigration policy differ substantially from the history of migration in Europe and in Germany more specifically. In the 1960s and early 1970s, many European countries recruited low-skill, short-term labour only to discover that return migration did not occur readily, particularly after the cessation of labour recruitment in 1973–4. Instead, in contradiction to the earlier position of admitting only (unattached) workers for short stays, most countries increasingly came to allow family migration, which both recognized and ensured that the migrants were there for good (Castles, 1984; also see United Nations, 1979, 1985a, 1985b).

Compared with Canada, Germany has very different views on the desirability of immigration and very different administrative regulations for admitting migrants. However, as in Canada, women are more likely than men to enter as family members and to have their economic histories shaped by administratively created dependencies on spouses.

Prorating Residency Rights

Administratively, systems of incremental residence rights distinguish European countries from settlement countries, where migrants are admitted as permanent residents at the outset, and where temporary migrants usually do not solidify their residency rights over time (Boyd, 1995). These distinctions are evident in the migration policy of Germany. On 26 April 1990 a new *Ausländergesetz* (Aliens Act) was passed in the German parliament, effective 1 January 1991. This law reaffirmed that 'the Federal Republic is not, nor shall it become, a country of immigration ... [and that] any further immigration of aliens from non-EC member states is to be prevented by all legal means' (quoted in Foerster, 1991–2: 89). Prior to this Aliens Act, migration of non-EC nationals in Germany was governed by the German Act of April 1965. While there have been some changes, notably in the easing of the conditions under which legal citizenship can be obtained and in the increasing security associated with the right-of-residence permit, the overall structure of residence permits has not changed appreciably. Table 6.2 summarizes the general parameters of the changes. In actuality, however, numerous and complex regulations govern work and residence permits, with variation existing for different types of migrants and their family members. As well, the migration of European Community nationals falls outside this legislation, handled through EC agreements and laws.

Under the earlier and current legislation, family reunification is permitted, but only of spouses and dependent children.[11] For foreigners who are not entering on family reunification grounds, such persons may be granted a permit only if their presence does not affect the interests of the Federal Republic of Germany. This meant, and continues to mean, that foreigners (not entering for family reasons) are required to obtain a residence permit in the form of a visa before entering Germany. This visa is issued only after it has been ascertained that the preconditions for employment are met and that the precedence accorded Germans and

TABLE 6.2
Germany (FRG) resident permits

	Worker	Spouse
Before January 1991 (Act of April 1965)		
Limited duration	Must meet preconditions for employment	Limited to worker status
Unlimited duration	May be granted after 5 years residence	
Right to stay (residence entitlement)	May be granted after 8 years residence	Limited to worker status
After January 1991 (Federal Act, April 1990)		
Limited duration	May meet preconditions for employment	Limited to worker status but may under certain conditions be granted permit in own right (see text)
Unlimited duration	May be granted after 5 years residence	
Right to stay (residence entitlements)	May be granted after 8 years residence	Same as above

EC-nationals have been satisfied (that is, they are favoured to fill employment slots first; Heyden, 1991: 285).

Residence status is consolidated as the duration of the stay increases. Under earlier 1965 legislation, a residence permit was initially granted for one year, then twice for a period of two years, and then, after five years, an unlimited permit could be issued. After eight years the right of residence could be granted provided certain conditions were met which included the securement of sustenance without recourse to unemployment benefits or social assistance benefits, sufficient knowledge of the German language, an appropriate home, and special work permits (Federal Republic of Germany, Federal Minister of the Interior, 1988: 18–19). These procedures are upheld in the new Aliens Act, which now requires applicants to demonstrate the ability to secure sustenance, simple verbal language knowledge, and appropriate housing; have a permit for gainful employment; make contributions to social security for at least five years (sixty months); and demonstrate non-existence of reasons for deportation (H. Kurthen, personal communication, 1996).

Men dominated the earlier guest-worker flows to the Federal Republic of Germany. Even in the 1980s, fewer than one out of three newly entered workers were women (Meyer, 1987: Table 2). Thus, as in Canada, women appeared more likely than men to enter on the basis of their relationship to a male already accorded a residence permit.[12] However, unlike the situation in Canada, where the right to remain is an individual right granted to all permanent migrant adults (excluding those cases involving fraudulent reporting on applications, criminal acts, terrorism, etc.), under German legislation prior to 1991, women were not granted a residence permit distinct from that of the person with whom they were reunited. If a divorce occurred or if a permit holder left Germany or failed to maintain the conditions necessary for the renewal of a residence permit, accompanying family members all lost their entitlement to stay. These regulations represent the fullest expression of dependency in which a dependent's right to remain in a country is determined solely by that of another resident (usually the husband).

This situation has been modified in the more recent (Ausländergesetz) legislation, in effect since 1 January 1991. Initially, the residence rights of a dependent are tied to those of the person already in Germany. However, with the granting of an unlimited residence permit (after five years of having limited permits), spouses may then acquire independent rights of residence. Separate legal positions also exist for living spouses of foreigners in case of marital dissolution. In case of separation or divorce after at least four years of a marital partnership existing in Germany (and in especially hard cases, three years), an independent residence permit is granted. At the death of the partner a separate residence permit is granted immediately.[13]

Family Dependency and Labour Market Access
In Canada labour market opportunities of immigrant women are reduced via the retarding effects of not knowing one of the two official languages and the eligibility requirements of past and current federally funded language training programs. Thus, the labour market impact of family dependency and entry status, as well as unpaid work roles is filtered through the eligibility requirements of language programs. In Germany, however, the linkage between mode of entry, family dependency, and labour market access is more overt. In the past, women entering Germany for family reunification faced reduced access to the labour market. However, like Canada, Germany too has recently modified various regulations in the direction of reducing restrictions.

As Heyden (1991: 285) observes, in principle the recruitment of foreign workers to Germany has been banned since 1973. However, there are exceptions such as the contractual employment of foreigners for purposes of training. The employment of seasonal workers is permissible for a limited time, and the employment for an unlimited period of time is permissible for specific categories of skilled workers if their employment is in the public interest (Heyden, 1991: 285). As indicated previously, a residence permit, necessary for entering Germany, is granted to such workers only after ascertaining that precedence in employment cannot be given to those defined as German or as nationals of the EC-12 countries. Precedence also is given to foreign workers holding a special work permit for which they are entitled to apply after five years' residence.

Like residence permits, work permits also solidify over time. The work permit is given only for limited periods of time and must be renewed. After five years' employment, a special work permit may be obtained which allows a worker to take up a job without establishing his or her entitlement to precedence. And, under the new legislation, effective January 1991, persons holding the 'right-to-residence permit' (see table 6.2) will no longer require work permits (Heyden, 1991).

For foreign-born spouses and dependants (for example, children) who are resident in Germany, other preconditions also exist for a work permit. Under the German Act of April 1965, spouses of foreign workers were required to wait four years (three if from Turkey) to apply for the initial work permit granted for first employment. Since January 1991, there has been no waiting period for family members joining foreigners already living in Germany and holding a residence permit of unlimited duration, attainable after five years (table 6.2).

The initial work permit policy (as well as the policy governing resumption of employment) of Germany ostensibly rests on the desire to protect employment opportunities for German nationals or foreigners who are nationals of EC member states (called foreign workers of equal status).[14] By restricting the employment permits of spouses for up to four years, this policy distinguishes between persons with entitlements to be in the labour market and those who are excluded. As in Canada, the impacts of these policies are not racially or ethnically neutral. They do not apply to nationals of the EC-12 countries. They do apply to all other groups. Migrants from Turkey form the largest resident population in Germany, and they represent a racial group in the view of many other Europeans. They also represent a sizeable working class (Castles, 1984). Much of this migration occurred in the 1960s and early 1970s to meet the German economy's demand for unskilled labour.

Structured Inequality

Countries vary considerably in immigration policies, family-based entitlements, and in the readiness with which civil, political, and social rights are extended to migrants. However, assumptions surrounding female dependency and family relationships often are found in, and sustained by, two features of international migration: type of migration and modes of entry. Through these conceptualizations and their enactments in administrative rules and regulations, women are more likely than men to migrate as domestic workers or on the basis of family membership.

In turn, how migrants administratively enter a country is not without consequences. Formal citizenship status can be denied or prorated and access to citizenship-based entitlements can be hampered, either directly by the terms of entry or indirectly when migrant economic incorporation, including labour force participation and type of work obtained, is affected by entry-related rules and regulations. Given the importance of economic status for life chances more generally, for formal citizenship, and for social entitlements in particular (Pateman, 1988), the link between dependency relations, entry status, and economic insertion acquires considerable importance for migrants.

Despite very different conceptualizations of the role of migration in both Canada and Germany, the policy-based administrative creation of 'dependency' categories indirectly affects migrant women more than migrant men. Further, in both countries, women appear more likely to bear the brunt of connections between entry status and select labour market policies. In Canada the past practice of disallowing basic training allowances meant that foreign-born women who do not know English or French were thwarted in utilizing labour market language training programs even when they were eligible. Not knowing the host language(s) reinforces an already tenuous labour market situation, as many women without knowledge of the English or French languages in Canada are employed in cleaning, manufacturing, and seamstress jobs where work may be irregular, low paying, and in onerous conditions. In Germany the incremental residency and work permits ensures that migrant women are absent from the formal labour force for a number of years.

In both countries, the linkages between dependency relations, entry status, and labour market status produce two conclusions. First, such linkages can perpetuate female dependency, either by formally tying the residency of a woman to that of her husband, by tying workers to a specific employer, or by situating migrant women in low-skill, marginal jobs. In the latter case, intrafamilial dependency is reinforced to the extent that the lower wages (or non-wages) of a woman render her dependent on the higher wages of her employed spouse. Second, from the perspective of feminist theorists, such outcomes are not surprising. State welfare policies are a mechanism of women's subordination not only in the way they link eligibility for welfare payments to family structure, but also in maintaining the economic marginality of women by relegating them to the private sphere and by treating them as second-class workers. From this perspective, it is not unusual to find that other forms of state policies, such as immigration policies, also carry with them the capacity to reconstruct dependency relations and create conditions of economic marginality.

Notes

1 Frequently used in the field of international migration, the terms 'immigration' or 'migration' policies refer to policies that govern the entry and conditions of admittance of would-be movers across national boundaries. The term 'migrant policy' refers to policies that are directed at these movers once they legally are admitted. Usually these policies are targeted at the integration, adaptation, acculturation, or other aspects considered important for the 'settlement' of migrants.

2 Other consequences of dependency exist, such as the difficulties in accessing social assistance faced by immigrant women who are victims of violence perpetrated by their sponsors (under Canadian law persons who sponsor the immigration of family members agree to assume financial responsibilities for a period of between five to ten years). This and other examples are discussed in Boyd (1989). In this essay I focus only on the consequences with respect to attaining citizenship status and labour market participation.

3 This chapter is a revision of a similarly titled paper presented at the annual meeting of the Canadian Sociology and Anthropology Association, Charlottetown, PEI, June, 1992. Policies described here are those in existence in Canada through 1994 and Germany through 1992.

4 Most of these claims are based on the number of annual temporary visas issued. However, to reiterate, many of these visas are issued to refugee claimants. Furthermore, the number of temporary visas cannot be equated with the number of persons in a country. A temporary visa can be issued for

short durations of time and undergo successive renewals. As a result, one person can generate multiple temporary visas over the course of a year (see Boyd, Taylor, and Delaney, 1986).

5 Spouses and dependants of principal applicants normally are issued visas allowing admission into Canada for up to twelve months following the admission of the principal applicants. After the expiration of these visas, close family members must satisfy admission criteria of the family (or less frequently) the independent class. Thus, if a woman enters to be reunited with a sponsor already in Canada (for example, a husband or offspring) and if her visa has expired, then she normally would be 'sponsored' by her husband for admission in the family class. If she is the sole adult in the group of family members being sponsored, she becomes the principal applicant for administrative purposes.

6 Gender stratification in the host country also can privilege men if entry is determined primarily by demand for male-typed occupations rather than female-typed occupations.

7 Other factors, not linked to entry status, also dampened access to the language training options of the Canadian Job Strategies program. Most problematic is the stipulation that English or French is required to perform the job. This prevented participation by workers in jobs such as office cleaning, restaurant kitchens, sewing, and some manufacturing where knowledge of the host language may not be considered essential to performing the tasks required (see Boyd, 1989, 1990 for further discussion).

8 In addition to the issue of training allowances, several barriers associated with participation in the Canadian Job Skills Strategies language program remain for women who seek to extend their language skills through LMLT. Participation in the Labour Market Language Training program still is dependent on the criterion that knowledge of English or French is necessary for the relevant occupation or employment and that workers are needed for employment in such occupations and jobs (see note 6 for exclusionary implications).

9 This is calculated from the 1991 Public Use Microdata file for Individuals. The percentages describe permanent residents age 15 to 55 who immigrated to Canada before 1988 if they resided outside of the Atlantic provinces and before 1980 if they resided in the Atlantic provinces (the latter selection was required by the pre coded categories available on the database). Since persons must reside in Canada for at least three years to establish eligibility for legal citizenship, the year 1988 was selected to demarcate the population that was eligible for legal citizenship in 1991.

10 I am grateful to Dr Hermann Kurthen and Dr Angelika von Wahl (University of North Carolina at Chapel Hill) for their comments on an earlier draft. Dr

Kurthen's review provided additional insight into German immigration law not always available from the documents I consulted. Any oversights or errors remain my responsibility.

11 The upper age limit varies somewhat across time and *Länder*, which are equivalents to states or provinces.

12 Indeed, the resident migrant had to have an unlimited residence permit in order to be entitled to reunification. Under the new Aliens Act, the criteria have changed to that of having a residence permit.

13 This is based on a direct translation of *Das Neue Ausländerrecht der Bundesrepublik Deutschland*, Minister of the Interior, and the overview of Germany in Jenks (1992).

14 It also deterred the migration of spouses since legal employment could not be obtained for up to four years.

References

Arat-Koc, Sedef. 1992. 'Immigration Policies, Migrant Domestic Workers, and the Definition of Citizenship in Canada.' In Vic Satzewich, ed., *Deconstructing a Nation: Immigration, Multiculturalism and Racism in the 1990s Canada*. Toronto: Fernwood Press, 229–42.

Bakan, Abigail B., and Daiva K. Stasiulis. 1994. 'Foreign Domestic Worker Policy in Canada: and the Social Boundaries of Modern Citizenship.' *Science and Society* 58 (Spring): 7–33.

– 1995. 'Making the Match: Domestic Placement Agencies and the Ritualisation of Women's Household Work.' *Signs 20* (Winter): 303–35.

Barbalet, J.M. 1988. *Citizenship: Rights, Struggle and Class Inequality.* Minneapolis: University of Minnesota Press.

Barber, Marilyn. 1991. *Immigrant Domestic Servants in Canada.* Booklet No. 16. Ottawa: Canadian Historical Association.

Barrett, Michele. 1980. *Women's Oppression Today.* Thetford: Thetford Press.

Boyd, Monica. 1989. *Migrant Women in Canada: Profiles and Policies*, Working Paper. Ottawa: Employment and Immigration. Immigration Policy Branch. Policy Analysis Directorate.

– 1990. 'Immigrant Women: Language, Socioeconomic Inequalities and Policy Issues.' In Shiva Halli, Frank Trovato and Leo Driedger, eds., *Ethnic Demography: Canadian Immigrant, Racial and Cultural Variations*. Ottawa: Carleton University Press, 275–96.

– 1991. 'Migrating Discrimination: Feminist Issues in Canadian Immigration Policies and Practices.' Working Paper No. 6. Centre for Women's Studies and Feminist Research, University of Western Ontario.

- 1992. 'Gender Issues in Immigration and Language Fluency: Canada and the United States.' In Barry R. Chiswick, ed., *Immigration, Language and Ethnic Issues: Public Policy in Canada and the United States*. Washington, DC: American Enterprise Institute, 305–72.
- 1994. 'Canada's Refugee Flows: Gender Inequality.' *Canadian Social Trends* 30 (Spring): 7–10.
- 1995. 'Migration Regulations and Sex Selective Outcomes in Settlement and European Countries.' In *International Migration Policies and the Status of Female Migrants*. New York: United Nations Population Division, 83–98.
- 1996. 'Immigrant Minorities, Language and Economic Integration in Canada.' Revision of an unpublished paper presented at the 1995 Conference on Old and New Minorities, Centre Jacques Cartier, Lyon France (Sponsored by Institut National d'Etudes Demographique).
- and Chris Taylor. 1986. 'The Feminization of Temporary Workers: The Canadian Case.' *International Migration* (Geneva) 24 (December): 717–34.
Boyd, Monica, Chris Taylor, and Paul Delaney. 1986. 'Temporary Workers in Canada: A Multifaceted Phenomenon.' *International Migration Review* 20 (Winter): 929–50.
Boyd, Monica, John deVries, and Keith Simkin. 1994. 'Language, Economic Status and Integration: Australia and Canada Compared.' In Howard Adelman, Allan Borowski, Meyer Burstein, and Lois Foster, eds., *Immigration and Refugee Policy: Australia and Canada Compared*, Vol. 2. Carleton, Australia: Melbourne University Press, 549–77.
Brand, Dionne. 1984. 'A Working Paper on Black Women in Toronto: Gender, Race and Class.' *Fireweed* 19 (Summer/Fall): 26–43.
Brubaker, William Rogers. 1992. *Citizenship and Nationhood in France and Germany*. Cambridge: Harvard University Press.
Bussemaker, Jet, and Kees van Kersbergen. 1994. 'Gender and Welfare States: Some Theoretical Reflections.' In Diane Sainsbury, ed., *Gendering Welfare States*. London: Sage, 8–25.
Calliste, Agnes. 1989. 'Canada's Immigration Policy and Domestics from the Caribbean: The Second Domestic Scheme.' In Jesse Vorst et. al., eds., *Race, Class, Gender: Bonds and Barriers*. Toronto: Between the Lines, 133–65.
Canada, Employment and Immigration Advisory Council. 1991. *Immigrants and Language Training: A Report presented to the Minister of Employment and Immigration*. Ottawa: Canada Employment and Immigration Advisory Council.
Canada, Employment and Immigration. 1992. *The Live-in Caregiver Programme*. Catalogue No. MP43-270/1992. Ottawa: Minister of Supply and Services.
Carby, Hazel. 1982. 'White Women Listen! Black Feminism and the Boundaries

of Sisterhood.' In Centre for Contemporary Cultural Studies, *The Empire Strikes Back*. London: Hutchinson, 212–35.

Castles, Stephen. 1984. *Here for Good: Western Europe's New Ethnic Minorities*. London: Pluto Press.

Collins, Patricia Hill. 1989. 'The Social Construction of Black Feminist Thought.' *Signs* 14 (Summer): 745–71.

Daly, Mary. 1994. 'Comparing Welfare States: Towards a Gender Friendly Approach.' In Diane Sainsbury, ed., *Gendering Welfare States*. London: Sage, 101–17.

Dill, Bonnie Thorton. 1979. 'The Dialectics of Black Womanhood.' *Signs* 4 (Spring): 543–55.

Esping-Anderson, Gosta. 1990. *The Three Worlds of Welfare Capitalism*. Cambridge: Polity Press.

Federal Republic of Germany, Federal Minister of the Interior. 1988. *Survey of the Policy and Law Regarding Aliens in the Federal Republic of Germany,* vii 1-937-020/15. Bonn.

Foerster, Viktor. 1991–92. 'Immigration in the Federal Republic of Germany.' *The Social Contract* 2, 2: 87–89.

Gordon, Linda. 1990. 'The New Feminist Scholarship on the Welfare State.' In Linda Gordon, ed., *Women, the State and Welfare*. Madison: University of Wisconsin Press, 9–35.

Heyden, H. 1991. 'South–North Migration.' *International Migration* 29: 281–90.

Jenks, Rosemary E. 1992. *Immigration and Nationality Policies of Leading Migration Nations*. Washington: Center for Immigration Studies.

King, Deborah K. 1989. 'Multiple Jeopardy: Multiple Consciousness: The Context of a Black Feminist Ideology.' In Micheline R. Malson, Jean F. O'Barr, Sarah Westphal-Wihl, and Mary Wyer, eds., *Feminist Theory in Practice and Process*. Chicago: University of Chicago Press, 75–105.

Kline, Marlee. 1989. 'Women's Oppression and Racism: A Critique of the "Feminist Standpoint."' In Jesse Vorst et al., eds., *Race, Class, Gender: Bonds and Barriers*. Toronto: Between the Lines, 37–64.

Kuhnle, Stein. 1991. 'Welfare States.' In Vernon Bogdanor, ed., *The Blackwell Encyclopaedia of Political Science*. Oxford: Blackwell, 636–7.

MacKenzie, Ian. 1988. 'Early Movements of Domestics from the Caribbean and Canadian Immigration Policy: A Research Note.' *Alternate Routes* 8: 124–43.

Macklin, Audrey. 1994. 'On the Inside Looking In: Foreign Domestic Workers in Canada.' In Wenona Giles and Sedef Arat-Koc, eds., *Maid in the Market: Women's Paid Domestic Labour*. Halifax: Fernwood Publishing, 13–39.

Marshall, Thomas Humphrey. 1981. *The Right to Welfare and Other Essays*. London: Heinemann.

Meyer, Heinrich. 1987. 'SOMPEMI Country Report on FRG,' unpublished report.

Mishra, Ramesh. 1981. *Society and Social Policy,* 2nd ed. London: Macmillian.

O'Connor, Julia S. 1993. 'Gender, Class and Citizenship in the Comparative Analysis of Welfare States Regimes: Theoretical and Methodological Issues.' *British Journal of Sociology* 44 (June): 501–18.

Orloff, Ann Shola. 1993. 'Gender and the Social Rights of Citizenship: The Comparative Analysis of Gender Relations and Welfare States.' *American Sociological Review* 58 (June): 303–28.

Pateman, Carol. 1988. 'The Patriarchal Welfare State.' In Amy Gutmann, ed., *Democracy and the Welfare State.* Princeton: Princeton University Press, 231–60.

Quadagno, Jill. 1990. 'Race, Class and Gender in the U.S. Welfare System.' *American Sociological Review* 55 (February): 11–28.

Shaver, Sheila. 1989. 'Social Policy Regimes: Gender, Race and the Welfare State.' Paper presented at the Conference on Women in the Welfare State, University of Wisconsin, Madison, 19–22 June.

– 1990. 'Gender, Social Policy Regimes and the Welfare State.' Paper presented at the Annual Meeting of the American Sociological Association, Washington, DC.

Silvera, Makeda. 1983. *Silenced: Talks with Working Class West Indian Women about their Lives and Struggles as Domestic Workers in Canada.* Toronto: Williams-Wallace.

Stasiulis, Daiva. 1990. 'Theoretizing Connections: Gender, Race, Ethnicity and Class.' In Peter S. Li, ed., *Race and Ethnic Relations in Canada.* Toronto: Oxford University Press, 269–305.

Thornhill, Esmeralda. 1989. 'Focus on Black Women!' In Jesse Vorst ed., *Race, Class, Gender: Bonds and Barriers.* Toronto: Between the Lines, 26–36.

United Nations. 1979. *Trends and Characteristics of International Migration since 1950.* Department of Economic and Social Affairs, Demographic Study No. 64. ST/ESA/ser.A/64, New York.

– 1985a. *World Population Trends, Population and Development Interrelations and Population Policies,* Vol. 1, *Population Trends.* Department of International Economic and Social Affairs, Population Studies No. 93. ST/ESA/SER A/93, New York.

– 1985b. *World Population Trends, Population and Development Interrelations and Population Policies,* Vol. 2, *Population and Development Interrelations and Population Policies.* Department of International Economic and Social Affairs, Population Studies No. 93. ST/ESA/SER A/93.Add.1, New York.

de Wenden, Catherine. 1987. 'National Policies and Practices of Entry Control in OECD Member Countries.' Annex B in *Continuous Reporting System on Migration, SOPEMI 1986.* Paris: OECD.

Williams, Fiona. 1989. *Social Policy: A Critical Introduction.* Cambridge: Polity Press.

7

The Shift to the Market: Gender and Housing Disadvantage

GERDA R. WEKERLE

Housing is generally left out of current debates on the welfare state. It is also notably absent in discussions of women's changing relation to the state and from the literature on women's political activism.[1] Yet access to affordable housing is an integral part of social welfare, affecting women's life chances, their security, and their access to services. The high cost of housing and women's relative poverty means that women as a group have considerably more circumscribed housing options than men. Access to affordable housing of a minimum standard is viewed by many as a social right that should be guaranteed by the welfare state. Writing on comparative social policy, Wilensky (1965: xii) argued that 'the essence of the welfare state is government-protected minimum standards of income, nutrition, health and safety, education, and housing assured to every citizen as a social right.'

Housing plays a key role within the wider social welfare system. Women are particularly hard hit by cutbacks to social welfare which affect the amounts of funding available for housing. They are further disadvantaged by the retreat from state-funded social housing programs and by the privatization initiatives that curtail government intervention in the housing market through a reduction in the provision of social housing or in the level of regulation, including rent controls, housing standards, or zoning provisions. Through these reprivatization initiatives, federal and provincial governments in Canada are reversing postwar welfare state policies that were intended to ensure access to affordable housing for low-income Canadians. In this process, women are left to the private housing market, a housing market where they are subject to systemic gender inequalities in access to housing and to discriminatory treatment within the housing system. As social rights and entitlements within the welfare state continue to be renegotiated and cut back, an examination of the role of housing within the wider social welfare system and its impact on women is warranted.

The prevailing discourse on housing as defined by the neo-conservative agenda seeks to focus on individuals and their inability to pay for housing in the private market. In analysing the British housing system, Clapham et al. (1990: 57) argue that housing disadvantage should, instead, be viewed as an impaired ability to participate fully in society and to exercise the rights of citizenship. Instead of focusing on the characteristics of individuals that confer disadvantage, they argue that we must instead pay attention to the processes conferring disadvantage. In evaluating the Canadian housing system within the wider context of the welfare system that creates and reinforces gender inequalities, this perspective directs us to examine housing policies within both the primary market sector and in the secondary social housing sector to determine how women gain and lose in each. Current proposals to streamline the housing system are presented as gender-neutral changes which mask the potentially harmful impact on women in the Canadian housing system.

Initial research on gender and housing in Canada focused on women's disadvantage and structured inequalities in access to residential space (McClain and Doyle, 1984)) or on women's 'special needs' as single parents for social supports and community services (Klodawsky et al., 1985). A few studies have also begun to document how women are discriminated against and sexually harassed in the housing system (Bourbonniere et al., 1986; Novac, 1993, 1992a, 1992b). Detailed case studies also document women's mobilizations at the local level to obtain better living conditions in public housing (Christiansen-Ruffman, 1995) and their efforts to develop women's housing projects controlled by women (Wekerle, 1988; Wekerle and Novac, 1989; Wekerle and Muirhead, 1991, Wekerle, 1994; Yasmeen, 1991). Only recently have we seen the emergence of the beginnings of a feminist housing analysis which critiques the systemic basis for the absence of a gendered perspective in Canadian housing policy (Novac, 1990; Wekerle and Novac, 1991; Andrew et al., 1994) and the impacts on women of a housing system that perpetuates gender inequalities. This chapter addresses the ways in which the Canadian housing system is deeply gendered, producing and reproducing gender-based inequalities.[2] It focuses on several dimensions of housing. First, I discuss the Canadian housing system as part of the larger social welfare system which produces and reproduces gender-based inequalities. Second, I develop a profile of gender inequalities in access to housing and the gendered nature of housing need. Next, I examine the changing policies and discourse around housing which seek to sharply delimit governments' responsibility for housing supply programs that create affordable housing for low-income households and shift responsibility to the private housing market. The complex interrelationship between restructuring of social welfare programs, reductions in social spending, and impacts on women's housing is illustrated by the cutbacks in housing programs implemented by the neo-conservative government in Ontario. The provincial government's withdrawal from provincial responsibility for social housing and attempts to deregulate the housing market provide a current example of the interconnection between housing, social welfare, and women's equality. And finally, the chapter focuses on the initiatives of women's movement organizations to develop alternative housing options for women that are controlled by women.

A Gendered Housing System

The housing system forms an integral part of the social welfare system. It represents the way a society has decided to produce, allocate, and maintain a physical stock of buildings used as shelter. Housing has a dual focus: it provides shelter to citizens as well as a myriad of social entitlements, including varying levels of shelter subsidies associated with the locational benefits of living in a specific municipality and province. Access to different kinds of housing, according to Clapham et al. (1990: 13), 'mediates access to that wider range of employment opportunities and social rights.'

The housing system forms an integral part of the dual welfare system which differentiates private benefits based on the market economy (that is, employment) from direct subsidies through public programs directed at both housing construction and subsidies of low- and moderate-income households to reduce their housing costs. The primary sector is market housing, serving the 63 per cent of Canadians who are homeowners and those households in the higher end of the rental market. Taken together, they comprise approximately 80 per cent of the housing market (Hulchanski, 1993c). The secondary sector comprises the other 20 per cent of Canadian households living in lower cost rental housing of poor quality and in the non-market social housing sector which comprises only 4.8 per cent of the total number of occupied units in Canada

(Hulchanski, 1993c: 6). Households in the secondary sector tend to have more limited choice of housing options, and, in many cases, any housing benefits they receive are means-tested.

The state's major role in housing is indirect, and it is played out through fiscal policies which affect mortgage rates, taxation policy (for example, there is no capital gains tax on a principal residence), a mortgage insurance program which reduces the risk to banks, various programs directed to job creation, incentives for the housing industry, and some limited programs directed at consumers that subsidize or support home ownership.

Governments have often viewed housing as a way to prime the economy and create jobs through support of home ownership and construction. Hulchanski (1990) points out that during the recession of the mid-1970s, when housing construction starts fell, the federal government responded with new programs designed to assist home owners. In the early 1980s, when mortgage interest rates hit highs of more than 20 per cent, the federal government provided short-term subsidies for home owners. In 1992, during the recession, the federal government created a Home Buyers Plan to lower the minimum down payment on mortgages insured under the National Housing Act (NHA) to 5 per cent and allow potential home owners to use up to $20,000 of a Registered Retirement Savings Plan (RRSP) for a down payment.

Historically, the Canadian housing system has been organized primarily to provide state support to the private, corporate, market sector of the housing system with only residual support provided to the non-market sector of the housing system. In the past few years, even this residual support has been substantially cut back. Those groups in Canadian society that are not primarily home owners are largely excluded from this system of benefits based on private property ownership.

Home Ownership

Households who are homeowners have access to universal entitlements, such as the capital gains exemption. They are also entitled to security of tenure and good quality housing at a price they can afford (Hulchanski, 1993c: 5). As housing economist Marion Steele (1993: 42) points out, a major advantage of home ownership is its role in wealth accumulation and its favourable treatment by the tax system.[3] Housing is, in effect, 'domestic capital,' to use a term coined by Cedric Pugh (1990) – capital that can be sold, traded up or down, and passed on to the next gen-

eration. Home owners can also control their housing costs, by defer-
ring maintenance, for example, in ways that tenants cannot. And,
most importantly, home owners enjoy greater security of tenure: they
are not subject to landlords or landlord–tenant regulations, as tenants
are.

The overwhelming reason for women's low home ownership rates is
their low incomes. This is likely to be exacerbated by current mortgage
lending practices which restrict people to spending no more than 30 per
cent of their income on housing, even though they may be spending
more in private rental accommodation.[4] Although CMHC has reduced
the amount of the required down payment for NHA-insured mortgages
to 5 per cent, this does not go far enough to meet the constraints of low-
income households.

Family status also affects the likelihood of women owning their own
homes. In 1994, 79 per cent of women living with a spouse lived in an
owner-occupied house. Only 48 per cent of unattached female seniors
and 31 per cent of female lone parents owned their own homes (Almey,
1995: 28). Over the years, there have been indications that women have
more difficulty gaining access to credit than men. As there are no Canadian data on mortgage discrimination against women heads of households, particularly if they are single women, newly divorced, or
working in the secondary sector of the economy at part-time, contract,
or other forms of employment, these reports remain anecdotal.

In many rural areas and small towns, home ownership is the only
housing option; there is little or no rental housing. Given the structure of
the Canadian housing system, home ownership is often the only viable
option for households that need space for larger families and access to a
range of amenities and job opportunities. Canadian housing policies
have had a chequered history of support of home ownership for low-
income households.[5] This has a particular impact on single women and
women who are single parents, since they have the lowest home ownership rates of all groups. Housing policy has addressed a limited range of
options: either social assistance to subsidize the private housing market
or housing supply programs to create housing that is targeted to groups
with affordability problems. This ignores a wider range of policy
options, including policies that might maintain women as heads of families in their own houses if their income drops after a divorce or separation, or regulation directed at the lending policies of banks to make it
easier for women of low and moderate incomes to obtain home mortgages. Steele (1993: 58) argues that housing policy should include home-
ownership programs targeted to low-income households, many of

which are non-traditional families headed by women. Supporting the increase in a household's net worth through home ownership reduces the need for income supplements in old age.

Social Housing

Social housing programs directed at low-income households are means-tested; as household income goes up, housing allowances are reduced dollar for dollar, thereby eliminating any benefit or opportunity to save. This has meant that low income households can easily be locked into subsidized housing because of limited incomes. Provincial social assistance regulations do not allow households to save money to buy a house in the private market. Such savings could take the form of a segregated fund, like a registered home-ownership program, which would not be considered 'income.' Regulations for determining the income of social assistance recipients must also be re-examined. Single parents who receive lump sum payments in divorce settlements often feel forced to invest them in a house, so that this money is not treated as income. A more liberal interpretation of the regulations might allow these funds to be used for higher education, job retraining, or to be put into a registered home ownership fund to save for more adequate housing.

The 'housing problem' has been defined as primarily a problem of housing affordability. Governments in Canada have commonly used two types of programs to assist households experiencing housing affordability problems: income supplement programs directed at households and housing supply programs which subsidize the construction of buildings. In the province of Ontario, for example, households receive social assistance either through General Welfare Assistance (GWA) or Family Benefits Assistance (FBA). Each program is means-tested and includes a shelter allowance component in which the ceiling often does not meet actual housing costs.[6] Up to 40 per cent of households in Ontario receiving social assistance in 1992–3 were paying housing costs above these shelter ceilings, while many others lived in substandard housing in order to stay within the shelter ceilings (Ontario Ministry of Housing, 1993). A remarkable indication of the inadequacy of shelter allowance ceilings in social assistance programs is that an estimated 83,000 households in Ontario received both a shelter allowance and a subsidized unit in rent-geared-to-income housing that was also subsidized (Ontario Ministry of Housing, 1993).

Over the past decade, the social housing sector in Canada has been substantially restructured as program delivery and financing have devolved from the federal to the provincial governments. From the mid-1960s to the mid-1970s, the federal government played a major role in housing policy. In 1973 amendments to the National Housing Act created the Nonprofit and Cooperative Housing programs. This provided funding for new non-profit and non-profit co-operative housing projects sponsored by municipal housing agencies, non-governmental organizations (NGOs), and community and ethnocultural groups. A commitment was made to the creation of socially mixed housing projects, that is, publicly subsidized housing where low-income and moderate-income households would live side by side, in contrast to the high concentrations of poor people in public housing that had been previously built. However, this commitment to the creation of a strong social housing sector was quickly eroded by changes in the economy, strong and active lobbying from the housing industry, and political shifts to the right.

Under a Conservative federal government, commitments to funding for social housing were cut back in favour of a greater reliance on the market to provide housing. Non-profit housing expenditures were substantially cut from a peak of 31,000 units funded in 1980 to a quarter of that in 1992. In the same year, the federal non-profit cooperative housing program was entirely eliminated (Dreier and Hulchanski, 1993).

A major shift in Canadian housing policy were the agreements made between the federal and provincial governments that jurisdiction for housing should be exclusively under provincial jurisdiction, with the exception of the federal government's continuing responsibility for housing for First Nations peoples. This devolution of responsibility to the provinces has resulted in a patchwork of housing programs across the country, with some provinces, most notably Ontario, British Columbia, and Quebec, setting up their own housing programs to fill the gap when the federal government withdrew, while other provinces have done little to produce new social housing. Shifting jurisdiction for social housing from the federal government to the provinces means increasing disparity of access to social housing across the provinces and territories as each sets its own political priorities for social expenditures. These priorities can change quite dramatically with each election. For instance, the province of Ontario constructed 86,354 social housing units between 1985 and 1995, with another 18,000 units under construction in 1995 (Donovan, 1995). A Tory electoral victory in 1995 resulted in the reversal of the government's commitment to social housing and a greater reliance on the private market to meet shelter needs.

The gender-based inequalities created by the housing system become apparent when we analyse where women are located in terms of housing tenure and access to different housing options. The key to understanding women's disadvantaged position in the Canadian housing system is to recognize their underrepresentation in the market sector as consumers, producers, and investors and their over-representation in the secondary sector of the housing market.

The Gendered Nature of Housing Need: A Profile of Women's Disadvantage

In the mid 1980s, McClain and Doyle (1984) produced the first slim volume detailing the extent and nature of Canadian women's housing disadvantage. Since then, it has been difficult to build up a picture of the linkages between women's inequality in the social welfare system and in the housing system because comparisons of men's and women's housing circumstances were not routinely collected, analysed, or made publicly available by either CMHC or Statistics Canada. One outcome of lobbying by women's groups and feminist housing analysts has been the generation of new data on housing differentiated by gender categories.[7]

According to Munro and Smith (1989: 4), 'Gender differences in housing attainment express not only the reproduction of patriarchy but also the reproduction of labour relations and of social inequality more generally.' They emphasize the existence of clear links between the labour market and the housing system: ability to pay affects housing choice, location, and tenure; the segmented labour market means that women, who are predominantly low paid, in part-time employment, and have low earnings compared with men, experience disadvantages in the housing market. Despite increases in women's labour force participation, women constituted 58 per cent of the proportion of Canada's population living in poverty in 1994 (National Council of Welfare, 1994: 1). This has an impact on women's chances in the housing system where ability to pay affects the choice of housing, its location, and its tenure options.

In Canada living arrangements and housing tenure are closely connected to women's family status and income. In 1991 some 16 per cent of all families with children were lone-parent families headed by women (Statistics Canada, 1995). An estimated 658,000 elderly women lived alone (Statistics Canada, 1991). Poverty levels are high in both groups. In 1994, 57 per cent of lone-parent families with at least one child under 18 had incomes below the low-income cut-off (defined as 'the poverty line' by Statistics Canada) compared with 11 per cent of two-parent families (National Council of Welfare, 1996). Among all unattached women who lived alone in 1994, more than 44 per cent had incomes below the poverty line (National Council of Welfare, 1994).

Within the housing system, housing supplements and rent-geared-to-income (RGI) units are allocated on the basis of 'core housing need.' Criteria include affordability (households that spend more than 30 per cent of their income on housing); suitability (households with more than one person per room); and adequacy (households without basic sanitary facilities). In 1990, 32 per cent of all Canadian households were claimed to be in core housing need, although this was the situation of 56 per cent of lone-parent families who spent an average 47 per cent of their income on shelter costs (CMHC, 1993).

A high percentage of all Canadian households in core housing need are women. Woman-headed households are disproportionately renters: in 1990, for example, 66 per cent of all lone-parent families with children younger than 18 were renters (Statistics Canada, 1991). The majority of households in core housing need are renters rather than owners of housing, and two-thirds of these renters are lone-parent families (CMHC, 1993). Among renters, the most likely renter households to experience housing need are female led: lone parents or women living alone (both elderly and non-elderly; CMHC, 1994c). As table 7.1 shows, female heads of households who rent were more than twice as likely to be in core housing need as male heads, while lone parents were 10.9 times as likely to be in need as male-led, two-parent families.

The extremely low incomes of female-led renter households mean that they comprise a disproportionate 43.6 per cent of all households in core housing need, although they comprise only less than 16 per cent of all households. Their average income in 1990 was only $12,600, 29.6 per cent of the income of male-led households not in core housing need (CMHC, 1994c). Among women-headed households who are not in the labour force and depend on government payments for their major source of household income, between 60 per cent and 70 per cent are in core housing need, as indicated by table 7.2. This rises to a high of 74 per cent of all lone-parent households receiving social assistance. This parallels the situation in Britain where Clapham et al. (1990: 75) note that women are far more reliant than men on the public sector to meet their housing needs as a result of the combination of low incomes, insecure employment, and their periodic absences from the workforce to care for children and the elderly.

TABLE 7.1
Susceptibility to housing need and low income – selected renter households, 1991

Household group	No. of HHLDS. in housing need	Comparative data on the incidence of need	Low-income status (bottom quintile)
All female-headed renter households	507,000 39%	female heads were 2.4 times as likely to be in need as male heads	725,000 55%
Elderly (65+) (90% living alone)	175,000 46%	female seniors were 1.4 times as likely to be in need as male seniors	286,000 75%
Non-elderly a) Lone parents	160,000 49%	lone parents were 10.9 times as likely to be in need as male-led two-parent families (most of which owned)	187,000 58%
b) Women living alone	148,000 31%	female individuals were 6.9 times as likely to be in need as male-led two-parent families (mostly owners)	225,000 47%
c) Females sharing with others	25,000 19%	sharing, with either other unattached individuals or related family members, keeps housing need lower among this small group	27,000 20%

Source: Adapted from CMHC. 'Low Income, Labour Force Participation and Women in Housing Need, 1991,' Research and Development Highlights, Socio-economic Series, Issue 16, September 1994.

Furthermore, as women are increasingly represented in the secondary labour market of part-time work or non-standard work, this also contributes to their low incomes and creates core housing need. When women are able to obtain full-time employment, their level of housing need drops substantially (CMHC, 1994c).

These national averages mask the extreme hardship experienced by lone parents renting housing in cities with high housing costs. A comparison of housing costs relative to income of married women, lone parents, and single women living in the Census Metropolitan Area of Toronto in 1986[8] shows that lone mothers who rent, pay, on average, 65.3

TABLE 7.2
Households in housing need by labour force (LF) status and major source of income, 1991

Type of household	LF Status[a]/source income	Households in need (%)	Average income ($)	Average STIR[b] (%)
All non-elderly	Head not in LF	57	11,600	50
female renters	Head in LF	26	13,500	48
333,000	Gov't. payments	71	11,600	51
	Non-gov't payments	22	13,800	46
a) Lone parents	Head not in LF	66	12,900	49
160,000	Head in LF	35	14,800	44
	Gov't payments	74	13,200	48
	Non-gov't. payments	28	14,900	45
b) Women living	Head not in LF	50	8,200	55
alone	Head in LF	25	12,200	50
148,000	Gov't payments	71	8,000	58
	Non-gov't payments	22	12,700	48

[a]LF status refers to labour force activity at survey time.
[b]STIR stands for the household's shelter cost-to-income ratio.
Source: CMHC. 'Low Income, Labour Force Participation and Women in Housing Need, 1991,' Research and Development Highlights, Socio-economic Series, Issue 16, September 1994.

per cent of their income for housing compared with 31 per cent for those who own their own homes. Lone women are paying 50 per cent of income to rent housing and 33 per cent as home owners (Wekerle and Novac, 1991: 26). In Ontario only about 18 per cent of social assistance recipients live in some form of rent-geared-to-income housing; the majority of recipient households, 70 per cent of which are headed by a female single parent, must compete for market rental housing (Social Assistance Review Committee, 1988: 32).

Because women-led households are overrepresented among households in core housing need, they now predominate in all forms of non-market housing. An evaluation of public housing in Canada by CMHC (1990) shows that 62.2 per cent of all residents are women, primarily female single parents and elderly women. In public housing family projects (excluding seniors housing) there are five times as many single-parent families as in the general population of renters. Approximately half of all households living in public housing family projects are single-parent families. This pattern is repeated in the social housing that is managed by municipal non-profit housing agencies. A survey of tenants living in non-profit housing owned and managed by the city of Toronto, for example, showed that between 60 per cent and 70 per cent of all residents were women (Lapointe Consulting and Norpark Design, 1991).

The concentration of female single parents and elderly women in publicly subsidized social housing affects their choice of housing, its location, and access to a range of services and public goods, such as schools and transportation. Obtaining a unit in subsidized social housing may take years on a waiting list, years during which women and their families pay a disproportionate amount of income on substandard housing. Choice of location, type of unit, or neighbours is extremely limited for women dependent on the social housing sector, and women and children who are vulnerable often find themselves placed in housing projects in areas with high crime rates and drug problems, thus exacerbating their vulnerability. In addition, women living in public housing, in particular, are subjected to the rules and regulations of a housing bureaucracy that strictly defines who may live in a unit, restricts activities, such as home-based businesses, and limits the amount of income residents can earn and still be eligible to remain in a subsidized unit. These restrictions contribute to women's dependency and are considerably more stringent than those generally imposed in private housing markets. The combination of women's lower incomes and their more limited ability to compete for housing in the private market leads to their concentration in the social housing sector, a sector subject to cutbacks and welfare state restructuring. The Canadian housing system, as this discussion has shown, perpetuates and sharpens already existing gender inequalities.

Restructuring the Housing System

As part of the wider restructuring of the welfare state during the 1980s, the role of housing was redefined from meeting housing needs to a focus on housing as a commodity, with the emphasis on capital accumulation through home ownership (Clapham et al., 1990: 49). Conservative governments in Canada and Britain attempted to reorient and cut back direct spending on housing. In the housing field, the discourse on the marketplace now tends to dominate both the primary, private sector and the secondary, social housing sector. This dominant discourse has been heavily influenced by housing economists who tend to limit the discussion of housing policy to questions of cost effectiveness, specifically the costs of serving needy households with affordability problems. This ignores other housing objectives such as increasing the supply of affordable housing and producing housing that is suitable and adequate to the needs of households – the rationale for publicly funded housing programs since the postwar period.

Since the end of the Second World War, the federal and, increasingly, the provincial governments in Canada have taken on the role of the housing provider of last resort for the poor, elderly, Aboriginal peoples, and people with special needs who are not served by the market. As part of the wider discourse of welfare state restructuring, this positive role of the state in the provision of housing and intervention in housing markets to provide affordable housing for the most disadvantaged households has been drastically reduced. Under the guise of deficit reduction, both the federal and provincial governments have argued that the state can no longer afford either the capital costs of new social housing construction or the ongoing subsidies involved in paying for existing social housing programs.

Neo-conservative provincial governments argue that the government should not be in the housing business at all. Housing, in their view, is the legitimate domain of the private market. This reflects a substantial retreat from the postwar policy of housing as job creation and an acceptance of government responsibility to assure adequate and affordable shelter for Canadians with the lowest incomes. Reprivatization initiatives take different forms, including defining housing need as an income security issue rather than a shelter problem; the creation of shelter allowance programs to subsidize housing in the private sector; and the withdrawal of government funding from the social housing sector. Housing allowance programs, which 'top up' the amount of money a household has available for shelter costs have been proposed by provincial governments as a more efficient way to make housing affordable for the most needy. As Hulchanski (1993a: 1) noted: 'At first glance, the idea of shelter allowances is very seductive. The subsidy can be targeted to specific groups to cover the gap between rising rents and the ability to pay. Renters would receive a direct cash subsidy calculated on the basis of income and rent level. Monthly checks would then be sent to those tenants who qualify.'

Neo-conservative provincial governments in Ontario and Alberta have proposed shelter allowances as a replacement for government-funded housing supply programs. But shelter allowance schemes still assume that government retains a responsibility for meeting the shelter needs of the poor. Proposals to privatize public housing, which are being considered in the province of Ontario, assume that the government can divest itself of ongoing responsibility for meeting the shelter needs of low-income households and that the market will provide adequate and suitable housing. These proposals do not take into account low vacancy rates in cities, particularly for low- cost housing, and the many forms of discrimination that limit the range of housing options available to women and racial minorities (Novac and Associates, 1992a, 1992b; Hulchanski, 1993b; Canadian Press, 1993). Many low-income, women-headed households cannot compete for housing in the private market because of their extremely low incomes and lack of a credit rating. Recent studies show that mother-led families, women living alone, and households receiving social assistance are discriminated against in housing. Immigrant women and women from ethnocultural communities are subjected to dual discrimination based on gender and race (Novac and Associates, 1992a, 1992b). Disabled women also face double discrimination in the housing market. Expecting these groups to find housing in the private market ignores these experiences of discrimination faced by various groups of women.

The strategy of defining housing need as an income security issue rather than as a shelter problem is an attempt to reduce existing claims for government provision and to reprivatize housing needs talk so that 'the housing problem' is not a community-wide problem arising from a combination of affordability, inadequate standards, or suitability, the criteria built into the definition of 'core housing need.' Instead, the 'housing problem' is redefined as an individualized problem related solely to an individual's inability to pay market costs. In keeping with a neo-conservative agenda, making this shift from where the right to housing brings with it rights to a minimum standard of shelter positions housing discourse away from the social rights of citizenship to a discourse of property rights. Such a shift supports the proposals to eliminate the provincial housing programs which direct government subsidies to construct new social housing and, instead, favours subsidies to the private property industry which seeks higher profits and rent deregulation. Critics point out that shelter allowances neither encourage the construction of new affordable housing nor do they meet the needs of people living in substandard housing or those with special housing needs (Hulchanski, 1993a).

In the past, housing programs have been protected, to some degree, from cutbacks because they have been identified with economic growth. The housing sector, and government-financed social housing supply programs, have been viewed as an important driving force in creating new jobs in the private sector, both directly in construction and related trades and indirectly as the stimulus to the goods-producing sectors that depend on new housing construction. Housing programs that are defined as primarily social welfare programs serving dependent and low-income populations may lose the support of the wider public and even that sector of the housing industry that has benefitted from social housing construction during times of recession.

Scrapping social housing supply programs also eliminates the opportunities to create alternative models of community life which have been supported by non-profit housing programs since the mid-1970s. Non-profit housing cooperatives, for example, have provided an alternative to home ownership, not only for the poor, but also for middle-income residents. These mixed-income projects, serving both low- and moderate-income households, help to ensure that low-income households are not stigmatized or concentrated. Focusing on housing subsidies only for the poor, many of them single-mother-led families, restigmatizes these households and denies them wider community support. By eliminating non-profit housing programs, especially the non-profit housing cooperative programs, governments also eliminate potential sites of mobilization and coalition-building between low- and moderate-income households.

Reprivatizing Initiatives and Women's Housing Security: The Ontario Example

Policy shifts in the housing system frequently occur in isolation from changes in the social welfare system. However, the interconnection between the two systems is made visible by recent changes in the province of Ontario which is proceeding with restructuring initiatives that involve both housing and social welfare simultaneously. In addition, these cutbacks are affecting virtually every layer of the complex of policies that address housing. Since the election of a Conservative government, cutbacks and the elimination of housing programs have threatened the housing security of low-income women. Funding has been withdrawn from the non-profit housing sector, a form of housing that provided an alternative to both the market housing model and to public housing. As well, the provincial government has cut funding to oppositional movements and advocacy groups within the housing sector.

Cutbacks in social assistance have had direct effects on housing. Cuts in Ontario welfare payments (22 per cent) included cuts to the housing allowance component of social assistance benefits, resulting in less money available for housing that welfare recipients were already occupying. This has resulted in an increase in evictions (Small, 1996) and an increase in the numbers of mother-led families turning to hostels (City of Toronto, 1996).

Other policy changes to strengthen the private housing market will negatively impact women because they are disproportionately concentrated in the low end of the rental housing market. Ontario's rent control legislation, initially passed in 1975, will be phased out over time. As units become vacant, they will turn to market rents (*Globe and Mail*, 1996). Cutbacks to the social housing sector will also reduce the numbers of subsidized housing units. In 1996 subsidies to 3,000 rent-geared-to-income units were eliminated when the units become vacant (Wright, 1996).

There are also proposals to privatize public housing in the province, either by selling the housing off to private landlords or to existing tenants. Modelled after Margaret Thatcher's wholesale privatization of British public housing in the 1980s, this would mean a withdrawal of the provincial government from ongoing subsidies of low-income tenants' shelter costs and repair and maintenance costs of the 84,000 units of public housing in the province. These initiatives threaten the housing security of public housing tenants in the province, more than 60 per cent of whom are households headed by women.

The Ontario government has also withdrawn its funding for non-profit housing and non-profit housing cooperatives funded under provincial programs. Besides eliminating funding for 385 non-profit housing projects that had already been approved for funding, which would have provided subsidized housing, several projects specifically targeted to single parents and low-income, older women lost their funding. This constitutes a loss to groups of low-income women, single mothers, and women from ethnocultural communities who have utilized the province's nonprofit housing program to develop housing projects that specifically meet women's needs.

Cutbacks to social services budgets also eliminated funding for social service provision in transitional housing for battered women. Current changes force a reversion back to an earlier model where funding is provided only for basic shelter needs. The elimination of funding to advocacy groups within the housing sector also affects women's options to fight discrimination. This has made it more difficult for women as tenants, as public housing residents, or as users of shelters to make their voices heard concerning major changes to the housing system in Ontario.

While Ontario may be the first province to travel the path of serious retrenchment, housing programs in other provinces are also under threat. To cut public expenditures, publicly funded housing programs that have been in place since the 1940s (public housing) and the 1970s (non-profit housing) are being re-examined, restructured and, in some provinces, eliminated altogether. The emphasis is on the market to provide housing for all households, despite the postwar experience that poverty and a combination of poverty and discrimination severely constrains the options of many households, and particularly households headed by women, in the housing market.

Women's Housing Activism

Throughout the 1980s some women's groups, particularly women's service and advocacy organizations, added housing to their list of issues requiring advocacy because the women they served – homeless women, young mothers, women living in public housing, immigrant and minority women, and disabled women – had experienced housing discrimination and had difficulties in obtaining affordable housing. The National Action Committee on the Status of Women, for instance, formed a housing committee that was active in forwarding proposals concerning federal housing policies.

The devolution of responsibility for housing to the provinces in the 1990s has meant that women's organizing around housing has taken place at the provincial and local levels. One of the best known groups, Mothers United for Metro Shelter (MUMS) in Halifax, spearheaded local demonstrations and actions that resulted in changes in housing policies affecting women living in public housing in Nova Scotia (Wekerle, 1988; Christiansen-Ruffman, 1995). Locally based groups, such as the Young Mothers' Resource Group in Toronto, lobbied for equal access to affordable housing for young mothers. They initiated meetings with the provincial Ministry of Housing and the Attorney General's Department to identify potential solutions to the housing needs of teenage mothers who cannot compete either in the private housing market or in the public sector (Community Concern Associates, 1988; Rahder, Doyle and Associates, 1991).

The Ontario Association of Interval and Transition Houses (OAITH) has been an organized voice for abused women. The organization, which has included housing as one of its core issues for its annual lobby of the Ontario legislature, framed this problem in terms of housing rights: 'Shelter is one of our basic human rights which is denied when women are unable to leave their partners and live on their own. This means abused women have lost both their human right to safety and their human right to shelter' (OAITH, 1990). Over the years OAITH has highlighted the shortcomings of both social welfare provisions for housing and housing policies. They have argued that social assistance payments are too low to adequately pay for housing, and cutbacks on housing allowances have reduced entitlements. The organization also has highlighted the difficulty in finding housing for women leaving emergency shelters, because of their low incomes and need for supportive services and assistance with housing searches. Although a few shelters have had housing advocates on staff, many of these positions have largely been eliminated in recent years. As a coordinating body for sixty-seven women's shelters in the province of Ontario, OAITH has itself been dependent on provincial funding, funding that was cut in 1995 on the grounds that the government of Ontario was prepared to fund battered women's shelters, but not advocacy organizations, especially those that publicly opposed the government (Morsebraaten, 1995; Toughill, 1995; OAITH, 1995).

Besides engaging in housing advocacy, women's groups have also been actively involved as developers and producers of housing under various federal and provincial housing programs. Throughout the 1980s women's shelters across Canada developed housing labelled 'second stage,' 'transitional,' or 'next step' housing. In contrast to the few weeks available in shelters, second-stage housing provided a woman and her children with housing for six months to three years with related supportive services including child care, counselling, and assistance in finding employment (Wekerle, 1988; Peters, 1990; CMHC, 1994a). In addition, various women's organizations across the country developed permanent housing targeted to serving the needs of battered women and their children.

Since the early 1980s more than 100 women-initiated and women-managed housing projects have been developed across Canada. Traditional women's organizations, such as the YWCA, and newly formed groups of women representing the interests of Aboriginal women, single parents, older women, or ethnic minority women, obtained funding from provincial and federal programs that encouraged community organizations to develop non-profit and cooperative housing for low- and moderate-income households (CMHC, 1994b). For example, a group of low-income women developed a 56-unit housing project, Ujama, located in Scarborough, Ontario, targeted to women of colour and female-headed households. Another non-profit housing project was designed to meet the housing needs of Filipina domestic workers. Anduhyaun II, in Toronto, houses First Nations women and their children in a 45-unit building that incorporates counsellors, a certified teacher, and child-care. In Winnipeg, Payuk Inter-Tribal Cooperative has developed 47 housing units for First Nations single parents and their families. In the province of Quebec a number of projects were built to meet the housing needs of low-income women, including the Cooperative d'habitation 'Le Fil d'Ariane' in Montreal, which serves the housing needs of single parents. In Vancouver the Entre Nous Femmes Housing Society, established by a group of single parents, has built six non-profit housing projects for women and their children (Wekerle, 1988; Wekerle and Muirhead, 1991; Yasmeen, 1991).

These housing projects developed by women's groups are a visible expression of feminist practice. Women have banded together to build housing that meets the housing needs of women who have not been adequately served by the existing housing markets in either the private or social sectors: battered women with children, single parents, and elderly women (Wekerle, 1988; Wekerle and Muirhead, 1991). Besides providing much needed shelter, these women-initiated housing projects also offer alternate models for housing that addresses the multiplicity of women's needs. Predicated on a view of housing as more than basic shelter, many of the women's housing projects incorporated some form of supportive services, community supports, and opportunities to participate in the management of the housing environment. For example, the Women's Community Cooperative, a 47-unit building in Hamilton, Ontario, was created by a group of women who are growing old together and providing one another with mutual support. Projects like Jessie's Centre for Teenagers in Toronto innovatively combined services for teen mothers, a child care centre, and a classroom, with housing units for young mothers and their children on upper floors. Entre Nous Femmes, in Vancouver, entered into partnership with Van City, a credit union, to produce a housing project built on the air rights of the credit union that combines housing for women and children and for seniors. In a Canadian housing system, where women are usually housing consumers at best (if they own housing or can rent it on the housing market) or recipients of increasingly inadequate forms of housing assistance, the ability to shape and control their own housing environments is a singular experience for women.

Women's voices in affecting Canadian housing policy have been muted and raised only sporadically in trying to change specific policies or regulations. A critique of the gendered nature of housing policy and markets that began to develop in the early 1980s was silenced when responsibility for housing devolved to the provinces, and governments began to withdraw funding from housing programs in favour of the marketplace. As the housing affordability crisis intensified for women throughout the 1980s, women's social service agencies were confronted with the choice of continuing and expanding their advocacy role to pressure government for more housing or to take up new funding opportunities and actually develop housing themselves. Given the daily crises experienced by women in obtaining housing, and the seeming inability of existing agencies to serve their client groups, small locally based women's service agencies often felt they had no choice but to become direct housing providers (Wekerle and Muirhead, 1991; Wekerle and Novac, 1991). This meant that women's housing advocacy work was redirected from public opposition to government policies to working within existing programs to obtain funding to build housing targeted to various groups of women. Developing housing is specialized and time-consuming. For many women's organizations, this project consumed five to ten years of their time and countless volunteer hours. Housing advocacy received less attention.

By the mid-1990s, cutbacks in social spending also jeopardized the remaining programs to produce social housing in those provinces (Ontario, Quebec, and British Columbia) that had continued to fund non-profit housing provincially. The pendulum has swung away from housing supply programs that offer opportunities for women's groups to develop locally based solutions to meet women's housing needs. In seeking to institute more market-based housing programs that are narrowly targeted to households in economic need, governments ignore the fact that housing is far more than basic shelter. Governments also do not address the essentially gendered nature of the housing system as a whole which reflects and perpetuates gender inequalities. The current restructuring of the welfare state is occurring at the same time as governments are withdrawing support for housing programs that have been targeted to low- and moderate-income households. Cutbacks in both these systems jeopardize Canadian women's housing security. Yet housing has effectively dropped off the agenda of national women's organizations. In the current mobilizations against cutbacks in the social welfare system, women's movements must also incorporate housing as part of their agenda for action. Otherwise, Canadian women will bear a disproportionate share of the costs of the current restructuring of the housing system.

Notes

1 The extent to which welfare rights groups have neglected housing as part of their agenda is reflected in the fact that the National Anti-Poverty Organization (NAPO) and the Canadian Council on Social Development (CCSD) only added housing to their agenda in the 1990s. The National Action Committee on the Status of Women (NAC) started a Housing Committee in the mid-1980s, but housing has not had much visibility as an issue in recent years.

2 Munro and Smith (1989) introduce the concept of the gendered nature of the housing system, and this is developed further in Clapham et al. (1990).

3 Marion Steele (1993: 54) reports that, especially in times of inflation, home-ownership results in a build-up of net worth. For those of about average income, when income is held constant, homeowners' net worth is more than five times as great as that of renters.

4 In 1992 a Collingwood, Ontario, woman filed a human rights complaint against a trust company alleging that its mortgage policies discriminate against single mothers and social assistance recipients because it would not grant her a mortgage on the grounds that she would pay more than 30 per cent of her income in housing costs (Aarsteinsen, 1992).

5 Throughout the 1940s, 1950s, and 1960s, Canada Mortgage and Housing Corporation took the view that its assistance to low-income families should be confined to rental housing (Steele, 1993: 46). In the early 1970s there was a large-scale subsidy program to encourage homeownership by low-income households. As mortgage rates skyrocketed and delinquencies rose, this program was eliminated in 1978. Since that period assistance to homeowners has been more indirect and targeted to moderate and higher income groups.

6 In 1993, in the province of Ontario, the shelter allowance component of social assistance was paid to 500,000 households at a cost of about $2.5 billion annually. Because of the cap on the Canada Assistance Plan, about 85 per cent of

this expenditure was funded by the province (Ontario Ministry of Housing, 1993).
7 Individual researchers have been required to purchase census data at high cost and to do custom analysis to extract data on gender and housing. Statistics Canada has convened a user group, including representatives of women's organizations, to discuss possible changes to the 1996 census. CMHC has included a gendered analysis of the relationship between housing, women's labour force participation, and incomes using data collected for the fedederal and provincial housing agencies on housing costs (CMHC, 1994c).
8 Based on analysis of 1986 Statistics Canada Public Use Sample Tapes, Individual File.

References

Almey, Marcia. 1995. 'Housing and Household Facilities,' in *Women in Canada: A Statistical Report*, 3rd ed. Statistics Canada. Ottawa: Ministry of Industry.

Andrew, C., P. Gurstein, F. Klodawsky, B. Moore-Milroy, J. McClain, L. Peake, D. Rose, and G.R. Wekerle. 1994. *Canadian Women and Cities*. Ottawa: CMHC.

Aarsteinsen, B. 1992. 'Bank Accused of Bias Against Single Mothers.' *Toronto Star*, 14 December.

Bourbonniere, L., M.Cote, J. Desrosiers, E. Ouellet. 1986. *Discrimination, Harcelement et Harcelement Sexuel*. Montreal: Comité Logement Rosemont.

Canada Mortgage and Housing Corporation (CMHC). 1990. *Public Housing Program Evaluation Report*. Ottawa: Program Evaluation Division.

– 1993. 'Families, Children and Housing Need in Canada, 1991.' *Research and Development Highlights*, Issue 12.

– 1994a. *Draft Final Report on the Evaluation of the Project Haven Program and Update on the Next Step Program Activities*. Ottawa: Program Evaluation Division.

– 1994b. *Women in Canada's Cities: Housing and Urban Services- Position Paper of Canada*. Ottawa: International Relations Divison.

– 1994c. 'Low Income, Labour Force Participation and Women in Housing Need, 1991.' *Research and Development Highlights*, Issue 16.

CMHC. 1994d. *The State of Canada's Housing*. Ottawa: CMHC.

Canadian Press. 1993. 'Ontario Rights Body Censures Landlords Over 30% Rent Rule.' *Toronto Star*, 23 February.

Christiansen-Ruffman, L. 1995. 'Womens Conceptions of the Political: Three Canadian Women's Organizations,' in M.M. Ferree and P.Y. Martin, eds., *Feminist Organizations: Harvest of the New Women's Movement*. Philadelphia: Temple University Press, 372–93.

City of Toronto. 1996. 'Tracking the Impacts of Provincial Cuts.' Report to City Neighbourhood Committee, Toronto, 26 February.

Clapham, D., P. Kemp, and S.J. Smith. 1990. *Housing and Social Policy*. London: Macmillan.

Community Concern Associates. 1988. *Young Mothers Resource Group Housing Study*, Toronto: Young Mothers Resource Group.

Donovan, K. 1985. 'Housing Millions Down the Drain.' *Toronto Star*, 20 May.

Dreier, P., and J.D. Hulchanski. 1993. 'The Role of Nonprofit Housing in Canada and the United States: Some Comparisons.' *Housing Policy Debate* 4, 1: 43–81.

Globe and Mail. 1996. Editorial. 'Last Rites for Rent Control,' 8 June.

Hulchanski, J.D. 1990. 'Canada's Incomplete Housing System: The Need to Address the Failure of the Rental Housing Market'. Toronto: School of Social Work, mimeo.

– 1993a. 'Here We Go Again: The Latest Lobby for a National Shelter Allowance Program.' *Canadian Housing*, Fall.

– 1993b. *Barriers to Equal Access in the Housing Market: The Role of Discrimination on the Basis of Race and Class*. Toronto: Ontario Human Rights Commission.

– 1993c. 'Trends in the Federal Role in Housing and Urban Affairs in Canada,' in *Papers Presented at Tri-Country Conference*. Washington, DC: Fannie Mae Office of Housing Policy Research.

Klodawsky, F., A. Spector, and D. Rose 1985. *Single Parent Families and Canadian Housing Policies: How Mothers Lose*. Ottawa: CMHC.

Lapointe Consulting Inc and Norpark Design. 1991. *Cityhome 40/40/20 Targeting Plan Evaluation Study of Tenant Satisfaction and the Effects of Social Mix*. Toronto: City of Toronto Housing Department.

McClain, J., with C. Doyle. 1984 *Women and Housing: Changing Needs and the Failure of Policy*. Ottawa: Canadian Council on Social Development and Lorimer Publishers.

Monsebraaten, Laurie. 1995. 'Ontario Cuts Funds to Women's Shelters.' *Toronto Star*, 2 November.

Munro, M., and S. Smith. 1989. 'Gender and Housing: Broadening the Debate.' *Housing Studies* 4, 1: 3–17.

National Council of Welfare. 1996. *Poverty Profile 1994*. Ottawa: Minister of Supply and Services.

Novac, S. 1990. 'Not Seen, Not Heard: Women and Housing Policy.' *Canadian Woman Studies* 11, 2: 53–7.

– 'Boundary Violations: Sexual Harassment within Tenancy Relations,' in H. Dandekar, ed., *Shelter, Women and Development: First and Third World Perspectives*. Ann Arbor: Wahr Publishers, 68–73.

– and Associates. 1992a. *Sexual Harassment of Tenants: Legal Remedies, Problems and Recommendations*. Toronto: Ontario Women's Directorate.

– 1992b. *The Security of Her Person: Tenants' Experiences of Sexual Harassment*. Toronto: Ontario Women's Directorate.

OAITH. 1990. *Balance the Power: Background Report, Annual Lobby*. Toronto: OAITH.

– 1995. 'Ontario's PC Government is Locking the Doors to Freedom for Abused Women and Their Children: Let's Take Back the Keys,' 20 November.

Ontario Ministry of Housing, Housing Policy Branch. 1993. *Social Assistance Shelter Allowance and Rent Geared-to-Income Subsidies*. Toronto: Ontario Ministry of Housing, 14 January.

Peters, E. 1990. *Second Stage Housing for Battered Women in Canada*. Ottawa: CMHC.

Pugh. C. 1990. 'A New Approach to Housing Theory: Sex, Gender and the Domestic Economy.' *Housing Studies* 5, 2: 112–29.

Rahder, Doyle, and Associates. 1991. *Non-profit Housing: Issues for Young Families*. Toronto: Young Mothers Resource Group.

Small, Peter. 1996. 'More Stay Longer at Hostels, Staff Find.' *Toronto Star*, 4 May.

Social Assistance Review Committee. 1988. *Transitions: Report of the Social Assistance Review Committee*. Toronto: Ontario Ministry of Community and Social Services.

Statistics Canada. 1991. *Family Incomes: Census Families 1991*. Cat. 13-208.

– 1995. *Women in Canada*, Cat. 89-503 E. Ottawa: Ministry of Industry.

Steele, M. 1993. 'Incomes, Prices, and Tenure Choices,' in J. Miron, ed., *House, Home and Community: Progress in Housing Canadians 1945-1986*. Montreal: McGill-Queen's Press, 41–63.

Toughill, Kelly. 1995. 'Foes Say Tories Threatened Them,' *Toronto Star*, 2 November.

Wekerle, G. R. 1988. *Women's Housing Projects in Eight Canadian Cities*. Ottawa: CMHC.

– 1991. *Gender and Housing in Toronto*. Toronto: Equal Opportunity Division, City of Toronto.

– 1994. 'Responding to Diversity: Housing Developed by and for Women.' *Canadian Journal of Urban Research* 2, 1: 95–113.

– and S. Novac. 1989. 'Developing Two Women's Housing Cooperatives,' in K.Franck and S. Ahrentzen, eds., *New Households, New Housing*. New York: Van Nostrand Reinhold, pp. 223–40.

– and B. Muirhead. 1991. *Canadian Women's Housing Projects*, Ottawa: CMHC.

Wilensky, H.L. 1965. 'The Problem and Prospects of the Welfare State,' in H.L.

Wilensky and C.N. Lebeaux, eds., *Industrial Society and Social Welfare*. New York: Free Press, v–lii.

Wright, Lisa. 1996. 'Not-for-profit Housing to Use Market Rents.' *Toronto Star*, 12 April.

Yasmeen, Gisele. 1991. 'Mutual aid Networks in Two Feminist Housing Co-operatives in Montreal,' MA thesis, Department of Geography, McGill University.

PART III

Women's Work and the State

8

Double, Double, Toil and Trouble ... Women's Experience of Work and Family in Canada, 1980–1995[1]

MEG LUXTON AND ESTER REITER

By the prickling of my thumbs,
Something wicked this way comes:
Macbeth, act 4, scene 1[2]

When it held power (1990–1995), the New Democratic Party (NDP) government in Ontario initiated discussions about ways to significantly reduce the 900,000 workers in the public sector. Arguing that the provincial debt and deficit were reaching crisis proportions, they proposed to lay off workers, roll back wages, reduce services to the public, and increase taxes while continuing to privatize a range of services from medical laboratories to land registry offices and roads. While such neo-liberal monetarist attacks on the welfare state have been the major political strategy for the conservative national governments in Britain, the United States and Canada since the early 1980s, the NDP collusion had a particularly bitter edge to it. The social democratic NDP both federally and provincially, in Ontario, had been the party of the organized labour movement, a promoter of basic feminist demands, and the political voice of those arguing for the growth and development of a welfare state. Thus, feminists in Ontario faced a severe attack on women's rights led by a government formed by the only political party which had advocated feminist goals and which had a number of prominent cabinet ministers who, prior to the election, were leaders and activists in the women's movement.

There was an irony in being forced to defend services and working conditions which only a few years before feminists had been attacking as insufficient and inadequate, and in resisting the dismantling of the welfare state by the very party which had fought so hard for it. But as women from Canada learned at the Fourth United Nations Conference and NGO Forum on women in Beijing, China, in August–September 1995, this experience in Ontario was not unique. Women from 186 countries reported that, internationally, the status of women has sharply deteriorated since the early 1980s as a direct result of international neo-liberal political and economic policies called 'structural adjustment' or 'restructuring.' These policies favour big business profit making at the expense of the standards of living of the majority of people. They support privatization, that is, turning over to private businesses a whole range of enterprises previously run in the collective public interest by government; these include such things as railways, electricity, student loans, garbage collection, and medical laboratory testing in hospitals. These neo-liberal policies are based on reducing or eliminating government regulations that protect national economies, environments, and health and safety, or that reduce major inequalities among people. They depend on creating conditions that force people to work for low wages with few benefits and little security. Since the 1980s most governments have adopted these policies; the Ontario experience under the NDP was typical. In this chapter we examine women's experiences of work and family between 1980 and 1995, arguing that this period of erosion of the welfare state subjected women to a double jeopardy, both as workers whose jobs were threatened and as people who used the threatened services.

While recognizing that women's experiences are significantly different, depending on their social locations as shaped by class, race, ethnicity or national origin, sexual orientation, or ability, we argue that throughout the twentieth century, in general, women's experiences of work and family have been centrally influenced by their attempts to deal with the competing demands of paid employment and domestic labour. In analysing the experiences of women juggling paid and domestic work, feminist activists and researchers argued that the majority of women work a double day, putting in one day's work at their paid workplace and a second at home. They also noted the way prevailing divisions of labour in both paid employment and family households trap most women in a 'double ghetto' and a 'double bind' (Luxton, 1990; Armstrong and Armstrong, 1984; Gannage, 1986). In this chapter we argue that the reciprocally related international policies in both the management of economies – 'structural adjustment' or 'restructuring' – and changes in the jurisdiction of nation states are putting women in a double jeopardy by intensifying their toil in both spheres. At the 1988 Canadian Labour Congress National Women's Conference, president Shirley Carr noted the impact of privatization on women: 'This attack from the right threatens all Canadians. Canadian women are doubly affected and often targeted by the privatizers. Not only is there a high percentage of women employed in public services, but they are also the recipients of more social programmes. As these are cut back or eliminated, women are hit the hardest' (Carr, 1988: 10).

But women are being hit not only by increased workloads. The public service has been particularly important as the main source of secure employment for women, and women in public sector unions have played a significant role in articulating and fighting for basic feminist demands. In addition, many of the rights and services of the welfare state, such as education, health care, or economic subsidies, have been the only available resources to relieve some of the worst tensions between paid employment and unpaid domestic labour. Thus, the efforts to privatize are also an attack on unionized women workers and their capacity to fight for women's rights such as pay and employment equity, parental leaves, regulations protecting women from racial discrimination, sexual harassment, discrimination on the basis of sexual orientation, and a range of other protections and gains for women both in the paid workplace and at home. This erosion of the unions means trouble for women's strength in the labour movement and for the organizing capacities of the women's movement.[3]

Paid Employment, Domestic labour, and the Sexual Division of Labour

The organization of capitalist employment, on the one hand, and of family households and domestic labour, especially child care, on the other, has resulted in a situation where the demands of one are contradictory to the demands of the other. In the early twentieth century the tension between the two spheres was mediated by the predominant sexual division of labour in marriage, where women as housewives and mothers did domestic labour and men as breadwinners did paid labour. Because household technology was limited, and there was no communal organization of services, housework was very labour intensive. At the same time, because women tended to have numerous children spread out over many years, child care responsibilities were intensive. As a result, to maintain an adequate standard of living, most households required a full-time person at home to do the cooking, cleaning, laundry, and child care.

While the majority of households depended on the male breadwinner's earning, the wage of the principal male earner in Canada was rarely adequate to sustain a family household. Male workers often fought for a 'family wage,' which promised married women some economic security, but only the most powerful unions were able to win such wage rates. The difference between the man's wage and the cost of survival was made up by various combinations of wage labour, income-generating activities, and intensifying the domestic labour of other household members. Thus, working-class households depended on children's earnings and expected children to contribute to the collective effort. Wives and other non-wage earners contributed by earning money in the informal economy and stretching incomes through unwaged labour (a mix of entrepreneurial sales and services and piecework such as taking in laundry, sewing, or boarders, peddling household products such as eggs, or running small businesses or stores out of the house). Most jobs in the informal economy were consistent with domestic roles and reinforced them, thus perpetuating the notion that women could extend family income by being good wives and loyal family members. Such work also tied women to networks of kin and neighbourhood activities that in turn tied family households into the social and economic life of a community.

The assumption that only men were the legitimate wage earners increased wives' dependency on husbands, thus providing an intrafamilial basis for women's oppression. Despite a situation where most women had always engaged in some form of income-generating activities, and a changing reality in women's formal involvement in paid labour, the dominant ideology persisted that women *should* marry and that marriage meant that women *should* work full time in their homes providing unpaid labour for their husbands and children. Even when employers preferred to hire women, they often felt compelled to defend their practices because the belief in a male breadwinner was so deeply entrenched (Parr, 1980). Employed women were subject to a certain degree of discrimination explained in terms of nuclear family, male breadwinner ideologies (Coontz, 1988: 292–321). Male unionists in the first half of the twentieth century often responded to employers' practices of hiring women at lower wages by insisting that women had no place in the paid labour force. Few chose the alternative of protecting male jobs by insisting on equal pay for the women (White, 1993).

Women's Paid Employment: Job Ghettos and Wage Inequalities

The assumption that women would be homemakers permeated socialization practices and educational systems with the consequence that
women were discouraged from obtaining the educational or training
credentials which would enable them to qualify for many jobs (Gaskell
and McClaren, 1987). The difficulties women have had both in obtaining
the education and training necessary to apply for paid work and in getting hired have limited women's employment opportunities. The hiring
practices of many workplaces prevented married women from holding
paid work; state regulations either explicitly prevented married women
from holding civil service jobs, or more generally made such employment difficult. In addition, a whole range of social conventions took for
granted that married women would work at home; those who had paid
employment were punished with varying degrees of intensity. The limitations on women's employment opportunities and their restricted earnings encouraged women to marry and to stay married. The assumption
that women should and would have husbands to support them was
used to justify the fact that employed women were restricted to certain
occupations ('women's work') thought to resemble the type of work
they were supposed to do in the home and that women were paid about
half of what men were paid.[4]

However, despite such constraints, the increased participation of
women in paid labour has been one of the most significant social
changes of the twentieth century. As table 8.1 shows, in 1901, 14 per cent
of all women were in the formal labour force, making up 13 per cent of
the total labour force. By 1995, 57 per cent of all women (compared with
73 per cent of all men) were in the formal labour force, making up 45 per
cent of the total labour force (Statistics Canada, 1995b). Most significantly, there has been an increasing trend of married women combining
responsibility for domestic labour with paid employment. By 1980 the
majority of married women were employed outside the home. By 1994,
63 per cent of women with children under 16 years of age and 56 per
cent of women with children under 3 years were in the paid labour force
(Statistics Canada, 1995a). Over two-thirds (68 per cent) of employed
women with children under 6 years of age worked full-time in 1991 (Statistics Canada, 1992d). The number of women who marry and then
work as housewives their whole life is rapidly decreasing. Simultaneously, increasing numbers of women, on leaving school, work for pay
until retirement. Thus, we find that fully 80 per cent of women between

TABLE 8.1
Canadian labour force participation rates of all men, all women, and married women,
1901–1995

Year	All men (%)	All women (%)	Married women (%)	Women as % of total labour force
1901	78.3	14.4	–	13.3
1911	82.0	16.6	–	13.3
1921	80.3	17.7	2.2	15.4
1931	78.4	19.4	3.5	16.9
1941	85.6[a]	22.9[a]	3.7	24.8
1951	84.4	24.4	9.6	22.0
1961	81.1	29.3	20.7	29.6
1971	77.3	39.4	33.0	34.4
1981	78.7	52.3	51.4	40.8
1991	75.1	58.5	61.7	45.4
1995	72.5	57.4	61.4	45.1

Population ≥ 15 years
[a]Includes those in active service
Sources: Statistics Canada, Historical Labour Force Statistics, 1995b, Cat. No. 71-201;
Labour Force Annual Averages Cat. No. 71–529; Women in Canada Cat. No. 89503E, 78;
1961 Census 94–536; 1991 Census 93–324; F.H. Leacy (ed.) 2nd ed. of M.C. Urquart (ed.)
and K.A.H. Buckley (assistant ed.), Historical Statistics of Canada (Toronto: Macmillan,
1965), 107–23.

the ages of 20 and 50 years of age were in the paid labour force in 1991
(Statistics Canada, 1993a). For immigrant women, the rates were comparable, although women of Aboriginal origin had a lower overall labour
force participation rate of 40 per cent in 1986 (Statistics Canada, 1990:
191).

Correlated to changing patterns of women's paid employment are
dramatic demographic changes. Women began marrying later, having
fewer children, and having them at a later age. In 1961 the age of first
marriage for women was 22.9 years; by 1990 it had gone up to 26 years.
Similarly, the age at which women had their first baby increased. In 1971
70.9 per cent of women having their first baby were between the ages of
20 and 25, while only 11.5 per cent of women doing so were between 30
and 34. In contrast, in 1988 only 48.1 per cent of women had their first
babies when they were between 20 and 25, while 22.3 per cent of women
did so when they were between 30 and 34, an increase of 94 per cent
(Statistics Canada, 1991b: Table 4).

The steady increase in women's labour force participation rates was

TABLE 8.2

Comparison of incomes for families (without children under 6 years of age) when the wife is/is not in the paid labour force, 1961–1988

Year	Average family income wife not in labour force ($)	Average family income wife in labour force ($)	% Greater income for family with wife in labour force
1961	5,652	6,387	13.0
1969	8,637	10,769	24.7
1971	9,424	11,136	18.2
1975	15,124	20,557	35.9
1982	28,902	41,062	41.1
1988	36,600	57,000	55.9

Source: Statistics Canada. *Income distributions by Size in Canada*, Cat. No. 13-207, various years. 1961 statistics from Jenny Podoluk, *Incomes of Canadians* (Ottawa: Dominion Bureau of Statistics, 1968), 132, cited by Larry Patriquin, 'The Changing Nature of Social Reproduction in Canada,' unpublished paper, York University, Toronto, April 1991.

related to a variety of other factors as well. As compulsory schooling kept children out of paid labour, their capacity to contribute to household earnings declined and their prolonged economic dependency increased their parents' expenses. With changes in household costs, particularly with the dramatic increase in the amount of money needed for taxes, housing, and heating, it became harder for people to meet their needs by intensifying their labour at home. Instead, they needed more cash, and so the economic necessity for married women's employment became more widespread. Their capacity to take on paid work was increased by the growth of consumer goods and services. The development of household technologies such as washers and dryers and consumer goods such as prepared foods potentially reduced the amount of housework and made those tasks remaining easier to do. The availability of a range of services outside the home such as day care, nursing homes, and restaurant meals gave household members greater flexibility in the ways they organized domestic labour. Most significantly, the growth of the clerical, sales, and service sectors, and particularly the public sector, created a demand for workers, so women were able to find employment (Marchak, 1987).

The importance of women's income to their family households has steadily increased throughout the century. Table 8.2 compares the

TABLE 8.3
Earnings of wives as a percentage of total income in dual-earner families, 1967–1992

1967	1985	1989	1990	1991	1992
26.4	28.1	28.7	29.4	29.9	30.7

Source: Statistics Canada, Cat. No. 13–215.

TABLE 8.4
Average earnings of women and men, 1971–1994, selected years

	Full-time, full-year workers			All earners		
	Women ($)	Men ($)	Ratio (%)	Women ($)	Men ($)	Ratio ($)
1971	21,449	35,953	59.7	13,557	28,926	46.9
1976	25,603	43,294	59.1	15,911	34,077	46.7
1981	25,265	39,639	63.7	16,800	31,323	53.6
1986	25,879	39,329	65.8	17,587	30,597	57.5
1991[a]	27,847	39,992	69.6	18,754	30,474	61.5
1993	28,580	39,572	72.2	19,145	29,754	64.3
1994	28,423	40,717	69.8	19,359	31,087	62.3

1971–1991 in constant 1991 dollars.
[a]The apparent reduction in the gap between women's and men's wages actually reflects a decline in men's earnings.
Source: Statistics Canada, Earnings of Men and Women 1994. Cat. No. 13–217 (Ottawa: Minister of Industry, 1995), Table 1.

incomes of families (without children under 6 years of age) when the wife was and was not in the paid labour force during the period when married women's labour force participation increased significantly. However, despite the dramatic increases in women's participation in the paid labour force and the increased significance of women's wages in family households (see table 8.3), serious discrepancies between male and female wages persist. Women generally are concentrated in low-paying jobs and receive 60 per cent to 65 per cent of the wages paid to men (White, 1993: 64). Women's earnings have consistently lagged behind men's earnings. As table 8.4 shows, while the figures are most dramatic when total earnings are considered, even looking only at full-time, full-year workers, there is considerable discrepancy.

Women's Double Day

As increasing numbers of women have entered the paid labour force, the sexual division of labour has shifted somewhat, but the fundamental incompatibility between paid labour and domestic labour remains. For the most part, because of the intimate association of women with domestic labour, and especially child care, it is women who most directly confront that incompatibility and whose lives are most immediately shaped by it.

Widespread complaints and study after study have shown that regardless of their paid employment, women retain primary responsibility for work in the home (Luxton 1990; Michelson, 1985, 1988; Bourdais et al., 1987). On any given day, 83 per cent of employed women spend an average of 2.25 hours a day on housework, compared with just 50 per cent of employed men who spend an average of 1.75 hours a day. The kinds of chores women and men do are different: 78 per cent of women had the sole responsibility for meal preparation, and 77 per cent for cleaning and laundry, while men tended to devote their time to activities such as outdoor maintenance that are usually more discretionary and do not need to be done regularly: 72 per cent of employed men took care of home repairs and outdoor clean-up (Statistics Canada, 1992d: 4).

Overwhelmingly, the activities and social relations of caregiving are women's responsibility. In 37 per cent of all families where both parents or the lone parent were employed women had heavy child care responsibilities (Lero et al., 1992). Mothers continue to spend more time on primary child care activities than fathers, and mothers remain responsible for the majority of the household chores at the same time. Despite years of organizing efforts by child care coalitions and the labour movement, Canada has no national child care system. Responsibility for preschool child care is left to individual parents and thus usually to women. There is a dramatic shortage in licensed child care spaces. For example, of those who relied on non-parental care arrangements in 1987, 49 per cent experienced some problems maintaining reliable, affordable care with which they felt secure (ibid.). In 1991 there were 2.2 million children 12 and younger requiring care for at least 20 hours per week, but only 15 per cent of these children could be serviced by licensed care arrangements (Health and Welfare Canada, 1991). In many families, the parents either arrange their paid employment so that one of them can always be available for the children or do paid work at home so they can be with the children while working.

General health care is also seen as women's responsibility. Even when employed full-time, 73 per cent of women surveyed by the Canadian Advisory Council on the Status of Women, reported that household health care was solely their responsibility (Heller, 1986). This is particularly true with respect to care for the elderly, sick, and/or disabled, and Canada has a growing population of elderly people. As Canadians live longer, women's elder care responsibilities are increasing. In addition, there are an estimated 2.3 million younger disabled adults in Canada in 1991, and these people live in private households as well. Of the 16 per cent of employees providing care to an elderly, disabled, or infirm family member, 60 per cent of the women reported primary responsibilities for the care, compared with 26 per cent of the men (MacBride-King, 1990). In a 1992 survey of 5,000 workplaces, fewer than one-fourth of the population (24 per cent) had neither child care or elder care responsibilities (Canadian Aging Research Network, 1992).

Thus, the studies document what most women know is the case. Experience of work–family conflict is common, and women report higher levels of this conflict compared with men. As might be expected, single mothers experience more tension than their married counterparts, and women who work for pay part-time experience less tension (Lero, 1991). Those who have both children and other dependent family members to look after have the most difficulty (MacBride-King, 1990). As a result of these activities, labour force participation and productivity are affected. Parents leave jobs, turn down job offers, reduce working hours, worry about their children while they are at work, and refuse overtime work. Mothers are three times more likely to be so affected than fathers (Lero et al., 1992). Absences connected with family-related responsibilities are considerably higher for women than for men, and employed mothers with preschoolers lose twice as many work days as women without children in this age range (Akyeampong, 1992). Women hold a disproportionate share of jobs in non-standard employment, part- time and/or part of the year; 25.4 per cent of all employed women worked part-time in 1991, making up 70.4 per cent of the part-time labour force (Statistics Canada, 1993c).

Women and Public Services

The growth of the welfare state in Canada in the period after 1945 until the early 1980s was important in transforming women's experiences of work and family. As women entered the paid labour force, some found relatively secure employment in jobs produced by the socialization of services which were formerly provided, if at all, in family households, for example, in nursing homes or child care centres. In turn, the provision of those services, to a limited extent, relieved household labour of the pressure to provide them at home. These programs, such as day care for elderly people, were based on a notion of shared responsibility and community reflected in the establishment of universal standards guaranteeing minimum rights and a notion of citizenship that included access to social services (Barlow and Campbell, 1995).

The introduction of universal medical care programs between the late 1950s and mid-1960s resulted in a considerable expansion of hospital and other related health care services. For example, in 1966, the federal government instituted the Medical Care Act extending public health insurance to cover physicians' fees. During the same period, regional development programs, the Canada and Quebec Pension plans, and the Canada Assistance Plan were introduced. Other services and programs such as education, unemployment insurance, housing, and transportation were greatly expanded (Daniel and Robinson, 1985). The federal government established a system of tax transfers and cash grants to cover 50 per cent of the operating costs. These cost-sharing arrangements remained in place until 1977, when the federal government converted this cost sharing to a system of cash payments and tax transfers to the provinces for health and education under the Established Program Financing Act.

As a result of this growth in public sector services, employment in this sphere almost doubled between 1960 and 1979, growing from 1.3 million workers (comprising 22 per cent of all employed people) to 2.4 million workers (representing 24 per cent of all employed people). During this period, the population increased from about 17.8 million to 23.6 million. Thus, while the private sector has always been the major source of employment, the public sector grew from about 27 per cent to about 31 per cent of total employment. By 1979 government employment as a percentage of total employment was the highest it has ever been. Table 8.5 documents the growth during the period when this rapid expansion took place (1962–79). Public schools were the largest single public sector employer, followed by public hospitals, and federal and provincial governments. The majority of these workers were women.

As women entered paid work in increasing numbers, the sexual division of labour at home did not alter dramatically. However, the development of services in the public sector, to a limited extent, assisted women

TABLE 8.5
Public and private sector employment in Canada during the period of
public sector expansion, 1962–1979

Total employment	1962	1979
Private sector	4,606,000	7,831,000
Total public sector	1,268,000	2,435,000
Public schools	254,000	661,000
Public hospitals	210,000	420,000
Federal government	200,000	348,000
Provincial government	139,000	334,000

Source: The Conference Board of Canada Employment Growth in the
Public Sector 1960–1979 Executive Bulletin No. 12, May 1985.

in meeting their responsibilities in paid and domestic work. Thus, while
there is no necessary reason why child care, care for the elderly, and
services for the physically handicapped and disabled are considered
'women's issues,' because of the sexual division of labour, women have
benefited more than men from the provision of such services. The universal provision of a monthly Family Allowance payment to mothers,
while never enough to support a child, was nevertheless often the only
money that non-wage earning mothers had in their own names
(National Council of Welfare, 1987). More importantly, it symbolized a
public recognition that raising children is not a private hobby, but a vital
social activity which benefits the whole society.

In a similar way, while state services played a role in mitigating the
contradictory demands on women, they also laid the basis for understanding the work of looking after people differently. Not just children,
but anyone needing special care – the disabled, the ill, old people, in
fact, the general well-being of the population was recognized as a social,
rather than an individual responsibility. The principle of universal entitlement to such benefits and services as family allowance payments and
medicare was understood as important for several reasons. It eliminated
a costly layer of bureaucracy and arbitrary moral judgments distinguishing deserving from non-deserving recipients of services. The tax
system was widely considered to be a simpler, more equitable way of
redistributing income between those who have more than they need,
and others who are poor, even though the taxation system has always
benefited corporate interests more than those in need (McQuaig, 1987).
Other features of welfare state provisions such as mothers' allowance
paid to mothers of young children without male support, or cushions
against unemployment, retraining, some subsidized housing, and wel-

fare which offered protection to both women and men, were all important in loosening women's dependence on individual men.

Thus, the growth of the welfare state created conditions in which
women made considerable gains in promoting equality for women.
They won improvements both in pay and working conditions in the
paid work sphere and in increased state support for relieving some of
the burdens of the double day. The various public sector unions, both
federal and provincial, played a vital role in facilitating both efforts.

Women's Unionization in the Public Sector

The major advances that women have made in achieving concrete gains
in paid employment have been through the union movement. As
nurses, teachers, civil servants at the federal and provincial levels,
municipal workers, and employees in schools and hospitals all joined
unions, the impact on the organized labour movement and on advancing the interests of women has been profound. Women's massive
increases in unionization occurred in the 1960s with the unionization of
the public sector. In 1962 the percentage of women in all unions was 16.4
per cent; in public sector unions the percentage of women was 29.4 per
cent. This increased steadily so that by 1979 women were 29.3 per cent
of all union members, but they were almost half of public sector unions
– 49.4 per cent. By the early 1990s women made up 40 per cent of all
union members in Canada: 62.3 per cent of union members employed in
public administration, health, and education, and 13.4 per cent of all
other industries (Statistics Canada, 1992c). In 1990, 71 per cent of the
female union membership worked in either educational services, health
and social services, or public administration. Thus, most unionized
women are to be found in these public sector occupations.

The right to bargain collectively in large workplaces has made the
most difference in improving wages and working conditions in
women's paid jobs. In fact, unionization has been an effective form of
pay equity for women. In 1987 union hourly wages on the whole were
22 per cent higher than non-union wages for both male and female
workers. However, while women's average hourly wages were only 71
per cent of men's, in unionized jobs, women's hourly wages were up to
85.3 per cent of men's. In 1988 the average weekly earnings for women
clerical workers, the largest single occupational category for women,
were 30 per cent higher for those who were unionized (White, 1993: 65,
87). The only occupations in 1991 where women's annual earnings

exceeded $30,000 (that is, the average earnings of men) were teaching, medicine and health, and management and administration. The first two are highly unionized, and largely female, while the third encompasses a wide range of duties in different industries. Unionized workers receive much better benefits than non-union workers. For example, while 62 per cent of unionized workers received maternity leave benefits, only 33 per cent of non-union workers did. Similarly over twice as many (83 per cent as opposed to 40 per cent) unionized workers had a workplace pension plan (Statistics Canada, 1992a: 93). Thus, it is not only the 'pink collar ghetto' or the resemblance to women's traditional responsibilities that is responsible for low wages, but often the inability to organize and bargain collectively.

Unions have also played an important role in winning other work-related benefits, many of them of direct interest to women. Unionized workers receive better coverage than non-union members on a whole range of benefits such as pensions, vacations, workers' compensation, sick leave, and paid holidays. While minimal maternity leaves were variously granted by provincial legislations and then funded through the federal unemployment insurance program, unions fought to extend and improve maternity leaves. In 1979 the Quebec Common Front first negotiated far more generous provisions (100 per cent paid leave for a longer period than the legal minimum). In 1981 the Canadian Union of Postal Workers went on strike for six weeks to become the first national union to win similar maternity provisions (White, 1990: 149). By 1992 almost one-half of all unionized workers had such provisions. Thus, 49.1 per cent of unions provide pay for maternity leave beyond that covered by Unemployment Insurance, while 63.9 per cent have provisions for adoption leave. Contract provisions related to domestic and family responsibilities that extend coverage beyond the legislated minimums have also been included in many union contracts. For example, over 30 per cent of union contracts provide for extended parental leave; 29 per cent have some provisions for paid family illness leave (Labour Canada, 1992). While the fight to include same-sex spouses, in gay or lesbian couples, for benefit coverage is still a contentious one, public sector unions have been among the most supportive of these claims.

Public sector unions have also led in the struggle to win support for a range of issues of particular concern to many women. Contract language offers public sector workers much better protection than their private sector counterparts against discrimination, sexual harassment, health and safety risks, and work reassignments. It provides for better arrangements for flexible hours, benefits for part-time workers, and training for disabled workers.[5]

There has been a close connection between the women's movement and women activists in the labour movement. Many activists from the women's movement in the early 1970s who got unionized jobs brought their activism as feminists to the labour movement. They have fought, on the one hand, to improve the situation of women inside unions and, on the other, to mobilize the union movement to fight for general feminist demands. To support women's struggles inside unions, women organized pan-union groups, such as Organized Working Women in Ontario and Saskatchewan, which encouraged women to speak up in their workplaces and unions, to take on positions of responsibility in their unions, and to make their unions take up women's issues. Women also organized women's caucuses and committees at various levels of the union movement from locals to the Canadian Labour Congress.

As they developed such bases inside the labour movement, trade union feminists played an important role in mobilizing labour's support for the political struggles of the women's movement around equity issues. Particularly in the national and government service unions in the public sector, where there are large concentrations of women, education and union policies on issues of concern to women has been strongest. Public sector unions including the Canadian Union of Public Employees (CUPE), the Public Service Alliance of Canada, and the Ontario Public Service Employees Union (OPSEU) have taken the initiative in supporting employment equity policies that challenge the inequities in hiring of all women, and women and men who are visible minorities, disabled, and Aboriginal peoples. Where ten years ago sexual harassment was not an issue, now union education on the subject is quite extensive, and in some unions it is dealt with as a violation of human rights, and attempts are made to deal with it both within the union movement and at the workplace. Some unions, such as the Canadian Auto Workers, have taken up issues of homophobia and sexual orientation, developing support for their gay and lesbian members, for example, in bargaining for same-sex benefits. The union movement has also supported more general feminist issues. For example, both the Ontario Federation of Labour and the Canadian Labour Congress now support women's rights to legal, safe, and available abortions and have called for a national child care plan including free, universal, quality child care. Provision of child care at union educationals is now a common practice. What these examples illustrate is the way in which the unions generally and the public service unions, in particular, have been a major force in advancing feminist demands and improving women's situations.

The Erosion of Good Jobs for Women

Fair is foul, and foul is fair:
Hover through the fog and filthy air.
Macbeth, act 1, scene 1

By the early 1990s the impact of the neo-liberal agenda was starting to show up in national trends. By the end of 1991 the steady increase in labour force participation for women that has occurred since the end of the Second World War came to a halt when the rate actually fell for the first time in decades. Between January 1992 and January 1993 the participation rate of women decreased by 2.3 per cent, as discouraged workers left the labour force when they could not find jobs. More insidiously, the wage gap between men and women seemed to be narrowing in 1991. However, this was not because of the growing equality of women. Instead, it was caused by the fact that young men, in particular, had suffered serious declines in their earning abilities. In 1991 the average earnings of men under 24 years of age were considerably below the average: men 20 to 24 years of age earned $14,165, more than $15,000 less on average than all men earned, and $4,000 less than all women. Young women had an even harder time, earning just $11,920 per year. While these figures include students, who only want part-time employment, they also reflect the fact that many young people are unable to find full-time work (Statistics Canada, 1993c). In 1994 the wage gap increased for the first time in thirty years; for every dollar a man earned, a woman working for pay full-time, full- year, earned 70 cents, 2 cents less than in 1993 (*Toronto Star*, 20 December 1995: A1).

There is a changing distribution of jobs in Canada. Employment growth has become skewed, so that there are now a few highly skilled, well-compensated jobs, and many unstable, relatively poorly paid jobs. The only types of jobs which are increasing are part-time and in the service sector where traditionally young women are employed. These are typically short-term work, temporary-help agency work, and own account self-employment, sometimes as relatively well-paid consultants, but more frequently in the informal sector, in occupations such as chip- wagon operators, news-stand owners, typing at home, and so on. Earnings of such workers tend to be lower than those of workers employed by others, and there are rarely any benefits (Economic Council of Canada, 1990). Such individualized occupations offer virtually no opportunity for collective education or organizing. It is very difficult for such workers to unionize.[6]

The impact on women's employment is illustrated by the recent changes in women's practices around part-time employment. Forty-nine percent of women worked less than a full-time, full-year basis from 1989 to 1991. Their average earnings fell by 8 per cent in that two-year period, averaging $8,890 in 1991. Thirty-six percent of women earned less than $10,000 a year (not enough to support even one person at poverty level), compared with 23 per cent of men (Statistics Canada, 1993b). The single most important reason for women working part-time has been reported as 'did not want full-time work,' although the number reporting that they could not find full-time jobs has been growing. While women over 45 years of age continue to report that they work part-time because they do not want full-time work, in January 1993 the most important reported reason for part-time work among women aged 25 to 44 years was listed as 'could only find part-time work.' In 1994, 34 per cent of all female part-time workers indicated that they wanted full-time employment but could not find it (Statistics Canada 1995a: 66). This reflects the high unemployment rate for both men and women, and a wage distribution where well-paid, full-time jobs are becoming increasingly scarce.

The impact of the changing political and economic agenda on the public service sector is particularly insidious. Federally and provincially, governments have identified their debts and deficits as reasons to reduce their operations. For example, soon after the Conservative government took power federally in 1984, there were cuts to transfer payments to the provinces which are responsible for providing these services. The rudimentary provisions for day care previously made under the Canada Assistance Plan are endangered. Funding for welfare, health, and post-secondary education to the provinces has been steadily cut. Simultaneously, eligibility for Unemployment Insurance (since July 1996 called Employment Insurance) has been restricted, while unemployment remains high. The Canada Health and Social Transfer (CHST) Act, which the Liberals implemented in the spring of 1996, proposed eliminating all federal transfers to the provinces by the turn of the century.

The different levels of government have reduced government services and spending through a variety of activities ranging from lay-offs and cutbacks to privatization. At the federal level, the Canadian Union of Postal Workers and CUPE documented cases of the contracting out of services ranging from garbage collection to cleaners. Predominantly female operations such as clerical, cleaning, and data processing occupations are often the first to be contracted out (Bakker, 1992). Thus, once again, women workers are among the most vulnerable and the most seriously exploited.

Both the labour movement and the feminist movement have argued that these reductions are not part of an economic strategy to reduce the debt and deficit, but a political attack on working people and the gains that they have made over the past several decades in Ontario. For example, a joint study by the Ontario Provincial Service Employee Union activists and the Management Board of the Ontario government found that in one eighteen month period, $900 million was spent by the government on private contractors. The union maintained that reducing the public service is not so much a cost-saving exercise as a redistribution of jobs from the public to the private sector. They also pointed out that some of the areas considered for privatization, such as land registry information and computer databases give the private sector undue control over public policy. When entire groups of workers are removed from the civil service, pay and employment equity initiatives are seriously weakened, even if the workers remain unionized. Since the 1995 change in Ontario labour law implemented by the Progressive Conservative government of Mike Harris, public service workers have been stripped of their successor rights which means that they lose their union rights, if their jobs are privatized. In addition, the process of getting certification as a union is now more difficult (OPSEU, 1995).

The provisions of the welfare state are also being undermined in many of the services provided to help care for people. Since the late 1970s there has been an effort to deinstitutionalize services in a number of areas such as homes for the physically or mentally disabled. In this arena there has been an overlap of the anti-state sentiments of those favouring citizen participation and self-management with the neo-conservative aims of downsizing government. Thus, government policy statements have been able to use this idea of shifting services from the institution to 'the community' as a justification for privatization. Even when such services remain in the non-profit sector, there are serious implications in the proliferation of fee-for-service contracts between the government and the non-profit sector. As unconditional grants are replaced by contracts, the ability of these voluntary agencies to reform, advocate, and innovate is seriously curtailed (Mishra et al., 1988). Thus, this form of privatization makes agencies accountable not to the service consumers, but to government bodies, and so rather than fostering the debureaucratization that is so appealing, critics maintain that the noxious features of institutional service delivery will devolve onto the private sector (Ismael, 1988). Inevitably, such services become less available, their costs increase, and the pressures on women to increase their unpaid domestic labour increases.

Thus, women's labour provides a double benefit for business interests. As paid workers, women remain a source of cheap labour. Privatization, which involves a lower rate of unionization for women, thus downgrades the wages of working women. With the decline in services, the assumption is that women will pick up the slack and intensify their unpaid caring duties for children, sick, incapacitated, or unemployed family members.

Challenges

For a charm of powerful trouble,
like a hell-broth boil and bubble.
Macbeth, act 4, scene 1

The welfare state was never able to dissolve the profound contradictions between unpaid and paid work responsibilities of women, nor did legislation or formal policy serve to eliminate discrepancies between male and female workers or even equalize treatment of women workers. Thelma McCormack (1990) maintains that the policies for the establishment of this state in the post–Second World War period, a mixed economy with a strong state-managed social insurance component, lacked a gendered consideration of the role of women in the paid labour force or a clear understanding of the changes in Canadian family structures. In the current period, when the welfare state is under attack, feminists face a contradictory challenge. We continue to develop critiques of the welfare state, while at the same time fighting hard to defend what exists from efforts to dismantle it. Its defence is vital for women. As unpaid workers, with the decline in services, the assumption is that women will pick up the slack and intensify their caring duties for children, sick, incapacitated, or unemployed family members. At the same time, despite criticisms that such ideas are crazy or utopian, or just too expensive, our fight against the neo-conservative agenda demands a revitalized feminist vision. Without such a vision, we remain stuck with accepting the inevitability of measures that are both anti-feminist and harmful to women.

Our consideration of the current situation leads us to a number of large questions, more easily asked than answered. Some of them have been part of feminist debates for many years; others are newly posed. The most basic questions centre on the nature of capitalist market economics, contemporary international economic policies, and national accounting systems. Feminists, as activists and as theoreticians, have challenged governments about the necessity of military expenditures which threaten the life of the planet. Why are these considered 'productive,' while life-nurturing domestic labour is not?[7] What would measures of gross domestic product look like if the object being assessed were the well-being of people instead of the rate of accumulation of capital? What would the world economy look like if it were organized, not for capital accumulation, but for socialized markets geared to meeting human needs (Elson, 1988)? Why is it that when governments do their accounting, institutions and services with tangible benefits – parks, roads, schools, and medicare – are counted as expenditures rather than assets and investments, but privately owned buildings and services, no matter what their purpose or how limited their accessibility, can be counted as assets and investments? Thus, by definition, only the private sector can create wealth, while the public sector is seen as the wasteful spender of that wealth. There is something quite flawed in the definitions, if the conclusions are so topsy-turvy.

As the Canadian government moves away from indivisible benefits – those decisions made for the common good such as clean air, water, equal access to education, justice, and peace – towards providing the support systems for private capital and promoting privatization, it justifies its actions on the basis of certain economic necessities. Social programs must be cut to reduce the debt and deficit. But as social action groups, the women's movement, and the labour movement have pointed out, we need to question established truths.

Thus, we need to question the premises of neo-liberal economics which argue that overly expensive public services are the cause of the debt and deficit, and that eliminating both must take precedence over jobs, health, child care, and education. This is presented as an argument about efficiency and affordability, when it is really a political and moral argument. As Fraser and Gordon (1994: 309–36) note, those who must rely on stingy government programs rather than the sale of their labour to an employer or a male breadwinner, no matter how abusive, are considered to be morally deficient. In the last half of the twentieth century we managed for a few decades to create a society in which everyone, male and female, of all ages and backgrounds was supposed to matter. We are all citizens with social rights – to health care, education, and a reasonable standard of living. How did the language become so quickly transformed from 'citizen' part of a collectivity, to one of 'customer,' the isolated individual in the marketplace (McQuaig, 1995; Saul, 1995)?

We need to consider the relationship between the women's movement, feminist demands for state-regulated reforms, and the possibilities and limits of state reformation. The pressures of the women's movement, both outside and inside organized unions, were influential in promoting state legislation such as human rights, maternity leave, and job and pay equity. Now that the state is dismantling these provisions, the importance of the political heart of these issues is once again in the fore.

Notes

1 An earlier version of this essay was presented at the Social Policy Research Centre in New South Wales, Australia. We acknowledge the support of the Canadian Government Programme for International Research linkages (PIR1). We thank Julia O'Connor, Department of Sociology, McMaster University, Hamilton, Ontario, and Sheila Shaver of the Social Policy Research Centre Centre in New South Wales for bringing together researchers from Canada and Australia
2 The quote 'Double, double, toil and trouble' is chanted by the three witches in William Shakespeare's play *Macbeth*, act 4, scene 1. While the phrase nicely captures the issues this chapter addresses, we also appreciate the symbolism of the three witches who might also represent women in the home, women as workers, and women as activist feminist troublemakers.
3 The Ontario Provincial Service Employees Strike in early 1996 was a significant counter-example. There was unprecedented unity between the public and private sector unions in opposition to the policies of the Conservative Harris government. Women as leaders, women as union members, and women's issues were at the forefront of this resistance.
4 The argument has often been made that female occupations such as child care, for example, are so low paying because they resemble women's unpaid work. However, there are some problems with this analysis. It could be maintained

that other highly skilled occupations, diagnosing and treating illnesses, or assisting in childbirth for example, also resemble what women were tradition- ally expected to do in the home. It seems that who has a monopoly over the jobs is also a relevant consideration, as well as the collective organization of the occupation.

5 Pradeep Kumar, 'Collective Bargaining and Women's Workplace Concerns,' in Linda Briskin and Patricia McDermott, eds. *Women Challenging Unions* (Tor- onto: University of Toronto Press, 1994, pp. 207–30.

6 But not impossible. The International Ladies Garment Workers Union has suc- cessfully organized about sixty-five homemakers into an association with legal affiliation to the ILGWU.

7 We think of the activities of women's peace groups such as Voice of Women in Canada, Women Strike for Peace in the United States, or the long occupation by the Women of Greenham Common in England. Marilyn Waring (1990) raised these issues in her criticisms of the United Nations System of National Accounts.

References

Akyeampong, E. 1992. 'Absences from Work Revisited.' *Perspectives* 4, 1: 47–53.

Arat Koc, S. 1990. 'Non-Citizen Domestic Workers and the Crisis of the Domestic Sphere in Canada.' In M. Luxton, H. Rosenberg, and S. Arat Koc, eds., *Through the Kitchen Window: The Politics of Home and Family.* Toronto: Garamond, 81– 103.

Armstrong, Hugh, and Pat Armstrong. 1984. *The Double Ghetto.* Toronto: McClel- land and Stewart.

Bakker, Isa. 1992. 'Pay Equity and Economic Restructuring.' In Judy Fudge and Pat McDermott, eds., *Just Wages.* Toronto: University of Toronto Press, 254–80.

Barlow, Maude, and Bruce Campbell. 1995. *Straight Through the Heart.* Toronto: HarperCollins.

Barrett, Michele, and Mary McIntosh. 1982. *The Anti-Social Family.* London: Verso.

Bourdais, C., P.J. Hamel, and P. Bemard. 1987. 'Le Travail et L'ouvrage: Charge et Partage des Toches Domestiques chez les Couples Québecois.' *Sociologie et Societies* 19, 1, 37–55.

Briskin, L., and P. McDermott. 1993. *Women Challenging Unions.* Toronto: Univer- sity of Toronto Press.

Briskin, L., and L. Yanz. 1983. *Union Sisters.* Toronto: Women's Press.

Burke, M.A. 1991. 'Implications of an Aging Society.' *Canadian Social Trends.* Sta- tistics Canada, Cat. No. 11-008E, Spring.

Canadian Aging Research Network (CARNET). 1992. 'Work and Eldercare

Research Group of CARNET.' Unpublished analyses, September, University of Guelph.

Carr, Shirley. 1988. Keynote Address, Canadian Labour Congress 6th Biennial National Women's Conference, 'The Equality Challenge: Taking Hold of our Future: Speeches, Workshop Report,' 27–30 January, Ottawa, 10.

Coontz, Stephanie. 1988. *The Social Origins of Private Life*. London: Verso.

Daniel, Mark J., and William E.A. Robinson. 1985. 'Employment Growth in the Public Sector 1960–1979.' Executive Bulletin No. 12, May, Conference Board of Canada.

Economic Council of Canada. 1990. *Good Jobs, Bad Jobs: Employment in the Service Economy*. Ottawa.

Ecumenical Coalition for Economic Justice (selected issues). *Economic Justice Report*. Toronto: ECEJ.

Elson, Diane. 1988. 'Market Socialism or Socialisation of the Market.' *New Left Review* 172 (Nov.–Dec.): 3–44.

Franklin, Ursula. 1990. *Real World of Technology*. Toronto: CBC Enterprises.

Fraser, Nancy, and Linda Gordon. 1994. 'A Genealogy of Dependency: Tracing a Keyword of the U.S. Welfare State.' *Signs* 19, 3: 309–36.

Frideres, James. 1988. *Native Peoples in Canada*, 3rd ed. Toronto: Prentice-Hall.

Gannage, Charlene. 1986. *Double Day, Double Bind: Women Garment Workers*. Toronto: Women's Press.

Gaskell, Jane, and Arlene McClaren. 1987. *Women and Education: A Canadian Perspective*. Calgary: Detsilig.

Health and Welfare Canada. 1991. *Status of Day Care in Canada*. Ottawa: National Child Care Information Centre, Child Care Programs Division, Health and Welfare Canada.

Heller, A. 1986. *Health and Home: Women as Health Guardians*. Ottawa: Canadian Advisory Council on the Status of Women.

Ismael, J.S. 1988. 'Privatisation of Social Services.' In Jacqueline S. Ismael and Yves Vaillancourt, eds., *Privatisation and Provincial Social Services in Canada*. Alberta: University of Alberta Press, 1–11.

Labour Canada. 1992. Bureau of Labour Information Collective Agreement database, January, Ottawa.

– Women's Bureau. 1990. *Women in the Labour Force*, 1990–1 ed. Ottawa.

Leacy, F.H., ed. 1965. *Historical Statistics of Canada*. 2nd ed. of M.C. Urquart, ed., and K.A.H. Buckley, assistant ed. Toronto: Macmillan.

Lero, D.S. 1991. 'Risk Factors in Work/Family Conflict: Preliminary Findings from the National Child Care Survey.' Paper presented to the Statistics Canada Workshop on Work Life, Family Life: Innovations in Human Resource Management, 6 September.

– A.B. Pence, H. Goelman, and L. Brockman. 1992. *Canadian Child Care Survey.* Ottawa: Statistics Canada.

Luxton, Meg. 1990. 'Two Hands for the Clock.' In M. Luxton, H. Rosenberg, and S. Arat Koc, eds., *Through the Kitchen Window: The Politics of Home and Family.* Toronto: Garamond, 39–55.

MacBride-King, J. 1990. *Work and Family: Employment Challenge of the 90s.* Ottawa: Conference Board of Canada.

Marchak, Pat. 1987. 'Rational Capitalism and Women as Labour.' In H.J. Maroney and Meg Luxton, eds., *Feminism and Political Economy.* Toronto: Methuen, 197–212.

McCormack, Thelma. 1990. *Politics and the Hidden Injuries of Gender.* Ottawa: CRIAW.

McQuaig, Linda. 1987. *Behind Closed Doors.* Toronto: Viking Press.

– 1995. *Shooting the Hippo.* Toronto: Viking.

Michelson, William. 1985. *From Sun to Sun: Daily Obligations and Community Structures in the Lives of Employed Women and Their Families.* Totowa, NJ: Rowman and Allanheld.

– 1988. 'The Daily Routines of Employed Spouses as a Public Affairs Agenda.' In L. Tepperman and J. Curtis, eds., *Readings in Sociology: An Introduction.* Toronto: McGraw-Hill Ryerson, 400–9.

Mishra, R., G. Laws, and P. Harding. 1988. 'Ontario.' In Jacqueline S. Ismael and Yves Vaillancourt, eds., *Privatisation and Social Services in Canada.* Calgary: University of Alberta Press, 119–39.

National Action Committee on the Status of Women (various years). *Review of the Situation of Women in Canada.* Toronto: NAC.

National Council of Welfare. 1987. *Tax Expenditures: Who Gets What.* Ottawa.

OPSEU Education and Campaigns Department. 1995. 'Bill 7 Kills Jobs.' OPSEU, Toronto, October.

Parr, Joy. 1990. *The Gender of Breadwinners: Women, Men and Change in Two Industrial Towns.* Toronto: University of Toronto Press.

Petersen, Jim, and David Rappaport. 1991. 'Contracting Out and Privatization in the Ontario Public Service: A Preliminary Report for Internal Discussion.' Unpublished paper, Ontario Public Service Employees Union, Toronto, September.

Reiter, Ester. 1991. *Making Fast Food.* Montreal: McGill-Queen's University Press.

Saul, John Ralston. 1995. *The Unconscious Civilization.* Toronto: Anansi.

Seccombe, Wally. 1992. *One Thousand Years of Family Formation.* London: Verso.

Statistics Canada. 1990. 'Housing, Family and Social Statistics Division.' *Women in Canada*, Cat. No. 89–503E, Ottawa.

– 1991a. *Labour Market Activities Survey for 1988.* Ottawa.

- 1991b. 'Canadian Centre for Health Information.' *Health Reports*, Cat. No. 82–003, 3, 2, Ottawa.
- 1992a. Household Surveys Division. *Labour Force Annual Averages 1991*, Cat. No. 71–220, Ottawa.
- 1992b. '1991 Health and Activity Limitation Survey.' *The Daily* 13 (4 October), Ottawa.
- 1992c. *Corporations and Trade Unions Return Act* (CALURA), Cat. No. 71–202, Ottawa.
- 1992d. *Initial Data Release from the 1992 General Social Survey on Time Use.* Ottawa.
- 1993a. *1991 Census*, Cat. No. 93–324, Ottawa.
- 1993b. *Earnings of Men and Women*, Cat. No. 13–217, Ottawa.
- 1993c. *Women in the Workplace*, Supply and Services Canada, Cat. Nos. 11–612 and 71–534, Ottawa.
- 1995a. *Women in Canada*. Ministry of Industry, Cat. No. 89–503E.
- 1995b. *Historical Labour Force Statistics*, Ministry of Industry, Cat. No. 71–201.
Toronto Star. 1995. 'Pay Gap Widens for Men, Women.' 20 December.
Waring, Marilyn. 1990. *If Women Counted*. San Francisco: Harper.
White, Julie. 1990. *Mail and Female: Women and the Canadian Union of Postal Workers*. Toronto: Thompson.
- 1993. *Sisters and Solidarity: Women and Unions in Canada*. Toronto: Thompson.

9

Towards a Woman-Friendly Long-Term Care Policy

SHEILA M. NEYSMITH

This chapter considers long-term care policies and programs in terms of their effects on women. Services can range from twenty-four-hour institutionally based care to social support offered to isolated individuals who live in the community. Long-term care programs cover people with disabilities and elderly persons in need of assistance because of their physical and/or cognitive impairments. Although long-term care policy is usually presented in gender-neutral terms, the overwhelming majority of service users and providers are women. Thus, long-term care policy is a particularly rich arena for examining the gendered nature of state, family, and market relationships. The chapter starts with an overview of current policy directions. Programmatic specifics of the Canadian situation will be considered alongside international trends, a useful approach for assessing policy choices being implemented in Canada. A comparative perspective helps in clarifying how priorities are framed and options constructed. Of particular interest is the transformation during the 1980s of a formerly institutionally based model of long-term care into a home-care model. Some of the resource and quality-of-life issues associated with this transformation have received considerable public attention. Less visible are the effects of this change on various groups of women.

In the next section, I assess just how 'woman-friendly' Canadian long-term care policy is by examining the consequences for various groups of women when community-based care is operationalized in terms of caring for people 'in their own homes.' These consequences suggest that such policies can actually be harmful to women.

The third section of the chapter explores a model of the welfare state that incorporates gender relations and thus allows for a consideration of the effects of long-term care policy on women. The absence of gender in theories of the state reinforces the traditional conceptual division of public and private social spheres. Thus, a policy of community care can be restricted to considering only the implications of formal services, and it does not have to take into account the informal services provided primarily by female kin. Although the costs of informal care are well documented, they continue to be viewed as the private troubles of family members rather than as equity issues that need to be addressed in public policy. As a consequence, arguments for entitlements arising from the work that women do for family members hold little credence in the public world of policy making where entitlements are determined. The final section of the chapter is less a conclusion than a consideration of future policy possibilities within the Canadian context.

Assessing the Issues

Long-term care policy covers a range of institutional and community-based services. Services may include meals-on-wheels, adult day care, group homes, homemaker services, home nursing care, community physiotherapy and occupational therapy, assessment and treatment, day hospitals, long-term residential or nursing home care, and chronic hospital care, as well as assistive device programs, nutritionists, and adult protection services (Health and Welfare Canada, 1992: 25–7). The term 'community-based care' is used to designate programs designed for people who are not living in institutional-type settings. Although some services may actually be delivered through institutions (Day Centres, for example), most programs coming under the community care conceptual umbrella are actually discrete services provided to people in their homes. In this chapter I will use the term 'home care' to refer to such services. This will free up the concept of 'community care' to cover a broader range of options that are absent from the medical model that underpins the current institutionally based care and home care programs that are shaped by traditional familial assumptions.

A perusal of the international literature on long-term care policy reveals a number of common themes (Lesemann and Martin, 1993). One important theme is costs. Program goals and rationales are routinely introduced with reminders that Canada's population is aging and the fiscal implications if health care costs are not controlled. The belief that Canada's health care costs are 'out of control' is questionable. We spend about the same percentage of our GNP on health care as other OECD countries, although compared with many of these countries our system is relatively expensive in terms of what it buys in improved health status. Japan, the Scandinavian countries, and the United Kingdom do better on indicators such as mortality rates and life expectancy. Only the United States has a more expensive health care system (Manga, 1994: 180). These observations notwithstanding, at the time of writing, Canada's political discourse is dominated by the spectre of a growing deficit. In the resulting urgency to 'get the debt under control,' U.S.-style approaches to privatizing and contracting out of services are being pursued in all provinces.

In Canada the 130 per cent increase in the population who are 85 years of age and older, which is expected to take place between 1991 and 2011, has added a sense of urgency to developing non-institutional alternatives (Health and Welfare Canada, 1992: 32). Since 1980 there has been a decrease in rates of institutionalization across countries, even though the percentage of the population older than 80 has been steadily increasing. Institutional care is no longer seen as a desirable option for more than a small group of elderly persons. Studies have documented the negative effects of institutional care on the well-being of many old people, but this is not the driving force in the development of community-based alternatives. It is concern over costs that powers, and thus shapes, long-term care policy debates (Denton and Spencer, 1995; Barer, Evans, and Hertzman, 1995).

The content, funding, and delivery of home care services has been part of health care cost debates for the past decade. The expansion of home care is seen as one response to funding formulas that now encourage early discharge from acute care facilities (Benjamin, 1993; Kenney, 1993; MacAdam, 1993; Swan and Estes, 1990). At the same time, the aging of the population and demographic trends in fertility, marriage, divorce, and migration suggest that for increasing numbers of old people the presence of an informal carer cannot be assumed. As one European observer put it, 'public policy everywhere is moving towards making home care pre-eminent even for the very frail just at a time when the family characteristics most suited to home care are changing and becoming much less predictable' (Baldock, 1993: 27).

At one level, then, policy recommendations to shift resources from institutional to community-based care are not controversial. Their implementation, however, raises important challenges to the traditional allocation of health care resources. In Ontario, for example, more than 50 per cent of the $17.5 billion of the provincial health budget in 1996–7 is allocated to institutional-type care, nearly 30 per cent goes to physician fees, and about 10 per cent is spent on drugs and appliances (Ontario, 1996: 127–43). This leaves very little for community-based services. Furthermore, these proportions have not significantly altered over the past decade despite an aging population and the pursuit, by the Ministry of Health, of an aggressive bed closure policy.

Compared with Europe, the United Kingdom, and Australia, home care in Canada is poorly organized. At the federal level, there is no home and community care policy equivalent of the Canada Health Act (CHA) of 1984 where a vision is articulated in terms of a set of principles about services to be guaranteed at point of access. Funding is tied to the enactment of these principles. Periodic challenges by different provinces to the feasibility of realizing the goals of the CHA serve to underline the importance of having federal regulations and funding capacity of a magnitude that make it financially unattractive for the provinces to compromise the principles in the CHA. In contrast, in the area of long-term care, although there were some federal funds available through the Established Program Financing Act (1957) and under the Canada Assistance Plan Act (1966), the conditions for receiving these funds were not related to national program standards such as universality, accessibility, or public accountability, as can be found in the CHA. In 1995 these pieces of legislation were superseded by the Canada Health and Social Transfer (CHST) Act.[1] This new act will reinforce the pattern where every province independently organizes and delivers a different mix of services (Beland and Shapiro, 1994). Not surprisingly, tracking costs at the national level is difficult because of the provincial variability in nomenclature and information systems (Neysmith, 1995). Despite these data limitations, we do know that across the country the development of home care programs does not match the policy rhetoric which suggests that they are central in health care planning. The overall slow rate of progress is captured in a sardonic concluding comment by Manga (1994: 198) in her recent review of health economics, 'It is encouraging to note that home care constitutes 0.8 per cent of total health care expenditure in 1987 compared to 0.3 per cent in 1975.'

It is important to keep these budget proportions in mind when examining the content and direction of the home care discourse. For instance, in the community consultations and committee hearings that preceded the planned implementation of Ontario's Long Term Care Act – Bill 173, there was much concern about the fragmented nature of services in the province (Deber and Williams, 1995).[2] Coordination was defined as the problem; case management and a single-point entry system were seen as the solution. While debate raged over how to coordinate services, there was little movement on reallocating resources from institutional to community-based services. Meanwhile research from the United States and the United Kingdom was showing that both the cost and models of case management could vary widely (Capitman, Haskins, and Bernstein, 1986; Hugman, 1994) with differential effects on consumers (Biggs, 1990–1; Kane et al., 1991). At the same time, a rapidly increasing demand for home care in these countries, as in Canada, is feeding an expanding service industry that relies on a labour pool of low-paid women to provide what some authors refer to as custodial-type home care services (Schmid and Hasenfeld, 1993).

A recent review of service delivery issues by Schmid and Hasenfeld (1993) summarizes the challenges facing the implementation of effective home care services. Although focused on the situation in the United States, similar issues are apparent in Canada, and for that matter in all Western countries with a mixed economy of welfare. First, home care exists in a turbulent political and fiscal climate which undermines organizational stability; second, service effectiveness depends on interpersonal relationships between worker and client; third, service is delivered outside of organizational boundaries and thus quality control is difficult; fourth, home care services rely on an unskilled labour force with staff instability. The point I wish to underline more forcefully than Schmid and Hasenfeld do is that the fiscal and political climate, such as the above-mentioned budget priorities, exacerbate the difficulties they note in other areas.

Although it remains a minuscule part of the total health care budget, the quantity of home care is in fact expanding. Several factors contribute to this. First, most of the daily services are provided by paraprofessional home care workers who perform a variety of tasks ranging from housekeeping to respite care to carrying out personal care regimes. These are relatively low-cost services provided by low-wage employees. Personnel are frequently part-time or on contract, thus keeping training and benefits costs to a minimum. Not calculated into the formal home care budget, however, is the labour of a second group of workers – elderly spouses and female kin. In addition, and even less frequently discussed, are the costs incurred when an elderly person has to 'do for herself' (Bond, 1992). I will discuss each group of carers. Guiding this discussion is a consideration of who these players are and their ability to take on the tasks and absorb the costs that our home care model places upon them.

The People Costs

Despite the acknowledged centrality of home care services in meeting the needs of frail elderly people, only limited attention has been given to the workforce which provides most of these services (for examples of research that does exist, see Bartoldus, Gillery, and Sturges, 1989; Eustis and Fisher, 1991; Feldman, 1993; Gilbert, 1991; Kaye, 1986). In large metropolitan centres like Toronto this new labour force of home care workers is increasingly composed of immigrant women. The stress related to the demands of the job and the working conditions that surround it have received some attention. We know that the work rates high on intrinsic measures of job satisfaction, but that extrinsic factors like salary, hours, and job structure are rated poorly (Bartoldus et al., 1989; Gilbert, 1991; Martin-Matthews, 1992; Neysmith and Nichols, 1994). Recently these quantitative indicators have been enriched by qualitative research which documents how the contradictory expectations in their jobs are experienced by paraprofessional personnel (Aronson and Neysmith, 1996; Diamond, 1990; Donavan, 1989; Neysmith and Aronson, 1996; Tellis-Nayek and Tellis-Nayek, 1989). Finally, home care workers receive lower wages than their counterparts in hospitals and nursing homes (Crown, MacAdam, and Sadowsky, 1992).

Furthermore, when quality control is addressed primarily through case management, it affects the way some issues get taken up, while equally pressing concerns are ignored. For instance, there is now a well-developed debate on the ethical dilemmas facing professional staff in case management positions which combine the roles of client advocate and resource gatekeeper (Kane, Caplan, and Thomas, 1993: 255). Less frequently heard are ethical concerns about the role of paraprofessional home care workers whose jobs combine heavy responsibility with minimal authority. Equally absent from the debate is a consideration of the effects on elderly clients and their families of a system in which nursing homes are defined as abhorrent even to those who might need them (Kane et al., 1993: 261).

Finally, it is acknowledged in most discussions of long-term care that persons who need assistance with the activities of daily living remain in the community by relying on informal supports (Havens, 1995). When an elderly individual can no longer personally perform an activity a spouse helps, if she or he is available. If not, then a daughter or daughter-in-law steps in. The gendered nature of this responsibility has been well documented (Dwyer and Coward, 1992; Hooyman and Gonyea,

1995). However, it is also clear that what occurs is not a simple substitution; rather the form of informal help provided varies along with the helpers (Penning, 1990). For example, national surveys show that both men and women provide care, but men provide it mainly to their spouses while women provide it to a variety of other persons (Health and Welfare Canada, 1993: 70, table 2). Furthermore, because informal caregiving is relationship based, its quality is completely unpredictable. We know that the condition of an elderly person in need of help is no predictor of caregiver response. The heaviest of care can be seen as relatively easy, while relatively light care can be intolerable. This raises questions about the appropriate criteria to use for determining 'at risk' situations.

Although demographic trends show otherwise, the availability of future cohorts of women to provide family care is seldom questioned in long-term care policy. It is perhaps not surprising, then, that in a recent overview of European home care policy Horl (1992), reviewing the Austrian situation, a demographically old country, was one of few writers to explicitly deal with assumptions about family in home care policy. Horl argued that policy that encourages more family care is no policy because the family is already the dominant source of help and there will be fewer, not more, female kin available in the future. He emphasized how partial relationships within the family will lead to the breaking up of the roles of mother, wife, and daughter as individuals go through several family constellations over a lifetime. Who is responsible for whom at any given moment will become an increasingly moot point.

In this section I have argued that funding is important because it declares where the priorities lie. Planning possibilities are influenced by the location of the funding authority. In health care, federal transfers, on the whole, have very few conditions attached to them. As a result, there has been no attempt to promote national standards as the provinces develop policy and set guidelines for program specifics. There is little likelihood of this changing with political pressure for more, not less, provincial policy-making autonomy combined with rapidly decreasing federal transfers to the provinces. In recent years, community-based services, in particular home care, have been proposed as cost-attractive alternatives as efficiency became the slogan for dealing with what was defined as the 'Fiscal Crisis of the Welfare State.' Since there has been little increase in the relative share of the budget going into home care services, one must conclude there has been no change in long-term care policy priorities – words to the contrary. The major players, and resource users, continue to be hospitals and allied interests such as pharmaceutical firms and test and supply services. Home care policy is shaped by these existing structures which limit what is feasible in the near future. The questions to consider, then, are: What is the impact of current programs on different groups of women? How do current policies affect future possibilities?

How Woman-Friendly Is Canadian Long-Term Care Policy?

Class analysts have repeatedly theorized, and documented, the role of the state in the decommodification of wage labour and the appropriation of non-wage labour. However, an appreciation of the gendered nature of this process suggests that it is not straightforward. In long-term care policy two processes of work transformation have occurred in recent years. One is the transferring of labour between different categories of paid workers that occurs, for example, when aides in chronic-care institutions are laid off and the employment of home care workers is expanded. The second is the appropriation of unpaid labour of family members as the tasks expected of them increase as formal services contract. Although I have touched on these earlier, I would like to spell them out in more detail.

Using Ontario as an example, in the 1989–90 long-term care budget nearly $8.00 out of every $10.00 went to institutional services such as nursing homes, chronic care facilities, and homes for the aged. The 1995–7 Budget Estimates of the Ministry of Health suggest that this gap is closing rapidly. In fact, if these estimates are on target, the proportion will be almost 50–50 *within the long-term care budget* (Ontario, 1996: 142). Although there has been a steady increase in home care funding, most of the change results from placing severe restraints on the number of nursing homes and chronic care beds allowed. Data from studies in the United States suggest that the effects on personnel of this changing location of care work will not be benign. First, the hours allotted per client are shrinking as a result of fiscal pressure. Not only is the work being speeded up, but the performance of tending tasks is emphasized at the expense of providing social support. Second, as paraprofessionals move from institutional to home-based care, working conditions change drastically. One of the more obvious differences is that the type of built-in supports available in facilities, such as immediate access to physicians, nurses, equipment, and auxiliary help, disappear. Also, although I used the expression 'personnel moved from,' in fact, it is seldom the same individuals who are involved. Employees tend to be drawn from different labour pools, with institutionally based aides requiring a set of credentials not required of the home care worker. At present, the entry level skills required for home care workers are minimal, although many take upgrading courses. Not surprisingly, aides in hospitals earn higher wages than those who work in chronic care facilities, with home care workers found at the bottom of the pay scale (Crown et al., 1992). Third, at the time of writing, many Ontario agencies have excellent employment practices. However, provincial funding is not increasing as rapidly as case loads. As hours of care are rationed to fit declining budgets, working conditions will deteriorate. At the same time, unionization of home care workers will continue to be difficult because of isolated work settings, the fact that many workers are on contract or are part-time employees, and the expanding number of small commercial agencies that are now included in the home care industry.

As part of the reform strategy accompanying Bill 173 – The Long-Term Care Act (1994) – the former Ontario NDP government released several policy documents. One of these proposed a systematized framework for training paraprofessionals (Ontario, 1993b). It goes without saying that training guidelines need to be put in place because home care workers are assuming increasingly complex tasks as more of the work formerly done in hospitals is transferred to the home. However, these types of proposals do not mean that increasing qualifications will translate into increased wages. As more tasks devolve to paraprofessionals, nurses are limiting their role to more technical and supervisory tasks. Thus, the bulk of home care work is becoming classified as semiskilled labour performed by large numbers of low-paid workers who perform tasks under the supervision of a small, relatively well-paid cadre of health care professionals. Hugman (1994) paints a similar picture following the implementation of community care in Britain. The case management model proposed in the legislation, and tested in large demonstration experiments, is being operationalized into care management where relatively few social work professionals supervise diploma-level practitioners who develop individual care plans but have little authority over resource allocations. On a more optimistic note, however, the financing of Canadian home care programs in most provinces seems to have avoided the gross budget distortions found in the United States. There the terms of the Medicare and Medicaid reimbursement schemes encourage the use of professional health care personnel such as physiotherapists, visiting nurses, and podiatrists even when home care workers, were they covered, could have done the work (Estes, Swan and Associates, 1993; Szasz, 1990). There are disagreements on where professional–paraprofessional lines are to be drawn. My point is that a funding formula, not client need, have influenced which type of labour was used. Under such circumstances tensions between these groups of women workers will be exacerbated.

Perhaps the contradictions inherent in this work-transformation process are most evident, however, when tasks previously classified as requiring the expertise of trained personnel are suddenly seen as appropriately handled by family caregivers. Everything from supervising medication to changing catheters can seemingly now be taught to aging spouses or harried daughters, and it is assumed these will be carried out competently. If this assumption proves faulty and a fatal mistake is made, the legal consequences when a family care giver is at fault are different than the accountability issues that must be faced when formal health care providers are involved. Thus, the concern to provide adequate training to reduce worker liability can be set aside. Again, this is not a question of whether kin (mostly women) can do this work, but rather a comment on how a fiscal crisis discourse can change practice and shift costs while pursuing the desirable goals of a home care policy. There is no question that the work being discussed needs doing; it does not disappear. The question is who is going to do it and under what terms and conditions?

Today women are in the labour force for most of their adult lives. The boundary between paid and unpaid work may continue to exist, but it is extremely permeable. Social policies such as home care not only affect both types of work, but such policies redefine the public/private boundary of caring responsibilities and, consequently, expectations about the labour of women. Finally, the effects of home care policies and programs are not experienced equitably by all women. Tracing the specifics of how this happens in a policy arena peopled by women reveals the power structures and social relations that undergird the visible workings of a patriarchal welfare state. These policies are gendered, but they are also enacted in a society with class and race cleavages. They can pit different groups of women against each other.

In conclusion, the Canadian version of the liberal welfare state shapes gender relations through policies and programs in the arenas of employment, day care, housing, economic development, transportation, and health care. These affect all women throughout their lives, but they also combine with the specifics of long-term care policy to differentially advantage and disadvantage groups of women depending upon their social location. Some of the recommendations made in the final section of the chapter would be ineffective if this broader context were not attended to. Becoming engaged in tactical struggles requires an analysis of current structures and processes in order to assess possibilities and locate windows of opportunity for effecting change. The Canadian state may be patriarchal, but the form this takes changes. The question, then, is not whether women will deal with the welfare state but how, with which tactics, and towards what goals? To do this, gender needs to be infused into our policy models – the focus of the next section.

Women, the Welfare State, and Gender Relations

A consideration of how long-term care policy affects women entails more than documenting how specific programs or pieces of legislation impact on different groups of women – as important as this might be. The cumulative effects of labour market, pension, and health care policies intersect in women's lives. If policies that are just to women are to be promoted, the underlying dynamics that produce gender inequities need to be integrated into the analysis. Instead of only examining, for instance, how pension and health benefits in old age are linked to class location through employment, such programs could be examined along gender lines, revealing that women receive benefits that are means-tested, like the Guaranteed Income Supplement (GIS), while men are better able to lay claim to richer benefits that are rights based, benefits associated with their status in the labour force, such as employer retirement packages, RRSPs, and higher payments from the Canada Pension Plan (CPP). Likewise, in the area of home care, there are gender and marital differences in receipt of services among individuals who have very similar functional capacity profiles. As agencies ration their increasingly scarce resources, the availability of family to provide needed care becomes part of the assessment. Based purely on mortality projections, the probability of men having access to a caregiving spouse greatly exceeds that of women. Thus, it is poor old women who are likely to need meagre public home care programs; if she has the income, she can access a rapidly growing, but largely unregulated, commercial home care service. Thus, systems of social protection reproduce gender as well as class differences. The following discussion explores the assumptions about family, labour market, and state relationships that underpin the operation of the Canadian welfare state.

Feminists may not yet have developed an adequate theory of the state grounded in the experiences of women, but these experiences show that full weight needs to be given to the structure of power and inequality in Canadian society while recognizing that complex differences exist among women. Fortunately, the institutionalization of dominance is never complete and possibilities for resistance can develop (Franzway, Court, and Connell, 1989: 35). First, a theory of the state that incorporates gender relations would see the state as a social process that operates across all arenas of life. It is not just a legal category or set of public institutions. Furthermore, the state is an actor in its own right, not just a vehicle for outside interests. It is the initiator of important dynamics, a place where interests are constituted as well as balanced (Franzway, Court, and Connell, 1989: 29). Such a model refutes the idea that the state is unitary or monolithic, but rather assumes that contradictions are embedded within its structures and processes. This rejection of structural determinism allows us to focus on the interplay between the state and its environment and, thus, envision possibilities for change.

Second, although the state is an important arena for the institutionalization of certain power relations, so is the family. In fact, feminist scholars in the 1970s argued so strongly that the family was the location of women's oppression that, by implication, power imbalances within the home seemed more important to the welfare of women than those in the public domain. This discourse, particularly strong in North America, diverted attention from how structures and processes of the state intervene between social needs and the way these are translated into political demands, between demands and state responses in the form of specific policies and the ability of groups to organize and raise new demands in the future (Franzway, Court, and Connell, 1989: 41).

Long-term care policy is presented as a policy focused on promoting the well-being of old people by moving the location of services out of institutions and into people's homes. The state might thus be seen as arbitrating between the interests of the health care system and the care needs of frail elderly citizens. In this model a progressive state, in the form of provincial governments, intervenes on behalf of a segment of the citizenry by articulating community care as a preferred political direction. Action takes the form of limiting the growth of hospital budgets and providing funds to promote the development of home-based services. In countries like Canada the 'good fight' is depicted as a struggle wherein the state, that is, policy makers, are cast as balancing the powerful forces of the health care system against the needs of senior citizens. What is not part of this picture are the social relationships within which senior citizens and health care providers are embedded. On the one hand, the senior citizen is redefined as a patient with kin ties that are available to provide ongoing care and support. However, he or she is essentially genderless and classless, belonging to no particular social or ethno-racial group. On the other hand, the health care system is depicted as a monolith wherein employment status differentials between, for example, physicians and nursing aides, acute and chronic care priorities, and disparate funding arrangements are ignored because they are considered extraneous to a home care policy. When programs are delivered, all these divisions within and between the long-term care system and old people come into play as powerful determinants of the content and organization of services that old people actually experience on a daily basis.

When Canada is described as a 'welfare state,' implied is a commitment to promoting the well-being of its citizens. In fact, countries are frequently compared on their social expenditure patterns as a measure for assessing how well they deliver on the implied promise. However, this line of research has been of limited use to feminists because it is not able to capture the relationships of power that are so critical to the welfare of women. For instance, state expenditures on housing and income security are presented as seemingly unrelated to patterns of woman abuse. Obviously, however, access to resources by women as they age is critical for escaping violent situations. Consequently, in recent years, feminist scholars have been trying to build analyses of the state that incorporate gender as an analytical dimension, rather than including it as just another variable to be considered when measuring the effects of policies on different groups of people.

Orloff (1993), for example, builds on the welfare state dimensions articulated by such authors as Esping-Andersen (1989). She notes that the assumed citizen in this model is male, and so the analytical focus has been on the public male world of state, market, and civil society relationships. Absent is any idea of families as significant providers of welfare. If the family were conceptualized as part of civil society, the triangle could be reconstituted so as to permit the examination of both paid and unpaid work. State provisions could then be examined in terms of their potential for shifting the burden of welfare from the family to the state or from women to men (Orloff, 1993: 312).

The review of directions outlined in the first section of this chapter suggests that community care is being transformed into home care where most of the work is done by female kin and thus poses little threat to established health interests. The social institutions that continue to provide most of the caring labour are families, households, social networks, and self-help organizations. These may shade into informal labour markets or the informal economy which includes both paid services and unpaid exchanges. The work is supplemented by paraprofessionals hired by health care organizations (Leira, 1994: 194). Charting informal labour markets is essential if we are not to conceal or marginalize the importance of provisions generated outside of formal schemes.

Conceptualizing care provision as work is important because it identifies what is overlooked, namely, that the structure of care provision affects citizen entitlements (ibid.: 186). The collective choice of men to leave caring to women is commonly considered an essential element in women's structurally inferior position in modern welfare societies (Connell, 1994). That women would care for dependents was an assumption in the design of all welfare states as the structure, and effects, of caring show in even the welfare progressive states of the Scandinavian countries where citizenship claims were modelled on the 'waged' worker. In analysing the distribution of welfare state entitlements, more rights are associated with wage than with care labour. In other words, access to benefits is differentiated according to a set of interrelated premises: the context of the work as either outside or inside formal employment; the welfare state decision to leave a considerable share of caring as a private responsibility; by the gendered division of labour – caring is for the most part ascribed to women (Leira, 1994: 198). What matters when entitlements are adjudicated is not the hours or the significance of the work, but the formal contract and the wage. Access to the full range of entitlements and to a better income when pensioned is accorded only to those who are attached full-time to the formal labour market in their adult years.

As care work seeps through the permeable membrane that divides the public and private lives of Canadian women, language becomes muddy. Concepts of domestic labour and social reproduction draw from a tradition that is built on the production of commodities and thus hides the fact that caring always involves relating personally to another human being. Such language encourages an emphasis on task performance rather than relationship skills – a work-transformation process now occurring in the job descriptions of home care workers (Aronson and Neysmith, 1996; Neysmith and Aronson, 1996). Providing care differs fundamentally from the production of objects, a difference that lies not in the hierarchial organization of the work, or of wages, but in the skills or accomplishments required by the different tasks, the normative requirements, and the social experiences that each entail (Leira, 1994: 188). On the other hand, focusing too much on personal relationships may underplay the considerable collective interests that are connected with the provision of care. Care is both public and private. It is not evident that better or more adequate care is provided if one set of emotions accompanies or is integrated with the activities than another; it is just different (ibid.: 190). If we could accept that care provision could entail different degrees of attachment, we could then rethink ways of assessing the work involved and the proper compensation for whomever does it, no matter what their relationship to the care recipient (Thomas, 1993: 663).

To get some appreciation of how such ideas might look if incorporated into policy, we might again usefully consider the Scandinavian approach (Andersson, 1992; Johansson and Thorslund, 1993) or that of Israel (Morginstin, Baich-Moray and Zipkin, 1992), albeit the two countries finance home care services differently. Nevertheless, in both the functional capacity of the person is the basis for determining claims for assistance, rather than the availability of informal kin care. The level of such guarantees or insurance schemes are always debatable and, in fact, have been reduced in Sweden over the past several years (Lagergren, 1994). The point to be made here is that their existence reflects a community obligation to meet need, which transcends a justification based on affective and kinship ties and avoids the dilemmas encountered when caring is projected as a labour of love. A model of rational caring rooted in the basic needs of a recipient is possible. Needless to say, such a model is not to be confused with a model based on bureaucratic rationality, which is seldom compatible with the caring needs of everyday life. Most importantly, this model situates the old person as citizen with legitimate claims to care and takes the focus off familial social relations as a source of care. In the long run it will facilitate our rethinking combinations of labour and feeling states that can exist in caring relationships, whether paid or unpaid. The study of family relationships is a legitimate area of inquiry in its own right, but quite tangential to the articulation of a long-term care policy that centres the needs of elderly persons.

Mapping Pathways for the Future

It follows from the foregoing discussion that policies which are presented as innovative because they place a priority on family-based care

are not woman-friendly. The very articulation of such a policy denies the reality that this is already the dominant form of care in Canada. It suggests that the amount of family care can be increased. It implies that families are not carrying their fair share of the costs of long-term care. This flies in the face of twenty years of research that documents the contrary. Similarly, referring to 'family' responsibility hides the fact that it is women who still perform most of the caring and domestic labour in the home while working full-time in the paid labour force – again a repeatedly documented fact (see Lero and Johnson, 1994). Deconstructing policy assumptions such as these is critical to opening up options that are more woman-friendly. If too much attention is given to how families can be helped to shoulder the costs of meeting the care needs of their members, little energy is available for mounting an informed debate on the fair share to be assumed by non-familial social institutions. Developing such a debate is essential for focusing the political spotlight on practices of hospitals, physicians, and drug and laboratory test companies, all players who currently consume most of the available health care resources. In this broader analysis questions are more easily raised about the power of the Canadian state to promote a sharing of the costs and responsibilities now carried disproportionately by women in their roles as paid and unpaid carers.

The development of a woman-friendly, long-term care policy will require that the discussion go beyond the boundaries of health care policy. One of the arenas pertinent to such discussions is labour force policy. By determining women's economic well-being earlier in their life cycle, women's experiences in the labour market affect the options available to them in their old age. Disparities between the income of men and women continue (Health and Welfare Canada, 1993: 131ff). Changing this will require more than pay equity legislation can deliver. The latter does not challenge the patriarchal tradition of defining individuals as employees only. A woman-friendly employment policy would assume that all employees, across sectors, have family responsibilities whether they be men or women. At a minimum this means that benefit packages would routinely contain dependent care provisions (for an in-depth discussion of such approaches see Neal et al., 1993). However, the current practice of leaving such decisions to companies and unions to negotiate means that only a few individuals fortunate enough to be employed within such firms benefit. Second, by relegating dependent care policy to this level, the message is given that, like personal insurance, this is a private responsibility, a benefit that may be negotiated in lieu of salary as part of the employment contract. It effectively denies the existence of a broader public issue. In this way, elder and child care share a common dilemma. The commonality is not in terms of their respective needs, as is sometimes suggested, but rather their common status as socially constructed problems in our society. Unlike health and income policy, where public and private responsibilities are recognized and the boundaries are debated, dependent care is still firmly lodged in the private sphere of family responsibility. A sign that these dynamics are changing would be job descriptions which assume that employees are social beings with multiple commitments to community and family life, as well as to their employer. Employment practices that did not take these into account would be challenged as discriminatory to the needs of both women and men. Recognizing that at any given moment some persons will be carrying heavier caring responsibilities than others, pension benefits would be tied less tightly to one's track record in the labour force, although under woman-friendly employment practices women would not suffer as much as they do at present.

For the aging citizen in need of care a woman-friendly long-term care policy means that there is an option not to choose family-provided care. Demographic projections indicate that kin carers will not be available to many elderly women. But even if they are, a policy that assumes the presence of informal carers puts elderly women in a socially created state of dependency. As Baldock (1993) points out, carer schemes need to be in addition to, not in lieu of, home care if they are to give elderly persons and their families choice. There is increasing evidence that old people do not want to be dependent on their children, especially for personal care (Phillipson, 1992: 265). This suggests that schemes focused on paying family carers will serve the needs of a limited group of persons (for a review of the strengths and weaknesses of these programs, see Linsk et al., 1993). Thus, policies that emphasize the role of informal carers are not woman-friendly because they familize women by making assumptions about women's relationships and the availability of their labour.

Housing and transport policy, although not elaborated within the limits of this chapter, are also integral to a woman-friendly long-term care policy. The goal of home care is to promote community living. Being confined to an ill-equipped apartment or remaining in a house that was originally designed for the post–Second World War suburban lifestyle, and requires a car to get around, means that elderly people, especially women, faced with mobility problems are extremely vulnerable to isolation. Living, rather than just existing, in the community requires interaction with others. Community integration has been one of the casualties of the transformation of community-based care into home care. Because community-based care programs have been limited to delivery of services into people's homes, little consideration is given to alternatives. For instance, in the United States, one of the more successful demonstration projects aimed at overcoming the isolation of inner city residents emphasized the importance of getting very frail people out of their homes and to senior health centres, where a combination of health, diet, exercise, and social programs were offered. One of these, the ON LOK program, has been extensively documented as a programmatic and financial success, yet such programs are a minor component of most community-based care strategies contemplated in Ontario (see Kushner and Rachlis, 1994).

The jockeying for position and professional turf battles that are part of the restructuring of health care economics and delivery systems (Manga, 1994; Ontario, 1994) produce waves that affect those who have little power to define the terms of the struggle, even though the outcome will affect the quality of their lives. This chapter has attempted to delineate who these less powerful players (mostly women) are, as well as assess the effects of current and future policy options on them. Because of their relatively powerless position, issues are constructed in ways that negatively affect the welfare of these various groups of women. For instance, in the fiscally precipitated ethical debates emerging around possibly setting limits to the health care entitlements of elderly persons, the elderly are positioned as questionable consumers of scarce resources. This social construction of the dilemma denies evidence showing that it is the content and delivery of services, not consumer behaviour, that increase health costs. In a recent incarnation of this idea, the elderly are exhorted to see this stage of life as a time to focus on giving to younger generations, not claiming. In a country where entitlements are defined by serious class, race, and gender disparities, the effects of such normative expectations have deleterious effects on already precarious groups within the elderly population. Spielman (1993) points out that the costs of this scenario would fall even more on women who have been doing unpaid caring all their lives. The foregoing discourse implies that they have not – an assumption that is not challenged in long-term care policy that emphasizes family responsibility.

As Canada approaches the twenty-first century all sectors of the population will need to become engaged in decisions about resource allocation. The importance of articulating priorities that are not mere reflections of the status quo will require imagination as well as commitment and politically strategic action. Fortunately, Canada is not alone in recognizing that the future of long-term care is a social and not a medical issue (Callahan, Ter Meulen, and Topinkova, 1995). Alternative voices will be heard most effectively, not in government advisory committees mandated as part of long-term care service structural reforms, but rather in the form of issues raised through organizations focused on promoting the well-being of their members. Thus, home care agencies that are unionized will enable paraprofessionals to articulate a set of concerns that can be brought to the bargaining table when health care priorities are being set and resources allocated. Groups of kin carers would bring a different set of priorities from those of formal care providers. The politicization of carer groups would also be an important arena for envisioning alternative scenarios. Likewise, the Community Living movement powered by analyses of the social construction of dependency for people with disabilities is questioning the very foundations of informal as well as formal care (Twigg, 1993).

The various segments of our aging population can be expected to take frequently conflicting positions on priorities. We should anticipate only limited agreement among aging middle-class white feminists, low-income immigrant women of colour, and lesbian and gay activists. The goal is to include their voices so as to mute those of much more powerful health care providers. The shape of future policy cannot be clearly sketched, but it is hoped that the gendered assumptions that permeate today's long-term care policy will not survive the critical onslaught from these multiple voices. The desired goal would be a long-term care policy firmly rooted in a concept of social citizenship where the rights and responsibilities of all actors do not reflect discriminatory assumptions about an individual's gender, class, race, sexual orientation, or country of origin.

Notes

1 Since the mid-1980s there has been much concern about the effects of steadily decreasing federal transfers (which comprise both cash and tax points) on the enforcement of national standards. The 1996 budget promised that the cash component of this transfer would not fall below $11 billion annually until at least 2003; its current level is $12.5 billion. The projected small increase in the

CHST from $25.1 billion in 1997 to $27.4 billion in 2003 will be realized by tax points (Canada, 1996). The certainty is that the provinces will be doing more health care financing, provincial variation in long-term care will increase, as will the mix of public, voluntary, and market sector services to be found across the country.

2 In 1995 the newly elected provincial Conservative government scrapped this bill. Nevertheless, the substantive issues discussed in the following paragraphs are generic to long-term care policy. The demise of Bill 173 has just once again put on hold long-term care reform for Ontario. Ontario, Canada's most populous province and one of the wealthiest, has the dubious record of having the most piecemeal approach to service provision (Deber and Williams, 1995: 300–1).

References

Andersson, L. 1992. 'Family Care of the Elderly in Sweden.' In J. Kosberg, ed., *Family Care of the Elderly: Social and Cultural Changes*. Newbury Park: Sage, 271–85.

Aronson, J., and S. Neysmith. 1996. '"You're not just in there to do the work": Depersonalizing Policies and the Exploitation of Home Care Workers' Labor.' *Gender and Society* 10, 1: 59–77.

Baldock, J. 1993. 'Some Observations on International Comparisons of Home Care Innovations.' In A. Evers and G.H. van der Zanden, eds., *Better Care for Dependent People: Meeting the New Agenda in Services for the Elderly*. Bunnik: Netherlands Institute of Gerontology, 25–37.

Barer, M., R. Evans, and C. Hertzman. 1995. 'Avalanche or Glacier?: Health Care and the Demographic Rhetoric.' *Canadian Journal on Aging / le Revue Canadienne du Viellissement* 14, 2: 193–224.

Bartoldus, E., B. Gillery, and P. Sturges. 1989. 'Job-related Stress and Coping among Home-Care Workers with Elderly People.' *Health and Social Work* 14: 204-10.

Beland, F., and E. Shapiro. 1994. 'Ten Provinces in Search of Long-Term Care Policy.' In V. Marshall and B. McPherson, eds., *Ageing: Canadian Perspectives*. Peterborough: Broadview Press, 245–67.

Benjamin, A.E. 1993. 'An Historical Perspective on Home Care Policy.' *Milbank Quarterly* 71, 1: 129-66.

Biggs, S. 1990–1. 'Consumers, Case Management and Inspection: Obscuring Social Deprivation and Need?' *Critical Social Policy*, Issue 30: 23–38.

Bond, J. 1992. 'The Politics of Caregiving: The Professionalization of Informal Care.' *Ageing and Society* 12, 1: 5–22.

242   Sheila M. Neysmith

Callahan, D., R. Ter Muelen, and E. Topinkova. 1995. 'Introduction: Special Issue on Resource Allocation and Societal Responses to Old Age.' *Ageing and Society* 15, 2: 157–61.
Canada, Department of Finance. 1996. *Budget in Brief*. March 6.
Capitman, J., B. Haskins, and J. Bernstein. 1986. 'Case Management Approaches in Coordinated Community-Oriented Long-Term Care Demonstrations.' *Gerontologist* 26, 4: 398–404.
Connell, R.W. 1994. 'The State, Gender and Sexual Politics: Theory and Appraisal.' In H.L. Radke and H.J. Stam, eds., *Power/Gender Social Relations in Theory and Practice*. London: Sage, 136–73.
Crown, W., M. MacAdam, and E. Sadowsky. 1992. *Caring* (April): 34–8.
Deber, R., and A.P. Williams. 1995. 'Policy, Payment and Participation: Long-Term Care Reform in Ontario.' *Canadian Journal on Aging / le Revue Canadienne du Viellissement* 14, 2: 294–318.
Denton, F.T., and B.G. Spencer. 1995. 'Demographic Change and the Cost of Publicly Funded Health Care.' *Canadian Journal on Aging / le Revue Canadienne du Viellissement* 14, 2: 174–92.
Diamond, T. 1990. 'Nursing Homes as Trouble.' In E. Abel and M. Nelson, eds., *Circles of Care: Work and Identity in Women's Lives*. Albany: State University of New York Press, 173–87.
Donovan, R. 1989. 'Work Stress and Job Satisfaction: A Study of Home Care Workers in New York City.' *Home Health Services Quarterly* 10: 97–114.
Dwyer, J., and R. Coward. 1992. *Gender, Families and Elder Care*. Newbury Park: Sage.
Esping-Andersen, G. 1989. 'The Three Political Economies of the Welfare State.' *Canadian Review of Sociology and Anthropology* 26, 1: 10–35.
Estes, C., J. Swan, and Associates. 1993. *The Long-Term Care Crisis: Elders Trapped in the No-Care Zone*. Newbury Park: Sage.
Eustis, N., and L. Fischer. 1991. 'Relationships between Home Care Clients and Their Workers: Implications for Quality of Care.' *The Gerontologist* 31, 4: 447–56.
Feldman, P. 1993. 'Work Life Improvements for Home Care Workers.' *Gerontologist* 33, 1: 47–54.
Franzway, S., D. Court, and R. Connell. 1989. *Staking a Claim: Feminism, Bureaucracy and the State*. Oxford: Polity Press.
Gilbert, N. 1991. 'Home Care Worker Resignations: A Study of the Major Contributing Factors.' *Home Care Services Quarterly* 12: 69–83.
Havens, B. 1995. 'Long-Term Care Diversity Within the Care Continuum.' *Canadian Journal on Aging / le Revue Canadienne du Viellissement* 14, 2: 245–62.
Health and Welfare Canada. Health Services and Promotion Branch. 1992. *Future Directions in Continuing Care*. Report of the Federal/Provincial/Territorial

Subcommittee on Continuing Care. Ottawa: Minister of Supply and Services Canada.

Health and Welfare Canada. Seniors Secretariat. 1993. *Ageing and Independence: Overview of a National Survey.* Ottawa: Minister of Supply and Services Canada.

Horl, J. 1992. 'Family Care of the Elderly in Austria.' In J. Kosberg, ed., *Family Care of the Elderly: Social and Cultural Changes.* Newbury Park: Sage, 235–51.

Hooyman, N., and J. Gonyea. 1995. *Feminist Perspectives on Family Care: Policies for Gender Justice.* Thousand Oaks: Sage.

Hugman, R. 1994. 'Social Work and Case Management in the U.K.: Models of Professionalism and Elderly People.' *Ageing and Society* 14, 2: 237–53.

Johansson, L., and M. Thorslund. 1993. 'Care of the Elderly in Sweden.' In F. Lesemann and C. Martin, eds., *Home-Based Care, the Elderly, the Family and the Welfare State: An International Comparison.* Ottawa: University of Ottawa Press, 151–83.

Kane, R., A. Caplan, and C. Thomas. 1993. 'CONCLUSION: Toward an Ethic of Case Management.' In R. Kane and A. Caplan, eds., *Ethical Conflicts in the Management of Home Care: The Care Manager's Dilemma.* New York: Springer Publishing, 249–62.

Kane, R., J. Penrod, G. Davidson, and I. Moscovice. 1991. 'What Cost Case Management in Long-Term Care.' *Social Service Review* 62, 2: 281–303.

Kaye, L. 1986. 'Worker Views of the Intensity of Affective Expression during the Delivery of Home Care Services for the Elderly.' *Home Care Services Quarterly* 7: 41–54.

Kenney, G. 1993. 'How Access to Long-Term Care Affects Home Health Transfers.' *Journal of Health, Politics and Law* 18, 4: 937–65.

Kushner, C., and M. Rachlis. 1994. 'Presentation to the Standing Committee on Social Development. Consideration of Bill 173, An Act Respecting Long-Term Care.' *Official Report of Debates (Hansard).* Legislative Assembly of Ontario. Third Session, 35th Parliament, October 3, S-2274–S-2278.

Lagergren, M. 1994. 'Allocation of Care and Services in an Area-Based System for Long-Term Care of Elderly and Disabled People.' *Ageing and Society,* 14, 3: 357–82.

Leira, A. 1994. 'Concepts of Caring: Loving, Thinking, Doing.' *Social Service Review* 68, 2: 185–201.

Lero, D., and K. Johnson. 1994. *110 Canadian Statistics on Work and Family.* Ottawa: Prepared for the Canadian Advisory Council on the Status of Women.

Lesemann, F., and C. Martin. 1993. 'Concluding Comments.' In F. Lesemann and C. Martin, eds., *Home-Based Care, the Elderly, the Family and the Welfare State: An International Comparison.* Ottawa: University of Ottawa Press, 251–71.

Linsk, N., S. Keigher, L. Simon-Rusinowitz, and S. England. 1993. *Wages for Caring: Compensating Family Care of the Elderly.* New York: Praeger.

MacAdam, M. 1993. 'Home Care Reimbursement and Effects on Personnel.' *Gerontologist* 33, 1: 55–63.

Manga, F. 1994. 'Health Economics and the Current Health Care Cost Crisis: Contributions and Controversies.' *Health and Canadian Society / Santé et Société Canadienne* 1, 1: 177–203.

Martin-Matthews, A. 1992. *Homemakers' Services to the Elderly: Provider Characteristics and Client Benefits, 1989–1992.* Guelph, Ontario: Gerontology Research Centre, University of Guelph.

Morginstin, B., S. Baich-Moray, and A. Zipkin. 1992. 'Assessment of Long-Term Care Needs and the Provision of Services to the Elderly in Israel: The Impact of Long-Term Care Insurance.' *Australian Journal on Ageing* 11, 2: 16–24.

Neal, M., N, Chapman, B. Ingersoll-Dayton, and A. Mlen. 1993. *Balancing Work and Caregiving for Children, Adults and Elders.* Newbury Park: Sage.

Neysmith, S. 1995. 'Would a National Information System Promote the Development of Canadian Home and Community Care Policy? An Examination of the Australian Experience.' *Canadian Public Policy* 21, 2: 159–73.

– and J. Aronson. 1996. 'Home Care Workers Discuss Their Work: The Skills Required to "Use Your Common Sense."' *Journal of Aging Studies* 10, 1: 1–14.

– and B. Nichols. 1994. 'Working Conditions in Home Care: A Comparison of Three Groups of Workers.' *Canadian Journal on Aging* 13, 2: 169–86.

Ontario, Legislative Assembly, Third Session, 35th Parliament. 1994. *Official Report of Debates.* Standing Committee on Social Development. Long-Term Care Act. Toronto: Hansard Reporting Services, October 3 and 4, S-2255–S-2368.

Ontario, Management Board Secretariat, 1996. *Expenditures Estimates, 1996–97,* Vol. 1. Toronto: Queen's Printer for Ontario.

Ontario, Ministry of Health, Ministry of Community and Social Services, Ministry of Citizenship. 1993a. *Partnerships in Long-Term Care: A New Way to Plan, Manage and Deliver Services and Community Support: A Policy Framework.* Toronto: Queen's Printer for Ontario, April.

– 1993b. *Partnerships in Long-Term Care: A New Way to Plan, Manage and Deliver Services and Community Support: An Implementation Framework.* Toronto: Queen's Printer for Ontario, June.

Orloff, A. 1993. 'Gender and the Social Rights of Citizenship: The Comparative Analysis of Gender Relations and Welfare States.' *American Sociological Review* 58, 3: 303–28.

Penning, M. 1990. 'Receipt of Assistance by Elderly People: Hierarchial Selection and Task Specificity.' *Gerontologist* 30, 2: 20–228.

Phillipson, C. 1992. 'Family Care of the Elderly in Great Britain.' In J. Kosberg, ed., *Family Care of the Elderly: Social and Cultural Changes*. Newbury Park: Sage, 252–70.

Schmid, H., and Y. Hasenfeld. 1993. 'Organizational Dilemmas in the Provision of Home-Care Services.' *Social Service Review* 67, 1: 40–54.

Spielman, B. 1993. 'Achieving Equity and Setting Limits: The Importance of Gender.' In G. Winslow and J. Walters, eds., *Facing Limits: Ethics and Health Care for the Elderly*. Boulder: Westview Press, 177–89.

Swan, J., and C. Estes. 1990. 'Changes in Aged Populations Served by Home Health Agencies.' *Journal of Aging and Health* 2, 3: 373–94.

Szasz, A. 1990. 'The Labour Impacts of Policy Change in Health Care: How Federal Policy Transformed Home Health Organizations and Their Labour Practices.' *Journal of Health Politics, Policy and Law* 15, 1: 191–210.

Tellis-Nayek, V., and M. Tellis-Nayek. 1989. 'Quality of Care and the Burden of Two Cultures: When the World of the Nurse's Aid Enters the World of the Nursing Home.' *Gerontologist* 29, 3: 307–13.

Thomas, C. 1993. 'De-Constructing Concepts of Care.' *Sociology* 27, 4: 549–669.

Twigg, J. 1993. 'The Interweaving of Formal and Informal Care: Policy Models and Problems.' In A. Evers and G. H. van der Zanden, eds., *Better Care for Dependent People: Meeting the New Agenda in Services for the Elderly*. Bunnik: Netherlands Institute of Gerontology, 115–31.

10

The State and Pay Equity:
Juggling Similarity and Difference,
Meaning, and Structures[1]

PAT ARMSTRONG

Pay Equity: Not Just a Matter of Money

In his Preface to Leonard Marsh's *Report on Social Security for Canada 1943*, Michael Bliss (1975: ix) describes the development of the welfare state as a 'transition from a society in which provision for destitution was largely an individual responsibility to one in which a variety of programs guarantees a level of social and economic security for all.' Bliss goes on to say that 'very little has been written about the nature of this transition, the concepts underlying it, the social, economic and political environment in which it took place, or the men involved.' He makes no mention of the women involved, or of the importance to women of the welfare state.

Yet women have been significant players in the development of social programs and welfare state policies at the federal, provincial, and local levels. Indeed, many programs have been introduced in direct response to women's conditions and concerns. And women are primary recipients of some state programs as well as the primary labour force in many state services. Of course, women have not always been successful in having their demands met. Moreover, even when women claim victory, the results are often contrary to their interests or at least to those of some women. As a result, women have had, and continue to look to the state for both protection and support, while remaining sceptical about, and critical of the protection and support the state provides.

Although women's demands on the state can be traced back to the earliest days of state formation, it has perhaps been most visible in the establishment of the Royal Commission on the Status of Women and in the subsequent developments around equity legislation. The commission was established as a result of pressure from various women's groups and was designed to address equity issues. The report of the commission (Status of Women, 1970) carefully documented women's inequality, but it was in general a very optimistic piece. There were certainly critics who argued at the time that the report did not go far enough. But many were hopeful that the very exposure of inequality would serve to improve women's conditions and that a state concerned with protecting democratic rights would take action to ensure that this was the case.

In the quarter century since the publication of the report, however, disillusionment has set in. Progress has been very slow. In some areas, the state has failed to introduce legislation, programs, or policies that would promote equality. In other areas, state action has failed to do the job. While there have been some improvements in women's conditions, most women continue to do women's work at women's wages in and out of the formal economy (Armstrong and Armstrong, 1984; Connelly and MacDonald, 1990). Housework and child care remain primarily women's responsibility (Luxton, 1980; Michelson, 1985; Parliament, 1989), and there has been little improvement in the availability, cost, and quality of child care facilities (Cook, 1986; McIntosh and Rauhala, 1989). Sexual harassment and physical abuse are still common, and there have been no significant advances in terms of women's ability to control their fertility (Guberman and Wolfe, 1985; MacLeod, 1986). While some changes have benefited some women, in general the state has failed to fulfil the expectations created by the royal commission's report.

This failure has given rise to both new theories about women's conditions and new strategies for change. Although often frustrated by the rate of progress, many women have continued to look to the state for legislative changes that would benefit women. Drawing on their experiences with existing legislation and with both state and private sector practices, some women have pressured for legislation that focuses on the structural basis of inequality rather than on the discriminatory ideas that had been a primary concern of the Royal Commission and of earlier legislation (Armstrong and Armstrong, 1978: 118–23).

The Ontario pay equity legislation of 1987 resulted from the efforts of such women. It reflected both their conviction that the state could provide the conditions for some fundamental change and their analysis of structural processes that kept women in their place. In calling for the legislation, however, the Equal Pay Coalition made it clear that 'this legislation is not a panacea and is only one, albeit a major step in achieving economic equality for women. Even when this legislation is in place, many women will still face discrimination at work which must be addressed through other means, such as mandatory day care, more retraining opportunities, higher minimum wage laws, and easier access to unionization' (1986: 1).

Especially within the universities, however, some women have become convinced that the state can and will do little to help women in different classes, races, and ethnic and age groups. Many of these women have been turning to approaches that can be collectively called postmodern. Although there are significant differences among and within various theories that fall under this rubric, the many versions of postmodernism grow out of some common criticisms and concerns. For many postmodernists, appealing to the state for help in gaining equal pay would simply be wrong-headed; inappropriate in part because there can be no policy that covers women, given that the very category women is rejected.

These theorists have emphasized the complexity of relations, structures, and processes, rejecting what they define as simple approaches or simple solutions based on grand theories that apply to all women. They have attacked what is frequently termed 'essentialism'; the notion that there are fundamental truths, shared values for assessing progress or rational action measured according to objective criteria (Fuss, 1991). Related to both these issues are their critiques of dichotomies such as women and men. Instead, they prefer to think in terms of a variety of sexual identities and to emphasize the differences among women. Their focus is on 'the importance of the subjective in constituting the meaning of women's lived reality' (Weedon, 1987: 8). Consequently, they 'make language the site of a struggle over meaning which is a prerequisite for political change' (ibid.: 9). For these theorists, it is critical to focus on meaning and to take action 'within the confines of some local determinism, some interpretive community' (Harvey, 1989: 52), rather than to develop legislative strategies at the provincial or national level. It is not clear, however, precisely what this would mean in terms of strategies to increase pay.

This essays evaluates the Ontario pay equity legislation primarily in terms of its impact on women's current pay and on women's future possibilities. It therefore assumes that there are criteria for assessing change that are related to concrete realities and that some legislative strategies can benefit women as a sex. In other words, it takes a perspective that is similar in many ways to that of the women who fought for the legislation. At the same time, it takes the critiques of postmodernists into account and assesses the impact of this legislation in terms of the emphasis on complexity, on differences among women, on the relative nature of worth, and on the importance of meaning.

It argues that, although many women will receive more pay as a result of the act, the recognition of complexity that is built into the act could lead to increased pay differences among women. In other words, in conforming to a postmodernist emphasis, the legislation may serve to increase inequality among women. At the same time, the experience of applying the legislation has supported the postmodernist claim that there are no objective, universal criteria establishing essential worth. Worth, to use their terminology, is socially constructed rather than objectively determined or measured. Indeed, the implementation process has also frequently served to transform the struggle into one over meaning, a struggle that postmodernists could applaud and a struggle that may have important long-term implications for women as a sex.

It concludes that the impact of this state legislation is not predetermined and is frequently contradictory. The Act could result in some gains for small numbers of women while creating the impression that the issue has been settled once and for all. But it could also legitimize women's right to better pay and transform the definitions of skill, effort, responsibility, and working conditions while challenging established, hierarchical ways of organizing work. The particular consequences will be determined by women's struggles at both the local and provincial level and by their struggles both over pay and over the meaning and value of work.

The argument is developed through an examination of the major features of the Ontario pay equity legislation. While many of the details are specific to this act, there are lessons to be learned that have a much broader application to state legislation in general and pay equity legislation in particular.

Complexity and Difference

The Ontario Pay Equity Act is a complicated and path-breaking piece of legislation. Like all legislation, it should be understood within a particular historical context. It reflects the efforts of a group known as the Equal Pay Coalition to make the legislation as inclusive and as compulsory as possible. It also reflects employers' attempts to limit the impact of the legislation as much as possible. It is the outcome of both a long struggle by a variety of women's groups and of a particular political and economic situation.

In the long history of demands for pay equity, the coalition of unions, community groups, and professional and business organizations that fought for the Ontario pay equity legislation is a relatively recent phenomenon (Armstrong and Armstrong, 1990a, 1990b; Lewis, 1988; Warskett, 1990). Formed in 1976, it represents more than a million women and men from widely divergent groups. Members of the Equal Pay Coalition have learned from experience that equal pay legislation requiring women to find identical or substantially identical work in order to establish inequity had a limited impact on women's pay. The problem was compounded by legislation that required individuals to initiate complaints, that allowed many exclusions, and that provided very small penalties for those few found guilty of discrimination (Armstrong and Armstrong, 1990a, 1990b).

The impact was limited because, for the most part, women and men are segregated in terms of jobs and industries, and women's work is consistently paid less than the work of men. It is also limited because employers benefit from women doing women's work at women's wages and thus have little incentive to change their practices (Armstrong and Armstrong, 1984; Connelly and MacDonald, 1990). The legislation was particularly ineffective in improving the pay for part-time workers and for immigrant or visible minority women who were concentrated in the private sector where unions have been either non-existent or inactive on this question. When the coalition sought new legislation, then, it wanted to ensure that it addressed the segregation of the labour force, the low value attached to women's work, the complexities that allowed for exclusions, the variations among workplaces, and the resistance of employers (Equal Pay Coalition, 1986: 2–3).

Although the coalition had enjoyed some successes in their efforts to work under the old legislation and to work for change through collective agreements, it had been in existence for almost a decade before a particular set of circumstances helped to overcome many of the remaining barriers to major legislative change. First, the accord that made it possible for the Ontario Liberals to form a government after the 1985 provincial election had the introduction of equal pay for work of equal value legislation as a condition of New Democratic Party support. Second, the Ontario economy was in the midst of an economic boom, making it somewhat easier to make demands on private sector employers and on public coffers. Third, a number of strong feminists who supported pay equity legislation were employed in the Women's Directorate of the provincial government, and it was this body which was mandated to chair the Interministerial Task Force on Pay Equity (Cuneo, 1988). Fourth, a series of rulings under the old legislation, backed by extensive research, had both demonstrated the need for new legislation that went well beyond individual complaints and laid the basis for such legislation by moving towards equal value and collective settlement. The Ontario Pay Equity Act that was introduced in 1987 included many concessions to employers' interests, but it marked a significant departure from existing legislation in responding to Coalition demands.

Unlike much of the legislation on pay equity introduced elsewhere, this Act applied to both the private and public sectors. The legislation required employers to produce pay equity plans and to negotiate these with unions when workplaces are unionized. It provided major penalties linked to time schedules, included part-time workers and all benefits, called for a job evaluation scheme free of gender bias, and established an independent tribunal to oversee the implementation of the Act. It clearly stated that the purpose 'is to redress systemic gender discrimination in compensation for work performed by employees in female job classes' (Ontario, 1987: 12). Systemic discrimination implied that, as a consequence of work structures, women shared a common problem in terms of pay. But the implementation of the Act was based on what postmodernists might call local determination. This local determination could mean that political issues are transformed into technical ones and that pay gaps among women increase. This problem is discussed in more detail later in the chapter.

The Impact of Local Determination and Difference

The inclusion of the private as well as the public sector was an important step in ensuring the coverage of all women. But the details of the Act mean that the women's sector of employment could have a significant impact on women's possibilities for pay increases. There are important differences in terms of when employers are required to post pay equity plans and of when they are to implement increases. As well, there are differences in terms of which employers are covered by the legislation and of what various employers are required to do by the Act. All of the public sector, but only those private sector employers with more than 500 employees, were required to post a plan two years after the Act came into effect, while employers with between 100 and 500 employees were given three years. Those with more than 9 but fewer than 100 employees 'may establish pay equity plans for any of the employer's establishments' (Ontario, 1987: 38) and can take five or six years to do so, depending on their size. If these employers decide not to set up pay equity plans, they are still required to demonstrate how they determined that a pay equity plan was not necessary, should a complaint be made. Those with fewer than 10 employees in the private sector must wait longer than public sector employees for their plans and payments. The estimated quarter of a million women in very small private sector establishments are excluded entirely (Harrington, 1987: 1), and many of those in small companies will have to complain in order to even see a plan. Many of those in these smaller workplaces are immigrant and visible minority women.

The Act emphasizes local determination of pay equity plans where these plans are required. According to the legislation, 'Each employer is responsible for implementing and maintaining the pay equity plan with respect to the employer's employees' (Ontario, 1987: 10). Many organizations contract out parts of their work, allocating, for example, some of the cleaning to one firm and some of the cooking to another, while hiring employees directly to do a large part of the remaining labour. As a result, women working in the same building, perhaps doing the same kind of job, could find themselves under different pay equity plans. Some may find themselves with no plan at all because their contracting firm is too small to be covered by the Act, even though they are employed in a large establishment.

Not only are there different plans for different employers, there may also be different plans for each of the employer's establishments if they are located in different 'geographic divisions' (ibid.: 4). This requirement could mean that employees paid by the same organization, but working in different parts of the province, could have quite separate and unequal pay equity plans. It could also mean that, by virtue of their geographic location, some quite large employers could avoid the Act altogether because each of the establishments in the various geographic regions is too small to be included under the legislation.

Within the establishments of the same employer, there may also be vast differences in the kinds of awards women receive. According to the Act, 'Pay equity is achieved when the job rate for the female job class that is the subject of the comparison is at least equal to the job rate for a male job class in the same establishment where the work performed in the two job classes is of equal or comparable worth' (ibid.: 12). Translated, this means that in order to have their wages raised under the Act, women have to go through the complicated process outlined below.

Implementing Pay Equity: Making Difference

The process of implementing pay equity is largely the responsibility of employers in non-unionized firms, although women can complain individually or collectively about the plan to the Pay Equity Commission. In unionized establishments the process is negotiated for each bargaining unit by the union. In many cases this means women are involved on the negotiating committees.

As the first step towards pay equity, women or their representatives have to establish that they are members of a female job class. What constitutes a job class may itself be a matter of dispute, given that the legislation (ibid.: 6) defines a job class in terms of positions that 'have similar duties and responsibilities and require similar qualifications, are filled by similar recruiting procedures and have the same compensation schedule, salary grade or range of salary rates.' A female job class is one that is at least 60 per cent female and is therefore somewhat easier to determine. However, the Act (ibid.: 10) allows for other agreements which consider 'the historical incumbency of the job class, gender stereotypes of fields of work and such other criteria as may be prescribed by the regulations.'

Next, it is necessary to find a male job class that is deemed to be of at least comparable worth. This means finding a job class that is at least 70 per cent male or is otherwise determined to be a male job class (ibid.: 6). Then female and male job classes must be compared in terms of 'the skill, effort and responsibility normally required in the performance of the work and the conditions under which it is normally performed' (ibid.: 12).

If there is a bargaining unit, women must first look for a comparable male job within their bargaining unit. Similarly, those outside a bargaining unit must first seek comparators outside any bargaining unit (ibid.: 14). If none can be found through this procedure, then women can search for other comparable male job classes within the establishment, but they may not go outside the establishment.

If women find a male job class that is of comparable value but is more highly paid, then they can claim the male job rate. If they find more than one comparable male job class, then they either get the lowest job rate for an equally valued male job class or the highest job rate of a male job class that is determined to be of less value than the female job class. If they find no male comparators or no male comparators that are more highly paid than the female job class, then they are out of luck.

Thus, as a result of these complex requirements, some women may find themselves a comparable male job class that is paid more while others, in the same location, working for the same employer, may find themselves unable to find an appropriate male job class. Those in bargaining units may be better protected by unions willing to challenge old schemes for establishing the value of skill, effort, responsibility, and working conditions or willing to challenge how establishment, employer, or job class is determined. Those 867,000 women that the Ontario Pay Equity Commission (1989: 16) estimates work in predominately female sectors without male comparators would, under the original legislation, receive no awards at all.

Amendments to the Act attempted to address some of the problems created by lack of comparators within the establishment. These amendments allowed women who were employed in female job classes in the public sector and who did not have a comparator in their establishment to seek a proxy in another public sector establishment. In other words, they could look to another, similar workplace that did have a comparable job class, one used in a pay equity plan, and replicate that comparison. Although proxies were not provided for in the private sector, the amendments did allow proportionate comparisons. This meant that it was not necessary to find a strictly comparable male job class in order to gain pay equity settlements. Instead, those developing the plans could argue for payments on the basis of the percentage of worth relative to a male job class. But these amendments, too, created very complicated requirements. And they still left many women without any comparators or pay equity settlements and still meant great differences among those who did receive payments under the pay equity plans.

The complex requirements – only some of which have been outlined here – not only mean that differences among women may increase under the Act as a result of the uneven coverage. They also mean that the determination of equity awards is so complicated that many women are excluded from even complaining about the implementation because they do not understand the process. The complicated and detailed regulations may transform a political process into a technical one, allowing only those with the time and the expertise to participate in the local determination.

The particular consequences of the Ontario Pay Equity Act will depend on the strength and resources of those negotiating with employers as well as on how the Act is interpreted and implemented. This necessarily means that the results will be uneven. Reports on the plans filed suggest that many women with strong negotiators, and in locations that make them eligible and make it possible to find comparators, will see significant gains. But these reports also suggest that differences among women will increase, leaving the weakest even weaker in relative pay terms.

Nurses provide just one example of the inequities that can result from the Act. Those at the University of Toronto, for example, were able to compare their work to that of professional engineering officers and received a 45 per cent pay hike that will increase their wages to more than $54,000 a year (Gorrie, 1990a). Meanwhile, the non-unionized nurses at Mississauga General Hospital were compared to pastry chefs and did not receive any compensation (Gorrie, 1990b). These nurses will continue to have wages that range between $35,000 and $40,000 a year.

Not surprisingly then, some nurses are fighting to define employer and establishment as broadly as possible in order to find a suitable comparator. A Supreme Court decision has upheld a Pay Equity Tribunal hearing decision which agreed with nurses working for the Region of Haldimand–Norfolk that the municipality was also the employer of the police force (Coutts, 1989). This decision means that these nurses can now compare their work to that of the more highly paid police officers, which may mean significant gains for these nurses. Whether or not this means that the definition of employer will be extended to benefit women in many other municipalities remains to be seen.

Similar patterns of disparity are evident in pay equity plans for women who do clerical work. Women who belong to the Ontario Public Service Employees' Union and who do clerical or secretarial work for the government added $1.32 to their average $14.70 hourly rate. At the same time, the non-unionized clerical workers at a community college received no addition to their maximum rate that ranges from $10.72 to $11.63 an hour (Centennial College of Applied Arts and Technology, 1989). These nurses and clerical workers are all part of the public sector, but the local determination of plans is increasing differences among them.

The case of day care workers suggests that the differences between public and private sector workers may even increase as a result of the legislation. Child care workers currently employed by municipalities may make up to twice as much as those employed in private centres. According to the government's pay equity plan, the child care workers employed by the province added $2.00 an hour to their wage as a result of the legislation (Coutts, 1989). Meanwhile, almost all private sector child care workers may be excluded from benefits under the legislation because they work in very small establishments or because they have no male comparators.

Many of the women who are employed in the major food chains and who belong to the United Food and Commercial Workers Union have also made significant gains in pay. Cashiers at A&P, for instance, were compared to stock clerks and, as a result, saw wage increases of $28.26 a week. The women working in the bakeries and at the deli counters in these stores were able to establish that their work was comparable to that of night crew foreman and, as a result, gained $36.00 a week (*Toronto Star*, 1990). The large number of women who work in small bakeries, corner delis, and many retail outlets that employ fewer than ten people, however, will not even have a chance to look for comparisons and make claims under the Act. Moreover, many in larger establishments will not find male comparators or will not have job evaluation schemes that demonstrate that their jobs are of equivalent worth. The result, as in the case of nurses and clerical workers, will be greater differences among women in terms of pay.

The Equal Pay Coalition wanted legislation that would acknowledge women are paid less than men and that would provide a compulsory but 'flexible approach permitting a range of bargaining options' to address this inequity (Equal Pay Coalition, 1986: 2–3). The coalition never spelled out exactly what this flexibility would mean. The legislation they got emphasized difference and local determination, in large measure as a result of pressure from employers. This emphasis has laid the basis for increasing disparities among women, even among women doing the same job and paid out of the same coffers, and even among those working in the same location. It has, at the same time, excluded many women from the process of negotiation, because the technical details involved overwhelmed many who did not have the time and resources necessary for such a complex task.

The Australian experience indicates that minimum wages set by occupation are much more effective in increasing women's wages and in decreasing the gap between average male and female wages (Adelberg, 1986). The Australian approach also involves much less complex and technical negotiations while recognizing the power struggles that are central to determining pay. The settlement of wages through sectoral bargaining, rather than through the application of complex legislation, means that much more emphasis is put on the politics of equality than on the techniques of measurement. The emphasis on difference, complexity, and local determination that is more in line with postmodernist thinking may well serve to further divide women from each other in terms of both pay and participation. It allows employers to pit women against each other and against men while limiting the overall gains for workers. If the legislation had carried through on the recognition of the systemic discrimination that keeps women's wages low, and gone on to develop a scheme that applied to all woman in particular occupations, it may well have been more effective at raising women's wages in ways that would not have such an uneven impact on women as a sex. The emphasis on difference is proving to be a double-edged sword, one that can be readily used against women.

The Struggle Over Meaning

For many postmodernists, the most important negotiations are those around discourse and meaning. Integral to the battles around the Ontario pay equity legislation have been struggles over meaning. All legislation involves negotiations over how terms, conditions, and actions are to be understood. But such negotiations have for the most part assumed a shared world-view, one based primarily on the perspectives of men with a common race and class background. This legislation fundamentally challenges many of those traditional ways of seeing.

Some of the battles have centred on how such terms as employer, establishment, job class, and job rate are to be understood. The significance of struggles around these interpretations and of the independence given to the Tribunal should not be underestimated. Both the wording of the legislation and the composition of the Tribunal have important consequences for negotiations around meaning. Women form the majority of Tribunal members, and each three-member Tribunal that hears cases has a member representing employees. The initial rulings of the Tribunal suggested that it would not simply be governed by old understandings. As Mary Cornish, a lawyer for the Ontario Nurses' Association, said of the decision to extend the meaning of employer in the Haldimand–Norfolk case, the decision supports the Pay Equity Tribunal's intent 'to interpret the pay equity act in a broad fashion so the maximum numbers of people benefit' (quoted in Coutts, 1989). The decision of the Tribunal in the case of Women's College Hospital also suggested a significant break with the past and made it clear that the legislation was intended to be interpreted as the basis for affirmative action. However, unlike the Haldimand–Norfolk case, the decision was not unanimous, and rulings since then have been less path breaking.

The case known as Women's College actually involved nurses from three major Toronto hospitals. A major issue was gender bias in the job evaluation scheme the employer was using to establish pay equity. In rejecting the proposed job evaluation plan, the Tribunal made it clear that 'sex stereotyping pervades the evaluation of work performed by women and men and thus affects the wages paid' (1992: 17). Citing the evidence on gender bias, the Tribunal went on to say that 'we are not left to wonder whether these findings can be generalized to the Ontario experience; that is, whether discrimination in compensation exists for the employees in female job classes in Ontario. The Act explicitly recognizes the existence of such legislation and is designed to remedy it.'

But, more important in the long term, are the struggles over how women's pay and women's work are to be understood and valued. The Equal Pay Coalition (1986: 2) won a major victory when the legislation included the 'strong introductory statement of principle and philosophy' that the coalition proposed. In stating that the purpose is 'to redress systemic gender discrimination in compensation performed by employees in female job classes' (Ontario, 1987: 12), the Act was acknowledging that the labour force is segregated and that this segregation is directly linked to women's low pay. Women's low pay was thus defined as a shared rather than an individual problem and as a problem that results from collective discrimination, rather than from women's individual capacities and contributions or from individual employer's minority views.

The notion of women's shared inequity is further reinforced by the requirement that compensation be paid to women as members of a female job class. This contrasts with legislation such as employment equity that begins with the assumption that women collectively face discrimination but seeks to remedy the problem by hiring or promoting individual women. Solutions designed for individual women may serve to divide women from each other and to integrate these individual women more fully into the existing hierarchy. They imply that there is nothing wrong with the structures, just with the allocation of people within those structures. In contrast, solutions that compensate all members of a job class have the potential, at least, to encourage women to work together for structural change.

That the Act required all large employers to develop a pay equity plan implied that all employers were assumed to be at least potential discriminators; that is, they were assumed guilty until proven innocent (Armstrong, 1988). This, too, marked an important departure from previous legislation that assumed employers did not discriminate against women. An employer 'was otherwise defined only if a woman complained and proved that an individual employer was guilty. The burden of proof was shifted by this proactive legislation and the relationship between employers and employees redefined.

Proactive legislation based on the assumption of systemic discrimination and requiring that women receive compensation by job class brings a new meaning to women's low pay. The implementation of such legislation could allow the problem to be defined as solved, even though many women will see little or no pay increases under the Act. But it could also mean that women's pay claims are seen as legitimate, and women could use this as the basis for not only extending the demands for decent pay, but also for expanding their claims into other aspects of their work.

Many of the current battles over meaning relate to the requirement that employers use 'a gender-neutral comparison system' (Ontario, 1987: 22) when evaluating the skill, effort, responsibility, and working conditions involved in female and male job classes. This requirement opens up the possibility for redefining how work is valued and structured.

Of course, this requirement does not necessarily lead to the emergence of new meanings and values. In some cases, gender neutrality is interpreted to mean a more universal application of existing job evaluation schemes to all male and female jobs classes. In other cases, it is understood to imply modifications to existing schemes, such as the inclusion of references to female-dominated jobs and of examples of tasks more common to women's work or the avoidance of sexist language.

This more careful and universal application of existing evaluation schemes, even in unmodified form, is likely to result in some compensation for women, given the large gaps in male and female wages and the past neglect of the content of women's work. But it is not likely to lead to a redefinition of women's work. Indeed, it may primarily serve to reinforce current values and meanings.

This result is likely because most of these job evaluation schemes have been developed and standardized on male-dominated jobs in the industrial sectors or on managerial positions in the service sector where few women work. In other words, they focus on what men do and are designed to measure what men do. When, for example, a scheme intended to measure the work of those men making cars is applied to the work of women caring for children, much of the work of women may simply disappear. Moreover, they have been designed as management tools, even though some have been negotiated with what are usually male-dominated unions. Thus, if management has traditionally paid women low wages or traditionally rewarded men who garden more than women who type, the job evaluation schemes are likely to justify these wages rather than challenge them. The existing job evaluation schemes reflect the content and structure of those male jobs as well as those methods of organizing work. And they reflect values that are more the result of power struggles over the worth of male-dominated work than they are the result of some universal and objectively determined components of jobs. In other words, job evaluation schemes are not simply a measurement of job components that have some universally agreed upon worth (Armstrong and Armstrong, 1990a). They embody negotiated values based on power relations and indicate the worth attached to what men do. They are also more likely to replicate the value attached to work in the private, goods-producing sector, where men dominate, than they are to assess adequately the services provided in the public sector, where women predominate.

Thus, the more universal application of old schemes may help to indicate how much of women's work is like men's work and pay them for what is similar. But, given the segregation of the labour force, it is unlikely to lead to a re-evaluation of what most women do. If this is the case, the implementation of the Pay Equity Act will not take us much beyond the equal pay for equal work legislation while implying that it does much more.

Recognizing the values built into current job evaluation schemes and backed by enough resources to mount a challenge, some women have begun to use the legislation to transform the way skill, effort, responsibility, and working conditions are evaluated. The Ontario Nurses' Association (ONA), for example, has argued before the Hearings Tribunal that the comparison system and methodology proposed by Women's College Hospital 'is gender-biased in its structure and design and cannot properly capture the job content of employees' (Ontario Nurses' Association, n.d.: 4). As they did in making a similar claim with regard to the scheme proposed by the region of Haldimand–Norfolk, the Association is maintaining that the job evaluation scheme is biased in terms of what is captured, how it is captured, and how what is captured is evaluated.

As the ONA is establishing, through their cases on current job evaluation schemes, much of the skill, effort, responsibility, and the working conditions central to many women's jobs remains invisible. The emphasis on discrete tasks makes it impossible to capture the overlapping and complex nature of women's skills or the caring that is a continuous part of many women's jobs. While the effort involved in lifting objects is recorded, that involved in convincing an elderly patient or a child to eat is not. Responsibility for money, goods, and supervising those lower on the formal hierarchy gets evaluated, yet cooperating and coordinating work with others and taking actual, as opposed to official, responsibility for people is usually ignored. The stress created by working outdoors or in excessive heat is often counted, but the stress of working with dying patients or demanding children does not get counted.

Capturing these aspects of women's work, the ONA is pointing out, requires a fundamental rethinking of how job evaluations are structured and carried out. Modelled on male work and hierarchical structures, the job evaluation schemes in use do not employ methods designed to reveal the invisible aspects of many women's work. Because both women and men have learned to think in terms of male models of work, capturing the content of women's work requires much more than adding new examples or removing sexist language. Current schemes have not been designed to have women or men think in alternative ways about what constitutes skill, effort, or responsibility or what constitutes difficult working conditions.

Even when aspects that are most common in women's work are captured, they are seldom highly valued. Responsibility for money is more highly valued than is caring for people. Garbage removal is considered more onerous than cleaning dirty diapers; police work more dangerous than dressing the wounds of patients with contagious diseases. As contentious as the question of what is captured in evaluation schemes is how what is captured gets evaluated. These women are not only fighting to expose the extensive skills, effort, responsibilities, and onerous working conditions involved in their work. They are also seeking to define these as valuable.

This struggle over the gender bias of job evaluation schemes is really a struggle over the meaning and value of women's work. But in order to negotiate this new meaning, women have to establish links to actual activities and to demonstrate that the job characteristics they describe are common to many women's jobs. Postmodernists have drawn our attention to the importance of the struggle over meaning. But they have also cautioned against focusing on women as a sex. Yet it may well be that the emphasis on defining the problems women face as collective ones, created by systemic discrimination, proves the most useful in women's long-term efforts to improve their conditions of work. The struggle over meaning that the postmodernists recommend is also a struggle over defining what women share in their daily work activities – a process that contradicts the postmodernist emphasis on difference. It could lead to better pay for women under the pay equity legislation. It could also have a much longer term and more pervasive effect if women's work is redefined. But in order to have a much more widespread impact, this new meaning will have to go beyond the hearing rooms of the Pay Equity Tribunal, beyond a struggle over language among a few, and get translated in concrete ways into job evaluation schemes as well as into shared meanings of the whole population.

Conclusion

The Ontario legislation, as the Pay Equity Coalition has pointed out, is not a panacea. The impact may well have contradictory consequences for women (Armstrong and Armstrong, 1990b). The long- and short-term consequences will depend, to a large extent, on how the legislation is applied and interpreted. This, in turn, will reflect women's collective efforts to transform the meaning attached to women's work and to extend the coverage of the Act to as many women as possible.

Certainly it is important, as the postmodernists make clear, to struggle over meaning and language. Such struggles can help transform both how we think and how women are paid. But, in order to be effective in changing women's conditions, this struggle needs to be connected to actual activities and often to activities that are common to many women. Emphasis on meaning can have a long-term impact on women's efforts to improve their conditions only if the struggles are successful in ensuring that these meanings are widely shared.

And while it is important, as postmodernists argue, to recognize complexity and difference, strategies intended to improve women's conditions involve thinking not only in terms of how women differ, but also in terms of what they share. Emphasizing difference can serve, as is the case with the Ontario Pay Equity legislation, to increase differences among women. At the same time, the legislation is based on an assumption of systemic discrimination that happens to women as a sex, and the success of the legislation, limited though it may be, can be attributed mainly to this assumption. While the results are inevitably contradictory and uneven, it could be argued that some of the greatest gains for women collectively and individually have come from the state intervening on behalf of women or of groups of women. This is becoming increasingly evident as states more often use a stress on difference and individual choice as a justification for withdrawing from traditional welfare state programs. The Pay Equity Act in Ontario can be seen as one of the last gasps of a welfare state prepared to recognize both systemic inequality that has an impact on women as a group and the responsibility of the state to intervene on their behalf. It has improved the wages of many women and transformed the attitudes of many others, even though it has not served to end wage inequality between women and men or among women.

There is much to be learned through the examination of particular legislation, as Michael Bliss (1975) made clear, about the more general implications for both the theory and practice of state intervention. But the lessons are not worth learning unless we recognize that the participants come with a variety of identities and attach a variety of meanings to the process. However, it is also necessary to recognize that an emphasis on difference and meaning is not without its own contradictions for women and can serve to work against women, especially in terms of the welfare state.

Note

1 Another version of this chapter is published in C. Andrew and S. Rodgers (eds.), *Women and the Canadian State*. Kingston: McGill–Queens, 1997, pp. 122–37.

References

Adelberg, Ellen. 1986. 'Australia's Pay Equity Law Is Tougher Than Ontario's – And It Works.' *The Ottawa Citizen* (November 29): B16.

Armstrong, Pat. 1988. *Predominately Female Sectors: Health Care*. Toronto: Ontario Pay Equity Commission.

– and Hugh Armstrong. 1978. *The Double Ghetto: Canadian Women and Their Segregated Work*. Toronto: McClelland and Stewart.

– 1984. *The Double Ghetto: Canadian Women and Their Segregated Work*. Toronto: McClelland and Stewart.

– 1990a. 'Lessons From Pay Equity.' *Studies in Political Economy* 3 (Summer): 29–54.

– 1990b. 'Limited Possibilities and Possible Limits for Pay Equity within and beyond the Ontario Legislation.' Paper presented at the Conference on Pay Equity: Theory and Practice. Osgoode Hall Law School, 10–12 May.

Bliss, Michael. 1975. 'Preface.' In Leonard Marsh, ed., *Report on Social Security For Canada 1943*. Toronto: University of Toronto Press.

Centennial College of Applied Arts and Technology. 1989. 'Pay Equity Plan for Non-Bargaining Unit Employees.' December. Mimeo.

Connelly, Patricia, and Martha MacDonald. 1990. *Women and the Labour Force*. Ottawa: Supply and Services Canada for Statistics Canada.

Cook, Katie. 1986. *Report of the Task Force on Childcare*. Ottawa: Supply and Services Canada for Statistics Canada.

Coutts, Jane. 1989. 'Court Ruling Widens Sweep of Equity Laws.' *Globe and Mail*, 25 November. A14.

Cuneo, Carl. 1988. *Pay Equity, The Labour-Feminist Challenge*. Toronto: Oxford University Press.

Equal Pay Coalition. 1986. 'Response to the Ontario Government's Green Paper on Pay Equity.' Toronto, 24 January, Mimeo.

Fuss, Diana. 1991. *Essentially Speaking: Feminism, Nature and Difference*. London and New York: Routledge, 5.

Gorrie, Peter. 1990a. 'Pay Equity Increases to Add 2% to Payroll.' *Toronto Star*, 20 January, C1 and C2.

– 1990b. 'Pay Equity Creating a Conundrum.' *Toronto Star*, 24 February; C1, C2.

Guberman, Connie, and Margie Wolfe, eds. 1985. *No Safe Place*. Toronto: Women's Press.

Harrington, Denise. 1987. 'Report to the Minister of Labour by the Ontario Pay Equity Commission on the Sectors of the Economy which are Predominately Female as Required under the *Pay Equity Act* Section 33(2) (c).' Toronto, 5 January, Mimeo.

Harvey, David. 1989. *The Condition of Postmodernity*. Oxford: Basil Blackwell.

Lewis, Debra. 1988. *Just Give Us the Money*. Vancouver: Women's Research Centre.

Luxton, Meg. 1980. *More Than a Labour of Love*. Toronto: Women's Press.

MacLeod, Linda. 1986. *Wife Battering in Canada*. Ottawa: Supply and Services Canada for the Canadian Advisory Council on the Status of Women.

McIntosh, Andrew, and Ann Rauhala. 1989. 'Day Care in Ontario Fall Short on Care.' *Globe and Mail*, 3 February; A1.

Michelson, William. 1985. *From Sun to Sun: Daily Obligations and Community Structures*. Ottawa: Rowman and Allenhead.

Ontario, Bill 154. 1987. An Act to Provide Pay Equity, Ontario Legislative Assembly, Toronto.

Ontario Nurses' Association. n.d. Applicant Union's Statement of Facts and Issues. Addressed to the Hearings Tribunal, with regard to Women's College Hospital.

Ontario Pay Equity Commission. 1989. 'Report to the Ministry of Labour by the Ontario Pay Equity Commission on the Options Relating to the Achievement of Pay Equity in Sectors of the Economy which are Predominately Female.' Toronto, 16.

Parliament, Jo-Anne B. 1989. 'How Canadians Spend their Day.' *Canadian Social Trends* 15 (Winter): 23–7.

Pay Equity Tribunal, Women's College Hospital (4 Aug. 1992) 30008-89, 200211-89; 20018-89; 20029-89; 20034-89; 20036-89 (PEHT).

Status of Women, Royal Commission on the. 1970. *Report*. Ottawa: Information Canada.

Toronto Star. 1990. 'Pay Equity Raises Go to Food, Stone Workers.' *Toronto Star*, 5, January, C3.

Warskett, Rosemary. 1990. 'Wage Solidarity and Equal Value: Or Gender and Class in the Restructuring of Workplace Hierarchies.' *Studies in Political Economy* 32 (Summer): 55–84.

Weedon, Chris. 1987. *Feminist Practice and Poststructuralist Theory.* Oxford: Basil Blackwell.

PART IV

Women Challenging the Welfare State

11

Challenging Diversity: Black Women and Social Welfare[1]

PATRICIA M. DAENZER

Within the Canadian welfare state, racial minority women are challenging their mainstream neo-colonization. Increasingly, they are establishing ethno-cultural services defined and controlled by their own communities. This rejection of traditional forms of oppression has a long history. This chapter, then, situates the community activism of contemporary Black women[2] within the history of Black women's equality struggles. The Black women's struggles that are discussed in this chapter pertain to more than organizing around welfare service delivery as it is conventionally understood. Social welfare has always been much more broadly defined by Blacks, and it includes action to break down the barriers to full citizenship, and the broad goals of racially specific social liberation. It is, in many ways, a struggle to relocate Blacks out of positions of racial oppression and into places of political and social equality. And, unlike the White women's movement against patriarchy, the struggle of Black women incorporates the additional dimension of anti-racist resistance.

In illuminating the relationship between activist Black women and the mainstream, I show that in the 1990s, Black women have grown particularly weary of institutional lip-service to their issues. Against great odds and with limited resources, Black women are organizing to create changes in welfare services and other institutional arrangements. In small numbers and with an evolving theoretical position, they are focusing on health care, community education, child care, services to abused women, legal services, services to new immigrants, and elementary and secondary school education. For a growing and active constituency, community self-definition and control of service delivery are important goals to achieve what Klaff (1980) refers to as symbolic community identity.

A small but growing body of Canadian literature suggests that when members of minority groups seek to use the services of mainstream agencies, the cultural insensitivity they confront in some agencies functions as a structural impediment to service accessibility (Teram and White, 1992; Lipsky, 1984; Doyle and Visano, 1987). Some authors explain this social distance between minority groups and mainstream agencies in terms of theories of alienation and social marginalization that have their roots in socioeconomic disadvantage and racial intolerance (Polakow, 1993; Staples and Johnson, 1993; Rodgers, 1987; Bronfenbrenner, 1986). In contrast, other perspectives argue that some forms of segregation are voluntary and essential to group development (Klaff, 1980).

This chapter develops the perspective that ethno-cultural social service agencies serve positive and community-building ends. Black women's support for their own separate services should be understood as a healthy sign of political emancipation and not as an indication of alienation or social 'dysfunction.' In this chapter, then, I explore Black women's activism and its relation to the welfare state. As a departure point for this discussion, I draw upon a recent participatory action research (PAR) project that was undertaken by a group of Black women. The PAR project provides a good illustration of the uneasy relationship between some Black women and the 'welfare state,' as well as with White women's concerns. In the next section of the chapter, this uneasy relationship is situated in a discussion of the racially gendered history that has helped to shape and locate the position of Black women today. In the section after that, Black women's activism and the issue of racially segregated welfare services is viewed against a historical backdrop of Black community relations in Canada and women-led emancipatory initiatives. I find that the current separatist trend has much in common with earlier Black movements, and I argue that it has the potential to transform aspects of social service delivery. This isolationist tactic, so seemingly 'disconnected' from the mainstream, is essential to the continued emancipation of all Black Canadians, women in particular.

Participatory Research: Black Women Define Their Issue

The PAR study began in 1992 with the cooperation of a group of eighteen Black sole mothers and the aid of a small research grant. The project, initially conceived, had three specific objectives. The first was to explore the 'community connectedness' of Black sole mothers through a structured qualitative questionnaire. This objective was identified by me without any input from the women, although following discussion with them, they agreed to this objective and added the second and third objectives that were important to them. Based on discussions and information sessions with representatives from selected agencies, the group was to prepare and publish a work-book for Black parents that would cover a variety of issues and concerns related to accessing social services and community institutions, including information, suggestions, and alternatives. Finally, the women planned to work towards the long-range goal of establishing their own social support and information network for Black mothers of school-aged children.

The PAR project evolved in two distinct phases. The first phase, beginning in 1992, involved eighteen Black women who were invited to participate by word of mouth and through ethno-specific agency contact.[3] During this initial phase, community affiliation was explored through their perceptions of their interaction with mainstream agencies, their social links with others in the community, their level of participation in community institutions (work, religion, services, and recreation). The second phase of the project began in 1993, during which time the group expanded to fifty-six mothers of Black children (including five women who were White), loosened its structure, and women attended as they were able.

Participants differed by socioeconomic backgrounds, education, and political and community knowledge. They shared a racial identity that was differentially lived and understood. Through discussions with each other, the participants came to understand that the circumstances of their social status, conditions, and relations were complicated by the intersecting issues of racial politics, gender, and social class. The PAR group seemed to offer the potential to empower the participants by encouraging them to reflect on their own position, and their discussion broadened to include issues of community politics.

This project was motivated by anecdotal community reports which suggested that increased tensions between some Black community members and some institutions existed, and that Black school-aged children might be more at risk of failure and economic marginalization in a variety of ways than is the case for White children. Based on these reports, two assumptions guided the research. First, if indeed there were greater risks to school-aged Black children, then indications of parental–community tensions might be particularly evident among those who are presumed to confront the greatest challenges – sole-parent, female-led families. Second, if there were growing Black community–mainstream tensions, these might also be reflected in relations between Black female-led families and the community institutions and services that were involved with their lives. A premise which flowed from these assumptions was that this disconnectedness from the mainstream could further diminish the opportunities for their children (Jackson, 1993; Alwin et al., 1985; Mirowski and Ross, 1980; Thompson and Ensminger, 1989). American researchers, for example, had found these connections among poor Black female sole parents (Mincy, 1989; McKendry and Fine, 1993; Dornbusch et al., 1991; Mahler, 1989; Olson and Haynes, 1993; McLanahan and Booth, 1989).

The first phase of the study measured connectedness by employing standard qualitative variables used in research which examines community affiliation and isolation and alienation (Alwin et al., 1985; Kalekin-Fishman, 1991; McKim et al., 1977; Kovacs and Cropley, 1975; Kuo, 1978). Black female parents have received particular attention in alienation studies since it is thought that racism and gender inequalities complicate Black female parents' lived experiences through rejection and isolation. These studies show that variables which are significantly related to alienation include economic marginalization, low levels of education, living in poor neighbourhoods, race, gender, and parenting in situations of poverty (Jackson, 1993; Wilson, 1987; Stevens and Duffield, 1986; Mirowski and Ross, 1980; Greene, 1990; Fine and Schwebel, 1988; Thompson and Ensminger, 1989; Mincy, 1989). But in all of these studies, the concept of alienation is constructed by the researcher. Unlike research methods that are feminist in their approach (Reinharz, 1992), women have not themselves been involved in defining how alienation may relate to their own, lived experiences.

On the surface, the findings of our PAR study seemed to parallel those of previous studies. The findings indicated that none of the participants had affiliations with any of the more than thirty-five agencies and social organizations that were providing services specifically for women. In addition, thirteen of the eighteen participants reported either limited or no contact at all with neighbourhood groups, community recreational facilities (YWCA programs, libraries, parks), only arm's-length relationships with service agencies, and very little knowledge about public health facilities. A number of the women with school-aged children had resisted active involvement with schools and educational institutional representatives. Most said that they would not call on White neighbours if they experienced an emergency, yet many did not report knowing other Black women in their neighbourhood on whom they could call on for help if needed. Only a few had someone in the wider community to call on if they had a problem (church minister, church member, acquaintances). Some sought affiliation with organizations (cultural, not service) of their own regional ethnicity. Of those who regularly attended church or other organized religion, many attended with other members of their own ethnocultural group.

Although the type of relationship that the PAR women had to their community has at times been labelled 'alienation,' the women themselves attach a very different meaning to their lack of involvement. They understand it as resistance to involvement with broader community services and agencies, rather than as passive lack of interest. They are more interested in racially specific community services and events, and they have limited interest in, and understanding of, mainstream educational, health care, welfare, legal/juvenile, and public services. They also frequently resent intrusive services such as social work. Some were angry that social workers frequently misunderstood their family values, and they believed that this misunderstanding contributed to tensions between the women and their teenaged children. Services related to social assistance were particularly singled out for criticism. However, although the majority preferred ethno-cultural organizations that were staffed by trained personnel from their own community, others accepted the alternative of their community sensitizing agency workers to their culture and values.

Following this preliminary phase of the study, which focused on connectedness, and was guided by the concepts of 'alienation and isolation,' I was compelled to reconceptualize my own theoretical framework and reassess the assumptions guiding the research. My initial assumption that the actions of Black women in their community constituted estrangement from the mainstream Canadian society, and might be symptomatic of social dysfunction, was rejected by the female participants in the study group as inaccurate and politically underdeveloped. The Black women rejected such terms as 'alienated,' 'estranged,' 'withdrawn,' and 'community dysfunction,' which they viewed as labels that belonged outside their own political and social contexts and were heavily influenced by Eurocentric social values and norms. These concepts, they argued, required debating, deconstruction, and reformulation into a more culturally appropriate and politically driven analysis of the meaning of integration. Their lived experiences, they felt, were not accurately understood by the staff in mainstream agencies.

These arguments helped to inform and broaden the focus of the study and led to the ongoing exploration of the definition and political history of social relations between Black women and the mainstream. While participation in the PAR project may have stimulated these women to focus on their social condition, their attention to segregated and ethno-specific services was also influenced by three events in the community.

The original PAR group of eighteen Black women was formed in 1992, amidst the well-publicized claims of racism at Nellie's, a women's hostel in Toronto. The information reported and discussed in the group was that some women of colour had accused White women of racism (Monsebraaten, 1994). During the same period, 1991–2, a needs assessment of a women's shelter in Hamilton was recommended, following a study that confirmed that their services were not responsive to the needs of racially and culturally diverse women who were victims of abuse. A breakaway-group of racial minority women wrested control of the needs assessment away from a predominantly White service agency and obtained public funding to engage in the Service Model Development Project for minority women (Working Group on Service Model Development, 1992). This victory made an impact which registered in the minds of many women observers.

A third event which received wide media attention in 1992 also influenced the women's self-exploration and community analysis. In that year, youths, both Blacks and others, rioted in the city of Toronto, and the media gave widespread coverage to what was viewed as a deterioration in relations between Blacks and mainstream society and institutions. In the post-riot period, some Blacks, through the community hearings held in Metropolitan Toronto, made public their demands for Blacks-only focused schools. Because education is such an important welfare and political issue for Blacks, this idea gained political credibility, and it was embodied as a recommendation in a report that had been the collaborative effort of the Black community and four levels of government (Canada, 1992). The press paid considerable attention to the proposal for Blacks-only schools, thereby granting it a certain legitimacy as a social alternative. It was not surprising that education was the catalyst which activated the discourse regarding racially segregated services. Of all the social welfare 'goods' delivered to Canadians, education has played, historically, a central and problematic role in the relations between Blacks and the Canadian mainstream.

The issues in the shelters and the riots in Toronto publicized the cleavages between the ethno-racial communities and the mainstream. The women in the PAR group focused their discussion on ethno-specific social services for Blacks, and some began to focus even more clearly on services for Black women. These discussions were kept alive throughout the course of the PAR study by the continuing attention the media paid to the apparent evidence of changing relationships between parts of the Black community and the mainstream. For example, media controversy erupted again in 1994 over the proposal by the Harriet Tubman Community Association to the Ontario Ministry of the Attorney General to establish separate community treatment services for young Black first-time offenders (Walkom, 1994). Also in 1994 a Black community legal clinic was launched, and this was accompanied by a fair amount of media coverage.

As the women in the PAR group came to understand so well, support for a separate existence from the mainstream organizations and institutions requires a deconstruction, and a culturally relevant reconstruction, of the notion of community integration. The PAR project provided a forum for the women to reconstruct these relations and examine their position within Canadian welfare-driven society. And, since the majority of the regular and active women in the group are immigrants, they have conceptualized their social condition and location in society within a somewhat bifurcated framework. They are Black and female, and they are also Black female immigrants – newcomers to Canada. Race, gender, and immigrant status, then, are important factors in understanding their social relations. The contemporary status of Blacks in Canada is historically linked to a history of antagonism engendered by the Canadian state. The fledgling movement of distancing from the mainstream, the uneasy alliances with feminism, and the continuing struggles of Black women are contextually rooted in this knowledge of *what has gone before*.[4]

Locating Black Women: Race and Gender in Canadian Society

Blacks in Canada include both recent immigrants and the descendants of American and Canadian African slaves who have lived here since the 1700s. In analysing the social history of Blacks in Canada, many of us acknowledge the important contribution of the Black woman, Harriet Tubman, who soldiered the underground railroad to guide, then free, thousands of American-enslaved Blacks into Canada during the 1800s (Hill, 1981).[5] For Black women in Canada, Tubman represents a symbol of the possible and a reminder of the unattained. In contrast to the slaves who sought refuge in Canada, the earliest arrivals of the contemporary group of Black women entered Canada as domestic servants. Both these histories are significant for understanding current Black women's issues.

Both Black immigrants and indigenous Black Canadians share this common legacy of slavery, but they differ in the post-slavery accommodations that were specific to their regions of births. Most immigrant Blacks were originally colonized and remained subordinated citizens after achieving institutional freedom from slavery. However, they forcefully challenged this continued colonization in the late 1950s and early 1960s, and many of them witnessed political liberation in their own countries before emigrating to Canada. On the other hand, in spite of an energetic tradition of community activism, Canadian Blacks were socially, politically, and economically oppressed until modest legislated changes occurred in the 1970s. The post-1960s immigrant population, then, entered Canada into social locations of subordination, but influenced by the growing resistance to it that they had witnessed in their countries of origin.

Following the period of Black slave migration in the 1800s, Blacks, except those from the United States, were prohibited general entry into Canada; they were seen as an undesirable race of people (Calliste, 1991; Satzewich, 1989; Daenzer, 1993). This remained the case until immigration policies were liberalized in the late 1960s. In 1967 Canada tabled new immigration legislation which, in principle, removed racial origin as an exclusionary criterion for entry into Canada. In that same year, one of a number of immigration amnesties quick-stepped immigrants who were in Canada on visitors' permits, and illegal immigrants, into landed-immigrant status. By the late 1960s Ontario had become the host province of the majority of racial minority immigrants all seeking 'the better economic life.' By 1989 the majority of new immigrants to Canada came from non-White countries. Between 1972 and 1989 the proportion of European immigrants declined markedly from 42 per cent to 27 per cent, while Asians, for example, increased from 22 per cent to 49 per cent of all immigrants. Racial minorities are projected to increase in Canada from 6 per cent in 1986 to 13 per cent in the year 2000 (Canada, 1991: 19).

Many of those who benefited from the immigration amnesty of 1967 were Black females who entered the country illegally as non-documented workers (NDW) in search of employment. These women were trapped in low-waged work, excluded from access to welfare, and indefinitely silenced by their illegal immigrant status (INTERCEDE, 1983). Their stories are not uncommon. Driven by their roles as the main economic providers for their families, and lacking the formal entry requirements for most Western nations, they continued a long tradition of illegal migration in search of work (Kessner and Caroli, 1982).

But even the Black women from the Caribbean who entered Canada legally as servants through the Domestic Workers Scheme of 1955 did not fare well (Daenzer, 1993; Calliste, 1991; Harris, 1988). The process was punitive, fraught with stereotypical assumptions, and represented an assault on the dignity of the Black women. Unlike White women who also entered the country as servants, Black women were subjected to extraordinary medical examinations justified by the stereotypical assumptions about Black women's lifestyles. Black women were also refused the usual assisted passage granted to women entering domestic service in Canada, and Black women were subjected to a special process of scrutiny to determine if any of them might leave domestic work, marry Canadians, or perform unsatisfactorily in their jobs (Calliste, 1991; Daenzer, 1993; Satzewich, 1989; Stasiulis, 1990; Timoll, 1989; Harris, 1988). This entry process for the earliest postwar Black immigrant women established a climate of antagonism between aspects of the Black community and aspects of the Canadian state.

The point of entry of Black women into Canada as servants is also historically significant for its emphasis on the gender differentiation between Black males and Black female immigrants. Black women entered Canada as servants partly through the support of Black males already resident in Canada, and partly through the complicity of the predominantly male Caribbean bureaucracies who agreed that Black females were ideally suited to the subjugated status of servants (Calliste, 1991; Daenzer, 1993). In subordinating Black women to a status inferior to theirs, Black men subscribed to the tradition of patriarchy which would thereafter shape relations between Black women and White women, Black women and the Canadian state, and Black women and Black men (Daenzer, 1993).

Female heads of families, therefore, were prominent among the 1950s and 1960s Black immigrants into Canada, and they engaged in a necessarily fragmented migration pattern. This was characterized by women-led migration in search of economic stability, followed by the subsequent sponsorship of their children (Daenzer, 1993; Arnopoulos, 1979; Silvera, 1989; Calliste, 1991). The process was often conflictual. The 1977 immigration attempt to deport seven of these women who were attempting to sponsor their children into Canada erupted into the much publicized protest by the International Coalition to End Domestic Exploitation (INTERCEDE) and others.[6] The deportation incident symbolized the power of patriarchy rampaging through the lives of women who had been used in the service of Canadian class interests (Harris, 1988; Ramirez, 1983/84).

The period of the 1960s and 1970s is known for the social challenges faced by Black female immigrants during the process of family reunification with children they had been forced to leave behind in their countries of origin. The family stress brought about by the years of separation caused child welfare agencies in particular to have a strong presence in some of these families' lives for varying periods. Some Black families were particularly at odds with child welfare agencies in Metropolitan Toronto during the 1970s, as agencies and families struggled to arrive at points of cultural accommodation regarding limits to discipline, the meaning of control and risks to children, and tensions resulting from the seeming intrusiveness of child welfare agencies. These encounters registered negatively with many families, and they likely influenced the current level of caution with which social service agencies are regarded by some minority women. But social tension and distance between some Black women and White Canadian society had an established history in Ontario and other parts of Canada. Long before the immigration of Blacks from the Caribbean, other Black Canadian women had been organizing and structuring their communities to minimize the effects of gender marginalization, racial subjugation, and institutional exclusions. The discussion in the next section explores the pioneering activism of these early Black women, and it suggests that the essence of this activism resonates among Black women today.

Black Women's Activism

Historical Roots

Regardless of the tensions associated with the entry of contemporary immigrant Black women into Canada, they arrived into a society which had already softened the hardest edges of its racism. This was the result of the work of Blacks who had lived in Canada for more than two centuries. Yet, what is so important and striking about the social history of both Black immigrant women, and their Black Canadian counterparts, is their invisibility in postmodern scholarship.

Until the work of Black scholars such as Brand (1991) and Bristow (1993, 1994) Black women's experiences and social struggles were absent in works such as Kealey (1979) and Pierson (1986), which recognized the contributions and struggles of women. Yet, Black women in Ontario have been actively pursuing improvements to their social conditions since the early nineteenth century. A broader social goal for early-century Black women was to synchronize their social status with White Canadian society (Bristow, 1993). This entailed inclusion into occupations and neighbourhoods and institutional participation without reference to or differentiation based upon their race and gender. A dominant theme in Black early-century struggle was the 'separate and unequal' issue that was central to attempts to demolish segregation (Brand, 1991; Bristow, 1993; Hill, 1981).

In the segregated Ontario of the 1850s, for example, Black women petitioned district school boards in St Catharine's, Hamilton, and Amherstberg, to allow their children to attend integrated schools. Segregated schools were seen as an arrangement which permitted social and educational resources to be focused on Whites at the expense of Black families. Segregated schools, the Black female reformers argued, offered a lower quality of social experience and education to Blacks (Hill, 1981).

The issue of the potential of state resources to enhance the life chances of minority populations has remained contentious into the late twentieth century. Education, viewed as a valued welfare good, is central to this debate. More than a century after the the Black women petitioned the school boards, the growth in the number of racial minorities in Ontario would give rise to a different debate – the separate but equal debate. The issue, however, appears to reflect contradictory interpretations over time. In the 1990s, as we saw in the previous section, Blacks are not only demanding the development of newly defined separate services and institutions, but some, such as the women in the PAR study group, are urging the transformation of current institutional arrangements, such as Black-focused schools restricted to Black students only. This is an apparent reversal of the turn-of-the-century debates, and some argue that this newer direction turns back the clock on historical social improvements. Careful analysis refutes that view.

The 1830s to 1850s segregation debate by Ontario's Black women was not a struggle premised upon the importance of forging relationships with Whites. It should be viewed, instead, as a struggle for resources to improve their social and economic condition. Black women such as Julia Turner in 1854, Mrs Levi Foster [sic] in the 1850s, and Mrs Henry Brant [sic] in the 1830s, reasoned that their children had a right to be educated where sufficient and appropriate resources were available (Hill, 1981). Since adequate resources were to be found in schools where Whites were educated, Blacks sought inclusion into these institutions for the benefits they promised.

Similarly, in 1934, fifteen Black Ontario women came together over a cup of tea and started a movement which still contributes to the political redefinition of Black social status in the 1990s. This group began with the title the Mothers' Club, but later became the Hour-a-Day Study Club (Bristow, 1993). In their early years, they addressed concerns about the social and economic future of Blacks through integrated education and the impact of the Great Depression on Blacks, who were already economically and socially marginalized (ibid.). In the 1990s, they continue to provide economic support to Black women relocating themselves through education in the professions (ibid.). They bridge economic gaps through scholarships and fill sociopolitical voids by providing support and encouragement for Black women. The Hour-a-Day Study Club is historically important for two reasons: Their work of redefining a political space for Black women in early Canadian society has resonated over time in spite of society's imposed obscurity; and, second, they established a tradition of self-help which caught on and which is currently undergoing political reformulation in postmodern welfare Canada.

Contemporary Tensions

The roots of contemporary Black social activism for equality and legitimacy within the Canadian welfare state lie in this history of Black female struggle for inclusion into mainstream Canada. Black women have a long history of exclusion and experience of the social costs associated with the struggle to locate ourselves in positions of relative parity with Whites. A position of relative parity requires similar though differentiated social statuses, political recognition for our participation, and economic outcomes which are proportional to those of the dominant populations. Implicit in the idea of relative parity is our rejection of a subordinated social status. Much of our current struggle, then, in the Canadian context, consists of a challenge to White domination. Since Black women have always occupied dominant economic positions in Black families (hooks, 1981), many of these struggles have been and continue to be female-driven. Black social movements are, however, neither homogeneous nor politically nor historically linear.

The starting point for postmodern Black movements in Canada has been this recognition that our social and political oppression owes its cogency both to systemic discrimination and to structural inequality. In addition to the disadvantaged socioeconomic position of Blacks, a deeper form of domination has eroded our political potential. This more insidious form of domination involves our intellectual suppression amidst institutional alienation. This intellectual suppression is embedded in the aims of Eurocentric education, and it is reinforced by popular media which promote a type of 'looking glass' psychology that results in the cultural discontinuity of minorities. A young Black student articulated it in the following way 'after you have been told for so long that you are inferior, there comes a point when you start to believe it' (Canadian Alliance of Black Educators, 1992). This form of suppression flourishes in social relations which alienate Blacks and other disenfranchised groups. Our struggle then is two-dimensional; it consists of peeling away these multilayered oppressions, and, second, creating sufficient distance from this oppression to be able to reclaim our intellectual and cultural selves. The latter, the process of self-emancipation, is qualitatively different from the former, the act of emancipation (Fanon, 1965). Self-emancipation involves liberation from the alien ideas and imposed culture of the oppressor, while emancipation is freedom from without, or the formal action of the oppressor in granting 'freer' status (Fanon, 1965). Without self-emancipation – the distancing and reclaiming – we can never transcend our social condition of institutional alienation. This transcendence has been central to early Black women's activism and is referred to as 'upliftment' (Brand, 1991; Bristow, 1994). Upliftment is a nineteenth-century term which imaginatively captures the activism of the Black women who, as we have seen, began the tradition of self-emancipation early in the nineteenth century by taking charge of lifting their community out of oppression by their own energies and sacrifices. As Peggy Bristow (1994: 115) comments about one of these women, 'The philosophy of "race uplift" ensured that sometime in the 1850s Sarah Grant would make space in her living-room to give Black children the rudiments of an education.'

Self-emancipation is not all that Black women must worry about. As women we are burdened with the additional challenges of liberating ourselves from White male patriarchy, White oppression, and Black male subordination (hooks, 1981). At various points in our histories we have disagreed on the priority of these different tasks. These disagreements still exist. Our struggles, then, embody contradictions, and our political approaches have been characterized by diversity and conflict. Some of us have shifted both towards and away from the feminist movement; some of us have also aligned ourselves with Black males and

then reverted to a form of Black womanism.[7] But what some of us manage to agree on is that the preconditions for our emancipation must
include the reclamation of our historical legitimacy through rewriting
our history and the ensuing exposure and negation of the historical
forces which produced this domination and alienation.

This process of self-emancipation is necessarily in conflict with the
notion of social integration as commonly understood. In order to join
forces with other movements such as feminism we must first stand
apart and reclaim our social and political selves from under White subordination; we must 'empower' ourselves through separateness and
control – the same notion of empowerment which serves as a theoretical
driving force for social welfare movements. This tension with feminism,
and the circumspection about current forms of institutional arrangements, is largely responsible for our self-imposed alienation. The
progress towards our emancipation is evident in the small-scale rejection of mainstream and a growing tendency towards separate services.

Although the feminist struggle and the struggle by Blacks to enhance
their social status bear similarities, they also differ in fundamental ways.
For Blacks, the efforts have been directed, first, to self-emancipation and,
second, to extract social emancipatory concessions from Whites, including White women (Fanon, 1965). Understandably, scholars differ in the
degree of compatibility they accord to feminist organizing and the movement to challenge racism (Das Gupta, 1991; Ng, 1991).[8] Yet, illumination
of this relationship between Black women and White women is essential
to a reconstructed epistemology of social relations which accounts for
the current marginalized condition of Black women. Not surprisingly, a
point of contention within feminist scholarship is the perception by some
Blacks that their experience, and the experience of other women of
colour, is silenced and negated by White women: 'Let us run our eyes
through the collage of female experience. We must quickly conclude that
Black women are not in the picture ... I invite you to come with me as I
aim the spotlight at the obfuscated image of Black women, buried under
cobwebs of oblivion, indifference, and racism' (Thornhill, 1991: 27).

Ethno-specific Agencies

Ethno-specific service agencies (ESAs) have also grown out of these
opportunities for collective action and deliberation. But while these are
fairly well developed in the Ontario Black community, they exemplify
only a tenuous distancing from mainstream control. The insecurity of

their funding base, and problems in the availability of staff to sustain their services, have always eroded the ability of ESAs to exert real control over the organization and development of their services. However, these ongoing difficulties have escalated enormously in the current environment, as the imposition of drastic cuts has threatened the very existence of some of these agencies. In addition to the issues of funding, communities themselves are politically unstable. The modern Black community, for example, shows a particular disposition for political mobilization and organization in the wake of specific crises. Nevertheless, some Black community ESAs have evolved and been sustained over shifting political and social climates.

The most notable of these are the 1980s Harambee Centres for Child and Family Services that are located in a number of Canadian cities and now function with mainstream support. Services like Harambee represent a revised relationship between ethno-specific groups and the welfare state because they function not only to address the immediate needs for service, but they also foster support for symbolic ethno-racial communities (Klaff, 1980). The primary focus of the ESAs in the immediate post-1960s was on bread-and-butter issues, and this helped to eclipse more radical forms of advocacy. The broader, and revisionist, function of today's ESAs actively supports and encourages the movement towards community emancipation. In addition, ESAs have been important to Black women's emancipation. Because many welfare service systems are still female-driven, minority women have taken leadership in many of the ethno-specific service agencies, and they are at the forefront in defence of the continued evolution of such services. While ethno-specific agencies function at the local level, Black women are also active in relation to the provincial and federal levels of government, and in these arenas they are similarly demanding control, rather than consultation.

Conclusion

In 1992 the Black women in the Participatory Action Research group began the process of self-redefinition by rejecting mainstream definitions of their community behaviours and by exploring their own social and political location in their community. They defined their political space by articulating preferences for community separateness and a greater control over institutions and services which had the potential to improve the life-chances of the next generation – their children. Reforms to the distribution of educational resources are a priority on their list of targeted initiatives. In 1994, for example, they made both oral and written submissions to the Ontario Royal Commission on Learning to demand structural segregationist changes in education to benefit Black students. In the same year they also made a formal request for inclusion on the newly formed Ontario Community and Social Services JobLink Planning Committee with a mandate to advise on comprehensive services for recipients of provincial welfare. In 1995 they planned and obtained funding for a series of health conferences focusing on misconceptions about Black women's health and identified the goal of redefining and articulating concerns of interest to a broader constituency of Black women. Throughout all of this work, the PAR women followed an established tradition of pursuing community welfare through empowerment, or 'upliftment,' the nineteenth-century term. Much of this early activism focused on enhancing community welfare. Over time, debates have shifted from equality through institutional integration, to equality by way of emancipatory segregation.

The debate over 'separate and un/equal' services for Blacks in Canada, therefore, has persisted and evolved over the last century. It has sometimes held different meanings for Black women than for Black men. The particular issues have changed, but the debate has variously focused on the right of Blacks to access services and participate in institutions on an equal basis with Whites. Equal access to resources means respecting entitlements as sister consumers and eliminating the ascribed supplicant status of the dispossessed. It also means entitlements to power sharing in institutional management. Finally, it means having the power to shift the focus of the critical lens towards the force of hegemonic dominance and away from minorities victimized by domination. And since education has always been seen as the gateway to economic independence, as well as to political and social liberation, it is not surprising that the focus of the earliest struggles was educational issues and institutions. Education continues to be an issue of importance in the work undertaken by Black women, such as the members of the Participatory Action Research group which has been used in this chapter as an important example of Black women's contemporary activism.

The brief historical glimpses provided in this chapter showed the similarities between the nineteenth-century struggles of Black Canadian women and the post-1970s movements. Both the earlier movements and the more recent struggles focused on improving the welfare, and thus social locations, of Black families in Canada; racism served as the organizing focal point in both periods. However, earlier Black movements sought inclusion into mainstream institutions as a way to equalize resources. Current community organizing departs from a strictly integrationist emphasis and instead redefines the terms of their involvement in society through empowered relationships and an insistence on control of their community. These emerging and redefined relationships have been critiqued as segregationist and limited by a loss of focus and of purpose; these intra-community debates continue. However, the analysis in this chapter suggests that the original political aims of emancipation and equality have been consistent across both periods. Earlier movements worked towards locating Blacks socially and economically beside White society; the current trend is to stand apart to effect greater control and self-directedness.

Small groups like PAR will not, by themselves, effect broad-scale improvement in welfare outcomes across the Black community. But they are registering their rejection of the mainstream into the public consciousness and passing on to their children the potential for continuing this emancipatory work. They have made public their aims of social support, advocacy, social action, and community organizing to strengthen Black women who are parenting and also their broader community. In so doing they stand some chance of decreasing Black female dependence on traditional welfare service agencies and wresting control of aspects of their lives from mostly privileged gatekeepers. Their growing rejection of traditional clientification is still evolving. Some services are resource intensive, and they are resource poor. But their greatest resource is their new consciousness. In the final analysis, this fledgling Black women's movement is continuing the work of Black woman self-emancipation towards greater political and social equality. Their work and struggle represents an example of the kind of challenge that Black women are making to the welfare state.

Notes

1 The author would like to acknowledge her appreciation of support for this research: an initial grant from McMaster University and subsequent funding from the Human Resources Department Canada, Women's Program, and the Ontario Women's Directorate.
2 The term 'Black women' is sometimes used interchangeably with African Canadian women. Women included in this group are those of Black African descent from the diaspora.

3 The Black sole mothers who responded to the invitation might well have been women who were already relatively active in community life. If this is the case, then the PAR findings may actually overstate the community connectedness of Black women as a whole.

4 This phrase is the title of an article by Beverly A. Greene (1990), who makes the case that the study of Black women's current sociopolitical condition must necessarily be grounded in knowledge of their history – what has gone before, originally quoted from Alice Walker (1990).

5 Tubman was aided in her work with the underground railroad, a secret passage through swamps and forests, by the Quakers and other reformers who also hated the idea of slavery.

6 The organization (INTERCEDE), International Coalition to End Domestic Exploitation, was born out of this process and comprises domestic workers and other women advocates from the wider community. The deportation of the women was stayed, but the incident further strained relations between some Blacks and Canadian immigration authorities. The women were to be deported because they attempted to sponsor their children into Canada and had not previously declared to immigration officials that they had children in their countries of origin.

7 'Womanist' or 'womanism' is a phrase coined by the author Alice Walker (1990) as an alternative to feminist.

References

Action Committee on Immigrant and Visible Minority Women. 1987. *Report.* Hamilton: ACIVW.

Alwin, Duane F., Philip. E. Converse, and Steven Martin. 1985. 'Living arrangements and social integration.' *Journal of Marriage and the Family* (May): 319–34.

Arnopoulos, Sheila McLeod. 1979. *Problems of Immigrant Women in the Canadian Labour Force.* Document prepared for the Canadian Advisory Council on the Status of Women. Ottawa: Canadian Advisory Council on the Status of Women.

Black Parent Community Group of Hamilton. 1994. *A Submission to the Ontario Royal Commission on Learning by the Black Parent Community Group of Hamilton.* Hamilton: BPCGH, March.

Brand, Dionne. 1991. *No Burden to Carry: Narratives of Black Working Women in Ontario 1920s to 1950s.* Toronto: Women's Press.

Bristow, Peggy. 1993. 'The hour-a-day study club.' In Linda Carty, ed., *And Still We Rise: Feminist Political Mobilizing in Contemporary Canada.* Toronto: Women's Press, 145–72.

– 1994. '"Whatever you raise in the ground you can sell it in Chatham": Black women in Buxton and Chatham 1850–65.' In Peggy Bristow, Dionne Brand, Linda Carty, Afua P. Cooper, Sylvia Hamilton, and Adrienne Shadd, eds., 'We're Rooted Here and They Can't Pull Us Up': Essays in African Canadian Women's History. Toronto: University of Toronto Press.

Bronfenbrenner, Urie. 1986. 'Alienation and the four worlds of childhood.' Phi Delta Kappan 67, 6: 430, 432–6.

Calliste, Agnes. 1991. 'Canada's immigration policy and domestics from the Caribbean: The second domestic scheme.' In Jesse Vorst et al., eds., Race, Class, Gender: Bonds and Barriers (rev. ed.). Toronto: Garamond Press and the Society for Socialist Studies, 136–68.

Canada, Department of Secretary of State, Ontario Ministry of Citizenship, The Municipality of Metropolitan Toronto, the City of Toronto, and the Working Group of African Canadians. 1992. Towards A New Beginning: Blacks in Metropolitan Toronto. Report of the Government and Community Four Level Working Group, Ottawa: Department of Secretary of State and Supply and Services Canada.

Canada, Employment and Immigration. 1991. PEAD – Planning Environment Assessment Document: Trends and Perspective. Ottawa: Employment and Immigration.

Canada, House of Commons. 1984. Equality Now: Report of the Special Committee on Visible Minorities in Canadian Society. Ottawa: Queen's Printer.

Canadian Alliance of Black Educators. 1992. Conference Report of Sharing the Challenge, Part 2: Report of Black High School Males in Conference. Toronto: Canadian Alliance of Black Educators.

Carty, Linda, ed. 1993. And Still We Rise: Feminist Political Mobilizing in Contemporary Canada. Toronto: Women's Press.

– and Dionne Brand. 1988. 'Visible minority women – A Creation of the Canadian state.' Resources for Feminist Research 17, 3: 39–42.

Daenzer, Patricia M. 1989. The Post-Migration Labour-Force Adaptation of Racial Minorities in Canada. Toronto: University of Toronto Publication Series: Working Papers on Social Welfare in Canada no. 28.

– 1993. Regulating Class Privilege: Immigrant Servants in Canada, 1940s–1990s. Toronto: Canadian Scholars' Press.

Das Gupta, Tania. 1991. 'Introduction and overview.' In Jesse Vorst et al., eds., Race, Class, Gender: Bonds and Barriers (rev. ed.). Toronto: Garamond Press and the Society for Socialist Studies, 1–11.

Doering, William. 1980. Is Life in a One-Parent Family Damaging to Children? A Look at Both Sides. U.S. Department of Health Education and Welfare, National Institute of Education. (ERIC Document Reproduction Service No. ED 193 546)

Dornbusch, Sanford M., and Philip L. Ritter. 1991. 'Community influences on the relation of family statuses to adolescent school performance: Differences between African Americans and non-Hispanic whites.' *American Journal of Education* 99, 4: 543–67.

Doyle, Robert, and Livy A. Visano. 1987. 'Inequalities within the Service Systems: A Case of Cultural Insensitivity.' *Currents: Readings in Race Relations* 4, 3: 3–5.

Fanon, Frantz. 1965. *Black Skin, White Masks*. Trans. Charles Lam Markmann, New York: Grove Press.

Fine, Mark A., and Schwebel, Andrew I. 1988. 'An emergent explanation of differing racial reactions to single parenthood.' *Journal of Divorce* 11: 1–15.

Greene, Beverly A. 1990. 'What has gone before: The legacy of racism and sexism in the lives of Black mothers and daughters.' *Women and Therapy* (Special Issue, *Diversity and Complexity an Feminist Therapy, Part II*) 9, 3: 207–230.

Harris, Ruth. 1988. *The Transformation of Canadian Policies and Programs to Recruit Foreign Labour: The Case of Caribbean Female Domestic Workers, 1950's–1980's.* Doctoral Dissertation. University of Michigan: Department of Sociology.

Hill, Daniel. 1981. *The Freedom Seekers: Blacks in Early Canada*. Agincourt, Ont.: Book Society of Canada.

hooks, bell. 1981. *Ain't I a Woman? Black Women and Feminism*. Boston: South End Press.

Intercede, 1983. 'Implementation of the Special Policy on Foreign Domestic Workers. Findings and Recommendations for Change.' A Brief to the Minister of Employment and Immigration. Toronto: Intercede.

Jackson, Aurora P. 1993. 'Black, single, working mothers in poverty: Preferences for employment, well-being, and perceptions of preschool-age children.' *Social Work* 38, 1: 26–34.

Kalekin-Fishman, Devorah. 1991. 'Systems, situations and the individual: An integrated view of alienation as related to migrants.' *International Journal of Sociology and Social Policy* 11, 6–8: 75–89.

Kealey, Linda, ed. 1979. *A Not Unreasonable Claim: Women and Reform in Canada, 1880s–1920s*. Toronto: Women's Press.

Kessner, Thomas, and Betty Boyd Caroli. 1982. *Today's Immigrants, Their Stories*. New York: Oxford University Press.

Klaff, Vivian Z. 1980. 'Pluralism as an alternative model for the human ecologist.' *Ethnicity* 7, 1: 102–18.

Kovacs, M.L., and A.J. Cropley. 1975. 'Alienation and the assimilation of immigrants.' *Australian Journal of Social Issues* 10, 3: 221–30.

Kuo, Wen H. 1978. 'Immigrant/minority status and alienation.' *Sociological Focus* 11, 4: 271–87.

Lewis, Stephen. 1992. *Report on Race Relations*. Toronto: Office of the Premier.

Lipsky, M. 1984. 'Bureaucratic disentitlement in social welfare programs.' *Social Service Review* 58: 3–27.

Mahler, Sara R. 1989. 'How working single parents manage their two roles.' *Journal of Employment Counselling* 26, 4: 178–85.

McKendry, Patrick, and Mark Fine. 1993. 'Parenting following divorce: A comparison of black and white single mothers.' *Journal of Comparative Family Studies* 24, 1: 99–111.

McKim, Judith L., Victoria F. Davison, and Lyle W. Shannon. 1977. 'Some cultural effects of the community on cultural integration.' *Sociological Quarterly* 18 (Autumn): 518–35.

McLanahan, Sara, and Karen Booth. 1989, August. 'Mothers-only families: Problems, prospects and politics.' *Journal of Marriage and the Family* 51: 557–80.

Mincy, Ronald B. 1989. 'Paradoxes in Black economic progress: Incomes, families, and the underclass.' *Journal of Negro Education* 58, 3: 255–69.

Mirowsky, John, II, and Catherine E. Ross. 1980. 'Minority status, ethnic culture, and distress: A comparison of blacks, whites, Mexicans, and Mexican Americans.' *American Journal of Sociology* 86, 3: 479–95.

Monsebraaten, Laurie. 1994. 'Why Metro Shelter for abused women was shut down.' *Toronto Star* A1, A10 (24 July).

Multicultural Advisory Group. 1987. *Report on Multiculturalism and Social Assistance*. Working Document prepared for the Ontario Provincial Social Assistance Review Committee. Toronto: Multicultural Advisory Group.

Ng, Roxana. 1991. 'Sexism, racism and Canadian nationalism.' In Jesse Vorst et al., *Race, Class, Gender: Bonds and barriers* (rev. ed.). Toronto: Garamond Press and the Society for Socialist Studies, 12–14.

Olson, Myrna, and Judith Haynes. 1993. 'Successful single parents.' *Families in Society* 74, 5: 259–67.

Pierson, Ruth Roach. 1986. *'They're Still Women After All': The Second World War and Canadian Womanhood*. Toronto: McClelland and Stewart.

Polakow, Valerie. 1993. *Lives on the Edge: Single Mothers and Their Children in the Other America*. Chicago: University of Chicago Press.

Ramirez, Judith. 1983/84. 'Good enough to stay.' *Currents* 1, 4: 16-20.

Reinherz, Shulamit. 1992. *Feminist Methods in Social Research*. New York: Oxford University Press.

Rodgers, Harrell R. Jr. 1987. 'Black Americans and the Ferminization of Poverty: The Intervening Effects of Unemployment.' *Journal of Black Studies* 17, 4: 402–17.

Satzewich, Vic. 1989. 'Racism and Canadian immigration policy: The government's view of Caribbean migration, 1962–1966.' *Canadian Ethnic Studies* 21, 1: 77–97.

Silvera, Makeda. 1989. *Silenced: Talks with Working Class Caribbean Women about Their Lives and Struggles as Domestics in Canada* (2nd ed.). Toronto: Sister Vision.

Staples, Robert, and Leanor Boulin Johnson. 1993. *Black Families at the Crossroads: Challenges and Prospects.* San Francisco: Jossey-Bass.

Stasiulis, Diva. 1990. 'Theorizing Connections: Gender, Race, Ethnicity and Class.' In Peter S. Li, ed., *Race and Ethnic Relations in Canada.* Toronto: Oxford University Press.

Stevens, Joseph H., Jr., and Barbara N. Duffield. 1986. 'Age and parenting skill among black women in poverty.' *Early Childhood Research Quarterly* 1: 221–235.

Teram, Eli, and Heather White. 1992. 'Strategies to address the bureaucratic disentitlement of clients from cultural minority groups.' *Canadian Journal of Community Mental Health* 12, 2: 59–70.

Thompson, Maxine Seaborn, and Margaret E. Ensminger. 1989. 'Psychological well-being among mothers with school age children; Evolving family structures.' *Social Forces* 67, 3: 715–30.

Thornhill, Esmeralda. 1991. 'Focus on Black Women!' In Jesse Vorst et al., eds., *Race, Class, Gender: Bonds and Barriers* (rev. ed.). Toronto: Garamond Press and the Society for Socialist Studies, 27–38.

Timoll, Andrea L. 1989. *Foreign Domestic Servants in Canada.* Unpublished Honours BA essay, Queen's University, Department of Political Science.

Vorst, Jesse, Tania Das Gupta, Cy Gonick, Ronnie Leah, Alan Lennon, Alicja Muszynski, Roxanna Ng, Ed Silva, Mercedes Steedman, Si Transken, and Derek Wilkinson, eds. 1991. *Race, Class, Gender: Bonds and Barriers* (rev. ed.). Toronto: Garamond Press and the Society for Socialist Studies.

Walker, Alice. 1990. 'Definition of Womanist.' In Gloria Anzaldúa, ed., *Making Face, Making Soul = Haciendo caras: Creative and Critical Perspectives by Feminists of Color.* San Francisco: Aunt Lute Books.

Walkom, Thomas. 1994. 'Bluntly, black legal program is racist.' *Toronto Star* (8 Nov.): A21.

Wilson, William J. 1987. *The Truly Disadvantaged: The Inner City, the Underclass, and Public Policy.* Chicago: University of Chicago Press.

Working Group on Service Model Development. 1992. Congress of Black Women, Hamilton chapter, the Immigrant Women's Action Group, and the Native Women's Centre. *Service Model Development Proposal: History of Group Making Proposal.* Working document from the files of the Immigrant Women's Centre.

12

Women, Unions, and the State: Challenges Ahead

NORENE PUPO

The structure of women's work and the nature of unionism are both at the brink of change. Within a climate of economic uncertainty and high unemployment, women's jobs are affected by economic and organizational restructuring, changes in technology, growth in part-time and contingent workforces, the increased use of home-based work, and an inequitable distribution of power and rewards. Individually and collectively, women are challenged by these issues at their workplaces while simultaneously they search for manageable ways of meeting their familial responsibilities. Many women are calling upon the labour movement to reformulate policies and practices to meet their needs within a restructured workplace and a reshaped labour force. Women are influencing the course of unionism in Canada by extending discussions on the meaning of insecurity and by underscoring the immediate need to address the work–family interconnection.

Women's challenges are shaking the boughs on which the traditional model of unionism rests. Since the 1960s Canadian women's membership in unions has grown at a tremendous rate, outpacing the rate of increase of their male counterparts. This growth in women's union membership reflects, in part, their increased participation in the labour force, but, perhaps more significantly, it also demonstrates the emergence of a new wave of unionism, symbolized by the developing partnership between women and labour organizations. The significance of the labour movement for women is not only to affect changes in the conditions of their work, but also to extend the 'welfare state' through the support and sponsorship of programs (child care, family services) which address the family–work interconnection.

In Canada, public sector unions are particularly characterized by sizeable female memberships. These unions are typically regarded as more progressive compared with their private sector counterparts, and they espouse a philosophy that is, at times, antithetical to the business union ethic frequently associated with the traditional model of unionism. Public sector unions have become sites of resistance for women, and they are broadening the scope of unionism in Canada. They are doing this through their adoption of more progressive policies, their greater willingness to address concerns lying outside the more traditional realm of the union (such as human rights and justice issues, lesbian and gay rights, community action, violence and social rights, to name a few) and their independent participation in the political arena separate from the NDP and the force of conventional party politics. This chapter explores the relationship of women to the state through their representation and actions in public sector unions and examines the ways in which women in the public sector are responding to economic insecurity by challenging both their employers and their unions. In particular, women's participation in the 1991 federal public service strike is highlighted as a strike that has served as a reference point because of the numbers involved and the special attention paid to the issue of job security. This chapter considers the issue of economic insecurity and unions' strategies, the changing profile and nature of unionism, the role of the state and the limitations of its present structure, and the future prospects that collective bargaining may offer to women.

Women and Unions: Shifting the Focus

The 1980s represents a difficult chapter in the history of the Canadian labour movement. During this time Canadian unions lost the relative comfort they enjoyed during the previous two decades when union rights were extended and workers openly challenged their employers' authority through a wave of strikes and collective action. During the 1980s labour came to represent the 'unwelcome house guest' as governments reversed hard-won labour legislation and created a less-than-hospitable climate in which to engage in collective bargaining. While leaving the structure of collective bargaining intact, Panitch and Swartz (1988) have argued that during the 1980s, the state introduced a series of measures which effectively and permanently restricted workers' rights and adopted an uncompromising position towards organized labour.

During this time of transition from 'an era of consent' to 'an era of coercion' (Panitch and Swartz, 1988), the face of both the labour force and the labour movement changed considerably. Union membership in Canada (as a percentage of the non-agricultural workforce) grew at a moderate rate over the 1970s and 1980s, peaking at 40 per cent in 1983, with some decline towards the end of the 1980s (cited in Panitch and Swartz, 1988: 98). During the mid-1980s the unionization rate of paid workers (including agricultural workers) declined from 34.4 per cent in 1985 to 33.3 per cent in 1987, but had grown to 34.7 per cent in 1990 (Statistics Canada, 1993: 35). Although a larger proportion of employed males are unionized in comparison with female paid workers, as noted earlier, women's share of union membership increased steadily from the 1960s through the 1980s (Labour Canada, 1990: 114; White, 1993: 56). Between 1962 and 1989 women's union membership grew by 510 per cent, while men's participation in unions grew by 86 per cent during the same period. In other words, only 16.4 per cent of all union members across Canada in 1962 were women, but by 1989 women accounted for 39.1 per cent of all union membership (cited in White, 1993: 56).

While the growth noted in women's union membership may be related to their increased labour force participation in general, it also reflects the survival tactics adopted by unions as manufacturing jobs were lost and their male membership declined. In response to plant closures and losses within the industrial sector, unions began organizing campaigns in the burgeoning service sector where women traditionally work. United Steelworkers, for example, traditionally a male-dominated union, has been organizing workers in nursing and retirement homes, in banking (VISA Centre), and in hotels and restaurants. Similarly, Canadian Auto Workers has organized some groups of clerical workers at auto plants and in mines, reservations and ticket agents, as well as workers in the hospitality industry. Despite these recent activities, a spokesperson for the women's caucus of one of these unions pointedly remarked that the union has 'not been very welcoming to women or traditional forms of women's work. The face of unions is not very female-oriented' (personal interview, November 1994).

The importance of union membership for women is also indicated by salaries. According to an International Labour Organization (ILO) study, Canadian unionized women earn an average of 83.7 per cent of men's earnings, compared with 69.6 per cent for non-union women. This union advantage is also apparent in the United States, but to a lesser degree. Union women in the United States earn 82.2 per cent of male earnings, compared with 73 per cent for non-union women (Galt, 1993: A6).

Within the unions, women have been instrumental in broadening the base of unionism to embrace a number of issues formerly considered to be outside the union's realm (see, for example, Briskin and McDermott, 1993; Cobble, 1993). For example, members of Women in Steel, in the Ontario district of the United Steelworkers of America, have pressed the union to adopt major policy statements on sexual harassment and violence against women. Women's efforts have propelled Canadian unions forward in a notably progressive direction which has resulted in, as the ILO suggests, Canadian unions 'show[ing] more innovative policies toward women workers, as well as more bargaining gains [than in the U.S.]' (cited in Galt, 1993: A6). Not only are Canadian women's caucuses more organized and allied more successfully with feminist concerns than is the case in the United States, but there have been more successful campaigns waged with a greater number of improvements earned in a number of areas, including pay equity, family leave, greater opportunities and respect on the job, and child-care provision. Women have also fought for their futures by developing leadership and retraining courses. Women in Steel, for example, sponsors a course combining skill development and political education through which women are trained for leadership positions in the union.

Unions and the State

The rapid growth in public sector unions has produced an important shift in the composition and representation within the labour movement. Not only has this meant an increase in the overall number of women holding union memberships in Canada, but it has also shifted the focus away from international unionism and the traditional (male-dominated) manufacturing sector to national unionism with emphasis on the service sector. By 1989, 46 per cent of union members in national unions and 48 per cent of all members in government unions were women. In the same year only 32 per cent of union membership (male and female) were members of international unions, while 54 per cent were in national unions and another 14 per cent were in government unions (cited in White, 1993: 58). International unions (representing male-dominated spheres and focusing almost exclusively on bread-and-butter issues and the family wage) are losing their dominance within the Canadian labour movement, and national and government unions (where female members are clustered) are setting the agenda for labour by defining the role of unions more broadly.

The growth of the public sector unions places the state in a compromising position, as employer called upon to bargain in good faith with the unions while representing its own corporate interests, and as 'neutral' legislator representing broadly both organization and employee interests. But the state's apparent neutrality unravels in the face of its primary imperative to maintain favourable economic conditions within the context of a capitalist structure. While the state maintains a degree of autonomy from capitalist interests, it works to promote the general advantage of capital and the rights of private property, and in this process tends to comprise the best interests of labour (see for discussion, Panitch, 1977; Pupo, 1994).

With respect to labour issues, the state is simultaneously charged with the task of maintaining its neutral appearance before the unions while proving its commitment to maintaining economic prosperity and corporate growth. The state is at once both employer and protector, contradictory positions. How the state negotiates with its own unions is most revealing of its overall commitments. Within the last decade, with the losses experienced in the manufacturing sector that resulted from recession, restructuring, and plant closures, the state has generally reacted to this fiscal situation by 'tightening its belt' around labour both through strategic negotiations with its own unions as well as through legislation affecting all unions. Nevertheless, public service unionists have remained steadfast in their attempts to create a more equitable and secure workplace.

Public service unions challenge the state on two fronts: directly, in terms of specific conditions of the workplace as their members' employer, and indirectly, through political activities and lobbying for changes in legislation. Compared with their counterparts in the private sector, workers in the public sector are more vulnerable to certain political decisions (wage restraints, for example). Yet, at the same time, the issue of insecurity has not, until relatively recently, been as intense, nor carried the same meaning for public as for private sector workers. Public sector workers may fear governments' decisions to downsize or streamline operations by declaring positions redundant, by attrition, or by leaving non-essential services unattended, thereby intensifying the work process for those remaining on the job. But private sector workers face additional fears of possible closures and moves as a direct consequence of competition within the global economy and from another workforce. While the state's decisions to restructure or to downsize become matters of public scrutiny and the cost to public service jobs is discussed in newspapers and in communities across the country, numerous plant closures costing thousands of permanent jobs are often unheralded, the result of decisions made in head offices frequently located outside Canadian borders.

At the same time, public sector workers are acutely aware of the state's policies of retrenchment and their reduced commitment to social welfare. The quality of everyday life in Canada has diminished, as growing numbers face job insecurity and the distinct possibility of requiring short- or long-term social assistance. In the context of sharply increasing concerns about their own job security, many public service workers are faced with contradictory circumstances: increasing caseloads as community and family resources are overstretched in the face of economic downturns, and shrinking resources within their workplaces as public services budgets are subjected to the state's spending restraints. Under these conditions, women's work in the public service as professionals (for example, social workers or health care providers) and as support staff (for example, clerical workers or technical service workers) has become intensified.

Studying activities of public service workers and their unions provides an indication of the effects of labour policies on the workforce. In particular it gives us insight into the impact on the female labour force of broad-based programs of retrenchment and economic restructuring since this often means replacing full-time, permanent jobs offering a modest degree of employment security, with part-time, temporary and/ or contractually limited jobs. These less secure and 'atypical' jobs characterize women's employment pattern.

When public service workers engage in struggles at the workplace, they force open public debate over central workplace issues, such as job security, the hours of work, pay equity, and workers' benefits. The outcome of confrontations within the public service helps to determine public sentiment not only towards government bureaucracy and inaction, but also towards unionism in general. It is with these strikes that 'cripple the nation' that public opinion is shaped. Often strategic alliances are formed with social action groups, such as the women's movement, community coalitions, or specific interest groups, thereby further empowering the striking workers by drawing the public's attention away from the inconvenience to the public caused by the strike to the losses of service and the implications of government cutbacks to the quality of life. Highlighting the concern over cutbacks, their effects on the public as well as on government service workers' jobs helps to curtail the public's perception of government workers as possibly unde-serving of raises in pay and benefits.

The actions of the state (as employer) are critically judged by other employers and labour unions. The manner in which the state bargains and considers workers' demands becomes a prototype for other em-ployers to emulate or reject. These actions come under close scrutiny by the press and the public at large, particularly since the question of whose interests are served or 'whose side are we on?' is often miscon-strued. While one may objectively or abstractly position himself or her-self on either labour or management's side, this alignment is sometimes shaken during public service workers' struggles when services are dis-rupted and individuals' needs are eclipsed by the concerns of the collec-tivity. This question of whose side to support is particularly relevant for women who are overrepresented in the public service domain both as employees in relatively low paid positions and as recipients of social welfare services. In their roles as members of public service unions, women have adopted a high profile by undertaking several recent actions, challenging their employer, the state, to reassess the issue of equity at the workplace.

Women in Action: Struggling for Security

The Context of Recent Struggles

The era of neo-conservativism ushered in by the 1983 election of the fed-eral Progressive Conservative government has been particularly diffi-cult for labour. Many labour analysts refer to the Mulroney years as the harshest period of anti-union sentiment and legislation in Canadian his-tory (Edwards, 1990: D1). During the reign of the federal Progressive Conservative party, workers have been confronted with a number of ini-tiatives with far-reaching implications: the dismantling of a large por-tion of VIA Rail service, alterations in the unemployment insurance system, the goods and services tax, free trade, economic recession, and the resulting downsizing and restructuring within public and private organizations, and global economic restructuring.

With the 1993 landslide victory of the federal Liberal Party led by Jean Chrétien, some labour analysts were hopeful that the anti-labour mes-sage of the previous government would be swept aside. However, the Liberal government has remained steadfast in its concern to decrease the federal deficit and has undertaken measures to reduce the number of federal employees, while limiting spending on unemployment insurance, pensions, and other social welfare programs.

Despite the intensity and range of these pressures, Canadian unions have adopted an increasingly political posture, aggressively organizing in the service sector, for example, to offset the losses of tens of thousands of jobs in manufacturing (Galt, 1992: A8). Between 1989 and 1990, 152,000 manufacturing jobs, 7 per cent of all jobs in this sector, were lost along with 46,000 jobs in textiles and clothing, and almost 10 per cent of all manufacturing jobs in Quebec (Carr, 1990: A15). In light of these losses in industries which are traditionally union strongholds, Canadian labour leaders have scrambled to develop a greater presence within the service sector and among part-timers and other workers who often had been overlooked in previous labour campaigns. Public service unionists (more so than private sector union leaders) are embracing a new and more progressive unionism which differs from the more conservative business unionism. Business unionism focuses mainly on the narrower bread-and-butter issues, while progressive unionism not only considers issues of pay and benefits as well as the conditions of work, but also moves beyond the immediate issues of the workplace to include alignments with the community and action in political, social, and economic affairs (Pupo and White, 1994).

In the late summer of 1991 federal public servants launched strike action against their employer in an effort to preserve job security. In an environment rife with job losses in the private sector, conversion of secure full-time jobs to part-time or contractually limited contingent jobs, technological change and job deskilling, downsizing, and general economic recession, federal employees risked a strike despite the threat of back-to-work legislation. The strike was a protest against the government's cost-saving measures, including proposed zero wage increases, workforce reduction, and the conversion of full-time to part-time or contractually limited jobs. Some observers argue that this strike was a matter of principle demonstrating the importance of job security, particularly among workers who have typically been among the least secure.

Eleven years earlier, in 1980, 40,000 government workers, members of the Public Service Alliance of Canada (PSAC), struck for a week, disrupting air traffic, shutting down government services, and plugging border crossings. But after a week the union support began to wane, and the strike was eventually settled for terms very close to what management had offered before the walkout (Papp, 1991b: A13). In 1991, however, fuelled by the gloomy economic forecast, the union gained a great deal of momentum, perhaps because the long-term stakes of job security and the permanent loss of full-time employment were so high. According to Jim MacEwan, vice-president of PSAC, job security is 'the scourge of the public sector,' or as Daryl Bean, PSAC president suggested, job security is 'the number one issue, with wages a close second' (Galt, 1991b: A7). The union and its membership were poised to fight back regardless of the consequences, including back-to-work legislation. What is significant about this struggle is the level of solidarity demonstrated by the strikers despite the risks they faced, including the imposition of back-to-work legislation, and its timing with respect to other labour actions. As the 1995 strike of health care workers in Alberta and the 1996 strike of members of the Ontario Public Service Employees' Union (OPSEU) so recently illustrated, public sector unions have become militant on the question of job security, as they witness the restructuring of the labour force with losses of full-time jobs in the primary sector and the emergence of part-time and casual employment in the service sector. This process of labour force restructuring is particularly salient for women. Although women now occupy a greater percentage of the public sector labour force, the sense of security that was once attributed to public service employment is vanishing as these jobs are restructured.

Public sector workers and unionists have witnessed losses as companies downsize their operations, demanding significant adjustments to their workforces. Workforce reduction often occurs without corresponding cutbacks in production or output, and this has heightened the experience of insecurity as organizations adopt measures of job intensification in response to diminished profits and shaky economic forecasts. Clerical jobs, occupied mainly by women, have been lost, and those remaining have been intensified by the introduction of new forms of technology. Public service employees have not been sheltered from exercises of downsizing. Between 1984 and 1990 the federal government decreased its payroll by 9.2 per cent (Freeman, 1991: B8),[1] and that reduction is growing with the federal and provincial cutbacks of the 1990s.

Within the public service, the process of downsizing has prompted discussion over two significant trends: contracting out work and shifting from full-time to part-time work.

While the reduction in the absolute numbers of public service workers over the past decade is a matter of serious concern, what is even more troublesome, according to union officials, is the governments' increased tendency to contract out various types of work, ranging from unskilled, blue collar jobs (for example, window washing, cleaning, and maintenance) to clerical work to encompass also more highly skilled and technical work (for example, computer programming and aircraft maintenance). Between 1984–5 and 1993–4 the cost of contracting out rose from $2.9 billion to $5.2 billion (Howard, 1994: A6).

Adopted as a cost-saving measure, this strategy of contracting out is of questionable value, given the increase in expenditures over the past decade and the higher cost of the services provided by outsiders. Moreover, some of the work is contracted out to companies in the United States and elsewhere. This practice has prompted union leaders to speculate that the government is side-stepping the union and in the process 'is creating a shadow civil service beyond accountability' (Bean, quoted in Howard, 1994: A6). The practice of contracting out, particularly at the blue collar and clerical levels, is a significant setback for women. Contract workers are usually paid minimum wages and enjoy few, if any, benefits. Moreover, these workers stand outside the public service and the union, and therefore they are unable to benefit from progressive policies regarding employment equity, pensions, or family caregiving that have been negotiated for public service employees.

The second significant trend over the past two decades has been a dramatic growth in the part-time labour force. In 1995, 16.6 per cent of the Canadian labour force worked part-time (Statistics Canada, 1996b: 35). While some may argue that part-time work is a lifestyle choice driven by a personal commitment to family work, others suggest that changes in the structure of the economy and the workplace leave individuals with little choice but to work on a part-time basis. The issue is complicated. Individuals are not usually presented with distinct choices regarding part-time or other forms of work. Rather their options are limited simultaneously by family circumstances and labour market considerations (Duffy and Pupo, 1992).

For increasing numbers of Canadians the option of part-time work versus full-time work is academic. In 1995, 25.3 per cent of women over the age of 25 who worked part-time indicated that they would prefer full-time work (Statistics Canada, 1996a). Growth in the number of part-time jobs and decreases in full-time work reflect the expansion of the service industry where the vast majority of the workforce – approximately 70 per cent – are employed and the decline of manufacturing and construction. Part-time, temporary, seasonal, and other 'non-standard' or 'atypical' forms of work pay less and have fewer benefits than full-time jobs. Women are vastly overrepresented in these marginalized positions, largely concentrated within the service industry. The greatest number of part-time jobs (87 per cent in 1993) are located in the service sector where the vast majority (86 per cent) of women work. Moreover, almost 70 per cent of all part-time workers are women (Pold, 1994).

Employers' use of part-time and other marginalized forms of work continues to be an outstanding labour issue for women. Referring to the matter of part-time work in connection with the 1991 public service workers' strikes, Linda Torney, head of the Metro Toronto Labour Council, concluded, 'There's a continuing attack on women's rights. It's insulting. People seem to assume that if you're a woman, it's okay to be used as a part-time worker' (quoted in Sweet, 1991: A23). Even nurses, who frequently preferred part-time work for the flexibility it offers, are increasingly experiencing more limited options as hospitals are trimming the size of their staff and employing contract and temporary workers to reduce costs. According to Kathleen Connors, president of the National Federation of Nurses' Unions, the number of nurses working as involuntary part-timers 'has really proliferated in the past five years. In fact, it's gotten so bad that 50 per cent of the nurses in Saskatchewan work part-time. Many can't live on part-time wages, so they're forced into splitting themselves between two jobs, two employers' (quoted in Sweet, 1991: A23).

Most women in the public sector are in clerical positions which are easily converted to part-time, temporary, or even home-based work. While employers often benefit through cost-savings from part-time and contingent work, recent research has pointed to the drawbacks of this form of employment (Duffy and Pupo, 1992). Although part-time employment may seem to provide a short-term solution to the tremendous work–family conflict women experience, it also carries heavy costs: lower wages, few benefits, limited opportunities to advance and learn, and lower levels of unionization, to name a few. Moreover, while organizations, including the state, rationalize the acceptance of part-time work by women, there is a tendency to view these workers as less committed to their paid employment than full-timers, and this attitude further entrenches women in marginalized and segregated job ghettos.

The Events

The issues of job security and part-time work were simultaneously fought in three major strikes over a three-week period in the fall of 1991:

against the federal government, the Canada Post, and the Toronto Transit Commission (TTC). The main thread connecting these three disputes is part-time work and job insecurity. According to Andre Kolompar, president of the Toronto local of the Canadian Union of Postal Workers (CUPW), 'This [part-time issue] is an attack on workers by all employers ... They say they need flexibility, but it's not a question of flexibility, it's a question of not having to keep full-time workers with pensions and other benefits' (quoted in Sweet, 1991: A23).

One of the central points of contention in the TTC dispute was that the management wanted to employ its retirees as summer relief workers and the union objected, fearing that this practice would eventually lead to greater use of part-time work, which has been a point of controversy at the TTC for a number of years. In this male-dominated workplace, the fight against part-time work may have been driven not only by the desire to protect highly coveted full-time work, but also by a rejection of the ways in which women's work is marginalized and cheapened by part-time schedules (Duffy and Pupo, 1992: 221–3). The union seems to associate part-time work, typically women's work, with a degradation of its labour force and maintains the notion of the family wage. The union's strategy, then, has been to fight against part-time work per se, rather than to negotiate pro-rated wages and benefits equivalent to those for full-timers for drivers on part-time schedules.

The postal workers' conflict was similarly aimed at 'slowing down or reversing a trend that is leading to a degradation and deterioration of the labour force,' according to Andrew Jackson, senior economist with the Canadian Labour Congress (CLC) (Galt, 1991b: A7). Both the CLC and CUPW were concerned that in addition to the increase in part-time work, a number of full-time jobs were shifted from full-time, full-year, secure jobs to temporary, insecure jobs with private contractors (Galt, 1991b: A7; see also White, 1990).

According to CUPW leader Jean-Claude Parrot, the union demanded a restructuring of part-time and casual jobs in order to create about 2,600 full-time jobs. By 1987 about 43 per cent of CUPW's members were women. While figures vary from year to year, well over 20 per cent of post office employees work part-time, and the majority of these part-timers (over 70 per cent) are women, many of whom would prefer full-time jobs (White, 1990). Parrot argued that even employees who had worked for the post office for as long as eight years were still considered to be casual staff. The union noted that in some areas of inside postal work, there was 'no operational reason' for the use of casual workers.

The union took the position that 'where casual employees are used in the same location to cover the same shift "on a continuous basis," the post office should use full-time workers' (Galt, 1991a: A5). Union leader Parrot extended the analysis to suggest that overall economic health was jeopardized by such careless labour market policy: 'Part-time and casual work is not good for our economy' (Papp, 1991a: A1). Elaborating on this sentiment a union bulletin warned: 'Any financial gains that Canada Post might get by turning full-time jobs into part-time jobs cannot compensate for the difficulties it creates for the workers. It's almost impossible to support a family when you are forced to live on part-time salaries' (quoted in Galt, 1991a: A5).

The federal government workers' action was largely a response to the government-initiated program of a wage freeze in 1991, followed by ceilings of 3 per cent for increases in each of the next two years. The government argued that such a freeze was necessary, warning workers that increased expenditures on salary could result in lay-offs. In addition, the struggle also extended the debate over the issue of insecure work, raising public awareness of the vulnerability of workers within a restructuring economy, since one of the government's key demands was guaranteed freedom to contract out work already done by public employees (Galt, 1991b: A7).

On Monday, 16 September 1991, the federal government was poised to legislate public service employees back to work and freeze their wages by introducing in Parliament 'one of the toughest anti-union bills since public servants were granted the right to collective bargaining 24 years ago' (Winsor and Galt, 1991: A1). The legislation would have extended the expired contracts of the striking employees, members of PSAC, rendering their strike illegal. Furthermore, the legislation moved beyond the particular workers affected at the time, since it also extended all other union contracts with the federal government for two years as they expired, thereby suspending any further discussion on the issue of wage and job security and, more significantly, obliterating collective bargaining rights in the federal public service. If union members and their leaders were non-compliant they would face stiff fines, but there were no provisions for jail sentences. Usually back-to work legislation entails binding arbitration or alternate dispute-settling procedures. However, this proposed legislation placed the government in full control, effectively suspending due process, by imposing a contract (Papp, 1991c: A14). While the government suspended the legislation in exchange for the union calling off the strike, the action sharpened criticism against the federal government and raised questions regarding the role and power of unions in the public sector, a question which was once again debated in Ontario in the fall of 1993 when the NDP government imposed its Social Contract.

Noting the profile of the public service as a female-dominated workforce, Canadian Labour Congress president Shirley Carr asked in reference to the federal government: 'How can they do this to someone who earns $21,000 a year? How can they do this to a single parent?' (quoted in Winsor and Galt, 1991: A2). Daryl Bean, PSAC president, calculated, based on the rate of inflation and cost of living, that 'the zero increase imposed on federal workers would mean a $1,500 cut in standard of living for a secretary earning less than $27,000 yearly' (Papp, 1991c: A14). According to the union, PSAC members' salaries ranged from $16,000 to $60,000 a year, and the majority, 60 per cent of members, are at the lower end of the salary grid, earning between $20,000 and $25,000 a year (Winsor and Galt, 1991: A2). The vast majority of those earning the lower salaries are women.

While union leaders were deeply concerned over the threat to collective bargaining posed by the proposed legislation, they also recognized that the government's actions aroused a new level of resistance among the workers towards arbitrary back-to-work orders and the conditions of work. Daryl Bean, PSAC president, for example, commented that the 'government could order its employees back to work but it could not force them to work once they got there' (Galt, 1991c: A8). Jim Chorostecki, PSAC's senior representative in Toronto, agreed that the government's exertion of power set the membership in motion. In their anger over the government's movements, union members, he observed, 'feel empowered and they want to do something with that power.' But the dilemma for the leadership was to find a safe balance between the government's power and the outraged members' needs. Chorostecki pondered, 'What do you do in the face of this kind of legislation? ... we don't want to see our members financially injured any more than they have already been by the strike. Can they afford to continue a strike if it does not appear they are going to gain something for this?' (quoted in Galt, 1991c: A8).

Although the strike was called off, the workers' actions 'sent a strong message to the government that its workforce was becoming radicalized with poignant implications for future relationships in the workplace' (Winsor, 1991: A4). The union considered the strike to be a victory. As one organizer reasoned: 'The suspension of back-to-work legislation is unprecedented in my experience' (Fraser and Galt, 1991: A4). Although the union leaders recognized their need to negotiate carefully and to exercise a measure of diplomacy in doing so, since the government could revert to implementing the back-to-work legislation, the workers' actions, their commitment to the union, and the struggle for greater security, may have shattered previous notions regarding the complacency of a female-dominated labour force. The women's commitment to changing the conditions of their work and the risk they took in raising public resentment towards government workers by engaging in strike action may have underscored the labour movement's need to re-evaluate its strategies.

Broadening the Scope: On the Hor(her)izons

Women's challenge to unions and the state is multifaceted. The driving force is the search for equality in the paid labour force and in the home. This will necessitate broad structural transformations, including shifts in social and labour market policy and unions' programs, as well as changes at the level of ideology and interpersonal relations.

With the second wave of the women's movement, women have challenged the state on issues of equality and rights and have made gains in a number of significant struggles. Feminists have raised awareness about the relationship between inequality in the home and in the paid labour force and have exposed the injustices women experience in both public and private domains. Moreover, they have demonstrated the ways in which outdated and patriarchal notions of family and gender permeate the foundations of public policy and organizational structures.

In recent years, women have waged successful campaigns for fairer social legislation which takes into account the differences in men's and women's lives and starts from the premise that compensating for this difference is crucial to the well-being of women and their families. In this regard, for example, women have worked to establish equality rights within the Charter of Rights and Freedoms, to reform custody and support legislation to check the number of women falling into poverty following divorce, and to amend family law.

On the labour front, women are affecting the nature and structure of the labour movement, pushing labour leaders to consider alternate modes of reaching workers and in organizing among groups of workers assumed to be uninterested in unions or too difficult to organize. With the growing number of female members and the drive to organize female-dominated workplaces particularly in the service sector, labour leaders will have to re-assess their strategies, recognizing that they have operated historically using definitions of membership and conceptions of the workplace derived from traditional male-dominated settings.

First, for labour leaders, one of the most important challenges in maintaining women's commitment to the labour movement is to seriously address the nature and structure of insecurity in women's work. This requires an appreciation of diverse needs regarding work scheduling, of work–family conflicts experienced particularly among workers with young children in the home and/or those caring for their elders, and of the need to promote community-based family support systems. Labour leaders must recognize that part-time and other forms of work should be available to those who want them, but that these forms of work should be subjected to the same legislative and union protection (including same wage scales, pro-rated benefits, and same opportunities) as full-time work. Rather than fighting against the principle of part-time work as they had in the past, and as the CUPW example illustrates, this means that labour leaders should welcome part-time and contingent workforces into bargaining units and should undertake contract negotiations regarding these workers as major players.

Another long-term challenge for the labour movement is to eliminate low wage jobs and to fight to reform the low wage labour market (Spalter-Roth and Hartmann, 1994). This will involve strategies to create jobs and decrease the high rate of unemployment which contributes to low wages and the ghettoization of workers. It also means lobbying legislators to increase the minimum wage and pressuring work organizations and governments to reform and implement equity legislation and procedures. It also involves continued efforts to organize low wage sectors and workers who have traditionally been overlooked by union activists.

Third, labour's campaigns should not narrowly focus on the workplace, but rather should take into account the constraints of family and workers' circumstances. This means bolstering services to support the need of workers to meet their family responsibilities, supporting legislative change and provisions for family leave and child care, and continuing efforts to end violence against women. The operational principle underlying such an agenda is that equity within the paid labour force rests on equity in the home, and educational programs based on this principle should be at the foundation of the unions' training practices. In short, a progressive social unionism should replace the more traditional business union philosophy. This progressive unionism would embrace a human rights and justice framework as the underlying conviction of the labour movement, and this principle would guide labour negotiations and contract bargaining in all workplaces.

Finally, the labour movement's ultimate challenge may be to reverse the pattern of restrictive labour practices and anti-union sentiment, demonstrating the strength of a radically changed labour movement and the willingness of members, such as the federal public service workers in the fall of 1991, and the OPSEU workers in Ontario in 1996, to challenge the government's power in order to preserve their dignity and safeguard their rights gained through previous hard-won labour struggles. If women are to continue to work towards change through their unions, they will need some proof that the labour movement is not only striving to improve pay and working conditions on a general level, but that labour activists will target the particular relations and conditions of women's work in developing their strategies. From a feminist perspective, only then will the labour movement prove its commitment to women's equality.

Note

1 Although the data clearly indicate that there has generally been a trend towards reducing the size of the federal public service over the past decade, the numbers are often quite confusing. Not only do different government agencies count personnel by different means (the number of actual people on the payroll regardless of the extent of their work versus the concept of the person-year which refers to the work of one person for one year), but a large percentage of federal work formerly undertaken by federal government employees is contracted out (Freeman, 1991: B8).

References

Briskin, Linda, and Patricia McDermott, eds. 1993. *Women Challenging Unions: Feminism, Democracy, and Militancy.* Toronto: University of Toronto Press.

Carr, Shirley. 1990 'Labour: "Don't Try to Make Us the Scapegoat."' *Globe and Mail* (2 August): A15.

Cobble, Dorothy Sue. 1993. *Women and Unions: Forging a Partnership.* Ithaca: ILR Press.

Duffy, Ann, and Norene Pupo. 1992. *Part-time Paradox: Connecting Gender, Work and Family.* Toronto: McClelland and Stewart.

Edwards, Peter. 1990. 'Last Chance for Labour?' *Toronto Star* (12 May): D1, D5.

Fraser, Graham, and Virginia Galt. 1991. 'PSAC Strike Called Off; Negotiations to Resume.' *Globe and Mail* (18 September): A1, A4.

Freeman, Alan. 1991. 'Downsizing, Government Style.' *Globe and Mail* (16 September): B8.

Galt, Virginia. 1991a. 'Strikes Called as Postal Talks Collapse.' *Globe and Mail* (24 August): A1, A5.

– 1991b. 'Public Servants Fight to Preserve What They Have.' *Globe and Mail* (13 September): A7.

– 1991c. 'PSAC Debate Over Returning Could Be Fierce.' *Globe and Mail* (17 September): A8.

– 1992. 'Labour Gaining Political Clout.' *Globe and Mail* (4 March): A1, A8.

– 1993. 'Unions Urged to Promote Women.' *Globe and Mail* (8 February): A6.

Howard, Ross. 1994. 'Federal Contracts Cost $5.3-Billion.' *Globe and Mail* (4 May): A6.

Labour Canada. 1990. *Women in the Labour Force.* 1990–91 Edition. Ottawa: Minister of Supply and Services.

Panitch, Leo. 1977. 'The Role and Nature of the Canadian State.' In Leo Panitch, ed., *The Canadian State.* Toronto: University of Toronto Press.

– and Donald Swartz. 1988. *The Assault on Trade Union Freedoms.* Toronto: Garamond Press.

Papp, Leslie. 1991a. 'Postal Workers Poised to Strike: Talks Break Off Without a Settlement.' *Toronto Star* (24 August): A1, A6.

– 1991b. 'Strike Awakens Labour's Sleeping Giant: Union Defies Threat of Back-to-Work Law.' *Toronto Star* (13 September): A13.

– 1991c. 'Ottawa to Order Federal Strikers Back.' *Toronto Star* (14 September): A1, A14.

Pold, Henry. 1994. 'Jobs! Jobs! Jobs!' *Perspectives on Labour and Income* 6, 3. Catalogue 75-001E. Ottawa: Statistics Canada (Autumn): 14–17.

Pupo, Norene. 1994. 'Dissecting the Role of the State.' In Dan Glenday and Ann Duffy, eds., *Canadian Society: Understanding and Surviving in the 1990s.* Toronto: McClelland and Stewart.

– and Jerry White. 1994. 'Union Leaders and the Economic Crisis: Responses to Restructuring.' *Relations Industrielles/Industrial Relations* 49, 4.

Spalter-Roth, Roberta M., and Heidi I. Hartmann. 1994. 'AFDC Recipients as Care-givers and Workers: A Feminist Approach to Income Security Policy for American Women.' *Social Politics: International Studies in Gender, State & Society* 1, 2 (Summer): 190-210.

Statistics Canada. 1993. 'Social Indicators.' *Canadian Social Trends* 28 Spring, 35.

– 1996a. *Historical Labour Force Statistics, 1995.* Ottawa: Minister of Industry.

- 1996b. 'Social Indicators,' *Canadian Social Trends*. Catalogue 11-008-XPE (Summer), 35.
Sweet, Lois. 1991. 'Why Unions Oppose Part-time Work.' *Toronto Star* (13 September): A23.
White, Julie. 1990. *Mail and Female: Women and the Canadian Union of Postal Workers*. Toronto: Thompson.
- 1993. *Sisters and Solidarity: Women and Unions in Canada*. Toronto: Thompson.
Winsor, Hugh. 1991. 'Saving Face for Both Sides.' *Globe and Mail* (18 September): A1, A4.
- and Virginia Galt. 1991. 'Back-to-work Law to Freeze Strikers' Pay.' *Globe and Mail* (14 September): A1, A2.

13

Institutionalizing Feminist Politics: Learning from the Struggles for Equal Pay in Ontario[1]

SUE FINDLAY

The introduction of Ontario's Pay Equity Act in 1987 was heralded as an impressive precedent in the development of pay equity legislation by feminist advocates. This legislation was regarded as a victory for the working women in Ontario and for the feminists in the Equal Pay Coalition who had been struggling for a policy to promote equal pay for work of equal value since 1976. Unlike most of the legislation that had been introduced up to that time, the Ontario legislation covered women in workplaces in the broader public sector and those with ten or more employees in the private sector, as well as women in the Ontario civil service. While the legislation, as it was introduced, did not cover many hundreds of thousands of women workers in the predominantly female sectors, included in the legislation was a proviso that made the investigation of ways to include these women a priority for the new Pay Equity Commission that was established to administer the legislation.

In spite of this victory, feminists have encountered quite massive and persistent resistance to the implementation of pay equity legislation from employers, from men in unions, and from government leaders themselves. Today, faced with demands from business for more flexible labour market policies, the Conservative government in Ontario seems to be preparing a rationale to abandon the commitments to pay equity altogether (New Democratic Party Office Memo, 18 July 1996). This resistance has undoubtedly limited its effectiveness as a strategy that can close the wage gap between women and men.

However, explanations about the limits of Ontario pay equity cannot be reduced to the resistance of men, to the lack of political commitment, or to the idea that the government is simply following the dictates of

employers. For, as we know from our own experiences in feminist struggles and the growing body of knowledge about the relationship
between feminists and the state that has emerged in recent years in Canada, the United States, Britain and Australia, ruling is a complex of
activities. In liberal democracies, feminists have, since the 1960s, played
an active role in constructing a consensus among feminists and between
feminists and the state (and other stakeholders) that contains the claims
that women make and the responses to them (Findlay, 1995; Ferguson,
1984; Ferree and Martin, 1995; Savage and Witz, 1992; Watson, 1990).

In this chapter, I look at the history of the struggles for equal pay to
see what we can learn from it about how feminists have been drawn into
a consensus with government (however uneasy and fragile), and the
limits of pay equity legislation as a strategy that can work for all of the
women workers in Ontario.

I begin the chapter with an outline of what I learned about wage discrimination in the community and social service sector from my experiences as a consultant in the Pay Equity Commission's investigation of
ways to extend pay equity legislation to women in the predominantly
female sector. I examine the tensions between the shared perspectives of
the Pay Equity Commission and trade union feminists about ways to
draw these women into the legislation and the perspectives of stakeholders from exclusively female agencies in this sector. I conclude this
section with some of the questions that were raised for me by these
experiences about the relationship between pay equity feminists and the
state, and a reflection on some of the explanations for the limits of policy
outcomes that analysts have offered in recent years.

In the second part of the chapter, I consider the struggle for equal pay
as it has evolved since the 1970s, exploring the way that the debates
among women, negotiations between feminists and union colleagues,
employers, and finally, state officials, shaped the definition of wage inequalities between women and men and how these might be addressed.

This section is exploratory, an account that pieces together information from selected documents that illustrate some of the particular 'battles' that shaped the longer struggle for equal pay. It is not intended to
be a comprehensive account, but an attempt to identify how a consensus
between feminists and state officials was forged in this particular case.
The difficulty that I have had in writing it has confirmed my view that
'making sense' is after all a collective process and reinforced my plea to
those who have been directly involved in various stages of this struggle
to write their own story.

The Problem with Pay Equity

In Section 33(2)(e) of the Province of Ontario's Pay Equity Act, 1987, the legislation stipulated that the Equity Office 'shall conduct a study with respect to systemic gender discrimination in compensation for work performed, in sectors of the economy where employment has traditionally been predominantly female, by female job classes in establishments that have no appropriate male job classes for the purpose of comparison ... and within one year of the effective date, shall make reports and recommendations to the Minister in relation to redressing such discrimination' (54).

In 1988 I was hired by the Pay Equity Commission as one of a team of consultants to prepare a background report on predominantly female workplaces in the community and the social service sector for this study (Findlay 1989a). In 1989 I was rehired to consult the 'stakeholder' in organizations in the broader public sector (such as libraries, child care centres, community and social service agencies, and health care units) about the workability of the commission's proposed 'proxy comparison approach' for women in exclusively female workplaces. This approach was intended to allow these women to compare their work with the work of men in selected 'proxy' organizations for purposes of establishing their claims for pay equity adjustments.

The difficulty of finding male comparators for women in predominantly female sectors had been an issue throughout the consultations about the development of the legislation. But in the pressure to introduce the legislation while the pro-equity New Democratic Party was the official opposition, feminists in the Equal Pay Coalition abandoned their search for a solution in exchange for a proviso in the legislation that the Pay Equity Office of the Pay Equity Commission would conduct studies of the predominantly female sector and make recommendations to the Minister of Labour about alternative methods to redress systemic gender wage discrimination.

In the consultations with stakeholders, I interviewed selected employers and representatives from unions and/or provincial associations. The stakeholders had mixed views on the commission's proposal, but many of those from the smaller, unorganized workplaces in the community and social service sector concluded that the proxy comparison approach was too complex for their workplaces. To implement the legislation, many of them would be forced to create new job descriptions and systematize their personnel procedures. Many lacked both the staff to manage the implementation process and the resources to hire consultants that could guide them in it. The legislation, modelled after legislation designed for state administrations in the United States, was really more suitable for large unionized workplaces with established systems of classification and personnel procedures.

Equally important, the implementation of pay equity adjustments would force their agencies to use already extended resources for pay equity adjustments. In most cases, employers would be forced to cut services or increase clients' fees. Wage increases for their workers have always competed with the resources they needed to serve their clients. They argued that if pay equity was to work at all in this sector, the government must establish a Pay Equity Fund to increase their operating grants.

There were more serious limits to the pay equity legislation for these workers. As I discovered, the real issue for these workers is parity with other government workers and a reorganization of the delivery of funding for social services, not pay equity. Wages in many of these agencies were shaped primarily by the government's funding practices and regulations rather than the decisions of their individual boards. The low wages of women workers in this sector reflect a set of compromises that have evolved over the decades in negotiations between community 'volunteers' (that is, men and women from a ruling class) and government officials about the funding and regulation of community responses to social issues. These compromises have been contained in a number of ways. The government's program delivery system isolates individual agencies and discourages collective action to challenge these compromises. Agency funding is determined by regional offices that negotiate budgets with individual agencies. The organization of provincial associations of these agencies is discouraged by the government. The government has provided little or no support for them. Unionization is discouraged by the agencies' management structure – one that tends to be dominated by members from the professional classes – and by their size.

As a strategy that limits comparisons to the workplace or to those between exclusively female workplaces and 'proxy' organizations, pay equity legislation cannot address or redress the discrimination that was rooted in government practices.

However, parity was not on the government's agenda, and pay equity was. To make the legislation work for these agencies, I suggested that for the purposes of implementing pay equity legislation for workers in agencies funded and regulated by the government that the more complex proxy comparison approach be abandoned and, instead, that the government be defined as their 'employer' (Findlay 1989b). This shift would then include employees of these agencies in the Ontario public service's pay equity plan and make the provincial government responsible for their pay equity adjustments.[2]

The staff of the Pay Equity Office defended the workability of the proxy comparison approach on technical grounds, warning me that I sounded like an 'advocate' rather than an objective analyst. Their responsibilities, as defined in the legislation, were limited to the task of finding male comparators for the women in the predominantly female sector. This was defined as a technical job, one that was grounded in the perspectives of experts in the field of job comparison, not the perspectives of either those who were responsible for implementing pay equity or those who represented their interests. The objective of the consultations, they reminded me, was to test the workability of the proxy comparison approach, not to invite critiques of the existing legislation. The issues that stakeholders raised about the pay equity fund, the questioning of the definition of employer that was raised by tribunal decisions, my questions about the suitability of pay equity as a strategy that could address wage discrimination for women in the government-funded agencies in the community and social service sector, were 'political' questions to raise with the minister and beyond the scope of the commission's technical mandate.

Feminist trade unionists who had been included in the consultations also defended the workability of the proxy comparison approach. They maintained that the proxy comparison approach could be made to work for women in these workplaces if the Pay Equity Office would agree to some minor technical adjustments and to the negotiation of the appropriate proxy organization.

The question that I was left with was 'Why did feminists support a government model that was clearly not adequate for women in exclusively female workplaces?' In their pursuit of similar questions over the years, feminists have turned to an examination of the relationship between feminists and the state. Some theorists have argued that feminists were co-opted by the programs that were developed in the late 1960s and early 1970s to 'increase the participation of citizens in decisions that affected their lives' (Loney, 1978; Schreader, 1990). Others, arguing against an instrumentalist perspective on the state, suggest that the members of feminist groups are 'willing partners in their own seduction' (Pal, 1993: 277).

More reflective of both my experience and my analysis of how feminists have been drawn into the ruling practices of the state, as they have organized themselves to represent women's interests in the policy processes of state institutions since the 1960s (Findlay, 1995), is the work of feminists who argue that feminist politics has been shaped by practices that organize feminist work and link women's issues to strategies that make sense to the dominant groups – to state officials, professionals, union leaders, and so on. In her analysis of a social service agency that feminists established to respond to the employment needs of immigrant women, Roxana Ng (1988) explains how the rules and regulations associated with government funding worked to reorganize the work of the agency to fit the needs of employers rather than the needs of immigrant women. While feminists had organized the work of the agency to respond to the particular requirements of immigrant women, in the end their work had been bureaucratized and professionalized, and immigrant women had become their 'clients.'

In *Family Violence and the Women's Movement* (1990), Gillian Walker points to another explanation for the institutionalization of feminist politics: 'As women again struggle to enter the public arena on our own terms, the processes of exclusion are being transformed into ones that absorb, appropriate, and reorganize our work' (Walker, 1990: 10). Arguing against the portrayal of the state as a monolith, Walker sees the institutionalization of feminist politics as one effect of a 'layered web of negotiated discursive relations' that feminists engage in when they try to act on women issues (ibid.: 63). The 'layers' in the 'web' include the struggles among feminists about defining women's experience, struggles between feminists and professionals with vested interests in defining these issues, and, lastly, between feminists and state officials to refine this definition in a way that ties the 'most radical aspects of feminist mobilization into a conservative law and order framework for social control' (ibid.: 78). In this process, the issues are individualized and hence depoliticized, and the specificity of women's experience is lost in definitions that are to be applied uniformly to 'women' as a group.

In the next section, I look at some of the ways that feminists were drawn into a similar process as they struggled for equal pay for working women: the negotiations among feminists, and between feminists and union leaders and state officials that led feminists to embrace the pay equity model; and the way that the implementation of pay equity worked to align feminists with the Pay Equity Commission in defence of the legislation and the proxy comparison approach.

Institutionalization: From Bargaining Equal Pay to Regulating Pay Equity

Defining the Issue

In the 1960s, women were increasingly conscious of the discrepancies between the wages they received and the wages that their male colleagues received for the same work. In its 1970 report, the Royal Commission on the Status of Women defined this problem as one that reflected the discrimination between women and men. Working within a framework that defined the issue of the status of women in terms of universal rights to equal opportunity between women and men, the commissioners based their argument on an appeal to these rights, rather than a more structural critique of the relations of production and their gendered nature or an exploration of what they could learn about wage-setting practices from the testimonies that some women gave about the more specific ways that these wage discrepancies worked. To guarantee these universal rights, they argued that the government should replace the interpretation of 'equal pay' as one that required equal pay for the same work with a definition that was 'more within the intent of the International Labour Organization Convention 100 which speaks of "work of equal value"' (Royal Commission on the Status of Women, 1970: 76).

However, they recognized that the low earnings of women in Canada also reflected the clustering of women workers in low wage ghettos. They made no recommendations to promote equal opportunities for women in the private sector, arguing that only 'radical changes in the attitudes of society can give them equal opportunities in employment and promotion' (Royal Commission on the Status of Women, 1970: 190). They recommended that the government adopt an equal opportunity program for women in the federal public service. These recommendations were based on a report that Kathleen Archibald prepared for the Public Service Commission. In this report, Archibald argued that wage discrimination was only a small part of the problem that accounted for the gap in the wages between women and men in the federal public service. The main problem was occupational segregation. To close the wage gap, she argued for an equal opportunity program that would address both 'equal access' and 'equal pay and promotional prospects when doing equivalent work' and recognize the specific responsibilities of married women with children (Archibald, 1970: 132). In the hopes of persuading managers in the public service to take up her recommendations, she rejected the need for quotas, distinguishing her equal opportunity model from the more contentious affirmative action model that had been created in the United States in the mid-1960s to redress the discrimination in employment that African Americans and women had historically faced.

In the latter half of the 1970s the issue of wage discrepancies was taken up by some of the feminist organizations that had emerged to lobby governments for the implementation of the recommendations of the commission. In 1976 the National Action Committee on the Status of Women was successful in its attempts to persuade the federal government to include equal value legislation in the new Canadian Human Rights Act. In this same year, the Equal Pay Coalition was organized in Toronto.

However, a more radical demand for wage reforms was coming from feminists who had taken the struggle for women's equality into the unions in the latter part of the 1970s. These feminists took up the claim for affirmative action as a strategy to address the issues of working women. For them, affirmative action included demands for equal pay. They appealed to union leaders for a debate within unions about 'the merits of affirmative action and the best strategies for winning gains in this area,' warning union leaders that feminists would and should turn to legislative strategies if they failed to respond (Larkin, 1983: 68). They organized inside unions: women's committees and women's caucuses were formed to pressure union leaders (Field, 1983). Some of them argued for gender parity on union executives. They organized outside the unions: Organized Working Women gave feminist trade unionists the opportunity to put collective pressure on their unions.

In 1982 the Ontario Federation of Labour sponsored a conference on affirmative action that was attended by 200 people. But, for the most part, labour leaders resisted women's demands for a program based on affirmative action, as it conflicted with the long-standing commitments that unions had made to seniority as a basis for promotions. Legislated affirmative action, programs were even worse. As they saw it, such programs challenged the bargaining power of unions.

Instead, they took up the demand for equal pay. By the mid-1980s, most unions had committed themselves to the principle of equal pay for work of equal value. Wage demands made more sense to unions: 'The demand for equal pay had already had a huge impact within and without the labour movement' (Larkin, 1983: 81). For example, in 1981, the clerical workers in the Canadian Union of Public Employees made equal pay the main issue in the civic worker's strike in B.C.'s Lower Mainland (Ainsworth et al., 1982: 135).

Commitments to equal value at trade union conventions did not necessarily translate into action. 'While some unions have actively pursued the issue, it must be conceded that the enthusiasm with which unions have integrated the principle into their practical union work has varied considerably' (Lewis, 1988: 49).

Legislating Equal Pay for Work of Equal Value: The Pay Equity Model

While feminists continued their struggle for union action, the leaders of Ontario's Equal Pay Coalition were shifting the focus of the Coalition from collective bargaining to a legislative model (ibid.: 71). This shift occurred for many reasons. In part it reflected the legalization of feminist issues that Walker describes in her account of the struggle to define wife abuse. In 1981 feminist lawyers had waged a successful battle for the inclusion of the equality clause in the Charter of Rights and Freedoms and were preparing themselves to use the courts as a way of removing various forms of discrimination against women. Legal solutions also dominated government responses to wife battering and to rape.

In a more practical sense, it made sense to the lawyers who played a leadership role in the Coalition. They were trained to rely on the law to eliminate discrimination, a training that could over-ride their understanding of the more systemic and structural roots of women's inequality. Their perspectives were supported by the success that feminists in Minnesota had achieved in persuading their state government to adopt pay equity in 1982, and at home by the recommendations for legislated equal pay that came from the Royal Commission on Equality in Employment in 1984. As the commissioner concluded, 'To ensure freedom from discrimination requires government intervention through law' (Royal Commission on Equality in Employment, 1984: 254). In 1985 the Manitoba government introduced pay equity legislation that was based on the Minnesota model (Lewis, 1988: 64). In this context, the pay equity model made sense to them, even though it had been developed specifically to redress gender discrimination for women in American state administrations.

What was most significant in taking up the legislative model was the impact it had on the work of the Coalition. Coalition members were absorbed in the work of specifying their demands to be embodied in the legislative model. Little time was left for the exploration of alternatives. Experts who understood these details dominated discussions, rather than those who represented the experience of women workers that could inform the Coalition about how this was implemented. Discussions of the structural issues that shaped women's wages in the workplaces in the Ontario economy were sidelined.

Negotiating Pay Equity: Feminists and the State

In 1985 members of the Coalition had a convincing argument for legislated pay equity as well as connections to – if not membership in – Ontario's major unions and the New Democratic Party. They were very instrumental in the decision that the New Democratic Party took to make the introduction of pay equity legislation part of the accord they negotiated with the minority Liberal government as the official opposition.

The government initiated a comprehensive round of consultations with representatives from employers, unions, and the feminist community in 1985 as the basis for defining pay equity legislation. The Coalition was clearly seen as the 'voice of working women.' By 1987 'the Ontario Equal Pay Coalition claimed to have 35 constituent groups in Ontario representing over one million women and men. Through one of its groups, the National Action Committee on the Status of Women (NAC), it claimed to represent nationally "over three million people and four hundred and fifteen groups"' (Cuneo, 1990: 8).

In their negotiations for pay equity, Coalition members won their demands for a pro-active model, in spite of the well-organized campaign that employers waged against it. But, they lost their bid for a method of establishing value that included comparisons between sectors or between branch plants of large multinationals. The comparison between female and male job classes was restricted to the individual workplace. Because of this restriction, the many hundreds of thousands of women in the predominantly female sector were not covered by the legislation, although the government did agree to a proviso in the legislation that committed the Pay Equity Commission to an investigation of ways to extend the legislation to this group. The Coalition also lost the fight to include workplaces with under ten employees in the legislation. The legislation that emerged was tied to the strategies that trade unionists, employers, and the government itself had negotiated over time to bargain for, regulate, and establish workers' wages. These practices were established by men for men. They also reflected the specificities of organized workplaces.

Members of the Equal Pay Coalition put considerable pressure on the feminist community to lobby members of the Ontario Legislature for the passage of the bill to introduce pay equity. At the workshop on pay equity at the 1987 socialist feminist conference on 'Women and the State' in Toronto, the representative from the Coalition argued that the legislation (with some modification) was a 'good first step.' Most of the participants at the workshop agreed. By 1987 the Coalition had established virtual 'ownership' of the pay equity issue. The authority this gave the Coalition, in addition to the very complex nature of the issue, discouraged feminists outside the Coalition from debating their positions. The one participant who dared to raise some questions at the workshop was quickly discounted. 'Are you crazy?' warned a prominent feminist (Findlay, 1987).

Implementing Pay Equity: Making It the Business of the State

The legislation specified a proactive model of pay equity that committed employers to the development of a pay equity plan and a process of developing this plan that included negotiations with their employees and their representatives. Many of the feminists who had struggled for equal pay over the years were now drawn into the implementation of the pay equity legislation. Feminists who worked in trade unions were called on to persuade their male-dominated unions to take up the legislation, to co-ordinate their unions' approach to pay equity, and to negotiate pay equity plans for their members. Feminist lawyers represented the interests of working women who took their disputes with their employers to the Pay Equity Tribunal. Feminists were appointed as representatives of labour on the Pay Equity Tribunal. Members of the Equal Pay Coalition were appointed to the Pay Equity Tribunal. Staff of the Ontario Women's Directorate joined the staff of the Pay Equity Office. Academic feminists were called on as expert witnesses in cases mediated by the tribunal. The key spokesperson for the Equal Pay Coalition was appointed to the Pay Equity Commissioner's Advisory Committee.

An independent agency, the Pay Equity Commission, was established to administer the act. The commission included the Pay Equity Hearings Tribunal that was established to hear complaints from employers and employees related to the implementation of the legislation; and the Pay Equity Office that was responsible for educational programs and related research. In Section 33(2)(e), the Pay Equity Office of the Commission was given the responsibility to undertake a study to develop recommendations for the minister on ways to extend pay equity coverage to the women in workplaces in the predominantly female sector.

Many social activists have regarded independent mechanisms such as commissions and councils as an essential part of the process of recognizing new social issues and carrying out reforms for groups that have historically been excluded from the policy process. They have relied on them to represent their interests in the development and implementation of policy and even to give them a voice in these processes. As soon as the legislation was passed, members of the Coalition began to pressure the Pay Equity Commission to begin its study. They were relying on the Commission to find ways to make pay equity work for all of the women workers in Ontario. As some of them argued, the office had both the resources they believed such a study required and the authority to hold government leaders to the commitments they believed they had made to the Coalition about the coverage of women in the predominantly female sector. And, they were 'tired of doing the government's work for it.'

Independent agencies such as the Commission are, in fact, more accountable to the government than activists might assume. Their mandates are defined by governments and reflect the priorities of governments. Their work is organized in a way that ensures its consistency with these priorities. In Section 33(2)(e), the government gave the Commission the authority to make recommendations to the Minister of Labour to cover women workers in the predominantly female sector, but it limited the Commission's investigation to the search for ways to identify male comparators for women in the predominantly female sector. In so doing, the government quite explicitly denied the Commission the freedom to investigate or challenge government practices that regulated the wages of women who delivered the programs and services of the welfare state through the small agencies in the community and social service sector or to challenge the very limited definition of 'employer' in the legislation that limited comparisons to the individual workplace.

These limits were reinforced by the way that the staff of the Pay Equity Office organized the investigation. This staff had been hired for the most part for their expertise in methods of comparison. The investigation they organized was one that rested heavily on their expertise, rather than the perspectives of the stakeholders from these agencies.

Although they initiated the investigation with a comprehensive set of sector studies, the information from these studies was used as background information about the 'workability' of options to extend the methods of comparison that were essentially shaped by their own expertise and the expertise of some outside consultants rather than the perspectives of either the employees or employers in these sectors.

Consultations were restricted to those who could advise the experts about the workability of the options they had prepared. Representative groups such as the Equal Pay Coalition had no voice in the implementation of the legislation. The voices of the stakeholders who were included were contained by a reliance on outside consultants (like myself) who mediated the relationship between these stakeholders and the experts inside. In this context, reservations about the proxy comparison approach were redefined as technical questions or referred to the minister as political issues. Arguments for the recognition of the government as the 'employer' for workplaces it funded and regulated were also dismissed.

In spite of the practices that tied the Commission's investigation to a government-defined mandate, its power to influence the development and implementation of government policy has been limited. The success of independent agencies like the Commission depends on their ability to 'make sense' to the powerful insiders in the bureaucracy who define and implement government policy and have the 'inside track' with their ministers. Bureaucratic rules and regulations about secrecy restrict the access that these agencies can have to the policy process inside government departments or ministries and to the documents that emerge from it. The overlap between their mandates and the mandates of advisers inside the bureaucracy work against their access to and influence on the minister.

In theory they are established to play complementary roles. In this case the Commission was established to administer the pay equity legislation; the Ministry of Labour was given responsibility for the longer term development of policy itself. In practice the distinctions between independent agencies and their bureaucratic counterparts are murky, and their mandates often overlap. In some cases they establish a co-operative relationship: they may work together in preparing proposals for their minister. But competition often characterizes their relationship. It is triggered by a number of factors. One is the role that the insiders play in monitoring the work of independent agencies. For example, the staff of the Policy Branch of the Ministry of Labour is responsible for advising the Minister of

Labour on practical and political implications of the recommendations made by the Pay Equity Commission. They were also responsible for preparing the minister's discussion paper on policy options noted above. In this work, the staff of the Policy Branch of the ministry actually repeated much of the work done by the staff of the Commission.

Competition between independent agencies and bureaucratic offices is also generated because their different locations in the policy process lead them to different understandings about how the government could best increase pay equity in predominantly female workplaces. They may represent different and conflicting interests.

When competition characterizes the relationship between the insiders and the outsiders (the independent agencies), the insiders have the advantage. Ministers rely on their advisers inside the bureaucracy more than on advisers from independent agencies. When faced with differences of opinion between her or his inside advisers and those in commissions and councils, it is likely that the advice from the insiders will make more sense to the minister. Insiders have more regular contact with their ministers; they are often in closer physical proximity. They know her or his perspectives. More importantly, as insiders, they are part of the 'policy environment' that influences Cabinet discussions and decisions that are the end point of a long process of debate and negotiation within the bureaucracy. Decisions reflect these negotiations as much as or more than carefully reasoned advice. The staff of independent agencies are effectively marginalized from these processes. Their proposals are often regarded as unrealistic in spite of their attempts to be pragmatic and to link them to the existing strategies and policies of the government.

Some theorists have argued that this marginalization of independent agencies like the Commission reflects the fact that they are 'captured' by the interests they are established to regulate. As Richard Schultz argues, 'Using regulation for positive public purposes results in a much closer integration of a regulatory agency with, rather than insulation from, other political processes such as those involved in lobbying Cabinet, members of Parliament, and departments' (Schultz, 1990: 475). However, in the case of the Pay Equity Commission, it was clearly in the interests of the government to limit the independence of the Commission. Pay equity threatened the interests of the business clients, and it also threatened the interests of the government in maintaining the low wages of women working in the welfare state.

The Commission, then, like other independent agencies appointed by government, suffered from its contradictory location in the policy process. It was a body that had neither the constituencies on the outside that give elected politicians their power in the definition of policies, nor the access to information and resources that gives provincial bureaucrats their power to control the development and implementation of government commitments. In the end, it depends on the interests of the government of the day and the willingness of ministers to take up their work, a dangerous dependency given the way that business interests were once again dominating government responses.

Dependent on government and limited to a technical mandate and a staff that relied on the expertise of job evaluation specialists to generate policy, the Pay Equity Commission defended the workability of the proxy comparison approach in spite of arguments from the stakeholders that the approach did not fit their organizations and evidence that this approach ignored the responsibilities that the government had for the low wages of women in agencies that delivered its commitments to community and social services.

Many of the feminists who had organized themselves to represent the interests of working women in Ontario also supported the workability of the proxy comparison approach and ignored the issues raised by the stakeholders. It became increasingly difficult for pay equity feminists to 'hear' the voices of unorganized women, as many of them were fully engaged in making the legislation work for organized working women. Feminists were depoliticized in this process. They were drawn into these new activities as professionals and as individuals, not as advocates. Their time was spent in representing the interests of their 'clients,' women who were members of their unions or who had the resources to pay the legal fees that were entailed in using the tribunal. As union staff, they were expected to work with organized women workers, or to organize the unorganized, not to support the struggles of the unorganized. As Coalition members, they had turned the search for ways to extend the coverage of the legislation to women in the predominantly female sector over to the Commission.

Conclusion

Feminist struggles for pay equity reflect the limited commitments that successive Ontario governments were prepared to make to wage reforms for women. But they also reflect a process of institutionalization in which feminists were drawn into a consensus about the workability of the government's pay equity legislation and a form of politics that supported their relationships with representatives from established groups, union leaders, and state officials rather than women workers. In taking up the 'reasoned' and 'reasonable' strategies required to unite the disparate interests of feminists, build alliances with the men who dominated the unions, and negotiate with government officials, feminists had little time for the ongoing dialogue that they needed to have with women workers about the way that wage discrimination really worked or for the debates they needed to have with each other about strategies that would work for these women.

The legislative commitment to investigate ways to extend pay equity to women in the predominantly female sector provided feminists in the Equal Pay Coalition with another opening that might have taken the model beyond the 'good first step' that they had argued the legislation represented. However enmeshed in strategies to make the legislation work, they came to defend the workability of the proxy comparison approach for women in exclusively female workplaces in spite of the reservations about it that were expressed by the stakeholders.

Given what we know today about the way that capitalist interests dominate our governing processes, it is easy to criticize the compromises that feminists have made in negotiations with state officials and representatives of the other major interests (unions and business) over the years to win wage reforms for women workers. But the truth is that in the context of the politics of reform that had emerged from the 1960s to shape the social movements of the 1970s and early 1980s and their relationships with governments, these compromises made a good deal of sense to feminists as strategies that supported the larger project of transformation. In the early 1980s, evidence that governments in the United States and other provinces across Canada were prepared to embrace a pay equity model simply sustained this point of view among the pay equity feminists in Ontario, as (in a more immediate sense) did the power that the NDP opposition exercised on their behalf during the Liberal minority government.

However, the political context that encouraged feminists to make the compromises necessary to promote the introduction of the government's pay equity model as a 'good first step' was changing in a very significant way by the time negotiations for the proxy comparison approach began in 1988. The Liberal government had won a majority and the new government was clearly more oriented to the interests of the business classes in Ontario than the equity claims advanced by the Equal Pay Coalition. Business leaders mounted a strong and successful campaign against the proxy comparison approach. The NDP opposition was no longer in a position to counter their arguments. Reflecting the pressure from the business leaders, the Minister of Labour rejected the Commission's recommendation for the proxy comparison approach (Ontario, Ministry of Labour, 1990: 4). Feminists may have breathed a sigh of relief when the NDP came to power in September 1990, but the NDP government took three years to deliver on its election promise to introduce the proxy comparison approach.

Today, claims from groups seeking equity are clearly subordinated to the interests of the business classes, as governments of all persuasions continue their retreat from the commitments to equality and social justice that were forged in the 1960s and early 1970s to create the more 'flexible' social and economic policies and programs that business argues must be the basis for Canada's effective participation in the global economy (Panitch, 1994). In 1995, the new Conservative government rescinded the proxy comparison approach, capped pay equity adjustments, and abolished the Pay Equity Advocacy and Legal Clinic. On 16 July 1996, the premier announced that he had been advised to abolish the Pay Equity Commission (NDP Office Memo, 18 July 1996).

The voices of the groups seeking equality have also been weakened by shifts in government policies. Initiatives have been taken to reduce the pressure that these groups can exert on politicians and bureaucrats alike. In many cases, governments have reduced or eliminated their funding of these groups. Partnerships between governments and community-based groups have replaced the more open-ended consultations of the 1970s (Phillips, 1991). Government machinery that was organized in the 1970s to reflect women's interests in the policy process (for example, federal and provincial advisory councils on the status of women) is being dismantled (Findlay, 1995).

By the late 1980s, however, the strategies that made sense to feminists in the 1970s and early 1980s were also challenged from within. The concept of 'sisterhood' had always been more tenuous than we wanted to believe in the early days of feminism, but by this time, feminists in Ontario (particularly in Toronto, where the struggle for pay equity was centred) were facing strong pressures from women of colour, Native women, and women with disabilities for organizations that could reflect the diversity of identities and interests among women. The effectiveness of coalitions such as the Equal Pay Coalition depended on creating a set of demands that reflected a unity and sameness among 'women' rather than the diversity and specificity of working women's wage discrimination. While claiming to represent the interests of all working women, the demands established by the Coalition tended to reflect the particular interests of women who were members of the more established groups that belonged to the Coalition (for example, the unions). As working women discovered during the implementation of the legislation, the pay equity model in Ontario worked better for organized working women than it did for unorganized women.

We have learned from our struggles for women's equality since the 1960s that 'Social justice entails democracy' (Young, 1990: 191). We have also learned how difficult it is to sustain the democratic project in this period of globalization. As Robert Cox argues in his exploration of this dilemma, 'The condition for a restructuring of society and politic in this sense would be to build a new historic bloc capable of sustaining a long war of position until it is strong enough to become an alternative basis of polity' (Cox, 1991: 349). What feminists can contribute to this project is our knowledge that this new historic bloc must be grounded in the recognition of difference. We can also contribute what we have learned about the need for more participatory forms of organizing that support this recognition. As feminists, we have learned about the importance of organizations in which women can speak for themselves rather than those that give some women the right to speak for other women; organizations that are more inclusive – organizations where women can build a 'horizontal voice' that reflects the diversity of our different cultures, ages, and interests; organizations where we can share our experiences and exchange our skills (Elshtain, 1993). We can and must make this learning part of the larger struggle for democracy.

Notes

1 This chapter is a revision of 'Making Sense of Pay Equity: Issues for a Feminist Political Practice,' in Patricia McDermott and Judy Fudge eds., *Just Wages*. Toronto: University of Toronto Press, 1991, 81–109. I would like to thank Gerda Wekerle for her very sensitive and persistent editing of this chapter.
2 The Pay Equity Tribunal had used a similar definition of 'employer' in its decision to allow nurses whose work was regulated by the Regional Municipality of Haldimand–Norfolk to compare their work to the work of police officers who were direct employees of the same government.

References

Ainsworth, Jackie, et al. 1982. 'Getting Organized ... in the Feminist Unions.' In

Maureen Fitzgerald, Connie Guberman, Margie Wolfe, eds., *Still Ain't Satisfied*. Toronto: Women's Press.

Archibald, Kathleen. 1970. *Sex and the Public Service*. Ottawa: Queen's Printer.

Cox, Robert. 1991. 'The Global Political Economy and Social Change.' In Daniel Drache and Meric S. Gertler, eds., *The New Era of Global Competition*. Montreal and Kingston: McGill-Queen's University Press, 335–50.

Cuneo, Carl. 1990. *Pay Equity: The Labour-Feminist Challenge*. Toronto: Oxford University Press.

Elshtain, Jean Bethke. 1993. *Democracy on Trial*. Concord, Ont: House of Anansi Press.

Ferguson, Kathy. 1984. *The Feminist Case against Bureaucracy*. Philadelphia: Temple University Press.

Ferree, Myra Marx, and Patricia Yancey Martin, eds. 1995. *Feminist Organization: Harvest of the New Women's Movement*. Philadelphia: Temple University Press.

Field, Debbie. 1983. 'The Dilemma Facing Women's Committees.' In Linda Briskin and Lynda Yanz, eds., *Union Sisters*. Toronto: Women's Press, 293–303.

Findlay, Sue. 1987. 'Equal Pay: Why No Debate?' *Cayenne* 11/12 (Spring/Summer): 36–40.

– 1989a. 'Pay Equity in Predominantly Female Establishments: The Community and Social Service Sector.' Research Report I, Report to the Minister of Labour by the Pay Equity Commission, January.

– 1989b. 'The Proxy Comparison Approach: Can It Work for the Broader Public Sector.' Report for the Pay Equity Commission of Ontario. September.

– 1991. 'Making Sense of Pay Equity: Issues for Feminist Political Practices.' In Judy Fudge and Patricia McDermott, eds., *Just Wages: A Feminist Assessment of Pay Equity*. Toronto: University of Toronto Press, 81–109.

– 1995. *Democracy and the Politics of Representation: Feminist Struggles with the Canadian State, 1960–1990*. PhD dissertation, University of Toronto.

Larkin, Jackie. 1983. 'Out of the Ghettos: Affirmative Action and Unions.' In Linda Briskin and Lynda Yanz, eds., *Union Sisters*. Toronto: Women's Press, 67–86.

Lewis, Debra. 1988. *Just Give Us the Money*. Vancouver: Women's Research Centre.

Loney, Martin. 1978. 'A Political Economy of Citizen Participation.' In Leo Panitch, ed., *The Canadian State*. Toronto: University of Toronto Press, 446–72.

New Democratic Party. 1996. Office Memo. 18 July.

Ng, Roxana. 1988. *The Politics of Community Service*. Toronto: Garamond Press.

Ontario, Ministry of Labour. 1990. *Policy Directions: Amending the Pay Equity Act*.

Pal, Leslie A. 1993. *The Interests of State: The Politics of Language, Multiculturalism and Feminism in Canada*. Montreal and Kingston: McGill-Queen's University Press.

Panitch, Leo. 1994. 'Globalization and the State.' In *Socialist Register, 1994*. London: Merlin Press, 60–93.

Phillips, Susan. 1991. 'How Ottawa Blends: Shifting Government Relationships with Interest Groups.' In Frances Abele, ed., *How Ottawa Spends*. Ottawa: Carleton University Press, 183-227.

Royal Commission on Equality in Employment. 1984. *Equality in Employment: A Royal Commission Report*. Ottawa: Supply and Services Canada.

Royal Commission on the Status of Women. 1970. *Report*. Ottawa Queen's Printer.

Savage, Mike, and Anne Witz, eds. 1992. *Gender and Bureaucracy*. Oxford: Blackwell.

Schreader, Alicia. 1990. 'The State-Funded Women's Movement: A Case of Two Political Agendas.' In Roxana Ng, Gillian Walker, Jacob Mueller, eds., *Community Organization and the Canadian State*. Toronto: Garamond Press, 184–99.

Schultz, Richard. 1990. 'Regulatory Agencies.' In Michael S. Whittington and Glen Williams, eds., *Canadian Politics in the 1990s*, 3rd ed. Toronto: Nelson, 468–80.

Walker, Gillian. 1990. *Family Violence and the Women's Movement*. Toronto: University of Toronto Press.

Watson, Sophie. 1990. *Playing the State: Australian Feminist Interventions*. London: Verso.

Young, Iris Marion. 1990. *Justice and the Politics of Difference*. Philadelphia: Temple University Press.